CHENG & TSUI

"Bringing Asia to the World"™

中文听说读写 · 中文聽說讀寫

INTEGRATED CHINESE

Simplified and Traditional Characters

3

Textbook

4th Edition

Yuehua Liu and Tao-chung Yao
Nyan-Ping Bi, Yaohua Shi, Liangyan Ge

Original Edition by Yuehua Liu and Tao-chung Yao
Yaohua Shi and Nyan-Ping Bi

CHENG & TSUI

"Bringing Asia to the World"™

Copyright © 2018, 2010, 2006, 1997 by Cheng & Tsui Company, Inc.

Fourth Edition 2018

6th Printing, 2023

27 26 25 24 23   6 7 8 9 10

ISBN 978-1-62291-159-2
[Fourth Edition, Simplified and Traditional Characters, Hardcover]

ISBN 978-1-62291-156-1
[Fourth Edition, Simplified and Traditional Characters, Paperback]

Library of Congress
Cataloging-in-Publication
Data [Third Edition]

Integrated Chinese = [Zhong wen ting shuo du xie]. Level 2, part 1 / Yuehua Liu . . . [et al.] – 3rd ed.
             p. cm.

Chinese and English.

Includes indexes.

Parallel title in Chinese characters.

ISBN 978-0-88727-680-4 (hbk.)
– ISBN 978-0-88727-679-8 (pbk.)
1. Chinese language–Textbooks for foreign speakers–English. I. Liu, Yuehua. II. Title: Zhong wen ting shuo du xie.

PL1129.E5I683 2009

495.1–dc22

Printed in the United States of America

The *Integrated Chinese* series encompasses textbooks, workbooks, character workbooks, teacher's resources, audio, video, and more. Content is available in a variety of formats, including print and online via the ChengTsui Web App™. Visit chengtsui.co for more information on the other components of *Integrated Chinese*.

Publisher
JILL CHENG

Editorial Manager
BEN SHRAGGE

Editors
MIKE YONG and LIJIE QIN
with LEI WANG

Creative Director
CHRISTIAN SABOGAL

Illustrators/Designers
KATE PAPADAKI and LIZ YATES

Photographs
© Adobe Stock
© Cheng & Tsui
© Shutterstock
© humphery/Shutterstock.com
© LP2 Studio/Shutterstock.com
© TonyV3112/Shutterstock.com

Cheng & Tsui Company, Inc.
25 West Street
Boston, MA 02111-1213 USA
Phone (617) 988-2400 / (800) 554-1963
Fax (617) 426-3669
cheng-tsui.com

This Fourth Edition of *Integrated Chinese* is dedicated to the memory of our dearest colleague and friend Professor Tao-chung (Ted) Yao.

Publisher's Note

When *Integrated Chinese* was first published in 1997, it set a new standard with its focus on the development and integration of the four language skills (listening, speaking, reading, and writing). Today, to further enrich the learning experience of the many users of *Integrated Chinese* worldwide, Cheng & Tsui is pleased to offer this revised and updated Fourth Edition of *Integrated Chinese*. We would like to thank the many teachers and students who, by offering their valuable insights and suggestions, have helped *Integrated Chinese* evolve and keep pace with the many positive changes in the field of Chinese language instruction. *Integrated Chinese* continues to offer comprehensive language instruction, with many new features, including the **ChengTsui Web App™**, as detailed in the Preface.

The Cheng & Tsui Chinese language program is designed to publish and widely distribute quality language learning materials created by leading instructors from around the world. We welcome readers' comments and suggestions concerning our publications. Please contact the following members of our Editorial Board, in care of our Editorial Department (email: editor@chengtsui.co).

Contents

Preface

The *Integrated Chinese* (IC) series is an internationally acclaimed Mandarin Chinese language course that delivers a cohesive system of print and digital resources for highly effective teaching and learning. First published in 1997, it is now the leading series of Chinese language learning resources in the United States and beyond. Through its holistic focus on the language skills of listening, speaking, reading, and writing, IC teaches novice and intermediate students the skills they need to function in Chinese.

What's New

It has been over eight years since the publication of the Third Edition of IC. We are deeply grateful for all the positive feedback, as well as constructive suggestions for improvement, from IC users. In the meantime, China and the world have seen significant transformations in electronic communications, commerce, and media. Additionally, the technology available to us is transforming the way teachers and students interact with content. The teaching of Chinese as a second language needs to keep pace with these exciting developments. Therefore, the time seems right to update IC across delivery formats.

In developing this latest edition of IC, we have consulted the American Council on the Teaching of Foreign Languages (ACTFL) *21st Century Skills Map for World Languages*. The national standards for foreign language learning in the 21st century focus on goals in five areas—communication, cultures, connections, comparisons, and communities. In addition to classifying the applicable **Language Practice** activities by communication mode (interpersonal, interpretive, and presentational), we have added a host of materials that address the 5 Cs. The delivery of IC via the new **ChengTsui Web App™** elevates the teaching and learning experience by presenting multimedia and interactive content in a truly blended and integrated way.

New, visually rich supplementary modules that recur in each lesson have been introduced. These can be taught in any sequence to serve as prompts for classroom discussion and student reflection:

- **Get Real with Chinese** draws on realia to situate language learning in real-life contexts. Students are required to analyze, predict, and synthesize before coming to conclusions about embedded linguistic and cultural meaning. Photos and questions connect the classroom to authentic Chinese experiences. To familiarize students with both character sets, students are exposed to realia in simplified characters and realia in traditional characters.

- **Chinese Chat** provides opportunities for language practice in the digital environment. Realistic texting, microblogging, and social media scenarios show students how the younger generation has adapted Chinese to new communication technologies.

- **Characterize It!** encourages students to approach Chinese characters analytically. Additional activities are provided on the ChengTsui Web App.

- **How About You?** has been revamped for the first two volumes and newly introduced in Volumes 3 and 4. This module encourages students to personalize their study of vocabulary and learn words and phrases that relate to their own interests and background. Visual cues, which prompt possible answers, promote vocabulary expansion and retention. In Volumes 3 and 4, questions appear in Chinese only, and encourage students to answer in a full sentence or short paragraph.

- In **A Way with Words**, students will find in the example sentence new words and phrases that, although unstudied, bear a cognate relationship to a word or phrase that they have just learned in the current lesson. Based on the provided context, students are encouraged to guess at the meaning of these new words or phrases. The exercise is designed to raise students' awareness of the latent semantic interconnections among different vocabulary items and to foster their ability to expand their vocabulary on their own.

While not new to the Fourth Edition, **Words & Phrases** is new to Volumes 3 and 4 of IC. This is because as students move up proficiency levels the number of new syntactic structures decreases while the study of semantics becomes more and more important. Unlike **Language Notes**, which sheds light on lexical nuances and idiomatic usage, **Words & Phrases** elaborates on versatile words and phrases with multiple examples and should be given the same weight as **Grammar**.

Moreover, per ACTFL guidelines, we have included **Compare & Contrast** activities in the **Cultural Literacy** (formerly Culture Highlights) section in order to promote students' awareness of cultural diversity in a world of rapid globalization. This section as a whole has been given a lavishly illustrated, magazine-style treatment to better engage students.

In Volumes 3 and 4, the **Text** has been updated for additional visual interest, including with icons of the characters. The **Before You Study**, **When You Study**, and **After You Study** segments have been revised to include questions in Chinese. **View & Explore**, meanwhile, encourages students to make use of short, supplemental video clips available through the ChengTsui Web App.

The **Vocabulary** list, as well as the Indexes, now provides simplified and traditional characters in full for each item in Volume 3.

Bringing It Together (formerly Let's Review) continues to help students review language forms and language functions previously introduced.

Finally, the new **Lesson Wrap-Up** section includes context-based wrap-up projects, developed in line with ACTFL standards. These projects encourage students to become active learners by requiring them to engage in research beyond the textbook, and additional projects for this section are available through the ChengTsui Web App. The ability to speak and write cohesively is a key attribute of advanced learners; building on Make It Flow! in IC1 and IC2, we have created a new segment, **Keep It Flowing**, to help students develop and apply strategies for coherently and cohesively organizing information in written and spoken discourse. The **Lesson Wrap-Up** activities can be used as assessment instruments for the **Can-Do Checklist**, which encourages students to measure their progress at the end of the lesson.

As previous users of IC will note, we have renamed the four-volume series. The new sequencing of Volumes 1 to 4 better reflects the flexibility of the materials and the diversity of our user groups and their instructional environments. However, we also recognize that Volumes 1 and 2 are often used together in the first year of language instruction, and Volumes 3 and 4 in the second. Thus, for ease of reference, we have retained the sequencing of the lessons from 1 to 20 in each half of the series.

We have also relabeled complex grammatical structures. Users will now find continuous Roman numerals applied across the four IC volumes. Students and teachers can now easily see that five segments are devoted to the particle 了, three to directional complements, and so on. Grammatical structures that are recycled for review purposes are marked "revisited," to allow teachers to decide how much time to spend on them. We hope that this new system brings greater organizational clarity and makes for easier cross-referencing.

As with the Third Edition, the Fourth Edition of IC features both traditional- and simplified-character versions of the Volume 1 and 2 textbooks and workbooks, and a combination of traditional and simplified characters in the Volume 3 and 4 textbooks and workbooks. However, in response to user feedback, we have updated the traditional characters to ensure they match the standard set used in Taiwan. For reference, we have consulted the Taiwan Ministry of Education's online *Revised Chinese Dictionary*. To reflect the predominance of simplified characters in Chinese language instruction, we have listed simplified characters first in the new edition of Volumes 3 and 4.

The most significant change in the Fourth Edition is the incorporation of innovative educational technology. Users of the print edition have access to audio (at chengtsui.co/resources), while subscribers to the ChengTsui Web App have access to audio plus additional, interactive content.

Users who choose to purchase the **Basic Edition** of the ChengTsui Web App will have access to:

- Audio (Textbook and Workbook)
- View & Explore video clips based on each lesson's theme
- Vocabulary flashcards
- Additional character practice
- Additional Lesson Wrap-Up projects

Users who choose to purchase the **Essential Edition** of the ChengTsui Web App will, in addition to the above, have access to the Workbook with automatic feedback for students and printable Character Workbook sheets for handwriting and stroke order practice.

In addition to the student editions, the ChengTsui Web App is available in an **Educator Edition**. The *Educator Edition* web-application overlay suggests teaching tips and strategies and conveniently makes connections between the Textbook and the additional resources provided in the Teacher's Resources, such as video activity worksheets, quizzes, and answer keys.

A key feature of the ChengTsui Web App is coherence. The innovative instructional design provides an integrated user experience. Learners can move seamlessly between the transmission, practice, application, and evaluation stages, navigating the content to suit their particular learning needs and styles. For more information about the Web App, please visit chengtsui.co.

Both in its print and digital versions, the new IC features a contemporary layout that adds clarity and rigor to our instructional design. Rich new visuals complement the text's revised, user-friendly language and up-to-date cultural content. We hope that students and teachers find the many changes and new features timely and meaningful.

Organizational Principles

In the higher education setting, the IC series often covers two years of instruction, with the first two volumes usually used in the first year of study and the final two volumes in the second. The lessons first cover topics from everyday life, then gradually move to more abstract subject matter. The materials do not follow one pedagogical methodology, but instead blend several effective teaching approaches. Used in conjunction with the ChengTsui Web App, incorporating differentiated instruction, blended learning, and the flipped classroom is even easier. Here are some of the features of IC that distinguish it from other Chinese language resources:

Integrating Pedagogy and Authenticity

We believe that students should be taught authentic materials even at the beginning stage of language learning. Therefore, authentic materials (produced by native Chinese speakers for native Chinese speakers) are included in every lesson.

Integrating Traditional and Simplified Characters

We believe that students should learn both traditional and simplified Chinese characters. However, we also realize that teaching students both forms from day one could be overwhelming. Our solution is for students to focus on one form during their first year of study, and to acquire the other during their second. Therefore, the first two volumes of IC are available in separate traditional- and simplified-character versions, with the texts presented in the alternative character form in the Appendix.

By their second year of study, we believe that all students should be exposed to both forms of written Chinese. Accordingly, the final two volumes of IC include both traditional and simplified characters. Students in second-year Chinese language classes come from different backgrounds, and should be allowed to write in their preferred form. However, it is important that the learner write in one form only, and not a mix of both. In keeping with the differing conventions for the punctuation of traditional and simplified characters, punctuation marks for simplified characters have been set at the baseline and close to the preceding character, while punctuation marks for traditional characters have been set at the median and centered within the following space.

Integrating Teaching Approaches

Because no single teaching method can adequately train a student in all language skills, we employ a variety of approaches in IC. In addition to the communicative approach, we also use traditional methods such as grammar-translation and the direct method.

Users of the ChengTsui Web App can employ additional teaching approaches, such as differentiated learning and blended learning. Students can engage in self-paced learning, a very powerful study strategy. The product also facilitates breaking down direct instruction into more engaging "bites" of learning, which improves student engagement. Moreover, the ChengTsui Web App allows students to interact with the content at home and practice and apply their learning in the classroom with corrective teacher feedback, which has the potential to improve student outcomes. Additionally, teachers and learners do not need to follow the instructional flow of the underlying book. They can navigate using multiple pathways in flexible and customized ways and at varying paces for true individualized learning.

Acknowledgments

We would like to thank users around the world for believing in IC. We owe much of the continued success of IC to their invaluable feedback. Likewise, we would be remiss if we did not acknowledge the University of Notre Dame for sponsoring and inviting us to a one-day workshop on IC on April 9, 2016. Leading Chinese-language specialists from across the country shared their experiences with the IC authors. We are especially indebted to Professor Yongping Zhu, Chair of the Department of East Asian Languages and Cultures at Notre Dame, and his colleagues and staff for organizing the workshop.

Professors Fangpei Cai and Meng Li of the University of Chicago took time out from their busy teaching schedules to compile a detailed list of comments and suggestions. We are profoundly touched by their generosity. In completing this Fourth Edition, we have taken into consideration their and other users' recommendations for revision. Indeed, many of the changes are in response to user feedback. The authors are naturally responsible for any remaining shortcomings and oversights.

For two summers in a row, Professor Liangyan Ge's wife, Ms. Yongqing Pan, warmly invited the IC team to their home to complete the bulk of the work of revising the IC series. Words are inadequate to express our thanks to Ms. Pan for her gracious hospitality and her superb cooking day in and day out.

We are deeply grateful to our publisher Cheng & Tsui Company and to Jill Cheng in particular for her unswerving support for IC over the years. We would also like to express our heartfelt appreciation to our editors Ben Shragge, Mike Yong, and the rest of the editorial team for their meticulous attention to every aspect of this new edition.

As we look back on the evolution of IC, one person is never far from our thoughts. Without Professor Tao-chung Yao's commitment from its inception, IC would not have been possible. Sadly, Professor Yao passed away in September 2015. Throughout the summer, Professor Yao remained in close contact with the rest of the team, going over each draft of IC 1 with an eagle eye, providing us with the benefit of his wisdom by phone and email. This Fourth Edition of IC is a living tribute to his vision and guidance.

Note: Prefaces to the previous editions of IC are available at chengtsui.co.

Series Structure

The IC series has been carefully conceptualized and developed to facilitate flexible delivery options that meet the needs of different instructional environments.

Component per Volume	Description	Print/Other Formats	ChengTsui Web App™
Textbook	• Ten engaging lessons per volume, each with readings, grammar explanations, communicative exercises, and culture notes	• Paperback or Hardcover • Simplified or Traditional Characters (Volumes 1 and 2) • Simplified and Traditional Characters (Volumes 3 and 4)	• *Basic, Essential,* and *Educator Editions*
Workbook	• Wide range of integrated activities covering the three modes of communication (interpersonal, interpretive, and presentational)	• Paperback • Simplified or Traditional Characters (Volumes 1 and 2) • Simplified and Traditional Characters (Volumes 3 and 4)	• *Essential* and *Educator Editions*
Character Workbook	• Radical- and character-writing and stroke order practice	• Paperback • Simplified and Traditional Characters	• *Essential* and *Educator Editions*
Audio	• Audio for Textbook vocabulary and lesson texts, and in Volume 1, pronunciation exercises • Audio for Workbook listening exercises, and in Volume 1, pronunciation exercises	• Audio available to print users at chengtsui.co/resources	• *Basic, Essential,* and *Educator Editions*
Video	• Volumes 1 and 2: acted dialogues and narratives presented in the Textbooks; also includes theme-related Culture Minutes sections in authentic settings • Volumes 3 and 4: documentary-style episodes correlating to the lesson themes in authentic settings	• One DVD per volume	• *Basic, Essential,* and *Educator Editions* • Streaming video
Teacher's Resources	• Comprehensive implementation support, teaching tips, sample syllabi, tests and quizzes, answer keys to the workbook exercises, and supplementary resources	• Downloadable resources that include core lesson guides along with ancillary materials previously on the companion website	• *Educator Edition*

Volume 3 Lesson Structure

All components of IC (Textbooks, Workbooks, and Teacher's Resources) are considered core and are designed to be used together to enhance teaching and learning. Recurrent lesson subsections are highlighted in the Textbook Elements column. Note that Supplementary Modules do not compose a separate section, but are rather discrete entities that appear throughout each lesson.

Section	Textbook Elements	Interactive Content	Workbooks	Teacher's Resources
Lesson Opener	• Learning Objectives state what students will be able to do by the end of the lesson • Relate & Get Ready helps students reflect on similarities and differences between Chinese culture and their own		• Opportunity for students to revisit learning objectives and self-assess	• Overview of language functions, vocabulary, grammar, pronunciation, and characters taught in the lesson • Sequencing recommendations and teaching aids
Text	• Chinese Text in each lesson demonstrates practical vocabulary and grammar usage • Before You Study includes two lesson-related questions for teachers to use as warm-up activities • When You Study provides three reading comprehension questions that students can answer after listening to and scanning the text • After You Study includes two summative questions that encourage students to produce discrete sentences • Language Notes sheds light on semantic nuances and idiomatic usage • *Pinyin* versions at the end of the lesson provide pronunciation support	• Audio builds receptive skills	• Listening comprehension and speaking exercises based on the dialogues • Reading comprehension	• Strategies for teaching the Text, plus question prompts

Section	Textbook Elements	Interactive Content	Workbooks	Teacher's Resources
Vocabulary	• Vocabulary lists define and categorize new words from the Text (proper nouns are listed last)	• Audio models proper pronunciation • Flashcards assist with vocabulary acquisition	• Handwriting and stroke order practice is provided in the Character Workbook • All exercises use lesson vocabulary to support acquisition	• Explanations, pronunciation tips, usage notes, and phrasal combinations
Grammar	• Grammar points, which correspond to numbered references in the readings, explain and model language forms		• Writing and grammar exercises based on grammar introduced in the lesson	• Explanations, pattern practice, and additional grammar notes
Words & Phrases	• Words & Phrases elaborates on useful words and phrases, highlighted in green in the lesson text, with multiple examples			
Language Practice	• Role-plays, pair activities, contextualized drills, and visual cues prompt students to produce language		• Exercises and activities spanning the three modes of communication (interpersonal, interpretive, and presentational), plus *pinyin* and tone practice, to build communication and performance skills	
Cultural Literacy	• Culture notes provide snapshots of contemporary and traditional Chinese-speaking cultures • Compare & Contrast draws connections between cultures		• Authentic materials develop predictive skills	• Background notes expand on the section and provide additional cultural information

Section	Textbook Elements	Interactive Content	Workbooks	Teacher's Resources
Lesson Wrap-Up	• Projects encourage review and recycling of lesson materials through different text types • Keep It Flowing develops students' ability to produce smooth discourse • Can-Do Checklist allows students to assess their fulfillment of the learning objectives	• Additional projects encourage students to produce written discourse	• Translation exercises provide opportunities to examine students' overall control of language forms and language functions in context	• Teaching tips for implementing self-diagnostic activities, answer keys for Keep It Flowing, and additional sample quizzes and tests
Supplementary Modules	• How About You? encourages students to personalize their vocabulary • Get Real with Chinese teaches students to predict meaning from context • Characterize It! explores the structure of Chinese characters • Chinese Chat demonstrates how language is used in text messaging and social media • A Way with Words raises students' awareness of the latent semantic interconnections among different vocabulary items	• Video, highlighted in the View & Explore segment, provides insight into non-verbal cues and communication plus context through authentic settings • Additional Characterize It! exercises increase understanding of characters	• Pattern exercises to build radical and character recognition	• Teaching tips and strategies for fully exploiting and implementing these new elements

Scope & Sequence

Lesson	Learning Objectives	Grammar	Words & Phrases	Cultural Literacy
1 开学/開學 **Starting a New Semester**	• Explain how to write your Chinese name • Say where you were born and grew up • Discuss the pros and cons of living on and off campus • Express a dissenting opinion politely	1. The particle 了 (IV) 2. Sentences with 是…的 (I) revisited 3. 除了…以外，都… 4. Connecting sentences (I)	A. 觉得/覺得 (to feel, to think) B. 方便 (convenient) C. 安全/安全 (safe) D. 省钱/省錢 (to save money, to economize) E. 自由 (free, unconstrained) F. 不见得/不見得 (not necessarily) G. 好处/好處 (advantage, benefit) H. 适应/適應 (to adapt, to become accustomed to)	• School relationships • Homonyms • Military training
2 宿舍生活 **Dorm Life**	• Name basic pieces of furniture • Describe your living quarters • Comment on someone's living quarters • Disagree tactfully	1. Existential sentences 2. Expressing relative degree or extent using 比较/比較 3. Indicating an extreme extent using …得很 4. Conjunctions	A. 恐怕/恐怕 (I'm afraid, I think perhaps, probably) B. 差不多/差不多 (about, roughly) C. 吵 (noisy; to quarrel) D. 安静/安靜 (quiet) E. 一般 (generally) F. 不怎么样/不怎麼樣 (not that great, just so-so) G. 地道 (authentic, genuine)	• Student housing • Campus dining • Accommodations for international students
3 在饭馆儿/ 在飯館兒 **At a Restaurant**	• Name four principal regional Chinese cuisines • Order food and drinks • Talk about what tastes you like and dislike • Describe your dietary restrictions and preferences	1. Topic-comment sentence structure 2. 一 + verb and 一…就… 3. 又…又… (both …and …) revisited 4. The reaffirmative 是	A. 正好 (coincidentally) B. 特别是/特別是 (especially) C. 有机/有機 (organic) D. 麻烦/麻煩 (to trouble; troublesome) E. 这（就）要看…（了）/這（就）要看…（了）(It depends on …) F. 比方说/比方說 (for example)	• Environmental influences on regional cooking • Restaurants • Dining conventions • Cooking essentials • Chopstick do's and don'ts

Lesson	Learning Objectives	Grammar	Words & Phrases	Cultural Literacy
4 买东西/ 買東西 **Shopping**	· Name basic clothing, bedding, and bath items · Describe your shopping preferences and criteria · Express discounts · Disagree with others tactfully	1. 无论…, 都…/ 無論…, 都… 2. Non-predicative adjectives 3. Adjective/verb + 是 + adjective/verb, 可是 or 但是… revisited	A. …什么的/ …什麼的 (…and so on) B. 大小, 长短/長短, 宽窄/寬窄 (kuānzhǎi)… (size, length, width…) C. 打折 (to discount, to sell at a discount) D. （要）不然 (otherwise) E. 只好 (can only, have to) F. 非…不可 (have to, must) G. 标准/標準 (criterion, standard) H. 在乎 (to mind, to care)	· Bargaining · New forms of payment · *Dongxi*
5 选课/選課 **Choosing Classes**	· State your major and academic department and some required general courses you have taken · Talk about your plans after graduation · Discuss what will enhance your future job opportunities · Explain whether your family members have an influence on your choice of major and career path · Share tips on how to save money for your education	1. 对…来说/對…來說 2. Resultative complements (III) 3. 另外 4. Comparing 再 and 还/還 5. 要么…, 要么…/要麼…, 要麼…	A. 只是 and 就是 (it's just that) B. 受不了 (unable to bear) C. 跟…打交道 (to deal with…) D. 这样/這樣 (in this way)	· Value of education · Graduate school · Declaring a major
Bringing It Together (L1–L5)	· Review of L1–L5			

Lesson	Learning Objectives	Grammar	Words & Phrases	Cultural Literacy
6 男朋友女朋友 **Dating**	· Say if you have an upbeat personality · State if you share the same interests or hobbies as others · Inquire if everything is OK and find out what has happened · Describe behaviors of a forgetful person · Give a simple description of what you look for in a friend · Tell what makes you anxious or angry	1. （在）…上 2. Verb 来/來 verb 去 3. Comparing 的, 得, and 地 (II) 4. 原来/原來 as adverb and adjective 5. Set phrases	A. 到底 (what on earth, what in the world, in the end) B. 根本 (at all, simply) C. 一干二净/一乾二淨 (completely, thoroughly, spotless) D. 实际上/實際上 (actually, in fact, in reality) E. 丢三拉四 (scatterbrained, forgetful) F. 一会儿…, 一会儿…, 一会儿又…/一會兒…, 一會兒…, 一會兒又… (one minute …, the next minute …)	· Valentine's Day and the *Qixi* Festival · Idealized traits · Courtship
7 电脑和网络/電腦和網絡 **Computers and the Internet**	· Find out if others are angry with you and apologize if so · Avoid tension in a conversation by changing the subject · Let people know about the trouble you had to go through because of their thoughtlessness or carelessness · Name and discuss the activities you use the Internet for · Discuss the pros and the cons of using the Internet	1. Potential complements (III) 2. Connecting sentences (II) 3. 过来/過來 and 过去/過去 (to come over/to go over)	A. 从…到…/從…到… (from … to …) B. 结果/結果 (as a result) C. 害得/害得 (to cause trouble so that, to do harm so that) D. 看起来/看起來 (it seems) E. 听起来/聽起來 (it sounds)	· Baidu, Alibaba, and Tencent · Internet lingo · Chinese character throwbacks

Lesson	Learning Objectives	Grammar	Words & Phrases	Cultural Literacy
8 打工 **Working Part-Time**	· Explain how people fund their education · Discuss if you work part-time and why · Name common jobs for students in China and in your country · Talk about how students spend their pocket money	1. Directional complements (III) 2. Connecting two verb phrases using 来/來 3. The particle 了 (V) 4. Rhetorical questions	A. 受到 (to receive) B. 压力/壓力 (pressure) C. 减轻/減輕 (to lessen) D. 适合/適合 (to suit) and 合适/合適 (suitable) E. 影响/影響 (to influence, to affect; influence) F. 取得 (to obtain) G. 说到/說到 (speaking of) H. 不是 X, 就是 Y (if it's not X, it's Y; either X or Y) I. 难怪/難怪 (no wonder) J. 多 (How … it is!)	· Tuition and scholarships · Working students · Mencius and manual labor
9 教育 **Education**	· Comment on whether your parents packed your schedule with activities as a child · Describe some typical classes offered in afterschool programs · Indicate agreement or disagreement · Present your opinions on children's education · Talk about parents' aspirations for their children	1. The adverb 才 before numbers 2. Adjectives as predicates 3. 不是X, 而是Y	A. 一直 (all along, continuously) B. Comparing 幸福, 快乐/快樂, and 高兴/高興 C. 厉害/厲害 (terrible, formidable) D. 最好 (had better, it's best)	· Respect for teachers · Parental aspirations · Cram school
10 中国地理/ 中國地理 **Geography of China**	· Locate major Chinese cities, provinces, and geographic features on a map · Compare basic geographic aspects of China and your own country · Describe features of a tourist sight that would attract or deter you · Discuss an itinerary for travel to China	1. Indicating the beginning of a state using 起来/起來 2. The conjunction 而 3. 最 adjective 不过了/最 adjective 不過了 4. The dynamic particle 过/過 revisited	A. 为了/為了 and 因为/因為 B. Comparing 理解/理解 and 了解/了解 C. 一下子 (all of a sudden, in an instant) D. 大多 (mostly) E. Indicating a pause in speech using 呢	· Regional differences · Xu Xiake · Major rivers
Bringing It Together (L6–L10)	· Review of L6–L10			

Abbreviations of Grammatical Terms

adj	adjective	pr	pronoun
adv	adverb	prefix	prefix
conj	conjunction	prep	preposition
interj	interjection	qp	question particle
m	measure word	qpr	question pronoun
mv	modal verb	t	time word
n	noun	v	verb
nu	numeral	vc	verb plus complement
p	particle	vo	verb plus object (for detachable compounds)
pn	proper noun		

Legend of Digital Icons

The icons listed below refer to interactive content. For readers who have purchased only the print edition, audio is available at chengtsui.co/resources and videos are available for separate purchase. All other digital content is available exclusively to ChengTsui Web App subscribers.

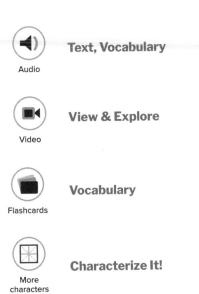

Text, Vocabulary
Audio

View & Explore
Video

Vocabulary
Flashcards

Characterize It!
More characters

Lesson Wrap-Up
More exercises

Cast of Characters

Zhang Tianming
张天明/張天明

An American college freshman whose parents immigrated to the United States from Nanjing, China. He's obsessed with sports and computers. Although he's outgoing and has many friends, his girlfriend thinks he spends too much time online.

Lisha
丽莎/麗莎

Lisa Cohen, an American college freshman. She and Zhang Tianming were high school sweethearts. Lisha loves music and is interested in all things Chinese.

Ke Lin
柯林

Al Collins, a graduate student and Lin Xuemei's boyfriend. He wants to study in China after he receives his master's degree in counseling. He is very warm and loves to help others.

Lin Xuemei
林雪梅

A graduate student from Hangzhou, China. She and Ke Lin are about four or five years older than Zhang Tianming and Lisha. Lin Xuemei and Lisha have quickly become good friends.

Li Zhe
李哲

Zack Ruiz, a senior and a good friend of Zhang Tianming's. He and Zhang Tianming like to hang out together and talk or play basketball. Li Zhe's older brother is an information technology specialist. His sister-in-law is originally from Hong Kong. Li Zhe has an eight-year-old niece.

第一课

第一課

开学
開學

STARTING A NEW SEMESTER

Learning Objectives

In this lesson, you will learn to:

- Explain how to write your Chinese name
- Say where you were born and grew up
- Discuss the pros and cons of living on and off campus
- Express a dissenting opinion politely

Relate & Get Ready

In your own culture/community:

- How do people disambiguate names?
- Do students prefer on-campus or off-campus housing?
- What services are provided for first-year students arriving on campus?

课文

Text

Audio

Before You Study

Answer the following questions in Chinese to prepare for the reading.

1 你是大学几年级的学生?

2 你住在学校宿舍里吗?

When You Study

Listen to the audio recording and skim the text; then answer the following questions in Chinese.

1 张天明是怎么介绍自己的名字的?

2 为什么有的人喜欢住在校内,有的人喜欢住在校外?

3 柯林住在哪儿?为什么?

张天明是大学一年级的新生[a]*。快开学了,他家离大学很远,得坐飞机去学校。他坐飞机坐了两个多小时,下飞机以后,马上叫了一辆出租汽车,很快就到了学校宿舍[1]。

人真多!

你是新生吧?

是,我是新生。你呢?

我是研究生。在这儿帮新生搬东西。请问,你叫什么名字?

我叫张天明。

张天明?是中文名字吗?

对,我爸爸妈妈是从中国来的。可是我是在美国出生,在美国长大的[2]。请问你的名字是……

我正在学中文,我的中文名字是柯林。你的名字是哪三个字?

张是弓长张,就是一张纸的张,天是天气的天,明是明天的明。

你是怎么来学校的?

課文

Audio

張天明是大學一年級的新生[a]*。快開學了，他家離大學很遠，得坐飛機去學校。他坐飛機坐了兩個多小時，下飛機以後，馬上叫了一輛出租汽車，很快就到了學校宿舍[1]。

人真多！

你是新生吧？

是，我是新生。你呢？

我是研究生。在這兒幫新生搬東西。請問，你叫什麼名字？

我叫張天明。

張天明？是中文名字嗎？

對，我爸爸媽媽是從中國來的。可是我是在美國出生，在美國長大的[2]。請問你的名字是……

我正在學中文，我的中文名字是柯林。你的名字是哪三個字？

張是弓長張，就是一張紙的張，天是天氣的天，明是明天的明。

你是怎麼來學校的？

Before You Study

Answer the following questions in Chinese to prepare for the reading.

1　你是大學幾年級的學生？

2　你住在學校宿舍裡嗎？

When You Study

Listen to the audio recording and skim the text; then answer the following questions in Chinese.

1　張天明是怎麼介紹自己的名字的？

2　為什麼有的人喜歡住在校內，有的人喜歡住在校外？

3　柯林住在哪兒？為什麼？

我先坐飞机，从机场到学校坐出租汽车。柯林，你也住在这儿吗？

不，这是新生宿舍[a]，我住在校外。

是吗？你为什么住校外？你觉得住在校内好，还是住在校外好？

有的人喜欢住在学校宿舍，觉得又方便又安全，有的人喜欢住在校外，因为校外的房子比较便宜。我住在校外，除了想省点儿钱以外[3]，还因为住在校外自由。再说，住在校内也不见得很方便。

真的吗？那我以后也搬到校外去。

你刚来，在学校住对你有好处[b]，可以适应一下学校的生活。要是你以后想搬家，我可以帮你找房子。

好吧，我以后要是搬家，一定请你帮忙。

天明，前边没人了，我帮你把行李搬进去吧。

好，谢谢。哎，我的电脑呢？……糟糕，电脑可能拉[c]在出租车上了！

Language Notes

a 新生

新生 (xīnshēng) (lit. new student) is the Chinese term for "freshman." The term 新鲜人/新鮮人 (xīnxiānrén), a perhaps initially facetious translation of the English term "freshman," is used in Taiwan. However, the adjective 新鲜/新鮮 (xīnxian) (fresh) typically describes food or things that are novel or unusual. Returning students are called 老生 (lǎoshēng) (lit. old student).

b 好处/好處

The opposite of 好处/好處 (hǎochu) (advantage, benefit) is 坏处/壞處 (huàichu) (disadvantage, harm).

c 拉

拉 (là) is used here in its colloquial sense to mean "to leave something behind." 拉 is otherwise pronounced "lā" and means "to pull." Some people prefer using the character 落/落, which is normally pronounced "luò" and means "to fall."

我先坐飛機，從機場到學校坐出租汽車。柯林，你也住在這兒嗎？

不，這是新生宿舍，我住在校外。

是嗎？你為什麼住校外？你覺得住在校內好，還是住在校外好？

有的人喜歡住在學校宿舍，覺得又**方便**又**安全**，有的人喜歡住在校外，因為校外的房子比較便宜。我住在校外，**除了**想省點兒錢**以外**[3]，還因為住在校外**自由**。再說，住在校內也**不見得**很方便。

真的嗎？那我以後也搬到校外去。

你剛來，在學校住對你有**好處**[b]，可以**適應**一下學校的生活。要是你以後想搬家，我可以幫你找房子。

好吧，我以後要是搬家，一定請你幫忙。

天明，前邊沒人了，我幫你把行李搬進去吧。

好，謝謝。哎，我的電腦呢？……糟糕，電腦可能拉[c]在出租車上了！

After You Study

Answer the following questions in Chinese.

1 請簡單地介紹一下張天明和柯林。

2 你喜歡住在校內還是校外？為什麼？

View & Explore

Video

For deeper language immersion and more cultural information, watch "Starting School," a short, supplemental video clip by Cheng & Tsui on this lesson's theme.

Vocabulary

Audio

Flashcards

No.	Simplified	Traditional	Pinyin	Part of Speech*	Definition
1	开学	開學	*kāi xué*	vo	to begin a new semester
2	新生	新生	*xīnshēng*	n	new student
3	辆	輛	*liàng*	m	(measure word for vehicles)
4	研究生	研究生	*yánjiūshēng*	n	graduate student
5	出生	出生	*chūshēng*	v	to be born
6	弓	弓	*gōng*	n	bow (for archery)
7	长	長	*cháng*	adj	long
8	校外	校外	*xiào wài*		off campus
9	校内	校內	*xiào nèi*		on campus
10	安全	安全	*ānquán*	adj	safe
11	比较	比較	*bǐjiào*	adv/v	relatively, comparatively, rather; to compare
12	省钱	省錢	*shěng qián*	vo	to save money, to economize
13	自由	自由	*zìyóu*	adj	free, unconstrained

* Parts of speech are indicated for most vocabulary items. Four-character phrases, idiomatic expressions, and other phrases that cannot be categorized by part of speech are left unmarked.

从张天明的家到学校坐飞机得坐两个多小时。你家离学校有多远？

從張天明的家到學校坐飛機得坐兩個多小時。你家離學校有多遠？

How About You?

While studying abroad in Taiwan, you plan to move to a new apartment. Your friend recommends a moving company to you and gives you their business card. Determine the manager's family name and the number to call. Check out the company's slogan on the right and explain how the company's name serves as an advertisement.

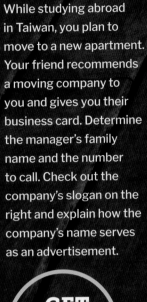

No.	Simplified	Traditional	Pinyin	Part of Speech	Definition
14	不见得	不見得	*bújiànde*		not necessarily
15	好处	好處	*hǎochu*	n	advantage, benefit
16	适应	適應	*shìyìng*	v	to adapt, to become accustomed to
17	生活	生活	*shēnghuó*	n/v	(day-to-day) life; to live
18	搬家	搬家	*bān jiā*	vo	to move (one's residence)
19	帮忙	幫忙	*bāng máng*	vo	to help
20	哎	哎	*āi*	excl	(exclamatory particle to express surprise or dissatisfaction or to remind)
21	拉	拉	*là*	v	to leave (something) behind inadvertently (colloq.)
22	张天明	張天明	*Zhāng Tiānmíng*	pn	(a personal name)
23	柯林	柯林	*Kē Lín*	pn	(a personal name)

Grammar

1	**The particle 了 (IV)**

The dynamic particle 了 can indicate that an action has occurred. It may appear after a verb; between a verb and a quantified object, as in (A) and (B); or after an unquantified object at the end of a sentence, as in (C).

A
　昨天晚上我看了一个电影。
　昨天晚上我看了一個電影。

　Last night I saw a movie.

B
　小王刚才在网上买了两本书。
　小王剛才在網上買了兩本書。

　Little Wang bought two books online a moment ago.

C　Q: 你昨天晚上做什么了？　　　　　A: 洗衣服了。
　　　　你昨天晚上做什麼了？　　　　　　　洗衣服了。

　　What did you do yesterday evening?　　　I did laundry.

In all the examples above, 了 signals that an action has occurred, but adding 了 is not equivalent to making a verb past tense. In some cases, 了 indicates that an action will actually occur in the future:

D
　明天我吃了早饭去机场。
　明天我吃了早飯去機場。

　Tomorrow, I'll go to the airport after breakfast.

Sentences with 了 that indicate the occurrence of an action usually have a time phrase, as in (A), (B), and (C). When the sentence does not have a time phrase, the time implied is the immediate past.

E Q: 这本书你看了吗?

这本書你看了嗎?

Did you read this book?

A: 我看了。

我看了。

Yes, I read it.

F Q: 你买明天的电影票了吗?

你買明天的電影票了嗎?

Did you buy tickets for tomorrow's movie?

A: 买了。

買了。

Yes, I did.

Q: 等了多长时间?

等了多長時間?

How long did you wait?

A: 人不多, 只等了五分钟。

人不多，只等了五分鐘。

There weren't a lot of people. I only waited five minutes.

When 了 appears between a verb and an object, the object is usually quantified, as in (A) and (B), but it need not be if one of three circumstances applies: if the object is followed by another 了, as in (G); if the object is followed by another clause, as in (H); or if the object refers to a definite person or thing, as in (I).

G   我给小李打了电话了。

我給小李打了電話了。

I called Little Li.

H 张天明买了机票就回家了。

张天明買了機票就回家了。

Zhang Tianming went home right after he bought the plane ticket.

I 昨天我在学校里看见了小王。

昨天我在學校裡看見了小王。

Yesterday, I saw Little Wang at school.

When 了 occurs at the end of a sentence, it may signify the occurrence or realization of an event, state, or new situation:

J 十月了，天气慢慢冷了。

十月了，天氣慢慢冷了。

It's October. The weather is gradually getting cold.

K 我想今天晚上看电影，可是明天要考试，所以不看了。

我想今天晚上看電影，可是明天要考試，所以不看了。

I wanted to go see a movie tonight, but I have an exam tomorrow, so I'm not going to.

When there are two verb phrases in a sentence and the first verb phrase is followed by the particle 了, the two actions denoted by the verbs are consecutive. The second action begins once the first one is completed.

L 我下了课再去找你。

我下了課再去找你。

After class, I'll go look for you.

M 昨天我搬进了宿舍就去餐厅吃饭了。

昨天我搬進了宿舍就去餐廳吃飯了。

Yesterday, as soon as I finished moving into the dorms, I went to eat at the cafeteria.

In (L), the action 去找你 occurs when the action 下课/下課 is completed. In (M), the action 去餐厅吃饭/去餐廳吃飯 occurs once the action 搬进宿舍/搬進宿舍 is finished.

2 | Sentences with 是...的 (I) revisited

We studied this construction in IC2 [see Grammar 4, Lesson 14, IC2]. Remember that when both the speaker and the listener know that an action or event has occurred and the speaker wants to draw attention to the particulars of the action—such as the time, place, manner, purpose, or agent—the 是...的 construction must be used. Notice that in the following examples the particle 了 is used to ask whether an action occurred. Once it's established that it did, the speakers immediately switch to using the 是...的 construction to get into the specifics of the action. Notice also that although we call it the 是...的 construction, 是 is, in fact, often optional.

A

Q: 柯先生来了吗?

柯先生來了嗎?

Did Mr. Ke come?

A: 来了。

來了。

Yes, he did.

Q: （是）什么时候来的?

（是）什麼時候來的?

When did he come?

A: （是）昨天晚上来的。

（是）昨天晚上來的。

Yesterday evening.

Q: （是）跟谁一起来的?

（是）跟誰一起來的?

Who did he come with?

A: （是）跟他姐姐一起来的。

（是）跟他姐姐一起來的。

With his older sister.

Q: （是）坐飞机来的还是开车来的？

（是）坐飛機來的還是開車來的？

Did they come by plane or by car?

A: 开车来的。

開車來的。

By car.

B 张天明（是）在美国出生的。

張天明（是）在美國出生的。

Zhang Tianming was born in the U.S.

If there is an object after the verb, 的 can be placed at the end of the sentence or before the object.

C **Q:** 你是大学生吗？

你是大學生嗎？

Are you an undergrad?

A: 不，我是研究生。

不，我是研究生。

No, I'm a grad student.

Q: 你是在哪儿上的大学？

你是在哪兒上的大學？

Where did you go to college?

A: 我是在纽约上的大学。

我是在紐約上的大學。

I went to college in New York.

In negative sentences, 是 cannot be omitted:

D Q: 你是在中国学的中文吗？

你是在中國學的中文嗎？

Did you study Chinese in China?

A: 我不是在中国学的中文，是在美国学的。

我不是在中國學的中文，是在美國學的。

I didn't study Chinese in China. I studied it in the U.S.

E Q: （是）谁跟你一起看的电影？是小张吗？

（是）誰跟你一起看的電影？是小張嗎？

Who went to the movie with you? Was it Little Zhang?

A: 不是小张跟我一起看的，（是）小李跟我一起看的。

不是小張跟我一起看的，（是）小李跟我一起看的。

No, Little Zhang didn't go with me. Little Li did.

3 | 除了…以外，都…

除了 means "not counting." As we learned in IC1, the structure 除了…以外，还/還… introduces something that is in addition to what is already known. [See Grammar 8, Lesson 8, IC1.]

A 他除了学中文以外，还学日文。

他除了學中文以外，還學日文。

or in other words:

他学中文，也学日文。

他學中文，也學日文。

In addition to Chinese, he's also studying Japanese.

B

我们班除了小王以外，还有小林去过中国。

我們班除了小王以外，還有小林去過中國。

or in other words:

小王和小林都去过中国。

小王和小林都去過中國。

In our class, in addition to Little Wang, Little Lin has also been to China.

C

昨天张天明除了搬家以外，还买东西了。

昨天張天明除了搬家以外，還買東西了。

or in other words:

昨天张天明搬家、买东西。

昨天張天明搬家、買東西。

In addition to moving, Zhang Tianming also went shopping yesterday.

On the other hand, the structure 除了⋯以外，都⋯ emphasizes that a group of people or things shares something in common, excluding the noted exceptions. It is usually translated as "except" or "except for."

D

除了小柯以外，我们班的同学都去过中国。

除了小柯以外，我們班的同學都去過中國。

or in other words:

小柯没去过中国。

小柯沒去過中國。

Except for Little Ke, every student in our class has been to China.
(Little Ke is the only one in our class who has not been to China.)

E

除了看书以外，晚上什么事我都愿意做。

除了看書以外，晚上什麼事我都願意做。

or in other words:

我晚上不愿意看书。

我晚上不願意看書。

Except for reading, I am willing to do anything in the evening.
(Reading is the only thing that I am not willing to do in the evening.)

Connecting sentences (I)

For flow and clarity, connecting words are necessary when we speak at length in multiple sentences. In the example from the Text shown below, take a look at how Ke Lin uses three connectives— 因为/因為, 除了…以外，还因为/除了…以外，還因為,and 再说/再說— to organize his sentences.

A **Zhang Tianming**

是吗？你为什么住校外？你觉得住在校内好，还是住在校外好？

是嗎？你為什麼住校外？你覺得住在校內好，還是住在校外好？

Is that so? Why do you live off campus? Do you think it's better to live on or off campus?

Ke Lin

有的人喜欢住在学校宿舍，觉得又方便又安全，有的人喜欢住在校外，**因为**校外的房子比较便宜。我住在校外，**除了**想省点儿钱**以外，还因为**住在校外自由。**再说**，住在校内也不见得很方便。

有的人喜歡住在學校宿舍，覺得又方便又安全，有的人喜歡住在校外，**因為**校外的房子比較便宜。我住在校外，**除了**想省點兒錢**以外，還因為**住在校外自由。**再說**，住在校內也不見得很方便。

Some people like to live on campus, thinking it's both convenient and safe. Others like to live off campus, as off-campus housing is relatively inexpensive. I live off campus. In addition to wanting to save some money, I also want freedom. On top of that, living on campus isn't necessarily that convenient.

Another way to connect sentences is by using ordinal numbers to enumerate each reason: 第一···，第二···，第三···.

Ke Lin　有的人喜欢住在学校宿舍，觉得又方便又安全，有的人喜欢住在校外，因为，第一，校外的房子比较便宜，第二，住在校外比较自由，第三，住在校内不见得很方便。

有的人喜歡住在學校宿舍，覺得又方便又安全，有的人喜歡住在校外，因為，第一，校外的房子比較便宜，第二，住在校外比較自由，第三，住在校內不見得很方便。

In (A), connecting words allow Ke Lin's reply to sound clearer and more organized. Take a look at another example:

B　妈妈告诉我当医生最好。因为除了好找工作以外，还挣钱多，再说家里人看病也方便。

媽媽告訴我當醫生最好。因為除了好找工作以外，還掙錢多，再說家裡人看病也方便。

Mom told me it would be best if I became a doctor because it would be easy for me to find a job, I would be able to make more money, and it would be more convenient for other family members to see the doctor.

Here as well, the sentences can be connected using ordinal numbers instead.

妈妈告诉我当医生最好。因为第一好找工作，第二挣钱多，第三家里人看病也方便。

媽媽告訴我當醫生最好。因為第一好找工作，第二掙錢多，第三家裡人看病也方便。

Characterize it!

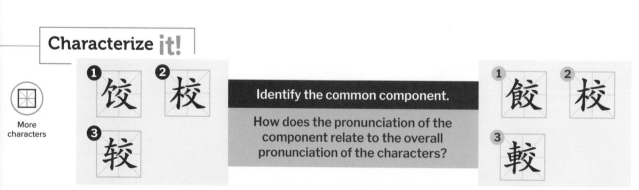

More characters

Identify the common component.

How does the pronunciation of the component relate to the overall pronunciation of the characters?

Words & Phrases

觉得/覺得 (to feel, to think)

觉得/覺得 can be used to express a feeling, as in (1).

1 我今天觉得有点不舒服，不能跟你一起去游泳了。

我今天覺得有點不舒服，不能跟你一起去游泳了。

I don't feel very well today. I can't go swimming with you. *[feeling]*

It can also be used to express an opinion, as in (2) and (3).

2 大家都说那个电影好看，可是我看了以后觉得不怎么样。

大家都說那個電影好看，可是我看了以後覺得不怎麼樣。

Everybody says that film is good, but I didn't think it was all that great after seeing it. *[opinion]*

3 很多美国人认为 (rènwéi) 十八岁以后就应该离开家搬到别的地方住，我觉得不一定。

很多美國人認為 (rènwéi) 十八歲以後就應該離開家搬到別的地方住，我覺得不一定。

Many Americans think that you should leave home and live somewhere else after you turn eighteen. I don't necessarily feel this is the case. *[opinion]*

When used to express an opinion, 觉得/覺得 is less formal than 认为/認為.

方便 (convenient)

As an adjective, 方便 can appear in a sentence as a predicate, as in (1) and (2).

1

住在城里买东西很方便。

住在城裡買東西很方便。

Living in the city, it's very convenient to shop. *[predicate]*

2

我想问您一个问题，您现在方便吗？

我想問您一個問題，您現在方便嗎？

I'd like to ask you a question. Is right now convenient for you? *[predicate]*

It can also appear as an attributive, as in (3).

3

方便的时候，请给我打个电话。

方便的時候，請給我打個電話。

Please give me a call whenever is convenient for you. *[attributive]*

A WAY WITH WORDS

叫出租汽车

昨天晚上她唱歌唱得不错，很多人为她叫好。

这个电影特别叫座，很多人想去看。

Using the word/phrase in orange as a clue, try to figure out the meaning of the words/phrases in blue; consult a dictionary if necessary. Consider how the literal and extended senses are related in each case.

叫出租汽車

昨天晚上她唱歌唱得不錯，很多人為她叫好。

這個電影特別叫座，很多人想去看。

安全/安全 (safe)

As an adjective, 安全/安全 can be used as a predicate, as in (1) and (2).

1
这栋楼很安全。

這棟樓很安全。

This building is very safe. *[predicate]*

2
你不必担心，她现在很安全。

你不必擔心，她現在很安全。

You don't have to worry. She's very safe now. *[predicate]*

It can also be used as an attributive, as in (3) and (4).

3
我们宿舍的安全问题很大。

我們宿舍的安全問題很大。

Our dorm has a big problem with safety. *[attributive]*

4
最安全的办法是下午五点以后不准人进公司。

最安全的辦法是下午五點以後不准人進公司。

The safest solution is to not allow people to enter the company building after 5:00 p.m. *[attributive]*

省钱/省錢 (to save money, to economize)

省钱/省錢 is a verb-object compound. Numerals and particles such as 了 can be inserted between the verb and the object.

1
每个星期少开一天车，一年可以省不少钱。

每個星期少開一天車，一年可以省不少錢。

If you drive one day less a week, you'll save a lot of money over a year.

2

这件衬衫周末打五折，可以省三十块钱。

這件襯衫週末打五折，可以省三十塊錢。

This shirt is half off this weekend. You can save thirty dollars.

3

我去年住在中国，吃饭很便宜，省了很多钱。

我去年住在中國，吃飯很便宜，省了很多錢。

I lived in China last year. Eating was very inexpensive. I saved a lot of money.

E

自由 (free, unconstrained)

自由 can be used as a noun, as in (1); as an adjective, as in (2); or as an adverbial with the addition of 地, as in (3).

1

Q: 在那个地方，你觉得人们有自由吗？

在那個地方，你覺得人們有自由嗎？

In that place, do you think people have freedom? *[noun]*

A: 我在那儿住了半年，觉得很自由。

我在那兒住了半年，覺得很自由。

I lived there for half a year. I found it very free. *[adjective]*

2

我妹妹住在表姐家里，她觉得很不自由。

我妹妹住在表姐家裡，她覺得很不自由。

My younger sister lives with my cousin. She finds it very restrictive. *[adjective]*

3

那个孩子快两岁了，可以在地上自由地走来走去。

那個孩子快兩歲了，可以在地上自由地走來走去。

That child is going to be two soon. He can walk around freely. *[adjective + 地 = adverbial]*

不见得/不見得 (not necessarily)

An adverb, 不见得/不見得 can be used to politely express a dissenting opinion.

1 **Q:** 她是在中国出生的，中文一定很好吧？

她是在中國出生的，中文一定很好吧？

She was born in China. Her Chinese must be very good.

A: 在中国出生的人，中文不见得好。

在中國出生的人，中文不見得好。

People who were born in China don't necessarily speak good Chinese.

2 报上说的不见得对。

報上說的不見得對。

What's said in the newspaper isn't necessarily right.

3 这个城市路上车多人多，开车不见得比走快。

這個城市路上車多人多，開車不見得比走快。

The streets in this city are packed with people and cars. Driving isn't necessarily faster than walking.

好处/好處 (advantage, benefit)

好处/好處 is a noun. It can be used as a subject, as in (1).

1 坐飞机的好处是很快。

坐飛機的好處是很快。

The advantage of flying is that it's quick.

It can also be used as an object, as in (2).

2　请你说说这样做的好处。

请你說說這樣做的好處。

Please tell us the advantage of doing it this way.

好处/好處 often occurs in this construction, meaning "X is advantageous for Y":

> X对Y（没）有好处
>
> X對Y（沒）有好處

3　少开车，多走路，对健康有好处。

少開車，多走路，對健康有好處。

Driving less and walking more is good for health.

4　这样做对你没有好处。

這樣做對你沒有好處。

Doing this has no advantages for you.

5　上过大学、会用电脑、会说外语，对找工作有好处。

上過大學、會用電腦、會說外語，對找工作有好處。

Having a college degree, being able to use a computer, and being able to speak a foreign language are advantages when it comes to looking for a job.

H　适应/適應 (to adapt, to become accustomed to)

The verb 适应/適應 must be used with a direct object.

1　你适应大学的生活了吗？

你適應大學的生活了嗎？

Have you gotten used to college life yet?

2　我来了两年了，到现在还不适应这里的生活。

我來了兩年了，到現在還不適應這裡的生活。

I've been here for two years, but I'm still not used to life here.

Alternatively, the object can be introduced by the preposition 对/對 and be placed before the verb 适应/適應.

3

你对这里的天气已经适应了吗？

你對這裡的天氣已經適應了嗎？

Have you gotten used to the weather here?

4

我们刚来美国，对美国的天气还不适应。

我們剛來美國，對美國的天氣還不適應。

We've just arrived in the U.S. We're not used to American weather yet.

Chinese Chat

A friend is texting you on WeChat to ask for a favor. How would you reply?

Lola:
我週末搬家。能幫忙嗎？

You:
...

Lola:
太好了！搬好了，我叫 pizza，怎麼樣？

You:
...

Language Practice

A | **Pleasure to meet you**   INTERPERSONAL |

Ask your teacher to give you a Chinese name if you don't already have one, then go around the class and introduce yourself. Explain the characters in your Chinese name and ask your classmates to explain how to write their own Chinese names.

B | **Back to school**   INTERPERSONAL |

In pairs, take turns asking questions about your trips back to school after summer break. Use the 是⋯的 structure to ask about the particulars of the trip, e.g.:

What date?

Q: 你是几号回学校来的?

你是幾號回學校來的？

A: 我是二十三号回学校来的。

我是二十三號回學校來的。

1   What day of the week?

2   How?

3   With whom?

C | **Apart from that**   INTERPERSONAL |

First, in pairs, take turns asking your partner what other courses he/she is taking this semester besides Chinese, using 除了⋯以外，还/還⋯. Use English to name courses you don't know how to say in Chinese.

Second, since you know your partner can speak Chinese, find out what other languages he/she can speak using 除了⋯以外，还/還⋯.

Au contraire

INTERPERSONAL

You're in a contrarian mood today. In pairs, practice disagreeing with everything that your partner says using 不见得/不見得, e.g.:

student dorm	convenient

Person A

住在学生宿舍很方便。

住在學生宿舍很方便。

Person B

住在学生宿舍不见得很方便。

住在學生宿舍不見得很方便。

1	what the teacher says	correct
2	living off campus	more freedom
3	writing English	easier than writing Chinese
4	airplane tickets	most expensive in August
5	people born in China	cook delicious Chinese food

E

It's good for you!

PRESENTATIONAL

Your friend is recovering from an illness. Offer him/her health advice using ⋯对⋯（没）有好处/⋯對⋯（沒）有好處, e.g.:

喝水对身体有好处。

喝水對身體有好處。

1 ✓   2 ✗   3 ✓

Another friend of yours has decided to take up learning Chinese as a hobby. Offer him/her three study tips, e.g.:

多听录音对学中文有好处。

多聽錄音對學中文有好處。

Missing in action

Based on the images, express your regret about leaving these items behind, e.g.:

糟糕，我把书拉在宿舍里了。

糟糕，我把書拉在宿舍裡了。

1

2

3

4

Newbie nerves

In pairs, brainstorm a list of things you can do to help first-year students feel more at ease when they first arrive on campus.

A WAY WITH WORDS

省钱

为了省事，他把三个月的房租一次付了。

这个孩子每天一回家就开始做功课，真让妈妈省心。

Using the word/phrase in orange as a clue, try to figure out the meaning of the words/phrases in blue; consult a dictionary if necessary. Consider how the literal and extended senses are related in each case.

省錢

為了省事，他把三個月的房租一次付了。

這個孩子每天一回家就開始做功課，真讓媽媽省心。

Pros and cons

PRESENTATIONAL   INTERPERSONAL

First, list the pros and cons of living on campus in a dorm and living off campus in an apartment or a house. Then survey three of your classmates and see who prefers living on campus or off campus. Record their reasons using ⋯⋯觉得住在校外比住在校内好。因为⋯⋯ / ⋯⋯覺得住在校外比住在校內好。因為⋯⋯ and report back to the class.

I   INTERPERSONAL

Stay or go

PRESENTATIONAL

In groups, discuss the pros and cons of living on campus vs. living off campus, then summarize your group members' opinions by using 有的⋯，有的⋯. Points for discussion can include safety, doing laundry, Internet access, shopping, expenses, and freedom, e.g.:

有的同学觉得住在校内，离教室近，上课很方便。有的同学觉得⋯⋯

有的同學覺得住在校內，離教室近，上課很方便。有的同學覺得⋯⋯

J   INTERPERSONAL

There's no place like home

PRESENTATIONAL

In pairs, take turns asking the following questions about living situations. Make sure you incorporate the expressions and constructions you've learned in this lesson.

1   Do you live on or off campus?

2   When did you move there?

3   What are the advantages of living where you do?

4   Do your friends live on or off campus as well?

5   What would you say to those who have made a different choice?

6   Next year, are you going to continue living on/off campus?

Then, based on your answers to the questions above, explain your choice of living on or off campus in a short, coherent paragraph. Don't forget to connect your sentences using 因为/因為, 除了⋯以外, 还/還⋯, 再说/再說⋯, and/or 第一⋯，第二⋯，第三⋯.

School Relationships

Relationships are very important in China. As one saying goes, "At home, we depend on our parents; when we travel, we depend on our friends" (在家靠父母，出外靠朋友). At college, away from their families for the first time, students often form special, sibling-like mentorship bonds based on seniority. Terms like 学长/學長 (xuézhǎng) (upperclassman), 学弟/學弟, 学姐/學姐, and 学妹/學妹 are frequently heard on Chinese college campuses. The unfortunate flip side to this strong sense of family and group belonging is occasional indifference to strangers.

COMPARE & CONTRAST

For students who are new to campus, not knowing one's way around and failing to blend in can be stressful and embarrassing. To avoid the awkwardness of being a 菜鸟/菜鳥 (càiniǎo) (newbie, lit. vegetable bird), new students often try to befriend a 学长/學長 to learn the ropes and meet new friends. While senior students do often play a central role in the social scene on campus, it is not uncommon for them to provide academic, personal, and professional advice to their younger peers. Do such relationships exist at your school? If not, what ways are there for new students to acclimate to their schools?

Homonyms abound in Chinese—for instance, Zhang Tianming's family name, 张/張 (Zhāng), sounds exactly like another family name, 章 (Zhāng). In conversation, it is common to disambiguate a family name by explaining how it is written. One way is to break the character into components: hence, Zhang Tianming's family name is said to be 弓长张/弓長張 (gōng cháng Zhāng), made up of 弓 (gōng) and 长/長 (cháng), and not 立早章 (lì zǎo Zhāng), made up of 立 (lì) and 早 (zǎo). A family name can also be disambiguated by presenting a disyllabic context in which it is used or by referencing a famous person with the same name. For instance, to differentiate the family name 江 (Jiāng) from 姜 (Jiāng), one might say 长江的江/ 長江的江，不是姜太公的姜 (Chángjiāng de Jiāng, bú shì Jiāng Tàigōng de Jiāng), ([it's] the Jiang in Changjiang [the Yangtze River], not the Jiang in Jiang Taigong [a semi-legendary figure from Chinese antiquity]).

江

姜

Homonyms

First-year students engaged in military training at Jiujiang University, Jiangxi Province

MILITARY TRAINING

Chinese law requires that all college students undergo basic military training. Since 1989, freshman orientation has included at least two weeks of on-campus military training overseen by officers of the People's Liberation Army. Since the academic year usually starts in September, when much of the country is still uncomfortably hot, many students find the experience grueling. The training consists of drill formations, crawling, strength building, and target practice, often under the harsh sun. Sometimes, nighttime cross-country hiking is also included in the program. While some students and parents find the requirement beneficial, others are more critical. However, there are no indications that military training will be phased out anytime soon.

Lesson Wrap-Up

Project

More exercises

You are on the University New Student Orientation Committee and have been tasked with helping a group of incoming Chinese students. Make a video for the new student orientation program. Look up information on the university website and incorporate it in your video. In your video, be sure to:

- extend a warm welcome to the new students, and introduce yourself—say what your name is, where you are from, what year you are, where you live, what your major is, and so on

- outline what you will go over in the video (i.e., the items below)

- describe the main facilities on campus—the library, computer center, athletic field, student activity center, student dorms, etc.

- explain when move-in day is and who will be helping new students move into their dorms (i.e., returning students)

- inform new students when they will meet their faculty adviser (指导教授/指導教授) (zhǐdǎo jiàoshòu) and what they will go over (classes and university life)

- remind them when classes begin

- tell them what fun activities the university has planned for new students before classes begin

- end by reiterating your welcome

Keep It Flowing

First, study the following description; pay particular attention to how the highlighted parts help the sentences flow smoothly from one to the next. Notice how:

- pronouns (他) replace corresponding nouns when the subject remains unchanged (张天明/張天明)

- identical subject pronouns in close proximity are omitted (他 in brackets)

- words and structures that indicate time or time relationships (⋯以后/以後, 马上/馬上, 快⋯了) and place (在那儿/在那兒) serve as connective devices

张天明上大学的第一天

张天明是大学一年级的新生，他家离大学很远。大学快开学了，他坐飞机去学校。他坐飞机坐了两个多小时，[他]下飞机以后，[他]马上叫了一辆出租汽车，[他]很快就到了学校宿舍。宿舍前边的人很多，在那儿，他认识了柯林。

張天明上大學的第一天

　　張天明是大學一年級的新生，他家離大學很遠。大學快開學了，他坐飛機去學校。他坐飛機坐了兩個多小時，[他]下飛機以後，[他]馬上叫了一輛出租汽車，[他]很快就到了學校宿舍。宿舍前邊的人很多，在那兒，他認識了柯林。

Second, describe your first day in college. Use as many of the cohesive devices in the example as possible to string together your answers to the questions:

- 你是大学几年级的学生？
  你是大學幾年級的學生？

- 你家离学校远不远？
  你家離學校遠不遠？

- 你是怎么从家里来学校的？坐飞机、开车，还是坐出租汽车来的？
  你是怎麼從家裡來學校的？坐飛機、開車，還是坐出租汽車來的？

- 从你家到学校要多少时间？
  從你家到學校要多少時間？

- 你到宿舍以后认识了谁？
  你到宿舍以後認識了誰？

Can-Do Check List ✓ **I can**

Before proceeding to Lesson 2, make sure you can complete the following tasks in Chinese:

- ☐ Disambiguate my Chinese name
- ☐ Ask and answer questions about where I was born and grew up
- ☐ Discuss my preferences for living on or off campus
- ☐ Express a contrary view politely

Zhāng Tiānmíng shì dàxué yī niánjí de xīnshēng[a]. Kuài kāi xué le, tā jiā lí dàxué hěn yuǎn, děi zuò fēijī qù xuéxiào. Tā zuò fēijī zuò le liǎng ge duō xiǎoshí, xià fēijī yǐhòu, mǎshàng jiào le yí liàng chūzū qìchē, hěn kuài jiù dào le xuéxiào sùshè[1].

 Rén zhēn duō!

 Nǐ shì xīnshēng ba?

 Shì, wǒ shì xīnshēng. Nǐ ne?

 Wǒ shì yánjiūshēng. Zài zhèr bāng xīnshēng bān dōngxi. Qǐng wèn, nǐ jiào shénme míngzi?

 Wǒ jiào Zhāng Tiānmíng.

 Zhāng Tiānmíng? Shì Zhōngwén míngzi ma?

 Duì, wǒ bàba māma shì cóng Zhōngguó lái de. Kěshì wǒ shì zài Měiguó chūshēng, zài Měiguó zhǎng dà de[2]. Qǐng wèn nǐ de míngzi shì . . .

 Wǒ zhèng zài xué Zhōngwén, wǒ de Zhōngwén míngzi shì Kē Lín. Nǐ de míngzi shì nǎ sān ge zì?

 Zhāng shì gōng cháng zhāng, jiù shì yì zhāng zhǐ de zhāng, tiān shì tiānqì de tiān, míng shì míngtiān de míng.

 Nǐ shì zěnme lái xuéxiào de?

 Wǒ xiān zuò fēijī, cóng jīchǎng dào xuéxiào zuò chūzū qìchē. Kē Lín, nǐ yě zhù zài zhèr ma?

 Bù, zhè shì xīnshēng sùshè, wǒ zhù zài xiào wài.

 Shì ma? Nǐ wèishénme zhù xiào wài? Nǐ juéde zhù zài xiào nèi hǎo, háishi zhù zài xiào wài hǎo?

 Yǒude rén xǐhuan zhù zài xuéxiào sùshè, juéde yòu fāngbiàn yòu ānquán, yǒude rén xǐhuan zhù zài xiào wài, yīnwèi xiào wài de fángzi bǐjiào piányi. Wǒ zhù zài xiào wài, chúle xiǎng shěng diǎnr qián yǐwài[3], hái yīnwèi zhù zài xiào wài zìyóu. Zàishuō, zhù zài xiào nèi yě bújiànde hěn fāngbiàn.

 Zhēn de ma? Nà wǒ yǐhòu yě bān dào xiào wài qù.

 Nǐ gāng lái, zài xuéxiào zhù duì nǐ yǒu hǎochu[b], kěyǐ shìyìng yí xià xuéxiào de shēnghuó. Yàoshi nǐ yǐhòu xiǎng bān jiā, wǒ kěyǐ bāng nǐ zhǎo fángzi.

 Hǎo ba, wǒ yǐhòu yàoshi bān jiā, yídìng qǐng nǐ bāng máng.

 Tiānmíng, qiánbian méi rén le, wǒ bāng nǐ bǎ xínglì bān jìn qu ba.

 Hǎo, xièxie. Āi, wǒ de diànnǎo ne? . . . Zāogāo, diànnǎo kěnéng là[c] zài chūzū chē shang le!

宿舍生活

DORM LIFE

Learning Objectives

In this lesson, you will learn to:

- Name basic pieces of furniture
- Describe your living quarters
- Comment on someone's living quarters
- Disagree tactfully

Relate & Get Ready

In your own culture/community:

- Do dorms and apartments usually come furnished or unfurnished?
- What facilities and services do dorms offer?
- Do dorms usually have air conditioning?

课文

Text

Audio

Before You Study

Answer the following questions in Chinese to prepare for the reading.

1 你平常自己带饭还是在学生餐厅吃饭?

2 学生餐厅的饭怎么样?

When You Study

Listen to the audio recording and skim the text; then answer the following questions in Chinese.

1 为什么宿舍房间里那么热?

2 柯林说住在这儿方便吗? 为什么?

3 张天明觉得美国的中餐馆儿怎么样?

张天明宿舍的房间不太大,住两个人。他的同屋[a]已经来了。房间里家具不多,靠窗户摆着两张书桌,每张桌子的前边有一把椅子。书桌的旁边是床[1],床上有被子和毯子。床旁边有两个衣柜,柜子里挂着一些衣服。门右边放着两个书架,书架还是空的。

真热! 房间里怎么没有空调[b]?

这栋楼比较[2]旧,我大一[c]的时候在这儿住过。

卫生间也比较小。住在这儿恐怕很不方便吧?

不,这儿很方便。学生餐厅[d]就在楼下,餐厅旁边有一个小商店,卖日用品和文具。教室离这儿不远,走路差不多五、六分钟。

洗衣服方便吗?

方便得很[3]。这层楼有三台洗衣机和三台干衣机。

这儿吵不吵?

不吵,这儿离大马路很远,很安静。

課文

Audio

　　張天明宿舍的房間不太大，住兩個人。他的同屋[a]已經來了。房間裡傢俱不多，靠窗戶擺著兩張書桌，每張桌子的前邊有一把椅子。書桌的旁邊是床[1]，床上有被子和毯子。床旁邊有兩個衣櫃，櫃子裡掛著一些衣服。門右邊放著兩個書架，書架還是空的。

真熱！房間裡怎麼沒有空調[b]？

這棟樓比較[2]舊，我大一[c]的時候在這兒住過。

衛生間也比較小。住在這兒恐怕很不方便吧？

不，這兒很方便。學生餐廳[d]就在樓下，餐廳旁邊有一個小商店，賣日用品和文具。教室離這兒不遠，走路差不多五、六分鐘。

洗衣服方便嗎？

方便得很[3]。這層樓有三台洗衣機和三台乾衣機。

這兒吵不吵？

不吵，這兒離大馬路很遠，很安靜。

Before You Study

Answer the following questions in Chinese to prepare for the reading.

1 你平常自己帶飯還是在學生餐廳吃飯？

2 學生餐廳的飯怎麼樣？

When You Study

Listen to the audio recording and skim the text; then answer the following questions in Chinese.

1 為什麼宿舍房間裡那麼熱？

2 柯林說住在這兒方便嗎？為什麼？

3 張天明覺得美國的中餐館兒怎麼樣？

听说学校餐厅的饭一般都不太好。这儿的呢？

你说对了，餐厅的饭真的不怎么样。

真的？那怎么办？

你别着急。附近有很多饭馆儿，还有一家中国餐馆儿呢。

我觉得美国的中国餐馆儿，好吃的不多。

那也不见得。附近那家中国餐馆儿的菜就很地道。我和我的女朋友常去。

真的吗？那么过几天你带我去那儿看看，好吗？

好，没问题。

View & Explore

For deeper language immersion and more cultural information, watch "Housing," a short, supplemental video clip by Cheng & Tsui on this lesson's theme.

Video

聽說學校餐廳的飯一般都不太好。這兒的呢？

你說對了，餐廳的飯真的不怎麼樣。

真的？那怎麼辦？

你別著急。附近有很多飯館兒，還有一家中國餐館兒呢。

我覺得美國的中國餐館兒，好吃的不多。

那也不見得。附近那家中國餐館兒的菜就很地道。我和我的女朋友常去。

真的嗎？那麼過幾天你帶我去那兒看看，好嗎？

好，沒問題。

After You Study

Answer the following questions in Chinese.

1 張天明的房間裡有些什麼傢俱？

2 你覺得住在張天明的宿舍裡有什麼好處和壞處？

Language Notes

a 同屋

Another word for roommate is 室友 (shìyǒu) (lit. room friend).

b 空调/空調

空调/空調 (kōngtiáo) is short for 空气调节器/空氣調節器 (kōngqì tiáojié qì) (air control or air adjustment machine), although the long form is almost never used. 空调/空調 can have both heating and cooling functions. However, by definition, 冷气机/冷氣機 (lěngqì jī) are only capable of cooling.

c 我大一

This phrase, short for 我是大学一年级的学生/我是大學一年級的學生, means "I'm a first-year college student." Among students, the shorter form is more common.

d 餐厅/餐廳

The term 餐厅/餐廳 applies to both small, independent restaurants and school and company cafeterias. School and company cafeterias are also called 食堂 (shítáng). In China, many schools and companies subsidize their own cafeterias; these are for the exclusive use of students or employees. Many accept meal cards rather than cash.

Vocabulary

Audio

Flashcards

No.	Simplified	Traditional	Pinyin	Part of Speech	Definition
1	同屋	同屋	tóngwū	n	roommate
2	摆	擺	bǎi	v	to put, to place
3	被子	被子	bèizi	n	comforter, quilt
4	毯子	毯子	tǎnzi	n	blanket
5	衣柜	衣櫃	yīguì	n	wardrobe
6	柜子	櫃子	guìzi	n	cabinet, cupboard
7	挂	掛	guà	v	to hang, to hang up
8	门	門	mén	n	door
9	空	空	kōng	adj	empty
10	空调	空調	kōngtiáo	n	air conditioning
11	栋	棟	dòng	m	(measure word for buildings)
12	旧	舊	jiù	adj	old (of things)
13	恐怕	恐怕	kǒngpà	adv	I'm afraid that, I think perhaps, probably
14	日用品	日用品	rìyòngpǐn	n	daily necessities
15	文具	文具	wénjù	n	stationery, writing supplies

张天明的房间里，靠窗户摆着两张书桌，书桌的旁边是床，床旁边有两个衣柜。你的房间里有哪些家具？

張天明的房間裡，靠窗戶擺著兩張書桌，書桌的旁邊是床，床旁邊有兩個衣櫃。你的房間裡有哪些傢俱？

How About You?

请大家也为"安全"充充电！

While studying abroad in Beijing, you see this poster in your dorm. What does it ask students to do in order to ensure everyone's safety?

GET
Real
WITH **CHINESE**

No.	Simplified	Traditional	Pinyin	Part of Speech	Definition
16	洗	洗	xǐ	v	to wash
17	层	層	céng	m	(measure word for stories of a building)
18	台	台	tái	m	(measure word for machines)
19	洗衣机	洗衣機	xǐyījī	n	washing machine
20	干衣机	乾衣機	gānyījī	n	clothes dryer
21	马路	馬路	mǎlù	n	road, street
22	一般	一般	yìbān	adv	generally
23	真的	真的	zhēn de	adv	really, truly
24	着急	著急	zháojí	v	to worry
25	餐馆儿	餐館兒	cānguǎnr	n	restaurant
26	地道	地道	dìdao	adj	authentic, genuine
27	过几天	過幾天	guò jǐ tiān		in a few days

Grammar

1 **Existential sentences**

Existential sentences indicate that something exists at a certain place. Such sentences have a non-typical word order and are structured as follows:

Place word/phrase + verb + (着/著 or 了) + numeral + measure word + noun

Let's look at some examples:

A
桌子上放着一本书。
桌子上放著一本書。
There is a book lying on the desk.

B
床前有一把椅子。
床前有一把椅子。
There is a chair in front of the bed.

C
书桌的旁边是衣柜。
書桌的旁邊是衣櫃。
Next to the desk, there is a wardrobe.

The verbs that can be used with this structure are limited to 有, 是, and verbs signifying bodily actions (e.g. 站, 坐, 躺, 拿, 放, 摆/擺, 挂/掛, and 贴/貼).

D
教室里有一些学生。
教室裡有一些學生。
There are some students in the classroom.

E

桌子上是一张地图。

桌子上是一張地圖。

On the desk is a map.

F

书架上摆着三张照片。

書架上擺著三張照片。

There are three photos on the bookshelf.

G

那个男孩子手里拿着一个小飞机。

那個男孩子手裡拿著一個小飛機。

That boy is holding a model plane in his hand.

H

床上坐着一个人。

床上坐著一個人。

Someone is sitting on the bed.

In existential sentences, 有 and 是 differ in their implications. 是 suggests that there is only one, or one type of, object or person at a particular place. By contrast, 有 suggests that at the location being referred to, there are multiple objects or types of objects or people. Compare:

I

桌子上有一枝笔，一份报和一些纸。

桌子上有一枝筆，一份報和一些紙。

There's a pen, a newspaper, and some paper on the desk.

[There may be other items on the desk as well.]

J

Q: 你看，桌子上放着什么？

你看，桌子上放著什麼？

Look, what's on the table?

A: 桌子上是一枝笔。

桌子上是一枝筆。

There's a pen on the table.

[There's nothing else on the table.]

Existential sentences can be used to describe what someone is wearing or what is in a space.

K

这个时候从前边走来一个人，他身上穿着一件白衬衫，手里拿着一条红毯子。

這個時候從前邊走來一個人，他身上穿著一件白襯衫，手裡拿著一條紅毯子。

At that moment, a man walked over from the front. He was wearing a white shirt and carrying a red blanket in his hand.

L

我住的地方非常漂亮，也非常安静。房子前边有很多花，房子后边是一个小山，山上有很多树。左边有一个小公园，右边有一条小路，从那条小路可以去学校。

我住的地方非常漂亮，也非常安靜。房子前邊有很多花，房子後邊是一個小山，山上有很多樹。左邊有一個小公園，右邊有一條小路，從那條小路可以去學校。

The place where I live is very pretty and very quiet. There are many flowers in front of the house. Behind the house is a small hill, and on this hill there are many trees. To the left is a small park, and to the right is a small road by which I can go to school.

2 | Expressing relative degree or extent using 比较/比較

The word 比较/比較 (relatively, comparatively, rather) is not used to make absolute comparisons such as "X is more [adjective] than Y" and "X is less [adjective] than Y." The term is more general, and is used in statements to indicate a relative degree or extent.

A

这把椅子比较贵，你别买了。

這把椅子比較貴，你別買了。

This chair is rather expensive. Don't buy it.

B 今天比较冷，你多穿点衣服吧。

今天比較冷，你多穿點衣服吧。

It's pretty cold today. You'd better put on more clothes.

C Q: 你喜欢什么运动？   A: 我比较喜欢打网球。

你喜歡什麼運動？   我比較喜歡打網球。

What kind of sports do you like?   I kind of like playing tennis.

(A), (B), and (C) all feature generalized rather than specific comparisons. Contrast these examples with (D):

D Q: 听说你这两天不太舒服，今天觉得怎么样？

聽說你這兩天不太舒服，今天覺得怎麼樣？

I heard that you were sick the last couple of days. How are you feeling today?

A: 好一点儿了。

好一點兒了。

A little better.

Because the questioner asks for a specific comparison of the respondent's current condition to his/her condition over "the last couple of days," it would be incorrect for the respondent to say:

[❌ 比较好。]

[❌ 比較好。]

As with (D), the sentence in (E) involves a specific comparison:

E 我很高，我哥哥更高。

我很高，我哥哥更高。

I'm very tall. My older brother is even taller.

Hence, it would be incorrect to say:

[❌ 我很高，我哥哥比较高。]

[❌ 我很高，我哥哥比較高。]

Indicating an extreme extent using …得很

…得很 is used after adjectives and certain verbs that denote thoughts or feelings to suggest an extreme extent. 冷得很, for example, suggests a much more intense degree of coldness than 很冷.

A

学校刚开学，大家都忙得很。

學校剛開學，大家都忙得很。

School just started. Everyone has been extremely busy.

B

今天搬进宿舍的新生多得很，我们明天再搬吧。

今天搬進宿舍的新生多得很，我們明天再搬吧。

There are way too many freshmen moving into the dorms today. Let's move tomorrow.

C

我们的宿舍安静得很，大家都很喜欢。

我們的宿舍安靜得很，大家都很喜歡。

Our dorms are very quiet. Everyone likes them a lot.

D

来学校一个多星期了，张天明想家得很。

來學校一個多星期了，張天明想家得很。

It's been over a week since Zhang Tianming arrived on campus. He's really homesick.

A WAY WITH WORDS

洗衣服

听说那个人洗钱，现在跑了，大家都在找他。

小白昨天刚从纽约回来，今天朋友们请她吃饭，为她洗尘 (chén)。

Using the word/phrase in orange as a clue, try to figure out the meaning of the words/phrases in blue; consult a dictionary if necessary. Consider how the literal and extended senses are related in each case.

洗衣服

聽說那個人洗錢，現在跑了，大家都在找他。

小白昨天剛從紐約回來，今天朋友們請她吃飯，為她洗塵 (chén)。

Conjunctions

Conjunctions are often omitted in spoken Chinese.

A | **Zhang Tianming**

真热！房间里怎么没有空调？

真熱！房間裡怎麼沒有空調？

It's so hot! How come there's no air conditioning in this room?

Ke Lin

（因为）这栋楼比较旧……

（因為）這棟樓比較舊……

(Because) this building is relatively old . . .

B | **Zhang Tianming**

这儿吵不吵？

這兒吵不吵？

Is it noisy here?

Ke Lin

不吵，（因为）这儿离大马路很远，（所以）很安静。

不吵，（因為）這兒離大馬路很遠，（所以）很安靜。

No, it's not noisy here. (Because) it's far from the major roads, (that's why) it's very quiet here.

Words & Phrases

| ## 恐怕/恐怕 (I'm afraid, I think perhaps, probably)

The adverb 恐怕/恐怕 is used to express an assessment or concern regarding a particular situation.

1　下雨了，恐怕我们不能打球了。

　　下雨了，恐怕我們不能打球了。

　　It's raining. I'm afraid we can't play ball.

2　十一点了，现在给他打电话恐怕太晚了。

　　十一點了，現在給他打電話恐怕太晚了。

　　It's eleven o'clock already. I'm afraid it's too late to call him now.

3　这儿没空调，恐怕夏天很热吧?

　　這兒沒空調，恐怕夏天很熱吧?

　　There's no air conditioning here. It's probably very hot in the summer, isn't it?

4　窗户外有一条马路，这儿恐怕很吵吧?

　　窗戶外有一條馬路，這兒恐怕很吵吧?

　　There's a street outside the window. It must be very noisy here, right?

People seldom say 我恐怕/我恐怕. For example, [❌我恐怕他不能去/我恐怕他不能去] would be incorrect. If someone says 我恐怕不能去了/我恐怕不能去了, what he or she really means is （我）恐怕我不能去了/（我）恐怕我不能去了 (I'm afraid I won't be able to go). One can also say 他恐怕不能去了/他恐怕不能去了, meaning （我）恐怕他不能去了/（我）恐怕他不能去了 (I'm afraid he won't be able to go). In other words, the implied subject is 我. In 他恐怕不能去了/他恐怕不能去了, 他 functions as the topic of the sentence.

差不多/差不多 (about, roughly)

差不多/差不多 means "roughly" or "approximately" and can be used as an adverbial.

1
我跟姐姐差不多高。

我跟姐姐差不多高。

I'm about the same height as my older sister. *[adverbial]*

2
教室离这儿不远，走路差不多五、六分钟。

教室離這兒不遠，走路差不多五、六分鐘。

The classroom isn't far from here. It's roughly a five- or six-minute walk. *[adverbial]*

3
Q: 你同屋的书架上一共有几本书？

你同屋的書架上一共有幾本書？

How many books are on your roommate's bookshelves?

A: 差不多有一百本。

差不多有一百本。

About a hundred. *[adverbial]*

4
电影两点开始，现在差不多一点半了，快走吧。

電影兩點開始，現在差不多一點半了，快走吧。

The film starts at two o'clock. It's almost one thirty. We'd better go now. *[adverbial]*

5
Q: 你多长时间给你母亲打一次电话？

你多長時間給你母親打一次電話？

How often do you call your mom?

A: 我差不多一个星期打一次。

我差不多一個星期打一次。

About once a week. *[adverbial]*

差不多/差不多 can also be used as an adjective meaning "almost the same." When used in this way, it can function as a predicate.

6 Q: 你弟弟长得什么样？

你弟弟長得什麼樣？

What does your younger brother look like?

A: 跟我差不多，好多人看见我常常叫他的名字。

跟我差不多，好多人看見我常常叫他的名字。

Very much like me. Many people call me by his name when they see me. *[predicate]*

7 今天的天气跟昨天差不多，不冷不热，很舒服。

今天的天氣跟昨天差不多，不冷不熱，很舒服。

Today's weather is very similar to yesterday's—not too cold, not too hot, very comfortable. *[predicate]*

A WAY WITH WORDS

同屋

他们一起上小学、中学和大学，是十几年的同窗。

小李和小王做的菜一样好吃。她们是同门，都是跟林师傅学的。

Using the word/phrase in orange as a clue, try to figure out the meaning of the words/phrases in blue; consult a dictionary if necessary. Consider how the literal and extended senses are related in each case.

同屋

他們一起上小學、中學和大學，是十幾年的同窗。

小李和小王做的菜一樣好吃。她們是同門，都是跟林師傅學的。

C 吵 (noisy; to quarrel)

When used as an adjective, as in (1) and (2), 吵 means "noisy."

1

外边很吵，我不能看书。

外邊很吵，我不能看書。

It's very noisy outside. I can't read. *[adjective]*

2

这儿很安静，一点儿也不吵。

這兒很安靜，一點兒也不吵。

It's very quiet here. It's not at all noisy. *[adjective]*

吵 can also be used as a verb meaning "to quarrel," as in (3) and (4).

3

他们两个人不知道为什么，吵起来了。

他們兩個人不知道為什麼，吵起來了。

The two of them started to quarrel. I don't know why. *[verb]*

4

别吵了！有什么问题，好好说。

別吵了！有什麼問題，好好說。

Stop quarreling! If there's a problem, talk it out. *[verb]*

D 安静/安靜 (quiet)

安静/安靜 is an adjective. It can be used as a predicate, as in (1), (2), and (3).

1

我们的宿舍很安静。

我們的宿舍很安靜。

Our dorms are quiet. *[predicate]*

2

这儿安静得很，我们就在这儿坐一下吧。

這兒安靜得很，我們就在這兒坐一下吧。

It's very quiet here. Let's sit here for a while. *[predicate]*

3

安静点儿，弟弟在睡觉。

安靜點兒，弟弟在睡覺。

Be quiet. My younger brother is sleeping. [*predicate*]

It can also be used as an attributive, as in (4).

4

我们找一个安静的地方聊聊，好吗？

我們找一個安静的地方聊聊，好嗎？

Let's find a quiet place to talk, OK? [*attributive*]

E

一般 (generally)

一般 is an adjective, often used as an adverbial.

1

我听说学校餐厅的饭一般都不太好。

我聽說學校餐廳的飯一般都不太好。

I hear that the school cafeteria food is generally not very good.

2

新生一般都没有车，差不多都找老生开车带他们去买东西。

新生一般都沒有車，差不多都找老生開車帶他們去買東西。

Freshmen usually don't have cars. Almost all of them ask upperclassmen to take them shopping.

3

周末学校宿舍一般都有一点吵，图书馆比较安静。

週末學校宿舍一般都有一點吵，圖書館比較安靜。

On weekends the dorms are generally a bit noisy. It's quieter in the library.

4

星期一到星期五，她一般都在学校餐厅吃饭，周末
常常去饭馆儿。

星期一到星期五，她一般都在學校餐廳吃飯，週末
常常去飯館兒。

From Monday through Friday, she usually eats at the school cafeteria. On weekends,
she often goes out to eat.

F

不怎么样/不怎麼樣 (not that great, just so-so)

Usually used as a predicate, 不怎么样/不怎麼樣 is a colloquial expression and means
"not that great" or "just so-so." It can sound a bit direct and dismissive, so it's often used among
friends or people who know each other well—that is, when there is no need to hold back.

1

这个图书馆不怎么样，书很少。

這個圖書館不怎麼樣，書很少。

This library is not that great. There are very few books.

2 Q: 你觉得这栋楼怎么样？

你覺得這棟樓怎麼樣？

What do you think about this building?

A: 不怎么样，又小又旧。

不怎麼樣，又小又舊。

Not that great. It's small and old.

3 Q: 你觉得这个房间的家具摆得怎么样？

你覺得這個房間的傢俱擺得怎麼樣？

What do you think about how the furniture in this room is arranged?

A: 不怎么样，床应该靠右，书桌应该靠窗户。

不怎麼樣，床應該靠右，書桌應該靠窗戶。

Not good. The bed should be on the right, and the desk should be against
the window.

地道 (authentic, genuine)

地道 is an adjective meaning "authentic." It implies that what's being referred to meets a certain standard. It is most often used to describe food or someone's accent. In Taiwan and southern Mainland China, 道地 is more common.

1

他说的北京话很地道。

他說的北京話很地道。

His Beijing dialect really passes muster. *[predicate]*

2

这是地道的中国菜。

這是地道的中國菜。

This is authentic Chinese food. *[attributive]*

3

我今天买了一些地道的日本茶。

我今天買了一些地道的日本茶。

I bought some authentic Japanese tea today. *[attributive]*

Chinese Chat

A friend is texting you on Facebook Messenger about your dorm. How would you reply?

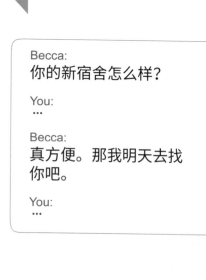

Becca:
你的新宿舍怎么样？

You:
...

Becca:
真方便。那我明天去找
你吧。

You:
...

Language Practice

Humble abode

INTERPERSONAL

In pairs, conduct a role-play about apartments. Pretend you have just moved into a new apartment, and your friend is asking you how things are. You like your place and would like to be positive about it, but at the same time, you don't want to brag too much. Formulate questions-and-answers using the prompts, e.g.:

客厅/客廳   大

Q: 你的公寓客厅很大吧?

你的公寓客廳很大吧？

A: 对，客厅比较大。

對，客廳比較大。

1   家具/傢俱   新

2   房租   便宜

3   附近   安静/安靜

4   买东西/買東西   方便

You don't want to do that

INTERPERSONAL

In pairs, practice dissuading your partner from engaging in the activities described in the prompts. Use ···得很 to emphasize the reason, e.g.:

eat at the cafeteria   awful food

Person A   我想去学生餐厅吃午饭。

我想去學生餐廳吃午飯。

Person B   别去，学生餐厅的饭难吃得很。

別去，學生餐廳的飯難吃得很。

1	go jogging in the park	freezing cold
2	study at the coffee shop	loud and noisy
3	get a part-time job at the bookstore	totally boring
4	go to the new store to shop	incredibly far away

<u>C</u>

You don't want to go there

INTERPERSONAL

In pairs, practice politely and indirectly expressing disagreement. Your partner wants to relocate to a different state, but you don't want him/her to leave. Attempt to dissuade him/her using 恐怕/恐怕, e.g.:

Alaska

Person A 我想搬到Alaska去。

我想搬到Alaska去。

Person B 是吗？ Alaska恐怕太冷了吧?

是嗎？ Alaska恐怕太冷了吧？

1	Florida	4	Texas
2	California	5	Michigan
3	New York		

Your partner is thinking of moving to a different dorm. Using 恐怕/恐怕, make a gentle attempt at convincing him/her that the other dorm is not as great as he/she thinks, e.g.:

small rooms

Person A 我想搬到 (name of a dorm) 宿舍去。

我想搬到 (name of a dorm) 宿舍去。

Person B 恐怕那儿的房间有点儿小吧?

恐怕那兒的房間有點兒小吧？

6	old furniture	8	noisy
7	restrictive	9	not convenient for having parties

D

Creature of habit

In pairs, use the prompts and refer to the schedule to discuss what Zhang Tianming and Ke Lin generally do on a weekly basis, e.g.:

星期一	星期二	星期三	星期四	星期五	星期六	星期天

Q: 张天明星期几买菜？

张天明星期幾買菜？

A: 张天明一般星期六买菜。

張天明一般星期六買菜。

1

2

3

4

Characterize it!

Identify the common radical.

How does the radical relate to the overall meaning of the characters?

More characters

Tough customer

In pairs, role-play two friends at the mall. You're both thoroughly dissatisfied with what's on offer. Form questions-and-answers and make it clear that you are unimpressed, e.g.:

Q: 这家店的文具怎么样?

這家店的文具怎麼樣？

A: 这家店的文具不怎么样，又贵又不好。

這家店的文具不怎麼樣，又貴又不好。

 1

 2

 3

 4

 5

Interior layout

Identify the furniture in the room, then take turns with your classmates describing the arrangement of the room. Make your description sequential, e.g., move from left to right.

Get your bearings

PRESENTATIONAL

Imagine that you're helping a group of freshmen get to know the layout of your campus. Pull up a map of your campus on your cell phone and work with a partner to identify where the main buildings/facilities are on the map, e.g., 运动场的南边是图书馆/運動場的南邊是圖書館.

H INTERPRETIVE

See what I'm saying

PRESENTATIONAL

Make a list of the furniture in your bedroom and share the list with your partner. Then bring in a picture or a sketch of your room. Work with a partner and describe your picture to him or her in Chinese, e.g., 房间的右边有一把椅子，椅子上挂着一件衣服/房間的右邊有一把椅子，椅子上掛著一件衣服, etc. Have your partner, without looking at your original picture or sketch, draw a picture of your room by following your description. Compare the original picture and your partner's drawing to see whether your descriptions were correct and whether your partner faithfully followed your descriptions.

I INTERPERSONAL

Dream house

PRESENTATIONAL

Imagine that you're working with an architect to build your dream house. Your partner will pretend to be your architect. He/she will ask questions and sketch your house based on your description and answers. Make your description as logical as you can, e.g., begin with the entrance and go from downstairs to upstairs, as well as from left to right.

J INTERPERSONAL

Upsides and downsides

PRESENTATIONAL

List the things that you do and don't like about your room/building, then share your list with a partner. Take turns explaining your list and reasons to each other, then politely agree or disagree with your partner's assessment.

喜欢/喜歡	不喜欢/不喜歡
_____	_____
_____	_____
_____	_____
_____	_____

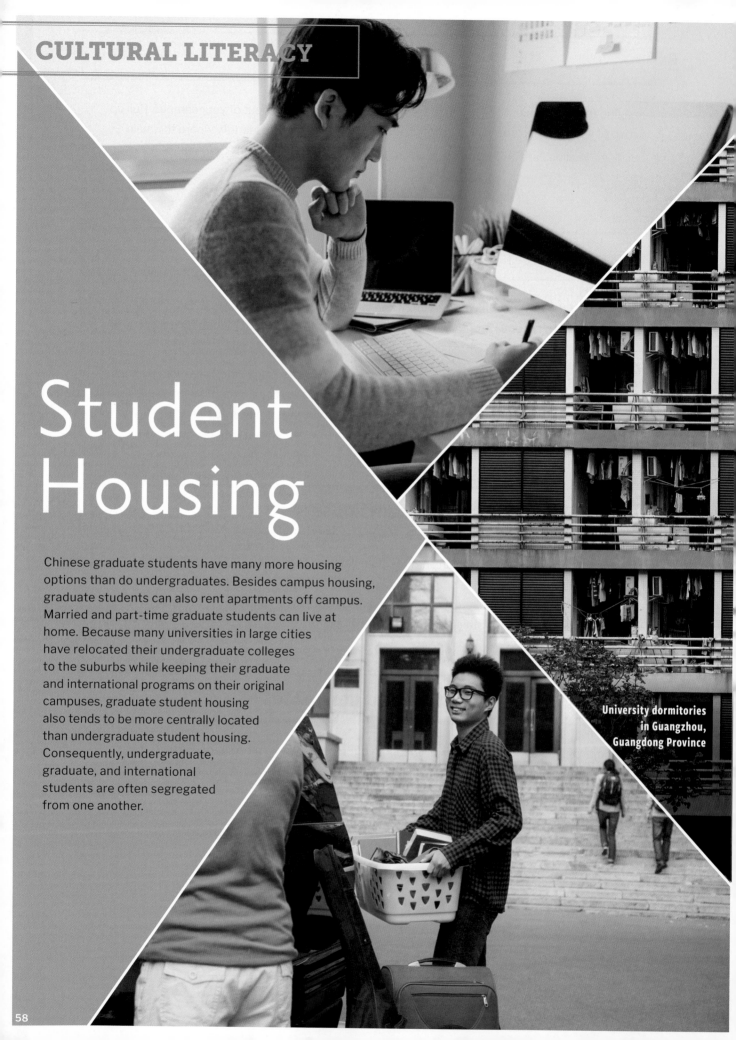

Student Housing

Chinese graduate students have many more housing options than do undergraduates. Besides campus housing, graduate students can also rent apartments off campus. Married and part-time graduate students can live at home. Because many universities in large cities have relocated their undergraduate colleges to the suburbs while keeping their graduate and international programs on their original campuses, graduate student housing also tends to be more centrally located than undergraduate student housing. Consequently, undergraduate, graduate, and international students are often segregated from one another.

University dormitories in Guangzhou, Guangdong Province

Campus Dining

The dining hall is an essential part of the Chinese college experience. Many colleges and universities try hard to please their students by offering a wide variety of dining options. Some even exchange chefs and host competitions with other local universities. One-upmanship of this kind is often called PK ("player killing," a term borrowed from combat video games) in colloquial Chinese. It's not unheard of for students to visit friends on other campuses in order to sample their food. The media also frequently report on novel creations by college chefs such as deep-fried mangos, stir-fried corn with grapes, stir-fried bitter and honeydew melons, fried wontons in salt and pepper, and so on. There are also numerous small and inexpensive eateries around most university campuses. Many people are nostalgic about dining on and around college campuses long after they graduate.

COMPARE & CONTRAST

Institutional spaces such as dorms are the product of available resources, but they're also conditioned by ideas about personal space and how people are supposed to relate to each other—that is, by ideas about how society is supposed to work. As one example, in dorms at many Chinese public universities, the electricity is turned off around eleven o'clock at night. Research Chinese dorm life online, and take a look at a few pictures. What ideas about how people are supposed to relate to each other in society are reflected in Chinese dorm rooms? Which of these ideas are shared in your own community/culture?

Accommodations for
INTERNATIONAL STUDENTS

If you study abroad in China, you will most likely stay in an international student dorm. You will probably share a room with another international student, or you may be paired with a Chinese roommate. Many universities have established international student dorms to avoid thrusting students into conditions dramatically different from those back home. However, China also has a history of segregating foreigners from the local population. For example, between about 1686 and 1856, Western traders were confined in a special area along the Pearl River in Canton (now Guangzhou). The so-called Thirteen or Canton Factories comprised the offices and warehouses of foreign mercantile agents. The establishment of these separate quarters arose from a desire to avoid the intermingling of foreigners and the native Chinese population, or 华洋杂处/華洋雜處 (huá yáng zá chǔ).

Lesson Wrap-Up

Project

More exercises

An educational consulting agency in China is creating a guide for Chinese students applying to American universities. They have hired you and some classmates as consultants to conduct a survey about living conditions at your school. Using the questionnaire below as a starting point, interview at least four students about their living conditions. Compare research results with a fellow consultant. As part of your conversation with your partner, be sure to elaborate in the following ways:

- the numerical breakdown of answers you received, e.g., 三个学生觉得……, 一个学生觉得……/三個學生覺得……, 一個學生覺得……
- how much a place costs, e.g., question #5, 住宿舍住一年……; the specific age of the building, e.g., question #6, 宿舍是……年盖/蓋 (gài) (to construct) 的; why a location is good or not, e.g., question #7, 宿舍离马路远不远/宿舍離馬路遠不遠…… or question #8, 宿舍旁边有没有小商店，买得到买不到……/宿舍旁邊有沒有小商店，買得到買不到……
- what you found students care most about with regard to their living conditions
- other relevant questions missing from this survey

QUESTIONNAIRE

1　你愿意住在校内还是住在校外?
　　你願意住在校內還是住在校外？

2　住在校内有什么好处，住在校外有什么好处?
　　住在校內有什麼好處，住在校外有什麼好處？

3　你愿意一个人住一个房间还是和同屋一起住?
　　你願意一個人住一個房間還是和同屋一起住？

4　一个人住有什么好处，和同屋住有什么好处?
　　一個人住有什麼好處，和同屋住有什麼好處？

5　你觉得你住的地方贵吗?
　　你覺得你住的地方貴嗎？

6 你觉得你住的地方旧不旧？

你覺得你住的地方舊不舊？

7 你觉得你住的地方安静不安静？

你覺得你住的地方安靜不安靜？

8 你觉得你住的地方买东西方便不方便？

你覺得你住的地方買東西方便不方便？

9 你觉得你住的地方洗衣服方便不方便？

你覺得你住的地方洗衣服方便不方便？

10 你喜欢不喜欢你住的地方？

你喜歡不喜歡你住的地方？

11 你觉得你的卫生间怎么样？

你覺得你的衛生間怎麼樣？

12 你最喜欢你的房间的什么？

你最喜歡你的房間的什麼？

13 你最不喜欢你的房间的什么？

你最不喜歡你的房間的什麼？

14 你觉得你住的地方缺 *(quē)* (to lack) 什么？

你覺得你住的地方缺 *(quē)* (to lack) 什麼？

Study the following description; pay particular attention to how the highlighted parts help the sentences flow smoothly from one to the next. Notice how:

- place words and phrases (**旁边**/**旁邊**, **这里**/**這裡**) can serve as connective devices
- conjunctions (**因为**/**因為**, **但是**) also join sentences together
- adverbs (**就**, **还**/**還**) serve as connective devices

张天明的宿舍很方便

　　张天明的宿舍很小，**因为**没有空调，很热，**但是**很方便。学生餐厅**就**在楼下，**旁边**有一个小商店，卖日用品和文具。**这里**洗衣服也方便得很，每层楼有三台洗衣机和三台干衣机。离教室也不远，走路差不多五、六分钟。**这里**离大马路很远，很安静。附近**还**有一家中国餐馆儿，菜很地道。

張天明的宿舍很方便

　　張天明的宿舍很小，**因為**沒有空調，很熱，**但是**很方便。學生餐廳**就**在樓下，**旁邊**有一個小商店，賣日用品和文具。**這裡**洗衣服也方便得很，每層樓有三台洗衣機和三台乾衣機。離教室也不遠，走路差不多五、六分鐘。**這裡**離大馬路很遠，很安靜。附近**還**有一家中國餐館兒，菜很地道。

Describe your dorm. Use as many of the cohesive devices highlighted in the example as possible to string together your answers to the questions:

你的宿舍……

你的宿舍……

- 大不大？

  大不大？

- 有没有空调？

  有沒有空調？

- 吃饭、买东西、洗衣服方便不方便？为什么？

  吃飯、買東西、洗衣服方便不方便？為什麼？

- 离教室远不远？

  離教室遠不遠？

- 安静不安静？为什么？

  安靜不安靜？為什麼？

- 附近有中国餐馆儿吗？如果有，菜怎么样？

  附近有中國餐館兒嗎？如果有，菜怎麼樣？

Can-Do Check List ✓

I can

Before proceeding to Lesson 3, make sure you can complete the following tasks in Chinese:

- ☐ Name the furniture in my room
- ☐ Describe my living quarters and where things are placed
- ☐ Talk about the facilities/amenities in my building
- ☐ Comment on the quality of food at my school's cafeteria
- ☐ Give opinions indirectly and politely

Zhāng Tiānmíng sùshè de fángjiān bú tài dà, zhù liǎng ge rén. Tā de tóngwū[a] yǐjīng lái le. Fángjiān li jiājù bù duō, kào chuānghu bǎi zhe liǎng zhāng shūzhuō, měi zhāng zhuōzi de qiánbian yǒu yì bǎ yǐzi. Shūzhuō de pángbiān shì chuáng[1], chuáng shang yǒu bèizi hé tǎnzi. Chuáng pángbiān yǒu liǎng ge yīguì, guìzi li guà zhe yì xiē yīfu. Mén yòubian fàng zhe liǎng ge shūjià, shūjià hái shì kōng de.

 Zhēn rè! Fángjiān li zěnme méiyǒu kōngtiáo[b]?

 Zhè dòng lóu bǐjiào[2] jiù, wǒ dà yī[c] de shíhou zài zhèr zhù guo.

 Wèishēngjiān yě bǐjiào xiǎo. Zhù zài zhèr kǒngpà hěn bù fāngbiàn ba?

 Bù, zhèr hěn fāngbiàn. Xuéshēng cāntīng[d] jiù zài lóu xià, cāntīng pángbiān yǒu yí ge xiǎo shāngdiàn, mài rìyòngpǐn hé wénjù. Jiàoshì lí zhèr bù yuǎn, zǒu lù chàbuduō wǔ, liù fēnzhōng.

 Xǐ yīfu fāngbiàn ma?

 Fāngbiàn de hěn[3]. Zhè céng lóu yǒu sān tái xǐyījī hé sān tái gānyījī.

 Zhèr chǎo bù chǎo?

 Bù chǎo, zhèr lí dà mǎlù hěn yuǎn, hěn ānjìng.

 Tīngshuō xuéxiào cāntīng de fàn yìbān dōu bú tài hǎo. Zhèr de ne?

 Nǐ shuō duì le, cāntīng de fàn zhēn de bù zěnmeyàng.

 Zhēn de? Nà zěnme bàn?

 Nǐ bié zháojí. Fùjìn yǒu hěn duō fànguǎnr, hái yǒu yì jiā Zhōngguó cānguǎnr ne.

 Wǒ juéde Měiguó de Zhōngguó cānguǎnr, hǎochī de bù duō.

 Nà yě bújiànde. Fùjìn nà jiā Zhōngguó cānguǎnr de cài jiù hěn dìdao. Wǒ hé wǒ de nǚpéngyou cháng qù.

 Zhēnde ma? Nàme guò jǐ tiān nǐ dài wǒ qù nàr kàn kan, hǎo ma?

 Hǎo, méi wèntí.

在饭馆儿
在飯館兒

AT A RESTAURANT

Learning Objectives

In this lesson, you will learn to:

- Name four principal regional Chinese cuisines
- Order food and drinks
- Talk about what tastes you like and dislike
- Describe your dietary restrictions and preferences

Relate & Get Ready

In your own culture/community:

- Are there different regional cuisines?
- How do people season their food?
- Do people prefer to steam, stir-fry, grill, or bake?

课文

Text

Audio

Before You Study

Answer the following questions in Chinese to prepare for the reading.

1 你爱吃辣的、酸的还是甜的？

2 你平常吃青菜吃得多还是吃肉吃得多？

When You Study

Listen to the audio recording and skim the text; then answer the following questions in Chinese.

1 柯林觉得这个餐馆儿什么菜做得特别好？

2 柯林告诉服务员在菜里少放什么？别放什么？

3 林雪梅喜欢吃中国什么地方的菜？柯林呢？

今天是周末，**功课也做完了**[1]，张天明就给柯林发微信，说他和他的女朋友丽莎想吃中国饭，问他想不想去。柯林说**正好**他也想吃中国饭，就让张天明和丽莎在宿舍门口等着，他开车来接他们。

半个钟头以后，柯林的汽车到了。张天明和丽莎上车一看[2]，车里还有一个女孩儿，柯林介绍说，她是从中国来的留学生，叫林雪梅。几分钟以后，他们四个人到了那家中国饭馆儿。

这是菜单。

谢谢。丽莎，天明，你们想吃点儿什么？

这儿什么菜好吃？

这儿鸡做得不错，鱼也很好，**特别**是清蒸鱼，味道好极了。

芥兰牛肉也挺好，又嫩又香[3]。

可以点[a]一个汤吗？

当然可以，这儿的菠菜豆腐汤做得很好，叫一个吧。

再来一个青菜吧。

課文

Audio

今天是週末，功課也做完了[1]，張天明就給柯林發微信，說他和他的女朋友麗莎想吃中國飯，問他想不想去。柯林說正好他也想吃中國飯，就讓張天明和麗莎在宿舍門口等著，他開車來接他們。

半個鐘頭以後，柯林的汽車到了。張天明和麗莎上車一看[2]，車裡還有一個女孩兒，柯林介紹說，她是從中國來的留學生，叫林雪梅。幾分鐘以後，他們四個人到了那家中國飯館兒。

這是菜單。

謝謝。麗莎，天明，你們想吃點兒什麼？

這兒什麼菜好吃？

這兒雞做得不錯，魚也很好，特別是清蒸魚，味道好極了。

芥蘭牛肉也挺好，又嫩又香[3]。

可以點[a]一個湯嗎？

當然可以，這兒的菠菜豆腐湯做得很好，叫一個吧。

再來一個青菜吧。

Before You Study

Answer the following questions in Chinese to prepare for the reading.

1 你愛吃辣的、酸的還是甜的？

2 你平常吃青菜吃得多還是吃肉吃得多？

When You Study

Listen to the audio recording and skim the text; then answer the following questions in Chinese.

1 柯林覺得這個餐館兒什麼菜做得特別好？

2 柯林告訴服務員在菜裡少放什麼？別放什麼？

3 林雪梅喜歡吃中國什麼地方的菜？柯林呢？

现在可以点菜了吗?

可以。一个清蒸鱼,一个芥兰牛肉,一个菠菜豆腐汤。今天你们有什么新鲜的青菜?

小白菜怎么样?

是有机的吗?

是。

好。服务员,菜要清淡一点儿,别太咸,少放油,别放味精。

麻烦你先来四杯冰水,给我们四双筷子,再多给我们一些餐巾纸。

好,没问题。对了,您要饭吗?

我们不"要饭"[b],我们要四碗米饭。

对,对,对,要四碗米饭。

对不起,和你开玩笑。

林雪梅,柯林说这儿中国菜很地道,是真的吗?

这个饭馆儿的菜是[4]不错,但是没有我们杭州的饭馆儿好。

我听我父母[c]说中国各个地方的菜不一样,哪儿的菜最好吃?

Top to bottom:
Stir-fried baby bok choy;
dim sum, including shrimp
dumplings and *shaomai;* and
boiled chicken and rice porridge

現在可以點菜了嗎？

可以。一個清蒸魚，一個芥蘭牛肉，一個菠菜豆腐湯。今天你們有什麼新鮮的青菜？

小白菜怎麼樣？

是有機的嗎？

是。

好。服務員，菜要清淡一點兒，別太鹹，少放油，別放味精。

麻煩你先來四杯冰水，給我們四雙筷子，再多給我們一些餐巾紙。

好，沒問題。對了，您要飯嗎？

我們不"要飯"[b]，我們要四碗米飯。

對，對，對，要四碗米飯。

對不起，和你開玩笑。

林雪梅，柯林說這兒中國菜很地道，是真的嗎？

這個飯館兒的菜是[4]不錯，但是沒有我們杭州的飯館兒好。

我聽我父母[c]說中國各個地方的菜不一樣，哪兒的菜最好吃？

Top to bottom:
Roast pork and duck; steamed
fish with ginger and scallions;
and oolong tea

这就要看你的口味了。比方说我爱吃甜的,就喜欢上海菜;柯林爱吃辣的,就喜欢四川菜、湖南菜。要是喜欢比较清淡的,就吃广东菜……

雪梅,我们寒假去中国吧。

去中国旅行,吃中国菜?可以考虑。

这个主意[d]不错,我也可以考虑。

有吃有玩儿?我当然可以考虑。

真的?那太好了!大家都去!

要是能去中国学中文就更好了。

哎,我们的菜来了。

Language Notes

a 点/點

点/點 (lit. to point) means "to order," i.e., from a menu. More casually, 要, 叫, or 来/來 can also be used.

b 要饭/要飯

Beggars are colloquially known as 要饭的/要飯的, and 要饭/要飯 means "to beg." This is why Lin Xuemei corrects the waiter, who meant to ask, "Do you want any rice?"

c 父母

In contrast with 爸爸妈妈/爸爸媽媽, the word 父母 has a literary flavor and is used as a collective noun meaning "parents."

d 主意

In this word, 主 changes from the third to the second tone and 意 is in the neutral tone.

這就要看你的口味了。比方說我愛吃甜的，就喜歡上海菜；柯林愛吃辣的，就喜歡四川菜、湖南菜。要是喜歡比較清淡的，就吃廣東菜……

雪梅，我們寒假去中國吧。

去中國旅行，吃中國菜？可以考慮。

這個主意[d]不錯，我也可以考慮。

有吃有玩兒？我當然可以考慮。

真的？那太好了！大家都去！

要是能去中國學中文就更好了。

哎，我們的菜來了。

After You Study

Answer the following questions in Chinese.

1 柯林他們點了些什麼吃的、喝的？

2 中國各個地方的菜不一樣，如果吃得清淡，點什麼地方的菜好？

View & Explore

For deeper language immersion and more cultural information, watch "At a Restaurant," a short, supplemental video clip by Cheng & Tsui on this lesson's theme.

Video

Vocabulary

Audio

Flashcards

No.	Simplified	Traditional	Pinyin	Part of Speech	Definition
1	正好	正好	*zhènghǎo*	adv	coincidentally
2	门口	門口	*ménkǒu*	n	doorway, entrance
3	留学生	留學生	*liúxuéshēng*	n	study-abroad student
4	菜单	菜單	*càidān*	n	menu
5	鸡	雞	*jī*	n	chicken
6	清蒸	清蒸	*qīngzhēng*	v	to steam (food without heavy sauce)
7	味道	味道	*wèidao*	n	taste, flavor (of food)
8	芥兰	芥蘭	*jièlán*	n	Chinese broccoli
9	嫩	嫩	*nèn*	adj	tender
10	香	香	*xiāng*	adj	fragrant, pleasant-smelling
11	菠菜	菠菜	*bōcài*	n	spinach
12	叫（菜）	叫（菜）	*jiào (cài)*	v (o)	to order (food)
13	新鲜	新鮮	*xīnxian*	adj	fresh
14	有机	有機	*yǒujī*	adj	organic
15	清淡	清淡	*qīngdàn*	adj	light in flavor
16	咸	鹹	*xián*	adj	salty
17	油	油	*yóu*	n/adj	oil; oily

No.	Simplified	Traditional	Pinyin	Part of Speech	Definition
18	餐巾	餐巾	*cānjīn*	n	napkin
19	筷子	筷子	*kuàizi*	n	chopsticks
20	开玩笑	開玩笑	*kāi wánxiào*	vo	to crack a joke, to joke
21	各	各	*gè*	pr	each, every
22	口味	口味	*kǒuwèi*	n	(personal) taste
23	比方说	比方說	*bǐfāng shuō*		for example
24	辣	辣	*là*	adj	spicy
25	考虑	考慮	*kǎolǜ*	v	to consider
26	主意	主意	*zhúyi*	n	idea

柯林学校附近的中餐馆儿的菜很地道，清蒸鱼的味道好极了。你们学校附近有没有中餐馆儿？哪些菜做得地道？

柯林學校附近的中餐館兒的菜很地道，清蒸魚的味道好極了。你們學校附近有沒有中餐館兒？哪些菜做得地道？

No.	Simplified	Traditional	Pinyin	Part of Speech	Definition
27	微信	微信	*Wēixìn*	pn	WeChat
28	丽莎	麗莎	*Lìshā*	pn	(a personal name)
29	林雪梅	林雪梅	*Lín Xuěméi*	pn	(a personal name)
30	杭州	杭州	*Hángzhōu*	pn	Hangzhou
31	四川	四川	*Sìchuān*	pn	Sichuan
32	湖南	湖南	*Húnán*	pn	Hunan
33	广东	廣東	*Guǎngdōng*	pn	Guangdong

波士顿-浦东B套

正餐菜单
开胃前菜
海鲜卷配海白菜沙拉
主菜
川酱狮子头配米饭鲜蔬
或
香煎豉汁鱼柳鲜蔬面
或
泰式扒鸡胸配香草土豆、蘑菇、西兰花及胡萝卜
芝士与饼干
甜点
黄桃芝士蛋糕
面包与黄油

轻食菜单
开胃前菜
凉拌鸡丝莲藕沙拉
主菜
蚝油牛肉莴笋炒面
或
香煎鱼排佐柠檬莳萝奶油汁配红粉土豆、四季豆及樱桃番茄

果汁
橙汁
椰子汁
番茄汁
杂色果汁

碳酸饮料
可乐
低糖可乐
雪碧
芬达

其他饮料
热巧克力及各种茶和咖啡

GET Real WITH CHINESE

You're on a long-distance flight to Shanghai and it's time for dinner. Choose what you want to eat from this menu. Thinking ahead to your return flight to Boston in a few months, what Chinese dishes would you like to see on the menu (including appetizers, main dishes, and desserts)?

Grammar

<table>
<tr><td>1</td><td>Topic-comment sentence structure</td></tr>
</table>

When someone, something, or some event is already known—in other words, if it is no longer new information to the speaker and the listener—this information typically appears at the beginning of a sentence. The positioning of known information at the beginning of a sentence is an important characteristic of Chinese and is an essential part of the way conversations in Chinese flow. Sentences with this structure are referred to as topic-comment sentences: the "topic" is mentioned in the first part of the sentence and commented on in the latter part of the sentence. Known information can also include information that has already been mentioned or activities that are taken for granted, such as eating and sleeping; for students, activities taken for granted can include going to classes, doing homework, etc.

A

今天是周末，功课也做完了……

今天是週末，功課也做完了……

Today is a weekend. Besides, (I've) already finished (my) homework . . .

[This is about a student. Everyone knows that students are supposed to have homework, so the fact that the student has homework is not new information.]

B

这儿的菠菜豆腐汤做得很好。

這兒的菠菜豆腐湯做得很好。

The spinach tofu soup here is very good.

C

Q: 你知道附近那个鞋店明天要打折吗？

你知道附近那個鞋店明天要打折嗎？

Did you know that there's a sale tomorrow at that shoe store nearby?

A: 这件事我早就知道了。

這件事我早就知道了。

I already knew about this.

["This" refers to the sale, mentioned in the previous statement, that the shoe store is putting on tomorrow.]

D

你去台北的飞机票买好了吗?

你去台北的飛機票買好了嗎?

The ticket for your flight to Taipei—have you booked it?

[The speaker knows that the listener is going to Taipei and that he/she needs a plane ticket.]

E

我们昨天在"小香港"吃了清蒸鱼,那个餐馆儿的清蒸鱼做得很好。

我們昨天在"小香港"吃了清蒸魚,那個餐館兒的清蒸魚做得很好。

Yesterday we had steamed fish at Little Hong Kong. That restaurant's steamed fish is really good.

["Steamed fish" appears in the first clause. Therefore, it's treated as a topic in the second clause.]

Sentences with the topic-comment structure differ from sentences with the basic Chinese word order of "subject + verb + object."

F

这本书你看完了吗?

這本書你看完了嗎?

Have you finished reading this book?

G

功课你做完了吗?

功課你做完了嗎?

Have you finished your homework?

H

饭要慢慢吃,吃得太快对身体不好。

飯要慢慢吃,吃得太快對身體不好。

Eat your food (more) slowly. Eating too fast is not good for your health.

I

Q: 听说学校商店的东西外面的人不能买了，是真的吗？

听說學校商店的東西外面的人不能買了，是真的嗎？

I hear that non-affiliates can no longer buy stuff at the school store. Is that true?

A: 谁说的？不可能吧。

誰說的？不可能吧。

Who said that? That can't be.

While many Chinese sentences follow a basic word order that is similar to that in English—i.e., "subject + verb + object"—the topic-comment structure should be used in certain circumstances.

2 | ─ + verb and ─···就···

─ before a verb (usually monosyllabic) expresses a brief action. It must be followed by a second clause:

A

外面有人叫我，我开门一看，是送信的。

外面有人叫我，我開門一看，是送信的。

Someone outside was calling my name. I opened the door and took a look, and it was the letter carrier.

─···就···, on the other hand, connects two consecutive actions. [See Grammar 8, Lesson 13, IC2.]

In this structure, 就 is required in some cases and optional in others. If the first action is closely followed by the second action, and if there isn't a pause in the sentence, 就 is usually required before the second verb:

B

老师刚才说的话，我一听就懂了。

老師剛才說的話，我一聽就懂了。

What the teacher just said—I understood it immediately.

C

我同屋每天一回宿舍就做功课。

我同屋每天一回宿舍就做功課。

Every day, my roommate does his homework as soon as he gets back to the dorm.

D　我一收到你发的短信就跑来了。

我一收到你發的短信就跑來了。

I came as soon as I got your text message.

If there is a pause in the sentence and there is an adverbial before the second verb, 就 is optional, as in (E) and (F).

E　他把毯子往床上一放，（就）很快地跑了出去。

他把毯子往床上一放，（就）很快地跑了出去。

He put the blanket down on the bed and quickly ran out.

In (E), 跑了出去 happened immediately after the previous action, 放.

F　回家以后，我把包往桌子上一放，（就）马上给小李打了一个电话。

回家以後，我把包往桌子上一放，（就）馬上給小李打了一個電話。

After I got back home, I put down my bag on the desk and gave Little Li a call right away.

If the subjects are different, 就 is usually required before the second action:

G　Q: 我们什么时候走？

我們什麼時候走？

When are we leaving?

A: 他一到，我们就走。

他一到，我們就走。

We'll leave as soon as he gets here.

H　下午我的朋友一来，我们就一起去滑冰了。

下午我的朋友一來，我們就一起去滑冰了。

This afternoon, as soon as my friend came, we went skating together.

The two actions in the 一⋯就⋯ pattern can be identical:

| I | 那个餐馆儿很容易找，我们一找就找到了。 |
| | 那個餐館兒很容易找，我們一找就找到了。 |

That restaurant was really easy to find. As soon as we started looking, we found it.

Sometimes, the first action expresses a condition. If the condition is met, then 就 is needed before the second verb:

| J | 他病了。一看书头就疼。 |
| | 他病了。一看書頭就疼。 |

He's sick. As soon as he tries to read, he gets a headache.

| K | 我一吃味精就得喝很多水。 |
| | 我一吃味精就得喝很多水。 |

I have to drink a lot of water whenever I eat MSG.

3 | 又⋯又⋯ (both . . . and . . .) revisited

We learned in IC2 that the 又⋯又⋯ pattern can be used with adjectives to indicate two simultaneous qualities. [See Grammar 6, Lesson 14, IC2.]

| A | 妈妈做的清蒸鱼又嫩又香。 |
| | 媽媽做的清蒸魚又嫩又香。 |

The steamed fish that my mother makes is tender and it smells delicious.

| B | 那个衣柜又旧又小。 |
| | 那個衣櫃又舊又小。 |

That wardrobe is old and small.

Verbs can also be used with this pattern to indicate two concurrent actions.

C

孩子们又跑又跳，玩儿得非常高兴。

孩子們又跑又跳，玩兒得非常高興。

The kids ran and jumped. They had a great time.

D

那个小孩又哭又吵，我们一点办法也没有。

那個小孩又哭又吵，我們一點辦法也沒有。

That child cried and fussed. We didn't know what to do.

Remember that when two adjectives are used in this way, they must be both positive or both negative in meaning. For instance, when describing people, we often say, "clever and pretty"; the weather can be "hot and stuffy" or "cold and humid." When two verbs are involved, the actions denoted must be concurrent—for example, "talk and laugh" and "cry and yell."

---

4 | The reaffirmative 是

Used before adjectives and verbs, 是 reaffirms the validity of a prior statement.

Note that when an adjective is used as a predicate, it generally cannot be preceded by 是. However, in speech, this special use of 是 for emphasis before an adjective requires that 是 be stressed, and the adjective should have already been mentioned, as seen in (A) and (B).

A   **Person A**   住在这个宿舍很方便。

住在這個宿舍很方便。

This dorm is really convenient.

Person B   住在这个宿舍是很方便，去上课，去医院，去餐厅都不远。

住在這個宿舍是很方便，去上課，去醫院，去餐廳都不遠。

This dorm is indeed very convenient. It's not far from school, the hospital, and restaurants.

B | **Person A** | 这个餐馆儿的上海菜很地道，我很喜欢。

這個餐館兒的上海菜很地道，我很喜歡。

The Shanghainese cuisine at this restaurant is quite authentic. I like it very much.

Person B | 他们的上海菜是很地道，可是太贵了。

他們的上海菜是很地道，可是太貴了。

Their Shanghainese dishes are quite authentic, but too expensive.

C | **Person A** | 听说你的同屋搬走了，不回来了。

聽說你的同屋搬走了，不回來了。

I hear that your roommate moved out and isn't coming back.

Person B | 没错，他是搬走了，他去了一个更有名的大学。

沒錯，他是搬走了，他去了一個更有名的大學。

That's right. He did move out, and went to another university with an even better reputation.

A WAY WITH WORDS

餐巾

这张餐桌太小了，坐不下八个人。

服务员，我们少一套餐具。

Using the word/phrase in orange as a clue, try to figure out the meaning of the words/phrases in blue; consult a dictionary if necessary. Consider how the literal and extended senses are related in each case.

餐巾

這張餐桌太小了，坐不下八個人。

服務員，我們少一套餐具。

Words & Phrases

A | 正好 (coincidentally)

正好 is an adverb.

1 我今天正好有时间，我跟你去买衣服吧。

我今天正好有時間，我跟你去買衣服吧。

I happen to have some free time today. Let me go with you to buy some clothes.

2 我去找他的时候，他正好要出门。

我去找他的時候，他正好要出門。

When I went to look for him, he happened to be about to go out.

3 我姐姐冬天正好要回中国，你跟她一起走吧。

我姐姐冬天正好要回中國，你跟她一起走吧。

Coincidentally, my older sister is going back to China this winter. You can go with her.

4 你找她跟你一起去买衣服吧，她今天正好没有课。

你找她跟你一起去買衣服吧，她今天正好沒有課。

Why don't you ask her to shop for clothes with you? As it happens, she doesn't have class today.

B | 特别是/特別是 (especially)

特别/特別 is often used together with 是.

1 这儿鱼做得很好，特别是清蒸鱼，味道好极了。

這兒魚做得很好，特別是清蒸魚，味道好極了。

The fish here is really good, especially the steamed fish. The flavor is just awesome.

2   王小姐喜欢买东西，特别是碗盘。

王小姐喜歡買東西，特別是碗盤。

Miss Wang likes to go shopping, especially for bowls and plates.

3   小柯不喜欢运动，特别是游泳。

小柯不喜歡運動，特別是游泳。

Little Ke dislikes sports, especially swimming.

4   李先生觉得中国菜很难做，特别是糖醋鱼。

李先生覺得中國菜很難做，特別是糖醋魚。

Mr. Li thinks Chinese food is difficult to prepare, especially sweet-and-sour fish.

c | 有机/有機 (organic)

有机/有機 is an adjective, but it can only be placed in front of a noun as an attributive.

1   有机水果比一般水果贵。

有機水果比一般水果貴。

Organic fruit is more expensive.

2   校内新开了一家咖啡馆，卖有机咖啡。

校內新開了一家咖啡館，賣有機咖啡。

There's a new coffee shop on campus. It sells organic coffee.

3   这几年，越来越多人买菜只买有机的（菜）。

這幾年，越來越多人買菜只買有機的（菜）。

In recent years, more and more people are only buying organic vegetables.

When it is used as a predicate, it must be embedded in a 是···的 construction.

4   我们饭馆儿的小白菜是有机的。

我們飯館兒的小白菜是有機的。

Our restaurant's baby bok choy is organic.

麻烦／麻煩 (to trouble; troublesome)

It's polite to preface a request or favor with 麻烦（你）／麻煩（你） ([May I] trouble [you]). Used in this way, 麻烦／麻煩 is a verb meaning "to trouble."

1
小张，如果有人来电话，麻烦你告诉他我去飞机场了。

小張，如果有人來電話，麻煩你告訴他我去飛機場了。

Little Zhang, if someone calls, could you please tell him that I went to the airport? *[verb]*

2
服务员，麻烦你给我一些餐巾纸。

服務員，麻煩你給我一些餐巾紙。

Waiter, could you please give me some napkins? *[verb]*

3
麻烦你告诉老师我病了，不能去上课了。

麻煩你告訴老師我病了，不能去上課了。

Could you please tell the teacher that I'm sick and can't go to class? *[verb]*

4 **Person A**
先生，这件行李我帮你拿进房间吧。

先生，這件行李我幫你拿進房間吧。

Sir, let me help you carry this luggage to your room.

Person B
不用，不麻烦你了。

不用，不麻煩你了。

That won't be necessary. I won't trouble you. *[verb]*

麻烦／麻煩 is also an adjective meaning "troublesome." It is often used as a predicate.

5
做中国菜很麻烦。

做中國菜很麻煩。

Making Chinese food is a lot of trouble. *[adjective]*

6

出国得办护照、办签证，很麻烦。

出國得辦護照、辦簽證，很麻煩。

To go abroad you have to get your passport and visa ready; it's quite a hassle. *[adjective]*

7

他这个人很麻烦，常常问一些很难的问题。

他這個人很麻煩，常常問一些很難的問題。

He can be quite a pain. He often asks questions that are very difficult. *[adjective]*

E

这（就）要看…（了）/這（就）要看…（了）
(It depends on . . .)

这（就）要看…（了）/這（就）要看…（了） can be used to give a flexible or indirect response to a question.

1

什么菜好吃？这就要看你的口味了。

什麼菜好吃？這就要看你的口味了。

What dishes are delicious? That depends on your taste.

2 Q: 明天的考试难不难？

明天的考試難不難？

Will tomorrow's test be hard?

A: 这就要看你准备得怎么样了。

這就要看你準備得怎麼樣了。

That depends on how well you prepare.

3 Q: 快放假了，寒假你打算去中国玩吗？

快放假了，寒假你打算去中國玩嗎？

It's almost vacation time. Do you plan on going to China this winter break?

A: 这就要看买得到买不到便宜的机票了。

這就要看買得到買不到便宜的機票了。

It all depends on whether I can buy a cheap plane ticket.

比方说/比方說 (for example)

比方说/比方說 is used before citing examples.

1 他去过很多国家，比方说英国、日本、中国……

他去過很多國家，比方說英國、日本、中國……

He's been to many countries, for instance, the U.K., Japan, China . . .

2 我们班的同学很多人唱歌唱得很好，比方说王朋，唱得棒极了。

我們班的同學很多人唱歌唱得很好，比方說王朋，唱得棒極了。

Many of our classmates sing really well. Take Wang Peng, for example. He's a great singer.

3 这里的饭馆儿很多，比方说东边的"好吃饭馆"，西边的"请再来"，南边的"最便宜"，北边的"大家喜欢来餐厅"。

這裡的飯館兒很多，比方說東邊的"好吃飯館"，西邊的"請再來"，南邊的"最便宜"，北邊的"大家喜歡來餐廳"。

There are many restaurants here, for example "Delicious" on the east side, "Come Again" on the west side, "Good Bargains" on the south side, and "Everybody's Favorite" on the north side.

Characterize it!

More characters

Identify the common radical.

How does the radical relate to the overall meaning of the characters?

Language Practice

A | **Flavor profile** | PRESENTATIONAL

Look at the foods and drinks listed and take turns with your partner to talk about how they usually taste, e.g.:

可乐/可樂→可乐/可樂一般很甜。

1　西瓜

2　苹果/蘋果

3　蛋糕

4　酸辣汤/酸辣湯

5　糖醋鱼/糖醋魚

6　清蒸鱼/清蒸魚

7　四川菜/四川菜

B | INTERPERSONAL | **To each his/her own taste** | PRESENTATIONAL

Ke Lin likes his food spicy and Lin Xuemei likes hers sweet. How about you and your classmates? Ask your classmates if they like their food spicy, sweet, salty, and/or sour, e.g.:

Q: 你爱吃辣的、甜的、咸的，还是酸的？
　　你愛吃辣的、甜的、鹹的，還是酸的？

A: 我爱吃＿＿＿的。
　　我愛吃＿＿＿的。

Then report back to the class:

Kevin、Tamara，……跟我一样，都爱吃＿＿＿的。 (same)

Kevin、Tamara，……跟我一樣，都愛吃＿＿＿的。

Diego 跟我不一样，他爱吃＿＿＿的。 (different)

Diego 跟我不一樣，他愛吃＿＿＿的。

Everyone's a critic

Imagine that you're a judge at a food-and-drink competition and you don't like to mince words.
Use the information provided to evaluate the competition entries frankly, e.g.:

酸辣汤/酸辣湯　　　　　⊕ 醋　　　⊖ 盐/鹽　⊗ 糖

这碗酸辣汤不怎么样。应该多放点儿醋，少放点儿盐，别放糖。

這碗酸辣湯不怎麼樣。應該多放點兒醋，少放點兒鹽，別放糖。

1	糖醋鱼/糖醋魚	⊕ 醋	⊕ 糖	⊗ 味精
2	芥兰牛肉/芥蘭牛肉	⊕ 油	⊖ 盐/鹽	⊗ 味精
3	菠菜豆腐汤/菠菜豆腐湯	⊖ 油	⊖ 盐/鹽	⊗ 醋
4	素饺子/素餃子	⊕ 青菜/青菜	⊖ 盐/鹽	⊗ 醋
5	冰茶/冰茶	⊕ 冰	⊖ 糖	

A WAY WITH WORDS

门口

去北京的汽车票在那个窗口卖。

我已经到了机场，在机场五号出口等你。

Using the word/phrase in orange as a clue, try to figure out the meaning of the words/phrases in blue; consult a dictionary if necessary. Consider how the literal and extended senses are related in each case.

門口

去北京的汽車票在那個窗口賣。

我已經到了機場，在機場五號出口等你。

Sales pitch

Write ad copy to help the following businesses promote their merchandise, e.g.:

| bookstore | numerous | new | Chinese books |

我们的书又多又新，特别是中文书。

我們的書又多又新，特別是中文書。

1	clothing store	pretty	inexpensive	shirts
2	furniture store	new	inexpensive	wardrobes
3	grocery store	fresh	inexpensive	spinach
4	fruit stand	big	fresh	apples
5	Chinese restaurant	pleasant-smelling	delicious	steamed fish
6	tea house	healthy	delicious	green tea

Model pupil

Alex is a model Chinese language student. By making use of various strategies—listening to audio recordings, practicing speaking with friends, studying new vocab, reviewing grammar, reading the textbook, writing characters, etc.—he wastes no time and takes every opportunity to improve his Chinese. State what he does as soon as he completes the following activities, e.g.:

上课/上課

Alex 一上课就说中文。

Alex 一上課就說中文。

1 起床/起床

2 下课/下課

3 回家

4 吃完晚饭/吃完晚飯

5 放假

Special meal

Mr. Li is throwing a dinner party, and has engaged the catering company owned by you and your partner to provide the food. Mr. Li has provided a chart of his guests' likes ✓, dislikes ✗, and dietary restrictions 🚫. Compare the chart with the list of dishes that your company specializes in. Discuss with your partner and choose dishes that will work for all guests. Give reasons. Next, list the dishes that shouldn't be served and explain why using 恐怕 / 恐怕. Finally, recommend a dish or two outside the menu that you and your partner think all guests would appreciate. Give reasons using 又 · · · 又 · · · .

	Guest 1	Guest 2	Guest 3	Guest 4
牛肉	✓	✓	✓	🚫
鸡/雞	✓	✓	✓	✗
鱼/魚	✓	✓	✓	✓
豆腐	✓	✗	✓	✓
菠菜/菠菜	🚫	✓	✗	✓
中国芥兰/中國芥蘭	✓	✓	✗	✓
辣的菜/辣的菜	✓	✗	✓	✓
味精	✗	✗	🚫	✗

Here are your catering company's specialties:

红烧牛肉/紅燒牛肉	芥兰牛肉/芥蘭牛肉	清蒸鱼/清蒸魚
家常豆腐	凉拌黄瓜/涼拌黃瓜	小白菜/小白菜
素饺子/素餃子	菠菜汤/菠菜湯	酸辣汤/酸辣湯
鸡汤/雞湯		

Comfort food

Using the adjectives you have learned in this lesson, list four reasons why you love your mom's or dad's cooking. Is it because it's not oily but flavorful, free of charge, etc.?

Then present to your class the reasons you love your mom's or dad's cooking. Include 第一…， 第二…, 除了…以外， 还/還 …, or other connectors to explain your reasons.

Chinese Chat

A friend is using iMessage to text you about plans tonight. How would you reply?

⟨ Messages   Contact

你想不想去学校旁边那家中餐馆儿吃晚饭？

...

我也喜欢吃四川菜。那家餐馆儿的四川菜做得很地道。我们几点去？

...

📷 [   ] Send

Friend:
你想不想去學校旁邊那家中餐館兒吃晚飯？

You:
...

Friend:
我也喜歡吃四川菜。那家餐館兒的四川菜做得很地道。我們幾點去？

You:
...

Environmental Influences on Regional Cooking

The so-called "Four Great Culinary Schools" (四大菜系/四大菜系) (*sì dà cài xì*) are identified by the abbreviated or historic names of the four provinces from which the cuisines originate. 川 (*Chuān*), 粤/粤 (*Yuè*), 鲁/魯 (*Lǔ*), and 苏/蘇 (*Sū*) refer to Sichuan, Guangdong, Shandong, and Jiangsu, respectively. The telltale fiery and tingling taste of Sichuanese cooking (川菜/川菜) (*Chuān cài*) comes from its two main seasonings: chili pepper and Sichuan peppercorn. Hot bean paste is another common ingredient. Best known outside China is far milder Cantonese cooking (粤菜/粤菜) (*Yuè cài*) from Guangdong (广东/廣東) (*Guǎngdōng*), which takes advantage of the region's bountiful fresh seasonal produce and seafood. Shandong (山东/山東), with its coastline in the east and mountains in the west, has a varied cooking tradition, 鲁菜/魯菜 (*Lǔ cài*), emphasizing broths, seafood, and poultry. Because of the region's proximity to the imperial court, Shandong cooking became the favorite of the Manchu aristocracy during the Qing dynasty (1644–1911). The long prosperity and cultural prominence of the lower Yangtze region also made its cuisine influential. 苏菜/蘇菜 (*Sū cài*) or 淮(扬)菜/淮(揚)菜 (*Huái[yáng] cài*) makes abundant use of the region's various types of tofu products and freshwater fish. Both 上海菜/上海菜 (*Shànghǎi cài*) and 杭州菜/杭州菜 (*Hángzhōu cài*) are considered subcategories of 苏菜/蘇菜 (*Sū cài*).

Restaurants

Although restaurants in China come in all shapes and sizes, many of the more popular establishments tend to be raucous and lavishly decorated multistoried affairs. They almost always include private banquet rooms, which may or may not include a ten- to fifteen-percent service charge or a minimum consumption charge. During Chinese New Year customers can also expect to pay a service fee at some restaurants because of high demand.

Many large restaurants have a membership system. Membership is free or automatic once a customer spends a minimum, usually very modest, amount and leaves a cellphone number. Some restaurants charge a small fee. Members receive a discount. At some restaurants customers can put money into their accounts and receive a bonus. The more money they put into their accounts, the bigger the bonuses.

To settle a restaurant bill is 结账/結賬 (*jié zhàng*) or more colloquially 买单/買單 (*mǎi dān*). Some write it as 埋单/埋單 (*mái dān*). No tips are expected. Some upscale restaurants include a cover charge, typically around fifteen percent.

DINING CONVENTIONS

Today, Chinese people typically eat family style, by sharing dishes. However, this wasn't always the case. The Chinese used to sit on floor mats as the Japanese and Koreans still do today; hence the set phrase "place a mat on the floor and sit on it" (席地而坐) (xí dì ér zuò). Food was served individually on small, low tables. Chairs were introduced to China from Central Asia through trade during the latter part of the Han dynasty (202 BCE–220 CE). Historians believe that Buddhism also played a role in the spread of chairs. Along with this new sitting position, tables also became elevated. Many scholars believe that the change from being served

individually (分餐) (fēn cān) to being served together (合餐) (hé cān) was in part the result of the gradual adoption of chairs over several centuries. Nowadays when dining out with friends, for hygienic reasons many Chinese expect or ask for an extra pair of serving chopsticks called 公筷 for each dish.

COOKING ESSENTIALS

The most basic and best-known technique in Chinese cooking is stir-frying (炒) (chǎo), traditionally done with a heavy cast-iron wok. Other common techniques include 红烧/紅燒 (hóngshāo) (braising in soy sauce) and 清蒸/清蒸 (qīngzhēng) (steaming with light seasoning). The three must-haves for Chinese cooking are green onion (葱/蔥) (cōng), ginger (姜/薑) (jiāng), and garlic (蒜/蒜) (suàn).

COMPARE & CONTRAST

1 How have dining conventions in your culture changed over time? What is the etiquette for using eating utensils? Have you ever felt intimidated by the elaborate table setting at a formal dinner?

2 Search online for a menu from a Chinese restaurant in your community. How do you think chop suey, crab rangoons, egg foo young, and fortune cookies ended up as part of the dining experience in certain Chinese restaurants in North America?

CHOPSTICK
Do's & Dont's

Hold chopsticks about a third of an inch from the thicker ends. Place the top stick between your thumb and index and third fingers and rest the bottom one on your fourth finger. Make sure that the chopsticks are even. Press the thinner ends on a plate if necessary to line them up. Apply a little pressure to the top stick with your thumb and pivot it with your index and middle fingers. The bottom stick remains stationary.

Do not eat from the thick ends of the chopsticks. Do not lick or suck them. Do not gesture with them. Do not stick them vertically into a bowl of rice and leave them there as one would when offering food to the spirit of a deceased person.

DO

DON'T

Lesson Wrap-Up

The owner of Great Wall, a small local Chinese restaurant, has asked you, a business major, to recommend an improvement plan in exchange for free meals. Research three Chinese restaurants in town and designate one of them Great Wall. The owner has requested that you complete the following tasks. Today is your meeting with the owner. Role-play the conversation with a partner, who will use the bullet points below to inquire about your research results. Make sure to:

- identify two competitors' locations—how they compare with Great Wall in terms of convenience and target customers, e.g., whether they are near colleges or businesses; if so, what kinds of businesses; and so on.

- research customer reviews—are there online reviews? How does Great Wall do in terms of general customer satisfaction compared with its competitors?

- note how customers rate the restaurant's level of hygiene and décor.

- pay attention to what customers say about the restaurants' prices, menu choices, and service.

- evaluate if Great Wall is on trend in terms of its offerings.

- come up with a business improvement plan for Great Wall with three to five points.

Keep It Flowing

Study the following description; pay particular attention to how the highlighted parts help the sentences flow smoothly from one to the next. Notice how:

- pronouns (他们/他們) replace corresponding nouns when the subject remains unchanged (张天明/張天明, 丽莎/麗莎, 柯林和柯林的女朋友林雪梅)
- definite references (那个/那個) replace indefinite references (一家)
- time (周末/週末) and place words (那儿/那兒) can serve as connective devices
- certain conjunctions (所以) introduce causal relationships
- certain phrases (特别是/特別是) single out specific items for emphasis
- certain adverbs (也, 还/還) indicate similarity or addition

在中国饭馆儿吃饭

周末，张天明、丽莎、柯林和柯林的女朋友林雪梅一起在一家中国饭馆儿吃饭。**那个**饭馆儿鸡做得不错，鱼**也**做得很好，**特别是**清蒸鱼，味道好极了。**那儿**的芥蓝牛肉**也**挺好，又嫩又香，菠菜豆腐汤做得**也**很好，**那儿**还有有机的小白菜。**所以他们**点了一个清蒸鱼，一个芥蓝牛肉，一个菠菜豆腐汤和一个小白菜。柯林告诉服务员，菜要清淡一点儿，别太咸，少放油，别放味精。他们的菜很快就来了。

在中國飯館兒吃飯

週末，張天明、麗莎、柯林和柯林的女朋友林雪梅一起在一家中國飯館兒吃飯。**那個**飯館兒雞做得不錯，魚**也**做得很好，**特別是**清蒸魚，味道好極了。**那兒**的芥蘭牛肉**也**挺好，又嫩又香，菠菜豆腐湯做得**也**很好，**那兒**還有有機的小白菜。**所以他們**點了一個清蒸魚，一個芥蘭牛肉，一個菠菜豆腐湯和一個小白菜。柯林告訴服務員，菜要清淡一點兒，別太鹹，少放油，別放味精。他們的菜很快就來了。

Describe a dining experience at a restaurant. Use as many of the cohesive devices highlighted in the examples as possible to string together your answers to the questions:

○ 你是什么时候，跟谁一起在饭馆儿吃饭的？
你是什麼時候，跟誰一起在飯館兒吃飯的？

○ 你听说或者知道那个饭馆儿的哪些菜做得比较好？
你聽說或者知道那個飯館兒的哪些菜做得比較好？

○ 你们是大家一起吃点的菜还是自己吃自己点的菜？
你們是大家一起吃點的菜還是自己吃自己點的菜？

○ 你们都点了些什么菜？
你們都點了些什麼菜？

○ 你们为什么点这些菜？
你們為什麼點這些菜？

○ 你们跟服务员说菜要怎么样，不要怎么样了吗？
你們跟服務員說菜要怎麼樣，不要怎麼樣了嗎？

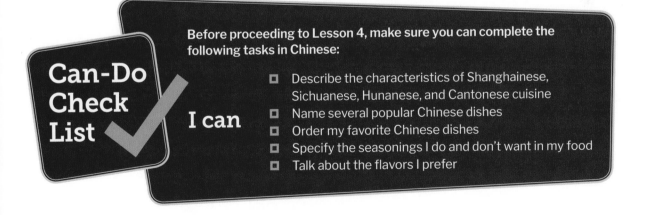

Can-Do Check List ✔

I can

Before proceeding to Lesson 4, make sure you can complete the following tasks in Chinese:

☐ Describe the characteristics of Shanghainese, Sichuanese, Hunanese, and Cantonese cuisine
☐ Name several popular Chinese dishes
☐ Order my favorite Chinese dishes
☐ Specify the seasonings I do and don't want in my food
☐ Talk about the flavors I prefer

Jīntiān shì zhōumò, gōngkè yě zuò wán le[1], Zhāng Tiānmíng jiù gěi Kē Lín fā Wēixìn, shuō tā hé tā de nǚpéngyou Lìshā xiǎng chī Zhōngguó fàn, wèn tā xiǎng bù xiǎng qù. Kē Lín shuō *zhènghǎo* tā yě xiǎng chī Zhōngguó fàn, jiù ràng Zhāng Tiānmíng hé Lìshā zài sùshè ménkǒu děng zhe, tā kāi chē lái jiē tāmen.

Bàn ge zhōngtóu yǐhòu, Kē Lín de qìchē dào le. Zhāng Tiānmíng hé Lìshā shàng chē yí kàn[2], chē li hái yǒu yí ge nǚháir, Kē Lín jièshào shuō, tā shì cóng Zhōngguó lái de liúxuéshēng, jiào Lín Xuěméi. Jǐ fēnzhōng yǐhòu, tāmen sì ge rén dào le nà jiā Zhōngguó fànguǎnr.

 Zhè shì càidān.

 Xièxie. Lìshā, Tiānmíng, nǐmen xiǎng chī diǎnr shénme?

 Zhèr shénme cài hǎochī?

 Zhèr jī zuò de búcuò, yú yě hěn hǎo, *tèbié shì* qīngzhēng yú, wèidao hǎo jí le.

 Jièlán niúròu yě tǐng hǎo, yòu nèn yòu xiāng[3].

 Kěyǐ diǎn[a] yí ge tāng ma?

 Dāngrán kěyǐ, zhèr de bōcài dòufu tāng zuò de hěn hǎo, jiào yí ge ba.

 Zài lái yí ge qīngcài ba.

 Xiànzài kěyǐ diǎn cài le ma?

 Kěyǐ. Yí ge qīngzhēng yú, yí ge jièlán niúròu, yí ge bōcài dòufu tāng. Jīntiān nǐmen yǒu shénme xīnxian de qīngcài?

 Xiǎo báicài zěnmeyàng?

 Shì *yǒujī* de ma?

 Shì.

 Hǎo. Fúwùyuán, cài yào qīngdàn yì diǎnr, bié tài xián, shǎo fàng yóu, bié fàng wèijīng.

 Máfan nǐ xiān lái sì bēi bīngshuǐ, gěi wǒmen sì shuāng kuàizi, zài duō gěi wǒmen yì xiē cānjīn zhǐ.

 Hǎo, méi wèntí. Duì le, nín yào fàn ma?

 Wǒmen bú "yào fàn,"[b] wǒmen yào sì wǎn mǐfàn.

 Duì, duì, duì, yào sì wǎn mǐfàn.

 Duì bu qi, hé nǐ kāi wánxiào.

 Lín Xuěméi, Kē Lín shuō zhèr Zhōngguó cài hěn dìdào, shì zhēn de ma?

 Zhè ge fànguǎnr de cài shì[4] búcuò, dànshì méiyǒu wǒmen Hángzhōu de fànguǎnr hǎo.

 Wǒ tīng wǒ *fùmǔ*[c] shuō Zhōngguó gè ge dìfang de cài bù yíyàng, nǎr de cài zuì hǎochī?

 Zhè jiù yào kàn nǐ de kǒuwèi le. Bǐfāng shuō wǒ ài chī tián de, jiù xǐhuan Shànghǎi cài; Kē Lín ài chī là de, jiù xǐhuan Sìchuān cài, Húnán cài. Yàoshi xǐhuan bǐjiào qīngdàn de, jiù chī Guǎngdōng cài . . .

 Xuěméi, wǒmen hánjià qù Zhōngguó ba.

 Qù Zhōngguó lǚxíng, chī Zhōngguó cài? Kěyǐ kǎolǜ.

 Zhè ge *zhúyi*[d] búcuò, wǒ yě kěyǐ kǎolǜ.

 Yǒu chī yǒu wánr? Wǒ dāngrán kěyǐ kǎolǜ.

 Zhēn de? Nà tài hǎo le! Dàjiā dōu qù!

 Yàoshi néng qù Zhōngguó xué Zhōngwén jiù gèng hǎo le.

 Āi, wǒmen de cài lái le.

买东西
買東西

SHOPPING

Learning Objectives

In this lesson, you will learn to:

- Name basic clothing, bedding, and bath items
- Describe your shopping preferences and criteria
- Express discounts
- Disagree with others tactfully

Relate & Get Ready

In your own culture/community:

- Is there a main shopping area where you can buy clothes and other necessities?
- Do people usually pay for their purchases in cash, by check, or with a credit card?
- Is there a sales tax?

课文

Text

Audio

Before You Study

Answer the following questions in Chinese to prepare for the reading.

1 你买衣服的时候，先看什么？样子、大小、牌子还是价钱？

2 你买东西的时候一般付现金还是刷卡？

When You Study

Listen to the audio recording and skim the text; then answer the following questions in Chinese.

1 张天明他们为什么要去购物中心？

2 柯林买衣服的标准是什么？

3 张天明、丽莎、林雪梅买东西的时候在乎什么？

张天明从家里来的时候，妈妈给他买了一些衣服，像T恤衫[a]、毛衣、牛仔裤[b]什么的，可是他觉得无论是样子还是颜色都不太好[1]。今天是星期日，正好林雪梅和丽莎也需要买卫生纸[c]、牙膏、毛巾、洗衣粉这些日用品，柯林就带他们来到附近一家最大的购物中心。

你要买什么衣服？

我想买一套运动服。

这边儿就是。你看看这一套，样子、大小、长短都合适，而且打八折。

颜色也不错。多少钱？是什么牌子的？

价钱不贵。这个牌子没听说过。

不过，是纯棉的[2]。

牌子不好不行，我想买名牌的。

你真时髦！穿名牌！那件好像是名牌的……哎呀，太贵了！

課文

Audio

張天明從家裡來的時候，媽媽給他買了一些衣服，像T恤衫[a]、毛衣、牛仔褲[b]什麼的，可是他覺得無論是樣子還是顏色都不太好[1]。今天是星期日，正好林雪梅和麗莎也需要買衛生紙[c]、牙膏、毛巾、洗衣粉這些日用品，柯林就帶他們來到附近一家最大的購物中心。

你要買什麼衣服？

我想買一套運動服。

這邊兒就是。你看看這一套，樣子、大小、長短都合適，而且打八折。

顏色也不錯。多少錢？是什麼牌子的？

價錢不貴。這個牌子沒聽說過。

不過，是純棉的[2]。

牌子不好不行，我想買名牌的。

你真時髦！穿名牌！那件好像是名牌的……哎呀，太貴了！

Before You Study

Answer the following questions in Chinese to prepare for the reading.

1. 你買衣服的時候，先看什麼？樣子、大小、牌子還是價錢？

2. 你買東西的時候一般付現金還是刷卡？

When You Study

Listen to the audio recording and skim the text; then answer the following questions in Chinese.

1. 張天明他們為什麼要去購物中心？

2. 柯林買衣服的標準是什麼？

3. 張天明、麗莎、林雪梅買東西的時候在乎什麼？

买东西，我只买名牌的，要不然就不买，因为名牌的衣服质量[d]好。

不错。有的衣服便宜是便宜，可是牌子不好[3]，穿一、两次就不想穿了，只好再买一件。这样买两件衣服的钱可能比买一件名牌的更多。

你说的有道理[e]。

买衣服只考虑便宜当然不好，但是也不一定非买名牌的不可。我买衣服的标准，第一是看穿着舒服不舒服，第二是质量好不好，第三是价钱合适不合适。是什么牌子的，样子时髦不时髦，我都不在乎。因为穿衣服是为了自己，不是为了给别人看。

我不同意。你喜欢看雪梅穿不好看的衣服吗？

雪梅穿什么衣服都好看，对不对？

好，好，好，别说了。

哎，柯林，你身上这件衣服怎么是名牌的，你不是不穿名牌的吗？

買東西，我只買名牌的，要不然就不買，因為名牌的衣服質量[d]好。

不錯。有的衣服便宜是便宜，可是牌子不好[3]，穿一、兩次就不想穿了，只好再買一件。這樣買兩件衣服的錢可能比買一件名牌的更多。

你說的有道理[e]。

買衣服只考慮便宜當然不好，但是也不一定非買名牌的不可。我買衣服的標準，第一是看穿著舒服不舒服，第二是質量好不好，第三是價錢合適不合適。是什麼牌子的，樣子時髦不時髦，我都不在乎。因為穿衣服是為了自己，不是為了給別人看。

我不同意。你喜歡看雪梅穿不好看的衣服嗎？

雪梅穿什麼衣服都好看，對不對？

好，好，好，別說了。

哎，柯林，你身上這件衣服怎麼是名牌的，你不是不穿名牌的嗎？

After You Study

Answer the following questions in Chinese.

1 请说一说张天明买衣服的标准是什么。

2 你自己买衣服的标准是什么？

我说不一定非买名牌的不可，没说过不穿名牌呀。这件是打折的时候买的。

哎，丽莎，我们去日用品那边看看。

你们去吧，我先去付钱，我们一会儿见。

（张天明在付钱……）

先生，付现金，还是用信用卡？

我刷卡。

先生，加上税一共是一百八十六块四。

好……谢谢！再见。

View & Explore

Video

For deeper language immersion and more cultural information, watch "Bargaining," a short, supplemental video clip by Cheng & Tsui on this lesson's theme.

我說不一定非買名牌的不可，沒說過不穿名牌呀。這件是打折的時候買的。

哎，麗莎，我們去日用品那邊看看。

你們去吧，我先去付錢，我們一會兒見。

（張天明在付錢……）

先生，付現金，還是用信用卡？

我刷卡。

先生，加上稅一共是一百八十六塊四。

好……謝謝！再見。

After You Study

Answer the following questions in Chinese.

1 請說一說張天明買衣服的標準是什麼。

2 你自己買衣服的標準是什麼？

Language Notes

a T恤衫

Words have entered Mandarin from a number of sources, including English and Chinese dialects. T恤衫 is a portmanteau composed of T恤, the Cantonese transliteration of the English "T-shirt" (pronounced *tiseot* in Cantonese), and the Mandarin morpheme 衫, "shirt."

b 牛仔褲/牛仔褲

牛仔褲/牛仔褲 (lit. cowboy pants) is the word for jeans. The word 仔 is used in several southern dialects to mean "boy." The word 牛仔, which has since been adopted into Mandarin, originated from Cantonese as a direct translation of the English word "cowboy."

c 卫生纸/衛生紙

卫生纸/衛生紙 (lit. hygiene paper) is also called 手纸/手紙 in northern spoken Chinese.

d 质量/質量

The word 质量/質量, meaning "quality," is used in Mainland China, whereas the word 品质/品質 is preferred in Taiwan, where it is pronounced *pǐnzhí*. In Mainland China, 品质/品質 is pronounced *pǐnzhì* and has a slightly different meaning—it refers to the essential qualities of a person or thing, such as a person's "moral fiber," 道德品质/道德品質 (*dàodé pǐnzhì*).

e 有道理

有道理 means "to make sense." It is often used to concur with someone else's opinion.

Vocabulary

Audio

Flashcards

No.	Simplified	Traditional	Pinyin	Part of Speech	Definition
1	像	像	xiàng	v	to resemble, to be like
2	T恤衫	T恤衫	tīxùshān	n	T-shirt
3	毛衣	毛衣	máoyī	n	woolen sweater
4	牛仔裤	牛仔褲	niúzǎikù	n	jeans
5	无论	無論	wúlùn	conj	regardless of . . . , whether it be . . . [See Grammar 1.]
6	需要	需要	xūyào	v/n	to need; needs
7	卫生纸	衛生紙	wèishēngzhǐ	n	toilet paper
8	牙膏	牙膏	yágāo	n	toothpaste
9	毛巾	毛巾	máojīn	n	towel
10	洗衣粉	洗衣粉	xǐyīfěn	n	laundry powder
11	购物	購物	gòuwù	vo	to shop
12	牌子	牌子	páizi	n	brand
13	价钱	價錢	jiàqian	n	price
14	纯棉	純棉	chúnmián	adj	pure cotton, one-hundred-percent cotton
15	名牌	名牌	míngpái	n	famous brand, name brand
16	时髦	時髦	shímáo	adj	fashionable, stylish
17	哎呀	哎呀	āiyā	interj	gosh, ah (an exclamation to express surprise)

No.	Simplified	Traditional	Pinyin	Part of Speech	Definition
18	质量	質量	*zhìliàng*	n	quality
19	只好	只好	*zhǐhǎo*	adv	to be forced to, to have no choice but
20	道理	道理	*dàoli*	n	reason, sense
21	非…不可	非…不可	*fēi … bù kě*		have to, nothing but … would do
22	标准	標準	*biāozhǔn*	n/adj	criterion; standard
23	在乎	在乎	*zàihu*	v	to mind, to care
24	同意	同意	*tóngyì*	v	to agree

张天明买东西的标准是只买名牌的。你呢?

張天明買東西的標準是只買名牌的。你呢?

While studying abroad in Taiwan, you go shopping with one of your friends. This is your friend's receipt from a clothing store. What did she buy, and what payment method did she use?

GET Real WITH CHINESE

女裝 風衣外套   2190.00 TX
02994857573

女裝 牛仔襯衫   590.00 TX
03294857874

女裝 V領T恤(短袖) 290.00 TX
09872857874

購買件數

小計   3件

合計   3070.00
信用卡   3070.00

No.	Simplified	Traditional	Pinyin	Part of Speech	Definition
25	好看	好看	*hǎokàn*	adj	nice-looking, attractive
26	一会儿	一會兒	*yíhuìr*	n+m	in a moment, a little while
27	现金	現金	*xiànjīn*	n	cash
28	加	加	*jiā*	v	to add
29	税	稅	*shuì*	n	tax

Grammar

<u>1</u> | 无论···, 都···/無論···，都···

无论/無論, meaning "regardless," signifies that a result will remain the same under any condition or circumstance. It must be used with either a question pronoun, as in (A) and (B), or an alternative construction, as in (C) and (D).

A 明天无论谁请客我都不去。

明天無論誰請客我都不去。

It doesn't matter who's paying tomorrow. I'm not going.

[谁/誰 is a question pronoun. Together with 无论/無論, it means "doesn't matter who" or "anybody."]

B Q: 你想去城里的哪个购物中心?

你想去城裡的哪個購物中心？

Which shopping center in town do you want to go to?

A: 城里的购物中心我都没去过，所以无论去哪个都可以。

城裡的購物中心我都沒去過，所以無論去哪個都可以。

I haven't been to any of the shopping centers in town, so going to any of them will be fine.

[哪个/哪個 is a question pronoun. Together with 无论/無論, it means "whichever" or "any."]

C 我们已经说好明天去买东西，你无论愿意不愿意都得跟我们去。

我們已經說好明天去買東西，你無論願意不願意都得跟我們去。

We've already decided to go shopping tomorrow. Whether you're willing or not, you have to go with us.

[愿意不愿意/願意不願意 is an alternative construction. Together with 无论/無論, it means "whether willing or not willing."]

D　他无论在家里还是在学校，都在学习，很少看见他玩儿。

他無論在家裡還是在學校，都在學習，很少看見他玩兒。

Whether he's at home or at school, he's always studying. You rarely see him have fun.

[在家里还是在学校/在家裡還是在學校 is an alternative construction. Together with 无论/無論, it means "whether at home or at school."]

2 Non-predicative adjectives

Some adjectives are primarily used as attributives, that is, before nouns or noun phrases. Unlike other adjectives, they cannot be qualified by words such as 很 or 非常. Their function is to categorize or distinguish the inherent traits or characteristics of people or things. Non-predicative adjectives that we have studied include 男, 女, 国际/國際, 有机/有機, and 纯棉/純棉, as in 男朋友 (boyfriend), 女朋友 (girlfriend), 国际足球/國際足球 (international football), 有机水果/有機水果 (organic fruit), 有机咖啡/有機咖啡 (organic coffee), 纯棉衬衫/純棉襯衫 (one-hundred-percent cotton shirt), and 纯棉运动服/純棉運動服 (one-hundred-percent cotton tracksuit).

When these adjectives are used as predicates, they must be embedded in a 是···的 construction:

A　李友的中国朋友是个男的。

李友的中國朋友是個男的。

Li You's Chinese friend is male.

[categorizing or distinguishing the gender of her friend]

B　小李买的水果都是有机的。

小李買的水果都是有機的。

The fruit Little Li buys is all organic.

[categorizing or distinguishing the method by which the fruit was farmed]

C　我穿的这件衬衫是纯棉的。

我穿的這件襯衫是純棉的。

This shirt I'm wearing is one-hundred-percent cotton.

[categorizing or distinguishing the composition of the fabric]

Adjective/verb + 是 + adjective/verb, 可是 or 但是… revisited

As you will recall from IC2, this structure is equivalent to "… is … (but) …" [See Grammar 6, Lesson 11, IC2.] It's used to express partial agreement. The speaker concurs with the other person's statement before going on to point out a different aspect that the other person may have ignored, as in (A) and (B), or warn the other person of possible contingencies, as in (C).

A   **Person A**   我打算学音乐。

我打算學音樂。

I plan to study music.

Person B   学音乐好是好，可是以后找工作不太容易。

學音樂好是好，可是以後找工作不太容易。

While it *is* good to study music, it may not be easy to find a job later.

B   **Person A**   这件衣服太贵了，别买!

這件衣服太貴了，別買！

This piece of clothing is too expensive. Don't buy it.

Person B   这件衣服贵是贵，可是牌子好。

這件衣服貴是貴，可是牌子好。

It *is* expensive, but it's a good brand.

C   Q: 明天晚上是林雪梅的生日晚会，你去吗?

明天晚上是林雪梅的生日晚會，你去嗎？

Lin Xuemei's birthday party is tomorrow night. Are you going?

A: 我去是去，可是会晚一点儿。

我去是去，可是會晚一點兒。

I *am* going, but I'll be a little late.

Words & Phrases

⋯什么的/⋯什麼的 (. . . and so on)

⋯什么的/⋯什麼的 (. . . and so on) is used to cap a series of items.

1　他要买毛衣、牛仔裤什么的。

他要買毛衣、牛仔褲什麼的。

He wants to buy sweaters, jeans, and so on.

2　妈妈昨天晚上请客，做了很多菜，像红烧牛肉、
清蒸鱼、家常豆腐什么的，都很好吃。

媽媽昨天晚上請客，做了很多菜，像紅燒牛肉、
清蒸魚、家常豆腐什麼的，都很好吃。

Mom invited people over last night. She made many dishes—beef braised in soy
sauce, steamed fish, home-style tofu, and so on. All of them were delicious.

3　我们这栋宿舍楼的家具不错，像床、桌子、
书架什么的，都又好又新。

我們這棟宿舍樓的傢俱不錯，像床、桌子、
書架什麼的，都又好又新。

The furniture in our dorm is quite nice. The beds, desks, bookshelves, and so on
are all good and new.

4　他床上放了很多东西，有被子、毯子、衣服什么的。

他床上放了很多東西，有被子、毯子、衣服什麼的。

There's lots of stuff on his bed: a quilt, a blanket, clothes, and so on.

大小, 长短/長短, 宽窄/寬窄 (kuānzhǎi)···
(size, length, width . . .)

Monosyllabic opposites such as 大 and 小; 长/長 and 短; and 宽/寬 (kuān) and 窄 (zhǎi) are combined to form the abstract nouns 大小 (size), 长短/長短 (length), and 宽窄/寬窄 (width), respectively.

1
你看看这一套，样子、大小、长短都合适。

你看看這一套，樣子、大小、長短都合適。

Take a look at this suit. The style, size, and length are all spot on.

2
这条裤子长短正好。

這條褲子長短正好。

The length of these pants is just right.

3
你穿中号的，这套运动服也是中号的，
大小正好合适。

你穿中號的，這套運動服也是中號的，
大小正好合適。

You wear a medium. This tracksuit is also a medium. The size is just right.

打折 (to discount, to sell at a discount)

打折 (to discount, to sell at a discount) means "on sale." When coupled with numbers, the phrase indicates a specific percentage off: e.g., （打）八折 is twenty percent off, （打）七五折 is twenty-five percent off, and （打）五折 or （打）对折/對折 is fifty percent off.

1
这个周末很多东西都打折，我们去买吧。

這個週末很多東西都打折，我們去買吧。

So much stuff is on sale this weekend. Let's go shopping.

2

这个书架上个月八十块，现在打七折，
是五十六块钱。

這個書架上個月八十塊，現在打七折，
是五十六塊錢。

This bookshelf was eighty dollars last month. Now it is thirty percent off.
It's fifty-six dollars.

3

我买了一张飞机票，打五折，一百二十五块钱。

我買了一張飛機票，打五折，一百二十五塊錢。

I bought a plane ticket at half price for one hundred and twenty-five dollars.

D | （要）不然 (otherwise)

（要）不然 means "otherwise." It is used to express a dire consequence if the advice or
course of action prescribed in the previous clause isn't taken.

1

这儿的冬天冷得很，你得再买一条毯子，
要不然容易感冒。

這兒的冬天冷得很，你得再買一條毯子，
要不然容易感冒。

The winter here is really cold. You've got to buy another blanket; otherwise, you'll
catch cold easily.

2

找房子不要找离马路太近的，要不然会很吵。

找房子不要找離馬路太近的，要不然會很吵。

When you are looking for a house, find a place that's not too close to the street.
Otherwise it'll be too noisy.

3

别吃那么多肉，多吃点青菜，要不然你会越来越胖。

別吃那麼多肉，多吃點青菜，要不然你會越來越胖。

Don't eat so much meat. Have more green leafy vegetables or you'll put on more
and more weight.

只好 (can only, have to)

只好 denotes the nonexistence of other options:

1　那个电影我想今天看，可是今天的票卖完了，只好明天看了。

那個電影我想今天看，可是今天的票賣完了，只好明天看了。

I wanted to watch that movie today, but the tickets were sold out. I can only watch it tomorrow.

2　我们去一个中餐馆儿吃饭，我想吃烤鸭，服务员说不卖烤鸭，我只好点别的菜了。

我們去一個中餐館兒吃飯，我想吃烤鴨，服務員說不賣烤鴨，我只好點別的菜了。

We went to eat at a Chinese restaurant. I wanted to order roast duck, but the waiter said they didn't sell it. I had to order something else.

3　我的车让妹妹开走了，我只好坐公共汽车去上班。

我的車讓妹妹開走了，我只好坐公共汽車去上班。

My younger sister was driving my car. I had to go to work by bus.

4　我们打算去海边玩，可是一看外边下雨了，只好不去了。

我們打算去海邊玩，可是一看外邊下雨了，只好不去了。

We had planned to hang out by the seashore, but when we saw it was raining, we had to call it off.

非…不可 (have to, must)

非…不可 can mean that if one doesn't do something, something negative is bound to happen.

1 你再不起床，上课非晚了不可。

你再不起床，上課非晚了不可。

If you stay in bed any longer, you'll definitely be late for class.

2 你得的这个病非打针不可，要不然会越来越重。

你得的這個病非打針不可，要不然會越來越重。

For this illness, you have no choice but to get an injection. Otherwise, it will get more and more serious.

非…不可 can also show strong resolution and will.

3 张天明买衣服非买名牌的不可。

張天明買衣服非買名牌的不可。

Zhang Tianming insists on buying only designer clothes.

4 我明年回国以后非找一个钱多的工作不可，要不然就再上学。

我明年回國以後非找一個錢多的工作不可，要不然就再上學。

I'm determined to find a lucrative job after I return to my country next year. Otherwise, I'll go back to school.

5 小林吃鱼非吃清蒸的不可，别的做法他不喜欢。

小林吃魚非吃清蒸的不可，別的做法他不喜歡。

When Little Lin eats fish, he insists on steamed fish. He doesn't care for fish cooked any other way.

标准/標準 (criterion, standard)

标准/標準 can be used as a noun, as in (1) and (2).

1

你认为一个好老师的标准是什么？

你認為一個好老師的標準是什麼？

What do you think are the criteria for a good teacher? *[noun]*

2

这个大学收研究生有什么标准？

這個大學收研究生有什麼標準？

What are the criteria for accepting graduate students at this university? *[noun]*

标准/標準 can also be used as an adjective—as an attributive, as in (3), or as a predicate, as in (4).

3

他说的是标准的北京话。

他說的是標準的北京話。

What he speaks is standard Beijing dialect. *[attributive]*

4

我说的上海话不太标准。

我說的上海話不太標準。

My Shanghainese is not very standard. *[predicate]*

A WAY WITH WORDS

合适

租这套房子付两百块押金不多，很合理。

这两件衬衫一共就二十块钱？太合算了！

Using the word/phrase in orange as a clue, try to figure out the meaning of the words/phrases in blue; consult a dictionary if necessary. Consider how the literal and extended senses are related in each case.

合適

租這套房子付兩百塊押金不多，很合理。

這兩件襯衫一共就二十塊錢？太合算了！

在乎 (to mind, to care)

在乎 is a verb. More often than not, it occurs in negative sentences.

1
别人说什么，我不在乎。

别人說什麼，我不在乎。

I don't care what other people say.

2
你的车不见了，你怎么一点都不在乎？

你的車不見了，你怎麼一點都不在乎？

Your car has disappeared. How can you not care at all?

3
他很在乎别人怎么看他。

他很在乎別人怎麼看他。

He cares a lot how other people see him.

A WAY WITH WORDS

Using the word/phrase in orange as a clue, try to figure out the meaning of the words/phrases in blue; consult a dictionary if necessary. Consider how the literal and extended senses are related in each case.

名牌

小白的姐姐演过电影，现在是名人了。

王先生上大学的时候就特别喜欢聊政治，现在成了电视上的名嘴了。

名牌

小白的姐姐演過電影，現在是名人了。

王先生上大學的時候就特別喜歡聊政治，現在成了電視上的名嘴了。

Language Practice

A | **Stocking up** | PRESENTATIONAL

In pairs, practice naming the basic household items depicted.

1  2  3  4

B | **New look** | PRESENTATIONAL

You'd like to give your wardrobe a makeover. Luckily, you've just received a gift card for your favorite clothing store. List the articles of clothing you'd like to purchase; for each, indicate the size and color you prefer as well as an estimated price. Then report your list to the class.

What a deal

Everyone's on a budget. In pairs, role-play a seller (Person A) and a prospective buyer (Person B). Based on the images, engage in some haggling over how steep a discount can be offered, and see if you can make a deal, e.g.:

Person A　这个冰箱多少钱你才买？

这個冰箱多少錢你才買？

Person B　这个冰箱打＿＿＿折我才买。

這個冰箱打＿＿＿折我才買。

Person A　打了＿＿＿折，是＿＿＿＿钱。好，卖了。

打了＿＿＿折，是＿＿＿＿錢。好，賣了。

 1 $500

 2 $300

3 $100

4 $1000 WWW

5 $50

6 $40

Discerning shopper

Everyone has different priorities when shopping. From among 样子/樣子, 颜色/顏色, 大小, 长短/長短, 价钱/價錢, 质量/質量, and 牌子, list your top five criteria when you shop for clothes, giving the most important criterion first. Then compare your list with that of your partner and explain your rankings to each other. Report your rankings using 第一…，第二…，第三…, etc.

Characterize it!

❶ 衬　❷ 衫

❸ 裤　❹ 被

Identify the common radical.

How does the radical relate to the overall meaning of the characters?

❶ 襯　❷ 衫

❸ 褲　❹ 被

More characters

Regardless

PRESENTATIONAL

Your friend Little Li is a voracious reader. Use 无论···都···/無論···都··· to describe his reading habits. He reads:

1 whether he's in or out of class

2 whether he's at the library or in his dorm

3 no matter what day of the week it is

4 no matter who he's with

Your friend has just invited you to dinner at seven o'clock tonight, but you have an exam early in the morning tomorrow. Use 无论···都···/無論···都··· to tell your friend that you cannot go, regardless of:

5 who's doing the inviting

6 which restaurant it is

7 whether the meal is Chinese or Japanese

8 whether the food is authentic or not

Fair and balanced

INTERPERSONAL

In pairs, role-play an amateur chef and his/her friend. The chef enjoys cooking Chinese food and wants a critique of the meal he/she has just prepared. The friend does not want to step on any feelings, but also wants to be honest, e.g.:

糖醋鱼/糖醋魚　　　　　香　　　咸/鹹

Q: 我做的糖醋鱼香不香?
　　我做的糖醋魚香不香？

A: 香是香，可是有点儿咸。
　　香是香，可是有點兒鹹。

1 菠菜豆腐汤/菠菜豆腐湯　　好喝　　咸/鹹

2 清蒸鱼/清蒸魚　　　　　　嫩　　　油

| 3 | 芥兰牛肉/芥蘭牛肉 | 好吃 | 甜 |
| 4 | 家常豆腐 | 香 | 酸 |

Switching roles, role-play a personal stylist and a client. In a mini-consultation, the personal stylist does not want to contradict his/her client, but wants to call the client's attention to details that he/she has overlooked, e.g.:

	good quality	length is not right
Person A	我觉得这条牛仔裤质量很好。	
	我覺得這條牛仔褲質量很好。	
Person B	质量好是好，可是长短不合适。	
	質量好是好，可是長短不合適。	

5	pretty color	sizing is off
6	cheap price	not one-hundred-percent cotton
7	perfect fit	not fashionable enough
8	nice style	too expensive

G | **My way or the highway** | PRESENTATIONAL

Mr. Zhang is extremely particular and very hard to please. Tell the class about some of Mr. Zhang's singular tastes, e.g.:

住房子/住房子	大房子/大房子

张先生住（房子）非住大房子不可。

張先生住（房子）非住大房子不可。

1	吃饭/吃飯	日本菜/日本菜
2	喝茶/喝茶	英国茶/英國茶

3	穿衣服	名牌的
4	开车/開車	跑车/跑車
5	打球	网球/網球

Do you know anyone who is extremely particular? Give an example or two.

H | **Strike a pose** PRESENTATIONAL

One of your classmates looks great and has a unique style, and you think he/she should become a model. Describe what he/she is wearing and what he/she looks like. Make sure that your description follows a certain logic. Describe his/her clothes from top to bottom and then his/her appearance—figure, hair, eyes, etc.

Chinese Chat

Little Bai and Little Li are chatting about shopping on Weibo. What is Little Li hinting at, and how does Little Bai reply?

小李:
手动点赞！不知道有没有我喜欢的颜色。

@小白:
晒一晒我刚买的衣服，打了七折，好开心！

小白:
有你喜欢的蓝色，但是只有大号的了，你穿着不合适。

 小李 ☆
7-6 10:36 AM 來自iPhone

手動點讚！不知道有沒有我喜歡的顏色。

@小白：曬一曬我剛買的衣服，打了七折，好開心！

↰ 轉發 | 💬 1 評論 | 👍 讚

小白：有你喜歡的藍色，但是只有大號的了，你穿著不合適。

Bargaining

Bargaining is expected almost everywhere in Mainland China. Even in mid-priced department stores, it doesn't hurt to ask whether a discount is possible, as department stores sometimes rent counter space to private vendors and manufacturers. How much you end up paying depends on your bargaining skills. Buyers often initiate haggling by offering as little as fifty percent of the original cost, particularly when buying clothes and shoes. However, there's no bargaining in supermarkets, large chain stores like Wal-Mart, or upscale department stores.

═ NEW ═
FORMS OF PA¥MENT

With the rise of the Internet and mobile technology, new forms of payment have become available to Chinese shoppers. As in the U.S., online shopping has become increasingly popular in China in recent years, especially among young people. However, unlike in many other countries, Chinese online shoppers as well as some online vendors have the option of holding off payment until the ordered item is delivered, a practice called 货到付款/貨到付款 (*huò dào fù kuǎn*) (payment on delivery) . To return an item ordered online, it is not uncommon to have it picked up from the shopper's home for free.

Paying by smartphone has become the preferred method for buyers and sellers alike. Alipay 支付宝/支付寶 (*Zhīfùbǎo*), and WeChat Pay, 微信支付/微信支付 (*Wēixìn zhīfù*), by Alibaba (阿里巴巴) and WeChat (微信/微信) respectively, can be used to pay for everything from takeout food to cabs. Many innovations from the Chinese mobile sector, from digital wallets to news feeds, appeared in China before anywhere else. Shipping is inexpensive or included and typically very fast. Last-mile delivery of merchandise is often completed by bicycle or moped.

Dongxi

The word 东西/東西 (*dōng xī*) has two meanings depending on how one pronounces the second character. When said in a high-level tone, 东西/東西 (*dōng xī*) literally refers to two opposing orientations. When the second character is pronounced with a neutral or soft tone, however, 东西/東西 (*dōngxi*) means "things" or "stuff." One modern scholar believes that the connection is trade. Since merchandise came from all directions, "east and west" became a stand-in for the exchange of goods. It is perhaps no accident that the Silk Road extended from China westward to the eastern Mediterranean. Another popular explanation points to the restriction of commerce to the East and West Markets in the Tang (618–907 CE) capital Chang'an (长安/長安). The smaller East Market located near the imperial palace sold luxury products, including products imported from the West, whereas the larger West Market situated in the plebeian quarters of the city sold daily necessities such as clothes, candles, cakes, and medicine.

COMPARE&CONTRAST

Dongxi is a good example of a compound word whose origins have been obscured by historical and etymological change. In English, many compound words are similarly intriguing. For example, do you know the original meaning of "aftermath" or "nightmare"? Why do you think the meaning of a word can evolve over time?

Lesson Wrap-Up

Project

More exercises

Role-play an intervention with two partners. One of you is a Chinese student with an online shopping addiction. Before you begin, research these terms on the Internet and write down their English equivalents: 剁手党/剁手黨 (duò shǒu dǎng), 光棍节/光棍節 (Guānggùn Jié), 淘宝网/淘寶網 (Táobǎowǎng). In your intervention session, be sure to:

· find out why your friend thinks he/she is a member of the so-called 剁手党/剁手黨.

· learn your friend's shopping habits: does he/she shop online every week, every day? How many times a week or a day? What does he/she like to buy?

· identify possible causes for your friend's shopping addiction. Why does he/she like to shop so much? Why is your friend out of control every November 11?

· ask your friend if he/she considers him/herself a 光棍.

· consider if there is any relationship between your friend's addiction and his/her status as a student away from his/her family.

· come up with practical ways to get your friend to quit being a shopaholic. What could he/she do more of instead of obsessively shopping online?

Keep It Flowing

Study the following description; pay particular attention to how the highlighted parts help the sentences flow smoothly from one to the next. Notice how:

· pronouns (他) replace corresponding nouns when the subject remains unchanged (张天明/張天明, 柯林)

· conjunctions (要不然, 因为/因為, 但是), adverbs (也, 就), and ordinal numbers (第一, 第二, 第三) also join sentences together

张天明和柯林买衣服的标准

张天明买衣服一定要买名牌的，要不然就不买，因为他觉得名牌的衣服质量好。柯林觉得买衣服只考虑便宜当然不好，但是不一定非买名牌的不可。他买衣服的标准，第一看穿着舒服不舒服，第二看质量好不好，第三看价钱合适不合适。他不在乎是什么牌子的，也不在乎样子时髦不时髦。他认为穿衣服是为了自己，不是为了给别人看。张天明看见柯林穿了一件名牌衣服，就问柯林为什么穿名牌的衣服？柯林说，他说过不一定非买名牌的不可，但是没说过不穿名牌呀。

張天明和柯林買衣服的標準

張天明買衣服一定要買名牌的，要不然就不買，因為他覺得名牌的衣服質量好。柯林覺得買衣服只考慮便宜當然不好，但是不一定非買名牌的不可。他買衣服的標準，第一看穿著舒服不舒服，第二看質量好不好，第三看價錢合適不合適。他不在乎是什麼牌子的，也不在乎樣子時髦不時髦。他認為穿衣服是為了自己，不是為了給別人看。張天明看見柯林穿了一件名牌衣服，就問柯林為什麼穿名牌的衣服？柯林說，他說過不一定非買名牌的不可，但是沒說過不穿名牌呀。

What are your criteria? Use as many of the cohesive devices highlighted in the example as possible to string together your answers to the questions:

○ 你买衣服一定要买名牌的吗？
你買衣服一定要買名牌的嗎？

○ 买名牌的衣服有什么好处？
買名牌的衣服有什麼好處？

○ 说说你买衣服有哪些标准，为什么。
說說你買衣服有哪些標準，為什麼。

○ 你朋友和你买衣服的标准一样不一样？
你朋友和你買衣服的標準一樣不一樣？

Can-Do Check List

I can

Before proceeding to Lesson 5, make sure you can complete the following tasks in Chinese:

- ☐ Name basic clothing items and household necessities
- ☐ State what I care about when shopping for clothes
- ☐ Express discounts on clothing and other items
- ☐ Disagree tactfully and express my perspective politely

Zhāng Tiānmíng cóng jiā li lái de shíhou, māma gěi tā mǎi
le yì xiē yīfu, xiàng tīxùshān[a], máoyī, niúzǎikù[b] shénme de,
kěshì tā juéde wúlùn shì yàngzi háishi yánsè dōu bú tài hǎo[1].
Jīntiān shì xīngqīrì, zhènghǎo Lín Xuěméi hé Lìshā yě xūyào
mǎi wèishēngzhǐ[c], yágāo, máojīn, xǐyīfěn zhè xiē rìyòngpǐn,
Kē Lín jiù dài tāmen lái dào fùjìn yì jiā zuì dà de gòuwù
zhōngxīn.

 Nǐ yào mǎi shénme yīfu?

 Wǒ xiǎng mǎi yí tào yùndòngfú.

 Zhèbianr jiù shì. Nǐ kàn kan zhè yí tào, yàngzi, dàxiǎo,
chángduǎn dōu héshì, érqiě dǎ bā zhé.

 Yánsè yě búcuò. Duōshao qián? Shì shénme páizi de?

 Jiàqian bú guì. Zhè ge páizi méi tīngshuō guo.

 Búguò, shì chúnmián de[2].

 Páizi bù hǎo bù xíng, wǒ xiǎng mǎi míngpái de.

 Nǐ zhēn shímáo! Chuān míngpái! Nà jiàn hǎoxiàng shì
míngpái de . . . Āiyā, tài guì le!

 Mǎi dōngxi, wǒ zhǐ mǎi míngpái de, yàobùrán jiù bù
mǎi, yīnwèi míngpái de yīfu zhìliàng[d] hǎo.

 Búcuò. Yǒude yīfu piányi shì piányi, kěshì páizi bù hǎo[3],
chuān yì, liǎng cì jiù bù xiǎng chuān le, zhǐhǎo zài mǎi
yí jiàn. Zhèyàng mǎi liǎng jiàn yīfu de qián kěnéng bǐ
mǎi yí jiàn míngpái de gèng duō.

 Nǐ shuō de yǒu dàoli[e].

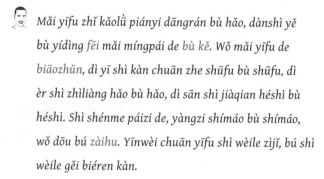 Mǎi yīfu zhǐ kǎolǜ piányi dāngrán bù hǎo, dànshì yě
bù yídìng fēi mǎi míngpái de bù kě. Wǒ mǎi yīfu de
biāozhǔn, dì yī shì kàn chuān zhe shūfu bù shūfu, dì
èr shì zhìliàng hǎo bù hǎo, dì sān shì jiàqian héshì bù
héshì. Shì shénme páizi de, yàngzi shímáo bù shímáo,
wǒ dōu bú zàihu. Yīnwèi chuān yīfu shì wèile zìjǐ, bú shì
wèile gěi biéren kàn.

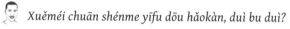 Wǒ bù tóngyì. Nǐ xǐhuan kàn Xuěméi chuān bù hǎokàn
de yīfu ma?

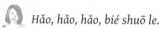 Xuěméi chuān shénme yīfu dōu hǎokàn, duì bu duì?

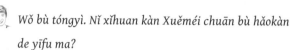 Hǎo, hǎo, hǎo, bié shuō le.

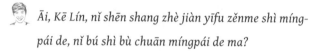 Āi, Kē Lín, nǐ shēn shang zhè jiàn yīfu zěnme shì míng-
pái de, nǐ bú shì bù chuān míngpái de ma?

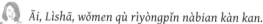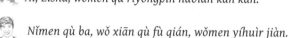 Wǒ shuō bù yídìng fēi mǎi míngpái de bù kě, méi shuō
guo bù chuān míngpái ya. Zhè jiàn shì dǎ zhé de shíhou
mǎi de.

 Āi, Lìshā, wǒmen qù rìyòngpǐn nàbian kàn kan.

 Nǐmen qù ba, wǒ xiān qù fù qián, wǒmen yíhuìr jiàn.

(Zhāng Tiānmíng zài fù qián . . .)

Xiānsheng, fù xiànjīn, háishi yòng xìnyòngkǎ?

Wǒ shuā kǎ.

Xiānsheng, jiā shang shuì yígòng shì yì bǎi bāshí liù
kuài sì.

Hǎo . . . Xièxie! Zàijiàn.

经济
ECON
19900

电脑
CMS
12100

第五课
第五課

选课
選課

CHOOSING CLASSES

Learning Objectives

In this lesson, you will learn to:

- State your major and academic department and some required general courses you have taken
- Talk about your plans after graduation
- Discuss what will enhance your future job opportunities
- Explain whether your family members have an influence on your choice of major and career path
- Share tips on how to save money for your education

Relate & Get Ready

In your own culture/community:

- When do college students declare a major?
- What are the most common schools/colleges found at universities?
- Approximately how many credits are needed to graduate from college?

课文

Text

Audio

Before You Study

Answer the following questions in Chinese to prepare for the reading.

1 你选专业了吗？你的专业是什么？/你打算选什么专业？

2 你这个学期选了几门课？哪一门课最花时间？

When You Study

Listen to the audio recording and skim the text; then answer the following questions in Chinese.

1 张天明为什么觉得这个学期的学习让他有点儿受不了？

2 张天明想选什么专业？他父母为什么不同意？

3 李哲想申请哪些学校？为什么？

张天明这个学期选了四门课：世界历史、电脑、政治学[a]和中文。这几门课都很有意思，他也学到了不少东西。因为张天明在家的时候常常跟父母说中文，所以一年级的中文课，对他来说[1]，听和说很容易，只是写汉字有点儿难。除了中文课以外，其他几门课都得花很多时间准备，还常常要写文章，所以他觉得有点儿受不了。这个学期已经过了一半，马上又得选下学期的课了，张天明希望下个学期能轻松点儿。后天要去见教授，讨论选课的事，他想先找别的同学聊聊，听听他们的意见。这一天下午，他在篮球场上正好碰见大四的李哲，就一边和李哲打球，一边聊了起来。

怎么样，下学期的课你选好[2]了吗？

还没有呢。你呢？

我一定要选中文，另外[3]两门课选什么，还没想好。对了，你还得再上几门课才能毕业？

我想拿双学位[b]，还[4]得上四门课。我想再[4]选一门化学、一门经济，另外[3]再选两门电脑系[c]的课，这样学分就够了。

对，我决定了，也选经济和电脑！我的问题解决了，太好了！我后天就去见我的教授，听听他的建议。李哲，你毕业以后打算做什么？

課文

Audio

張天明這個學期選了四門課：世界歷史、電腦、政治學[a]和中文。這幾門課都很有意思，他也學到了不少東西。因為張天明在家的時候常常跟父母說中文，所以一年級的中文課，對他來說[1]，聽和說很容易，只是寫漢字有點兒難。除了中文課以外，其他幾門課都得花很多時間準備，還常常要寫文章，所以他覺得有點兒受不了。這個學期已經過了一半，馬上又得選下學期的課了，張天明希望下個學期能輕鬆點兒。後天要去見教授，討論選課的事，他想先找別的同學聊聊，聽聽他們的意見。這一天下午，他在籃球場上正好碰見大四的李哲，就一邊和李哲打球，一邊聊了起來。

怎麼樣，下學期的課你選好[2]了嗎？

還沒有呢。你呢？

我一定要選中文，另外[3]兩門課選什麼，還沒想好。對了，你還得再上幾門課才能畢業？

我想拿雙學位[b]，還[4]得上四門課。我想再[4]選一門化學、一門經濟，另外[3]再選兩門電腦系[c]的課，這樣學分就夠了。

對，我決定了，也選經濟和電腦！我的問題解決了，太好了！我後天就去見我的教授，聽聽他的建議。李哲，你畢業以後打算做什麼？

Before You Study

Answer the following questions in Chinese to prepare for the reading.

1 你選專業了嗎？你的專業是什麼？/你打算選什麼專業？

2 你這個學期選了幾門課？哪一門課最花時間？

When You Study

Listen to the audio recording and skim the text; then answer the following questions in Chinese.

1 張天明為什麼覺得這個學期的學習讓他有點兒受不了？

2 張天明想選什麼專業？他父母為什麼不同意？

3 李哲想申請哪些學校？為什麼？

我想念研究生，要么上工学院，要么[5]上管理学院，我还没跟我的教授谈。天明，你想选什么专业？

我想学文学。可是我妈妈说，学文学将来找工作不容易，而且挣钱也少，她希望我念金融。但是我对金融没有兴趣，整天跟数字打交道，多没意思。

我的父母跟你的父母差不多。如果让我自己选专业，我选哲学，因为我喜欢想问题。我们班很多同学比我们自由，他们的父母不太管孩子选什么专业。

你要申请哪些学校？

我想申请离我姐姐家比较近的学校，这样我就可以搬到她家去住，把房租跟饭钱省下来。

不过在姐姐家里住可能不太自由。

你的话没错，但是住在姐姐家的好处也不少。我再考虑考虑。

Language Notes

a 政治学／政治學

学／學 is used as a suffix meaning "studies," as in 政治学／政治學 (political science), 经济学／經濟學 (economics), 医学／醫學 (medical science), and 化学／化學 (chemistry).

b 双学位／雙學位

双学位／雙學位 literally means "double degree." 双／雙 means "double." It can only be used before a noun as an attributive, as in 双手／雙手 (both hands) and 双人床／雙人床 (double bed). It can't be used as a predicate.

c 电脑系／電腦系

In Mainland China, while the formal term for "computer" is 计算机／計算機 (jìsuànjī), in conversation, people often say 电脑／電腦 instead. "Department of Computer Science," however, is always 计算机系／計算機系, not 电脑系／電腦系, as is the case in Taiwan.

我想念研究生，要麼上工學院，要麼[5]上管理學院，我還沒跟我的教授談。天明，你想選什麼專業？

我想學文學。可是我媽媽說，學文學將來找工作不容易，而且掙錢也少，她希望我念金融。但是我對金融沒有興趣，整天跟數字打交道，多沒意思。

我的父母跟你的父母差不多。如果讓我自己選專業，我選哲學，因為我喜歡想問題。我們班很多同學比我們自由，他們的父母不太管孩子選什麼專業。

你要申請哪些學校？

我想申請離我姐姐家比較近的學校，這樣我就可以搬到她家去住，把房租跟飯錢省下來。

不過在姐姐家裡住可能不太自由。

你的話沒錯，但是住在姐姐家的好處也不少。我再考慮考慮。

After You Study

Answer the following questions in Chinese.

1 請說一說張天明這個學期的課怎麼樣。

2 李哲大學畢業以後有什麼計劃？你會給他什麼建議？

View & Explore

For deeper language immersion and more cultural information, watch "College," a short, supplemental video clip by Cheng & Tsui on this lesson's theme.

Video

Vocabulary

Audio

Flashcards

No.	Simplified	Traditional	Pinyin	Part of Speech	Definition
1	选	選	xuǎn	v	to choose
2	门	門	mén	m	(measure word for academic courses)
3	世界	世界	shìjiè	n	world
4	历史	歷史	lìshǐ	n	history
5	其他	其他	qítā	pr	other, else
6	文章	文章	wénzhāng	n	essay, article
7	受不了	受不了	shòu bu liǎo	vc	cannot take it, unable to bear
8	轻松	輕鬆	qīngsōng	adj	light, relaxed
9	教授	教授	jiàoshòu	n	professor
10	讨论	討論	tǎolùn	v	to discuss
11	意见	意見	yìjiàn	n	opinion
12	碰见	碰見	pèng jiàn	vc	to run into (a person by chance)
13	毕业	畢業	bì yè	vo	to graduate
14	学位	學位	xuéwèi	n	academic degree
15	化学	化學	huàxué	n	chemistry
16	经济	經濟	jīngjì	n	economics, economy
17	系	系	xì	n	academic department (of a college or university)
18	学分	學分	xuéfēn	n	academic credit
19	决定	決定	juédìng	v/n	to decide; decision
20	解决	解決	jiějué	v	to solve, to resolve

No.	Simplified	Traditional	Pinyin	Part of Speech	Definition
21	建议	建議	*jiànyì*	n/v	suggestion; to suggest
22	要么···， 要么···	要麼···， 要麼···	*yàome . . . ,* *yàome . . .*	conj	if it's not . . . it's . . . , either . . . or . . . [See Grammar 5.]
23	工学院	工學院	*gōng xuéyuàn*	n	school of engineering
24	管理学院	管理學院	*guǎnlǐ xuéyuàn*	n	school of management
25	谈	談	*tán*	v	to talk, to discuss
26	文学	文學	*wénxué*	n	literature
27	将来	將來	*jiānglái*	n	future
28	挣钱	掙錢	*zhèng qián*	vo	to earn money
29	金融	金融	*jīnróng*	n	finance, banking
30	整天	整天	*zhěng tiān*		all day long
31	数字	數字	*shùzì*	n	numeral, figure, digit

张天明想学文学，但是他妈妈希望他念金融。你想选什么专业？你父母同意吗？

张天明想學文學，但是他媽媽希望他念金融。你想選什麼專業？你父母同意嗎？

This is your friend's graduation certificate from Minzu University, a top-ranked university in Mainland China. Which part of the certificate references your friend's academic department, and what was her major?

中央民族大学

毕业证书

学生　白海文，　性别女，1995年01月26日出生，于2013年09月至2017年07月在本校文学院　汉语言文学　专业学习，学制四年，修完教学计划规定的全部课程，成绩合格，准予本科毕业。

校长：陈理

中央民族大学：

二〇一七年七月十日

编号：100521201705671489

No.	Simplified	Traditional	Pinyin	Part of Speech	Definition
32	打交道	打交道	*dǎ jiāodào*	vo	to deal with
33	哲学	哲學	*zhéxué*	n	philosophy
34	管	管	*guǎn*	v	to control, to manage, to mind, to care about
35	申请	申請	*shēnqǐng*	v	to apply (to a school or job)
36	省下来	省下來	*shěng xia lai*	vc	to save (money, time)
37	李哲	李哲	*Lǐ Zhé*	pn	(a personal name)

Grammar

1 | 对…来说/對…來說

对…来说/對…來說 is used to suggest that the opinion expressed is valid only with regard to a particular person. When speaking, the word indicating the person (i.e., the personal pronoun or proper noun) is stressed.

A
对她来说，今年最需要做的事情是选一个好大学。

對她來說，今年最需要做的事情是選一個好大學。

For her, the most urgent thing this year is to pick a good college.

B
对小王来说，今年找到工作最重要，要不然吃饭、住房子都会有问题。

對小王來說，今年找到工作最重要，要不然吃飯、住房子都會有問題。

For Little Wang, the most important thing this year is to find a job. Otherwise, both food and housing will become problematic.

As (C) shows, this structure can also be used together with 觉得/覺得.

C
（我觉得）对他来说，有工作比没工作好，可是他觉得工作不好比没有工作更糟糕。

（我覺得）對他來說，有工作比沒工作好，可是他覺得工作不好比沒有工作更糟糕。

(I think that) for him, it's better to have a job than have no job. However, in his view, having a lousy job is worse than having no job.

Resultative complements (III)

The use of resultative complements is an essential feature of the Chinese language. Generally speaking, resultative complements are necessary as long as an action produces a certain result. The structure of a sentence containing a resultative complement is:

Subject + verb + resultative complement (+ object)

For example, when the action of writing a character, 写字/寫字, results in an error, a resultative complement is used: 写错字/寫錯字. Similarly, since washing clothes, 洗衣服, results in them being in a state of cleanliness, a resultative complement is used: 洗干净衣服/洗乾淨衣服.

Whether a verb can be combined with an adjective or another verb to form a "verb + resultative complement" is not random, but rather follows certain patterns. Therefore, it is best to memorize each verb + resultative complement as a set phrase.

Resultative complements fall into one of three categories. First, resultative complements relating to the verb that provide additional information about the action itself:

A 我搬完家就去购物中心买日用品。（我—搬家，搬—完）

我搬完家就去購物中心買日用品。（我—搬家，搬—完）

I'll go get some household necessities at the shopping center as soon as I finish moving.

[The result, 完 (completed), refers to the action 搬 (moving).]

B 下学期的课你选好了吗？（你—选课，选—好）

下學期的課你選好了嗎？（你—選課，選—好）

Have you finished selecting classes for next semester?

[The result, 好 (properly finished), refers to the action 选/選 (selecting).]

In (B), the resultative complement 好 means "properly carried out," in the sense that another action can now begin.

Second, resultative complements relating to the subject that indicate an impact on or a change in the person who has carried out the action:

C
老师说的话我听懂了。（我—听，我—懂）

老師說的話我聽懂了。（我—聽，我—懂）

I understood what the teacher said.
(My listening resulted in my understanding.)

D
张教授写文章写累了。（张教授—写，张教授—累）

張教授寫文章寫累了。（張教授—寫，張教授—累）

Professor Zhang was tired from writing articles.
(Professor Zhang wrote, and he became tired.)

Third, resultative complements relating to the object that describe an impact on or change in the person affected by the action:

E
你怎么把妹妹打哭了？（你—打妹妹，妹妹—哭）

你怎麼把妹妹打哭了？（你—打妹妹，妹妹—哭）

Why did you hit your sister and make her cry?
(You hit; your younger sister started to cry.)

F
他搬走了一把椅子。（他—搬椅子，椅子—走）

他搬走了一把椅子。（他—搬椅子，椅子—走）

He took away a chair.
(He moved the chair; the chair is now gone.)

G
你要把衣服洗干净才能去看电影。（你—洗衣服，衣服—干净）

你要把衣服洗乾淨才能去看電影。（你—洗衣服，衣服—乾淨）

You have to wash the clothes clean (finish the laundry) before you can go see the movie.
(You wash the clothes; the clothes will be clean as a result.)

3

另外

There are three ways to use 另外. First, 另外 can be used before a numeral or demonstrative pronoun + noun, as in (A), (B), and (C).

A

下个学期我打算选三门课。一门电脑课，另外两门课选什么，还没决定。

下個學期我打算選三門課。一門電腦課，另外兩門課選什麼，還沒決定。

I plan to take three courses next semester. One will be computer science. As for the other two, I haven't decided yet.

B

这里有两个大学，一个是男校，另外一个是女校，都很不错。

這裡有兩個大學，一個是男校，另外一個是女校，都很不錯。

There are two colleges here. One is a men's college and the other is a women's college. Both are quite good.

C

他三个妹妹都有工作，一个是律师，另外两个是大学教授。

他三個妹妹都有工作，一個是律師，另外兩個是大學教授。

All three of his younger sisters have jobs. One is a lawyer and the other two are college professors.

另外 can also be used as an adverb before a verb phrase, as seen in (D), (E), and (F), or as a conjunction at the beginning of a sentence, as in (G).

D

下个学期我要选一门化学课，另外再选两门电脑系的课，学分就够了。

下個學期我要選一門化學課，另外再選兩門電腦系的課，學分就夠了。

Next semester I'll take a chemistry course, plus two more computer science courses. Then I'll have enough credits.

E

在这个州买吃的东西，除了东西的价钱以外，
另外还得付百分之八的税。

在這個州買吃的東西，除了東西的價錢以外，
另外還得付百分之八的稅。

When you buy food in this state, you have to pay eight percent in tax on top of the price.

F

上个周末我买了一些日用品，另外还买了
一件T恤衫。

上個週末我買了一些日用品，另外還買了
一件T恤衫。

Last weekend I bought some household necessities. I also bought a T-shirt.

G

请你给我订两张飞机票，另外，麻烦你再帮我买一个
大一点儿的包。

請你給我訂兩張飛機票，另外，麻煩你再幫我買一個
大一點兒的包。

Please book two plane tickets for me. And also, may I trouble you to get a slightly bigger bag for me?

---

4 | **Comparing 再 and 还/還**

再 indicates the repetition or continuation of an action. When it is used in the sense of continuation, it usually refers to the future:

A

先生，您刚才点的菜我没听清楚，麻烦您再说一次。

先生，您剛才點的菜我沒聽清楚，麻煩您再說一次。

Sir, I didn't hear clearly what dishes you just ordered. Would you mind repeating yourself one more time?

B

因为工作，我去年去了一次上海，明年要再去两次。

因為工作，我去年去了一次上海，明年要再去兩次。

For business, I went to Shanghai once last year, and will go twice again next year.

C

上课需要买的书，我已经买了两本，
再买一本就行了。

上課需要買的書，我已經買了兩本，
再買一本就行了。

Of the textbooks for my classes, I've bought two. I'll buy one more and be done with it.

D

那个店的衣服样子不错，我姐姐昨天买了两件，
她说想再买几件。

那個店的衣服樣子不錯，我姐姐昨天買了兩件，
她說想再買幾件。

The clothes in that store are pretty stylish. My older sister bought two things yesterday. She said she'd like to get a few more.

还/還, on the other hand, denotes an increase in number or an expansion of scope. It can refer to the past or the future.

E

历史课我选了一门了，还得选一门。

歷史課我選了一門了，還得選一門。

I've already taken one history class. I have to take one more.

F

我点了一个清蒸鱼，一个家常豆腐，
还点了一盘饺子。

我點了一個清蒸魚，一個家常豆腐，
還點了一盤餃子。

I ordered steamed fish, home-style tofu, and also a plate of dumplings.

G

我明天去购物中心，要买毛巾、牙膏，
还要买洗衣粉。

我明天去購物中心，要買毛巾、牙膏，
還要買洗衣粉。

I'll go to the shopping center tomorrow for towels, toothpaste, and also powdered detergent.

If there is a modal verb—such as 想, 要, 能, or 会/會—in the sentence, it precedes 再 as in (B) and (D), but follows 还/還 as in (G).

要么…，要么…/要麼…，要麼…

要么…，要么…/要麼…，要麼… is a selective conjunction. It indicates that there are (at least) two possibilities or desires from which one must or will choose.

A
你要么学医，要么学经济，就是不能学文学。
你要麼學醫，要麼學經濟，就是不能學文學。

You have to study either medicine or economics. You just can't study literature.

B
Q: 你这个寒假打算做什么？
你這個寒假打算做什麼？

What do you plan to do this winter break?

A: 要么打工，要么实习。
要麼打工，要麼實習。

Either work part-time or get an internship.

C
Q: 今天晚饭想吃点什么素菜？
今天晚飯想吃點什麼素菜？

What veggie would you like with dinner tonight?

A: 要么吃菠菜，要么吃芥兰，要么吃小白菜。
要麼吃菠菜，要麼吃芥蘭，要麼吃小白菜。

Spinach, Chinese broccoli, or baby bok choy.

A WAY WITH WORDS

轻松

我每天都带电脑去上课，所以需要一个轻便的电脑。

住在校内很方便，你不应该那么轻易地决定搬到校外去住。

Using the word/phrase in orange as a clue, try to figure out the meaning of the words/phrases in blue; consult a dictionary if necessary. Consider how the literal and extended senses are related in each case.

輕鬆

我每天都帶電腦去上課，所以需要一個輕便的電腦。

住在校內很方便，你不應該那麼輕易地決定搬到校外去住。

Words & Phrases

只是 and 就是 (it's just that)

只是 and 就是 signify a turn in thought; they are similar to 不过/不過 in usage, and milder in tone than 但是 or 可是. Note that 只是 and 就是 usually appear in the last clause of a sentence. The first clause is often positive in meaning, whereas the second clause modifies the first clause, pointing out a flaw in something that might otherwise be perfect. In this respect, 只是 and 就是 differ from 但是, 可是, and 不过/不過.

1
你要搬到校外去住，我不是不同意，
只是觉得太早了一点儿。

你要搬到校外去住，我不是不同意，
只是覺得太早了一點兒。

It's not that I object to your moving off campus, it's just that I think it's a little bit too soon.

2
那件毛衣样子好是好，只是价钱太贵。

那件毛衣樣子好是好，只是價錢太貴。

It's true that the sweater is stylish, it's just that it's too expensive.

3
这个饭馆儿很好，也不贵，就是常常没有位子。

這個飯館兒很好，也不貴，就是常常沒有位子。

This restaurant is very good, and it's not expensive either. It's just that there often aren't any tables available.

Characterize it!

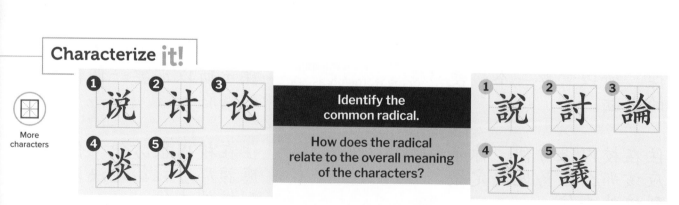

Identify the common radical.

How does the radical relate to the overall meaning of the characters?

More characters

B | 受不了 (unable to bear)

1 今天太热，我真的受不了。

今天太熱，我真的受不了。

It's so hot today. I really can't take it.

2 很久没吃中国菜了，小张快受不了了。

很久沒吃中國菜了，小張快受不了了。

It's been a while since Little Zhang had Chinese food. He won't be able to stand it for much longer.

3 我的同屋每天夜里两三点才睡觉，我真受不了。

我的同屋每天夜裡兩三點才睡覺，我真受不了。

My roommate doesn't go to bed until two or three in the morning. I can't stand it.

C | 跟…打交道 (to deal with …)

This phrase is typically used when describing what a person has regular dealings with because of the nature of his/her work or other reasons.

1 购物中心的售货员整天跟买东西的人打交道。

購物中心的售貨員整天跟買東西的人打交道。

The salespeople at the shopping center deal with customers all day long.

2 我妈妈在银行 (yínháng) 工作，天天跟钱和数字打交道。

我媽媽在銀行 (yínháng) 工作，天天跟錢和數字打交道。

My mom works at a bank. She deals with money and numbers every day.

3

我现在在小学教英文，每天跟小孩儿打交道，很高兴。

我現在在小學教英文，每天跟小孩兒打交道，很高興。

I now teach English at an elementary school. I deal with children every day. I'm very happy.

D | ## 这样/這樣 (in this way)

这样/這樣 refers to the fact mentioned in the previous statement. It connects two consecutive clauses.

1

我想申请离家比较近的学校，这样我就可以搬回家去住。

我想申請離家比較近的學校，這樣我就可以搬回家去住。

I'd like to apply to a school that's closer to home. This way I can move back home.

2

学外语得常常听录音、念课文，这样才能提高听和说的水平。

學外語得常常聽錄音、念課文，這樣才能提高聽和說的水平。

To learn a foreign language, you have to frequently listen to audio recordings and read lessons aloud. This way, you can improve your listening and speaking abilities.

3

选课以前你应该听听教授的意见，这样你的课才能选得合适。

選課以前你應該聽聽教授的意見，這樣你的課才能選得合適。

Before you select courses you should consult with your professor. This way, you can choose courses that are suitable.

4 买东西应该等商店打折的时候去买，这样才能买到便
宜的东西。

買東西應該等商店打折的時候去買，這樣才能買到便
宜的東西。

You should shop when the stores are having sales. This way you can find good bargains.

Chinese Chat

Teacher Chang just posted this on Twitter. How would you reply?

11:04 AM 74%

< **Tweet** ✑

Teacher Chang
@Teacher_Chang66

下个学期的课你们都选好了吗？
8:07 PM - 14 Nov

↩ ⇄ 12 ♥ 17

| 140 | Reply

Teacher Chang:
下個學期的課你們
都選好了嗎？

A WAY WITH WORDS

自由

他太自大了，一直觉得
自己是班上最好的学
生。

她跳舞跳得很自然，一
点儿都不紧张。

Using the word/phrase in orange as a clue, try to figure out the meaning of the words/phrases in blue; consult a dictionary if necessary. Consider how the literal and extended senses are related in each case.

自由

他太自大了，一直覺得
自己是班上最好的學
生。

她跳舞跳得很自然，一
點兒都不緊張。

Language Practice

| Staying the course | INTERPERSONAL |

In pairs, ask each other these questions to find out which courses your partner has taken and which courses your partner has been most and least interested in.

○ 你选过什么课？

你選過什麼課？

○ 你对哪一门课最有兴趣？

你對哪一門課最有興趣？

○ 你对哪一门课最没有兴趣？

你對哪一門課最沒有興趣？

Then, ask your partner which courses he/she wants to take next semester and which courses he/she expects will benefit his/her future job search.

○ 下个学期你想选什么课？

下個學期你想選什麼課？

○ 什么课对将来找工作很有好处？

什麼課對將來找工作很有好處？

○ 还有什么课对将来找工作也很有好处？

還有什麼課對將來找工作也很有好處？

Dash to the finish line

In pairs, tell each other what your major is, whether you wish to double major, how many credits you still need to graduate, and whether you plan to find a job or apply to graduate school after graduating, e.g.:

Major	Double Major	Credits	Job	Graduate School
✓ (finance)	✗	30	✓	✗

我的专业是金融，我不打算拿双学位。我还需要三十个学分才能毕业。毕业以后，我打算找工作，不打算念研究生。

我的專業是金融，我不打算拿雙學位。我還需要三十個學分才能畢業。畢業以後，我打算找工作，不打算念研究生。

Note: If you haven't chosen a major yet, you can say:

我还不知道选什么专业。

我還不知道選什麼專業。

C ┃ INTERPERSONAL ┃ **Too much of a good thing** ┃ PRESENTATIONAL

Go around the class and ask your classmates what kind of course load in a semester is manageable or unmanageable for them.

。一个学期上几门课会让你受不了？

一個學期上幾門課會讓你受不了？

。一个学期上几门课你觉得会比较轻松？

一個學期上幾門課你覺得會比較輕鬆？

Tally your classmates' answers, and report back to the class, e.g.:

____个同学觉得上____门课会让他们受不了。____个同学觉得上____门课会比较轻松。……

____個同學覺得上____門課會讓他們受不了。____個同學覺得上____門課會比較輕鬆。……

Based on the images, describe what or who these people have regular dealings with due to the nature of their jobs, e.g.:

经济学教授整天跟数字打交道。

經濟學教授整天跟數字打交道。

 **1**

 **2**

 3

In pairs, form question-and-answers about whether your partner has a parent, sibling, teacher, or friend who is concerned about every detail of his/her work, studies, and life in general. Does this person try to micromanage? Report the information to the class, e.g.:

parents   wardrobe

Q: 你父母常常管你穿什么衣服吗？

你父母常常管你穿什麼衣服嗎？

A: 我父母常常（or 不常）管我穿什么衣服。

我父母常常（or 不常）管我穿什麼衣服。

1   siblings   wardrobe

2   parents   food

3   friends   classes

4   teachers   major

5   parents   work

F | ## Makes "cents" | INTERPERSONAL

Brainstorm with your partner and come up with at least three ways to save money to pay for your education, e.g.:

Q: 怎么样可以把钱省下来付学费？

怎麼樣可以把錢省下來付學費？

A: 住在家里可以把钱省下来付学费。

住在家裡可以把錢省下來付學費。

G | ## Getting schooled | INTERPRETIVE

Draw lines to connect the Chinese words with their English equivalents.

人文学院/人文學院   school of engineering

医学院/醫學院   school of management

工学院/工學院   business school

理学院/理學院   medical school

药学院/藥學院   college of humanities

法学院/法學院   college of sciences

商学院/商學院   law school

管理学院/管理學院   school of pharmacology

Value of EDUCATION

There is an influential old saying in China, "Nothing ranks higher than studying" (万般皆下品，唯有读书高/萬般皆下品,唯有讀書高) (*Wàn bān jiē xià pǐn, wéi yǒu dú shū gāo*). It came from an anthology of poems by child prodigies compiled during the Song dynasty (960–1279). What does it reveal about the value that the Chinese traditionally placed on education? Another familiar saying, "With books come houses of gold; with books come jade-like beauties" (书中自有黄金屋，书中自有颜如玉/書中自有黃金屋,書中自有顏如玉) (*Shū zhōng zì yǒu huángjīn wū, shū zhōng zì yǒu yán rú yù*), also dates from the Song and came from the third Song emperor, Zhenzong 真宗 (968–1022), no less. In a poem intended to encourage people to improve their circumstances through studying, Zhenzong stresses that the key to improving one's life is through education. One historian has called the imperial service examination system "the ladder of success" in premodern China.

Graduate School

The word for "graduate school" in Mainland China is 研究生院, whereas in Taiwan, it is 研究所. However, 研究所 can mean either "graduate school" or "research institute." In Mainland China, the word 研究所 refers only to research institutes, which may or may not be affiliated with universities. In fact, most of the top research institutes in Mainland China are affiliated with the Chinese Academy of Sciences or the Chinese Academy of Social Sciences, and many of them offer postgraduate education. "To go to graduate school" is 念研究生 in Mainland China and 念研究所 in Taiwan. Like in many countries, people apply to graduate school by submitting an application to one or more schools. However, in both Mainland China and Taiwan, admission is given based on people's scores on the graduate school entrance exams.

COMPARE&CONTRAST

1 Does education provide the same kind of opportunity for advancement in your country as it does in China?

2 What do you think of the Chinese sayings introduced in this section—especially the one emphasizing the material and practical benefits of studying? How do they contrast with the ideals of a liberal arts education?

Declaring a major

Humanities Sciences

The Chinese educational system is highly compartmentalized. Typically, high school students are streamed into one of two separate tracks: sciences or humanities. College applicants have to declare their majors on their college application forms. Thus, when high school graduates are admitted to colleges or universities, they are admitted directly into specialized academic departments. Because a student's college application can have a crucial impact on his/her future career, parents usually play a large role in the application process. Once students are in college, it is generally difficult to switch majors. However, in recent years some universities have attempted to be more flexible by allowing students the opportunity to explore their options before declaring a major. There is also a move to put more emphasis on general education, 通识教育/通識教育 (tōngshí jiàoyù), so that students will become well-rounded in both the humanities and sciences.

Lesson Wrap-Up

Project

More
exercises

Spring course registration is next week, and you are meeting with your faculty adviser, who is also your Chinese teacher. Before the meeting, you reviewed your academic status by logging into your university degree audit program. On a worksheet, jot down courses you've already taken (已经选了/已經選了), courses you have yet to take (还需要选/還需要選), and courses you plan to take next semester (下个学期打算选/下個學期打算選). Also, look up a few words in order to carry out the meeting in Chinese: "required course," "elective," and the words for biology, physics, sociology, accounting, etc. Role-play the meeting with a partner using these suggested questions.

QUESTIONS:

- 你已经选了多少学分的课了？
  你已經選了多少學分的課了？

- 你还需要多少学分才能毕业？
  你還需要多少學分才能畢業？

- 下个学期你打算选什么课？
  下個學期你打算選什麼課？

- 哪些课对你来说可能比较难？
  哪些課對你來說可能比較難？

- 哪些课得花很多时间准备？
  哪些課得花很多時間準備？

- 你父母希望你学什么？
  你父母希望你學什麼？

- 你希望选什么专业？
  你希望選什麼專業？

- 你打算毕业以后做什么？
  你打算畢業以後做什麼？

- 你想不想念研究生？
  你想不想念研究生？

- 你计划五年、十年、二十年以后做什么？
  你計劃五年、十年、二十年以後做什麼？

Study the following description; pay particular attention to how the highlighted parts help the sentences flow smoothly from one to the next. Notice how:

- pronouns (**他**, **他们/他們**) replace corresponding nouns when the subject remains unchanged (**张天明/張天明**, 李哲)
- identical subject pronouns in close proximity are omitted (**他** in brackets)
- time words (**现在/現在**, **这一天下午/這一天下午**) and certain adverbs (**然后/然後**) serve as connective devices
- certain conjunctions (**可是**) indicate contrast or causal relationships (**因为/因為**)
- certain verbs (**听说/聽說**, **⋯说/說**) introduce hearsay and speech

下个学期选什么课?

张天明这个学期选了四门课：世界历史、电脑、政治学和中文。**他**觉得这几门课都很有意思，也学到了不少东西。**现在**得选下学期的课了，**他**希望下个学期能轻松点儿。**这一天下午**，**他**跟李哲聊选课的事。**听说**李哲要选经济和电脑课，**他**很高兴，[**他**]也决定选这两门课。**然后他们**又聊选专业的事。张天明**说他**喜欢文学，**可是他**妈妈非叫他学他不喜欢的金融不可。李哲**说他们**班很多同学选专业很自由，**因为他们**的父母不太管孩子选什么专业。

下個學期選什麼課?

張天明這個學期選了四門課：世界歷史、電腦、政治學和中文。**他**覺得這幾門課都很有意思，也學到了不少東西。**現在**得選下學期的課了，**他**希望下個學期能輕鬆點兒。**這一天下午**，**他**跟李哲聊選課的事。**聽說**李哲要選經濟和電腦課，**他**很高興，[**他**]也決定選這兩門課。**然後他們**又聊選專業的事。張天明**說他**喜歡文學，**可是他**媽媽非叫他學他不喜歡的金融不可。李哲**說他們**班很多同學選專業很自由，**因為他們**的父母不太管孩子選什麼專業。

What are you taking this semester? Use as many of the cohesive devices underlined in the example as possible to string together your answers to the questions:

○ 你这个学期选了几门课？哪几门？

　　你這個學期選了幾門課？哪幾門？

○ 你觉得那几门课有意思吗？你学到了什么东西没有？

　　你覺得那幾門課有意思嗎？你學到了什麼東西沒有？

○ 你这个学期忙不忙？

　　你這個學期忙不忙？

○ 你下个学期想选几门课？想轻松点儿，还是忙点儿？

　　你下個學期想選幾門課？想輕鬆點兒，還是忙點兒？

○ 你想学什么专业？为什么？

　　你想學什麼專業？為什麼？

○ 你父母管你选什么专业吗？

　　你父母管你選什麼專業嗎？

Can-Do Check List ✓ **I can**

Before proceeding to Lesson 6, make sure you can complete the following tasks in Chinese:

- ☐ Name my major and other required courses
- ☐ Talk about my plans after graduation
- ☐ Talk about ways to enhance my future job prospects
- ☐ Discuss whether my parents have a say in choosing my major and career path
- ☐ List ways to save money for school

Zhāng Tiānmíng zhè ge xuéqī xuǎn le sì mén kè: shìjiè lìshǐ, diànnǎo, zhèngzhìxué[a] hé Zhōngwén. Zhè jǐ mén kè dōu hěn yǒu yìsi, tā yě xué dào le bù shǎo dōngxi. Yīnwèi Zhāng Tiānmíng zài jiā de shíhou chángcháng gēn fùmǔ shuō Zhōngwén, suǒyǐ yī niánjí de Zhōngwén kè, duì tā lái shuō[1], tīng hé shuō hěn róngyì, zhǐshì xiě Hànzì yǒu diǎnr nán. Chúle Zhōngwén kè yǐwài, qítā jǐ mén kè dōu děi huā hěn duō shíjiān zhǔnbèi, hái chángcháng yào xiě wénzhāng, suǒyǐ tā juéde yǒu diǎnr shòu bu liǎo. Zhè ge xuéqī yǐjīng guò le yí bàn, mǎshàng yòu děi xuǎn xià xuéqī de kè le, Zhāng Tiānmíng xīwàng xià ge xuéqī néng qīngsōng diǎnr. Hòutiān yào qù jiàn jiàoshòu, tǎolùn xuǎn kè de shì, tā xiǎng xiān zhǎo bié de tóngxué liáo liao, tīng ting tāmen de yìjiàn. Zhè yì tiān xiàwǔ, tā zài lánqiú chǎng shang zhènghǎo pèng jiàn dà sì de Lǐ Zhé, jiù yì biān hé Lǐ Zhé dǎ qiú, yì biān liáo le qǐ lai.

 Zěnmeyàng, xià xuéqī de kè nǐ xuǎn hǎo[2] le ma?

 Hái méiyǒu ne. Nǐ ne?

 Wǒ yídìng yào xuǎn Zhōngwén, lìngwài[3] liǎng mén kè xuǎn shénme, hái méi xiǎng hǎo. Duì le, nǐ hái děi zài shàng jǐ mén kè cái néng bì yè?

 Wǒ xiǎng ná shuāng xuéwèi[b], hái[4] děi shàng sì mén kè. Wǒ xiǎng zài[4] xuǎn yì mén huàxué, yì mén jīngjì, lìngwài[3] zài xuǎn liǎng mén diànnǎo xì[c] de kè, zhèyàng xuéfēn jiù gòu le.

 Duì, wǒ juédìng le, yě xuǎn jīngjì hé diànnǎo! Wǒ de wèntí jiějué le, tài hǎo le! Wǒ hòutiān jiù qù jiàn wǒ de jiàoshòu, tīng ting tā de jiànyì. Lǐ Zhé, nǐ bì yè yǐhòu dǎsuàn zuò shénme?

 Wǒ xiǎng niàn yánjiūshēng, yàome shàng gōng xuéyuàn, yàome[5] shàng guǎnlǐ xuéyuàn, wǒ hái méi gēn wǒ de jiàoshòu tán. Tiānmíng, nǐ xiǎng xuǎn shénme zhuānyè?

 Wǒ xiǎng xué wénxué. Kěshì wǒ māma shuō, xué wénxué jiānglái zhǎo gōngzuò bù róngyì, érqiě zhèng qián yě shǎo, tā xīwàng wǒ niàn jīnróng. Dànshì wǒ duì jīnróng méi yǒu xìngqù, zhěngtiān gēn shùzì dǎ jiāodao, duō méi yìsi.

 Wǒ de fùmǔ gēn nǐ de fùmǔ chàbuduō. Rúguǒ ràng wǒ zìjǐ xuǎn zhuānyè, wǒ xuǎn zhéxué, yīnwèi wǒ xǐhuan xiǎng wèntí. Wǒmen bān hěn duō tóngxué bǐ wǒmen zìyóu, tāmen de fùmǔ bú tài guǎn háizi xuǎn shénme zhuānyè.

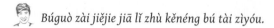 Nǐ yào shēnqǐng nǎ xiē xuéxiào?

Wǒ xiǎng shēnqǐng lí wǒ jiějie jiā bǐjiào jìn de xuéxiào, zhèyàng wǒ jiù kěyǐ bān dào tā jiā qù zhù, bǎ fángzū gēn fànqian shěng xia lai.

Búguò zài jiějie jiā lǐ zhù kěnéng bú tài zìyóu.

Nǐ de huà méi cuò, dànshì zhù zài jiějie jiā de hǎochù yě bù shǎo. Wǒ zài kǎolǜ kǎolǜ.

Bringing It Together (L1–L5)

Chinese character crossword puzzles

Many of the new words and phrases from Lessons 6–10 share the same characters. In these puzzles, the common character is positioned in the center of the cluster of bubbles. The triangular points indicate which way you should read the words. Work with a partner and see how many association bubbles you can complete, adding more bubbles if you can think of additional words/phrases, e.g.:

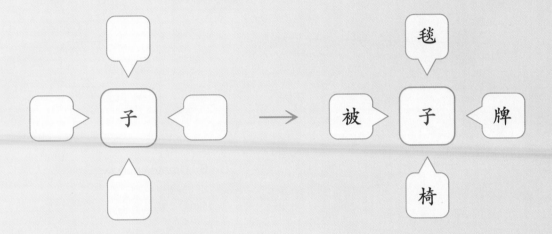

1   **2**

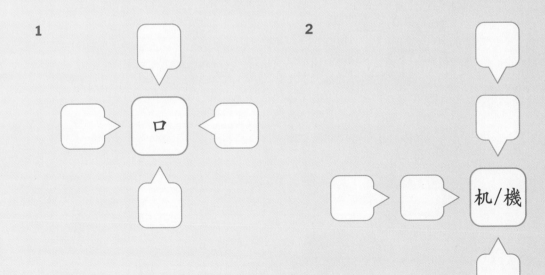

3

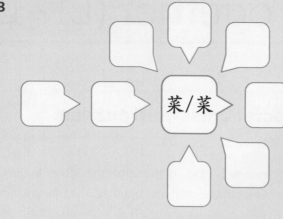

菜/菜

4

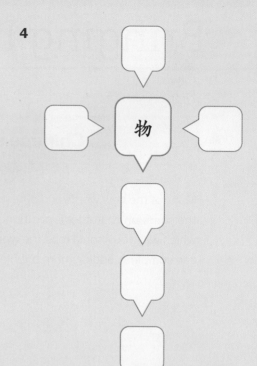

物

5

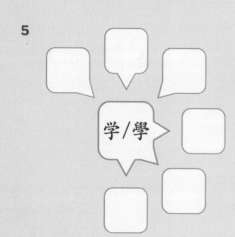

学/學

6 Create your own

Make a word list

First, brainstorm with a partner and ask each other what words come to mind when you want to:

- describe your dorm room/apartment
- prioritize your criteria when shopping
- specify your preferences when ordering food
- talk about your studies

Then, brainstorm with your partner and ask each other what words or phrases will help when you want to:

- agree with someone
- politely disagree with someone
- discuss the pros and cons of something
- make a polite request
- voice your disagreement rhetorically

C

Organize your thoughts

Select a topic from the first list in (B). In pairs, discuss

- what you want to say
- what words or phrases from the second list in (B) will help you express your opinion
- what should be said first, next, and last
- what transitions may be needed
- what cohesive devices should be used to connect your sentences

It's a good idea to jot down sentences that you wish to say, then number them in the order you think they should be presented. Consider how you can make your list into a coherent discourse. Once you've finished, present your work to the class.

Let me explain myself

How would you help make Person B sound logical while justifying his/her choice of major?
Use the following conjunctions where appropriate to complete the following paragraph.

另外　　因为　　虽然　　可是　　所以　　再说

Person A　你想好选什么专业了吗?

Person B　想好了。我决定学化学。

Person A　为什么选化学?你昨天不是说要跟我一样,上管理学院吗?

Person B　＿＿＿管理学院的课不难,＿＿＿很没有意思。＿＿＿我对数字、金融也没什么兴趣。＿＿＿上管理学院的人太多了,毕业以后找工作不见得容易。我听说学药学找工作比较容易。＿＿＿我打算先学化学专业,将来念药学研究生。

另外　　因為　　雖然　　可是　　所以　　再說

Person A　你想好選什麼專業了嗎?

Person B　想好了。我決定學化學。

Person A　為什麼選化學?你昨天不是說要跟我一樣,上管理學院嗎?

Person B　＿＿＿管理學院的課不難,＿＿＿很沒有意思。＿＿＿我對數字、金融也沒什麼興趣。＿＿＿上管理學院的人太多了,畢業以後找工作不見得容易。我聽說學藥學找工作比較容易。＿＿＿我打算先學化學專業,將來念藥學研究生。

男朋友女朋友

DATING

Learning Objectives

In this lesson, you will learn to:

- Say if you have an upbeat personality
- State if you share the same interests or hobbies as others
- Inquire if everything is OK and find out what has happened
- Describe behaviors of a forgetful person
- Give a simple description of what you look for in a friend
- Tell what makes you anxious or angry

Relate & Get Ready

In your own culture/community:

- Is dating common?
- What do people look for in a date?
- Do people introduce their dates to their parents?
- Is it common for friends to start dating?

课文

Text

Audio

Before You Study

Answer the following questions in Chinese to prepare for the reading.

1 你和哪位朋友、同学的兴趣爱好一样？

2 要是你跟好朋友吵架了，一般谁先跟谁说对不起？

When You Study

Listen to the audio recording and skim the text; then answer the following questions in Chinese.

1 丽莎跟张天明之间到底发生了什么事？

2 丽莎为什么觉得张天明心里还是有她？

3 林雪梅说柯林这个人怎么样？

丽莎这几天好像有什么[a]心事。昨天林雪梅问了她好几[b]次，她才说她跟张天明吵架了。

雪梅刚认识丽莎的时候，听丽莎说，她和张天明在高中就是同学。天明人很好，很开朗，学习也不错。在兴趣上[1]她跟天明不太一样，天明是个球迷，电视里一有球赛，他就非看不可，丽莎是个歌迷，一有演唱会就去听。丽莎说，他们的兴趣爱好虽然不同[c]，但是一直相处得很好。

林雪梅想来想去[2]，想不出他们到底发生了什么事儿。是因为文化背景不同吗？还是天明有了新的女朋友？正好今天晚上有空，雪梅就去找丽莎。

你跟天明怎么了？

别提了[d]，他心里根本没有我。

到底是怎么了？

課文

🔊 Audio

麗莎這幾天好像有什麼[a]心事。昨天林雪梅問了她好幾[b]次，她才說她跟張天明吵架了。

雪梅剛認識麗莎的時候，聽麗莎說，她和張天明在高中就是同學。天明人很好，很開朗，學習也不錯。在興趣上[1]她跟天明不太一樣，天明是個球迷，電視裡一有球賽，他就非看不可，麗莎是個歌迷，一有演唱會就去聽。麗莎說，他們的興趣愛好雖然不同[c]，但是一直相處得很好。

林雪梅想來想去[2]，想不出他們到底發生了什麼事兒。是因為文化背景不同嗎？還是天明有了新的女朋友？正好今天晚上有空，雪梅就去找麗莎。

👩 你跟天明怎麼了？

👩 別提了[d]，他心裡根本沒有我。

👩 到底是怎麼了？

Before You Study

Answer the following questions in Chinese to prepare for the reading.

1 你和哪位朋友、同學的興趣愛好一樣？

2 要是你跟好朋友吵架了，一般誰先跟誰說對不起？

When You Study

Listen to the audio recording and skim the text; then answer the following questions in Chinese.

1 麗莎跟張天明之間到底發生了什麼事？

2 麗莎為什麼覺得張天明心裡還是有她？

3 林雪梅說柯林這個人怎麼樣？

两个星期前我跟他约好去看一个演唱会，没想到他那天晚上一直玩儿电脑，把演唱会的事儿忘得一干二净。你说我能不生气吗？

别生气了，柯林也常常这样，一看球赛就什么事儿都忘了。

还有更叫[e]人生气的呢。上个星期六我找他陪我去看电影，他很高兴地[3]答应了，可是八点的电影，我等到八点一刻他还没到。打他手机，才知道他跑[f]到另一家电影院去了。这些虽然都是小事儿，但是叫我非常生气，觉得他根本不在乎我。真想跟他分手。

原来[4]是这样。这个天明，怎么这么[g]马虎！后来呢？

后来他见到我，不停地给我道歉，说对不起，态度特别好。这让我觉得他心里还是有我。

是啊，别生气了！马虎跟心里没有你根本不同。如果有一天不吵了，说不定你们就

兩個星期前我跟他約好去看一個演唱會，沒想到他那天晚上一直玩兒電腦，把演唱會的事兒忘得一乾二淨。你說我能不生氣嗎？

別生氣了，柯林也常常這樣，一看球賽就什麼事兒都忘了。

還有更叫[e]人生氣的呢。上個星期六我找他陪我去看電影，他很高興地[3]答應了，可是八點的電影，我等到八點一刻他還沒到。打他手機，才知道他跑[f]到另一家電影院去了。這些雖然都是小事兒，但是叫我非常生氣，覺得他根本不在乎我。真想跟他分手。

原來[4]是這樣。這個天明，怎麼這麼[g]馬虎！後來呢？

後來他見到我，不停地給我道歉，說對不起，態度特別好。這讓我覺得他心裡還是有我。

是啊，別生氣了！馬虎跟心裡沒有你根本不同。如果有一天不吵了，說不定你們就

真的会分手。实际上，柯林跟天明差不多，常常忘这忘那[h]、丢三拉四[5]的。他一会儿忘了我的生日，一会儿找不到钥匙，一会儿又……有的时候真让人着急。

是吗？原来柯林也有马虎的时候。对了，你交男朋友的事儿，家里知道吗？

这个吗……我还没把我跟柯林的事儿告诉家里呢。

View & Explore

Video

For deeper language immersion and more cultural information, watch "Relationships," a short, supplemental video clip by Cheng & Tsui on this lesson's theme.

真的會分手。實際上，柯林跟天明差不多，常常忘這忘那[h]、丟三拉四[5]的。他一會兒忘了我的生日，一會兒找不到鑰匙，一會兒又……有的時候真讓人著急。

是嗎？原來柯林也有馬虎的時候。對了，你交男朋友的事兒，家裡知道嗎？

這個嗎……我還沒把我跟柯林的事兒告訴家裡呢。

After You Study

Answer the following questions in Chinese.

1 張天明和麗莎在興趣上有什麼不同？

2 如果你是麗莎，你會跟張天明分手嗎？為什麼？

Language Notes

a 什么/什麼

In colloquial Chinese, 什么/什麼 can be used as an indefinite reference rather than as a question pronoun. Here, it can be omitted without affecting the meaning of the sentence.

b 好几/好幾

好 can be used as a mild intensifier, e.g., 好几个人/好幾個人 (quite a few people). Here, 几/幾 is not a question pronoun, but suggests a small, indefinite number: "a few."

c 同

同 is an adjective meaning "same" or "alike." It doesn't usually appear by itself.

d 别提了/別提了

Here, 提 means "to mention." When someone is in a bad mood and says, 别提了/別提了, the speaker is not so much asking the other person to drop the topic as indicating his/her emotional response to the subject.

e 叫, 让/讓

叫 and 让/讓 are interchangeable when they are used in the sense of "making [someone] do [something]."

f 跑

Here, 跑 is used colloquially to mean "to go."

g 这么/這麼

这么/這麼 is usually pronounced *zème* rather than *zhème* in northern China.

h 忘这忘那/忘這忘那

In 忘这忘那/忘這忘那 (forget this and forget that), both 这/這 (this) and 那 (that) are indefinite references, just like their English equivalents.

Vocabulary

Audio

Flashcards

No.	Simplified	Traditional	Pinyin	Part of Speech	Definition
1	心事	心事	*xīnshì*	n	something that weighs on one's mind
2	吵架	吵架	*chǎo jià*	vo	to quarrel
3	高中	高中	*gāozhōng*	n	senior high school
4	开朗	開朗	*kāilǎng*	adj	extroverted, open and sunny in disposition
5	迷	迷	*mí*	n/v	fan; to be infatuated with
6	演唱会	演唱會	*yǎnchànghuì*	n	vocal concert
7	爱好	愛好	*àihào*	n/v	hobby, interest; to love (something)
8	不同	不同	*bù tóng*		different, not the same
9	相处	相處	*xiāngchǔ*	v	to get along
10	到底	到底	*dàodǐ*	adv	what on earth, what in the world, in the end
11	发生	發生	*fāshēng*	v	to happen, to occur, to take place
12	背景	背景	*bèijǐng*	n	background
13	提	提	*tí*	v	to mention, to bring up
14	心	心	*xīn*	n	heart, mind
15	根本	根本	*gēnběn*	adv	at all, simply
16	一干二净	一乾二淨	*yì gān èr jìng*		completely, thoroughly [See Grammar 5.]
17	生气	生氣	*shēng qì*	vo	to get angry
18	叫	叫	*jiào*	v	to make (someone do something)
19	陪	陪	*péi*	v	to accompany
20	答应	答應	*dāying*	v	to agree (to do something), to promise, to answer

No.	Simplified	Traditional	Pinyin	Part of Speech	Definition
21	电影院	電影院	*diànyǐngyuàn*	n	movie theater
22	分手	分手	*fēn shǒu*	vo	to break up, to part company
23	原来	原來	*yuánlái*	adv/adj	as a matter of fact; original, former [See Grammar 4.]
24	马虎	馬虎	*mǎhu*	adj	careless, perfunctory, mediocre
25	不停	不停	*bùtíng*	adv	continuously, incessantly
26	道歉	道歉	*dào qiàn*	vo	to apologize
27	态度	態度	*tàidu*	n	attitude
28	说不定	說不定	*shuōbudìng*	adv	perhaps, maybe
29	实际上	實際上	*shíjìshang*	adv	in fact, in reality, actually
30	丢三拉四	丢三拉四	*diū sān là sì*		scatterbrained, forgetful [See Grammar 5.]
31	钥匙	鑰匙	*yàoshi*	n	key
32	交朋友	交朋友	*jiāo péngyou*	vo	to make friends

柯林常常忘这忘那、丢三拉四的，一会儿忘了雪梅的生日，一会儿找不到钥匙。你也常常忘这忘那吗？

柯林常常忘這忘那、丢三拉四的，一會兒忘了雪梅的生日，一會兒找不到鑰匙。你也常常忘這忘那嗎？

Grammar

<table>
<tr><td>**1**</td><td>（在）…上</td></tr>
</table>

（在）…上 can be combined with an abstract noun to mean "in terms of," for instance, in terms of character, interests, studies, work, etc.

A
在兴趣上，丽莎跟天明不太一样。

在興趣上，麗莎跟天明不太一樣。

In terms of interests, Lisha and Tianming are not really the same.

B
小林最近在学习上有很多问题，所以不太高兴。

小林最近在學習上有很多問題，所以不太高興。

Little Lin has had a lot of problems with his studies lately, so he is not very happy.

C
在生活上，如果有什么问题，就告诉我。

在生活上，如果有什麼問題，就告訴我。

In terms of daily life, if you encounter any problems, let me know.

<table>
<tr><td>**2**</td><td>Verb 来/來 verb 去</td></tr>
</table>

The construction "verb 来/來 verb 去" signifies a repetitive action, as in 走来走去/走來走去 (walk back and forth), 飞来飞去/飛來飛去 (fly here and there), 想来想去/想來想去 (think about again and again), 说来说去/說來說去 (say again and again), 讨论来讨论去/討論來討論去 (discuss again and again), and 研究来研究去/研究來研究去 (consider/research again and again).

A
你别在房间里走来走去，大家都睡觉了。

你別在房間裡走來走去，大家都睡覺了。

Don't pace back and forth in the room. Everybody's sleeping.

B

这个问题我们讨论来讨论去，最后还是没有办法
解决。

這個問題我們討論來討論去，最後還是沒有辦法
解決。

We discussed this problem over and over. In the end, we still couldn't find a way
to solve it.

C

妈妈叫我学经济，我想来想去还是选了化学。

媽媽叫我學經濟，我想來想去還是選了化學。

My mother wanted me to study economics. After thinking about it again and again,
I decided to study chemistry.

GET Real WITH CHINESE

You want to watch a movie
with your Chinese friend in
the Zhongguancun area of
Beijing. Your friend is showing
you how to buy movie tickets
at a lower price on a 团购/
團購 *(tuángòu)* (group
purchasing) app. Identify
the offers at the two movie
theaters. Decide which
offer you would take and
explain why.

Comparing 的, 得, and 地 (II)

These three structural particles are pronounced the same, but are used differently.

的 links an attributive with a noun, as in (A), (B), and (C).

Attributive + 的 + noun (phrase)

A
请帮我买点新鲜的青菜水果。

請幫我買點新鮮的青菜水果。

Please help me buy some fresh vegetables and fruits.

B
妈妈给我买的衣服是纯棉的。

媽媽給我買的衣服是純棉的。

The clothes that my mom bought for me are one-hundred-percent cotton.

C
你说的那位教授我不认识。

你說的那位教授我不認識。

I don't know the professor you are talking about.

得 links a verb or adjective to a descriptive complement, as in (D), (E), and (F).

Verb/adjective + 得 + complement

D
教授说我选课选得很好。

教授說我選課選得很好。

My professor said I chose my classes well.

E
我是个不怕热的人。今天热得连我都受不了了。

我是個不怕熱的人。今天熱得連我都受不了了。

I'm not a person who's scared of heat, but it's so hot today that even I can't stand it.

F

孩子们玩儿电脑玩儿得忘了吃饭。

孩子們玩兒電腦玩兒得忘了吃飯。

The children had such a good time playing on the computer that they forgot to eat.

地 links an adverb with a verb, as in (G) and (H).

Adverbial + 地 + verb (phrase)

G

女儿的病还不好，王太太着急地给医生打了一个电话。

女兒的病還不好，王太太著急地給醫生打了一個電話。

Mrs. Wang's daughter's illness wasn't getting better. Mrs. Wang anxiously called the doctor.

H

看完电视，爷爷奶奶慢慢地走上楼去休息。

看完電視，爺爺奶奶慢慢地走上樓去休息。

After watching TV, Grandma and Grandpa slowly went upstairs to rest.

4 | 原来/原來 as adverb and adjective

原来/原來 has two meanings. First, it is used at the beginning of a clause to convey a sudden realization, as in (A), (B), and (C). Second, it can be used as an adjective before a noun, as in (D) and (E), or as an adverb before a verb, as in (F), (G), and (H), meaning "in the past, before a change occurred." Note that when it is used as an adjective, 原来/原來 must be followed by 的.

A

我早就听说有一个新同屋要来，原来就是你呀。

我早就聽說有一個新同屋要來，原來就是你呀。

I heard that a new roommate was coming. So it was you!

B

房间里热得很，原来窗户没开。

房間裡熱得很，原來窗戶沒開。

The room was really hot. It turned out that the window wasn't open.

C

我觉得好像在哪儿见过你，原来你是我的同学的姐姐。

我覺得好像在哪兒見過你，原來你是我的同學的姐姐。

I thought that I had seen you somewhere. Turns out that you're my classmate's older sister.

D

你还住在原来的宿舍吗？

你還住在原來的宿舍嗎？

Are you still living in the same dorm where you used to live?

E

这栋楼还是原来的样子，又小又旧。

這棟樓還是原來的樣子，又小又舊。

This building is still the same as it used to be—small and old.

F

他原来住在学校的宿舍里，后来搬到校外去了。

他原來住在學校的宿舍裡，後來搬到校外去了。

He used to live in a dorm on campus, but later he moved off campus.

G

她原来吃肉，现在吃起素来了。

她原來吃肉，現在吃起素來了。

She used to eat meat. Now she's a vegetarian.

H

我的同屋原来不喜欢吃菠菜，后来听说菠菜对身体健康有好处，就开始吃菠菜了。

我的同屋原來不喜歡吃菠菜，後來聽說菠菜對身體健康有好處，就開始吃菠菜了。

My roommate didn't originally like spinach. Then he heard that spinach was good for health. After that, he started to eat spinach.

Set phrases

There are many set expressions in Chinese. Their form is often fixed and they are not meant to be taken literally. In other words, their overall meaning is not the sum of the individual words. For this reason, it's best to memorize the whole expression. These set expressions are typically composed of four characters, and many of them are idioms, e.g., 一干二净/一乾二淨 and 丢三拉四 from this lesson.

Set phrases function like words, but often in limited grammatical contexts. For example, 一干二净/一乾二淨 is adjectival, but it's most often used as a complement [see Words & Phrases C]. 丢三拉四, which functions like a verb, can be used as a predicate, but it can't have an object or complement [see Words & Phrases E].

Chinese Chat

Your friend Little Wang just posted this on WeChat. What's troubling him?

小王:
小高，演唱会马上就要开始了，你到底在哪里？

小高:
不是约的明天吗？怎么，是今天？

9:21 AM   85%

‹ Discover   Moments

小王

小高，演唱會馬上就要開始了，你到底在哪裡？

6 hours ago

小高: 不是約的明天嗎？怎麼，是今天？

Words & Phrases

A | 到底 (what on earth, what in the world, in the end)

The word 到底 is often used in questions to press the other speaker for an answer.

1   Q: 你明天去看演唱会吗？

你明天去看演唱會嗎？

Are you going to the concert tomorrow?

A: 我想去，可是……

我想去，可是……

I'd like to go, but …

Q: 你到底去不去？

你到底去不去？

Are you going or not?

2   他们俩到底为什么分手？没有人知道。

他們倆到底為什麼分手？沒有人知道。

What's the real reason those two broke up? No one knows.

Note the embedded question in (3). The word 到底 implies that the speaker has been agonizing over coming to a conclusion.

3   毕业以后到底念研究生还是找工作，我还没考虑好。

畢業以後到底念研究生還是找工作，我還沒考慮好。

Whether I really should go to graduate school or find a job after graduation, I still haven't thought it through.

根本 (at all, simply)

根本 is often used in negative sentences.

1
老师今天介绍的语法，我根本不懂。

老師今天介紹的語法，我根本不懂。

I simply don't get the grammar that the teacher introduced today.

2
他们俩吵架的事儿我根本没听说，你别问我。

他們倆吵架的事兒我根本沒聽說，你別問我。

I've heard nothing at all about their fight. Don't ask me.

3
你根本不认识他，怎么知道他的兴趣爱好是什么？

你根本不認識他，怎麼知道他的興趣愛好是什麼？

You don't know him at all. How could you know what his interests and hobbies are?

一干二净/一乾二淨 (completely, thoroughly, spotless)

This idiom is mostly used after 得 as a complement. It means one of two things: either completely, thoroughly, "with nothing remaining," which is the meaning used in this lesson and in (1) and (2) below; or very clean, as in (3).

1
上个学期学的汉字，他已经忘得一干二净了。

上個學期學的漢字，他已經忘得一乾二淨了。

He has forgotten every single character that he learned last semester.

2
他请我们去饭馆儿吃饭，我去晚了一会儿，到那儿的时候，他们已经把菜吃得一干二净了。

他請我們去飯館兒吃飯，我去晚了一會兒，到那兒的時候，他們已經把菜吃得一乾二淨了。

He invited us to dinner. I was a little bit late. When I got there, they had already eaten everything.

3

他把房间打扫得一干二净。

他把房間打掃得一乾二淨。

He made the room spotless.

D | 实际上/實際上 (actually, in fact, in reality)

1

很多人以为我同屋比我大，实际上我比她大多了。

很多人以為我同屋比我大，實際上我比她大多了。

A lot of people think my roommate is older than I am. Actually, I'm much older than she is.

2

我以前一直以为整天跟数字打交道没什么意思，后来才知道，实际上挺好玩儿的。

我以前一直以為整天跟數字打交道沒什麼意思，後來才知道，實際上挺好玩兒的。

I always had a misconception that it was boring to handle numbers and figures all day long. I got to know later that it was actually quite fun.

3

小王实际上学分已经够了，但他还想选两门电脑课，明年春天再毕业。

小王實際上學分已經夠了，但他還想選兩門電腦課，明年春天再畢業。

Little Wang actually has enough credits already, but he wants to take two more courses in computer science and graduate next spring.

Characterize

More characters

1 想 2 态
3 意 4 虑

Identify the common radical.

How does the radical relate to the overall meaning of the characters?

1 想 2 態
3 意 4 慮

丢三拉四 (scatterbrained, forgetful)

This means to be so scatterbrained as to leave things behind—that is, to be careless and absentminded. [See also Language Note C, Lesson 1.]

1 我哥哥常常丢三拉四的，我看有一天他会把自己也丢了。

我哥哥常常丢三拉四的，我看有一天他會把自己也丟了。

My older brother is so scatterbrained. I wouldn't be surprised if he lost himself one day.

2 你再这么丢三拉四的，你女朋友非跟你分手不可。

你再這麼丢三拉四的，你女朋友非跟你分手不可。

If you continue being so forgetful and absentminded, your girlfriend will break up with you sooner or later.

一会儿…, 一会儿…, 一会儿又…/一會兒…, 一會兒…, 一會兒又… (one minute ..., the next minute ...)

Used in this way, 一会儿…, 一会儿…, 一会儿又…/一會兒…, 一會兒…, 一會兒又… suggests two or more alternative actions or states. If it is repeated three times, there needs to be a 又 after the third 一会儿/一會兒. The implication is that someone or something is constantly changing or unpredictable.

1 小张觉得他哥哥很麻烦，一会儿叫他洗衣服，一会儿叫他出去买东西，一会儿又叫他做饭，小张根本没办法做自己的事。

小張覺得他哥哥很麻煩，一會兒叫他洗衣服，一會兒叫他出去買東西，一會兒又叫他做飯，小張根本沒辦法做自己的事。

Little Zhang finds his older brother to be a lot of trouble. One minute he's asking him to do laundry, the next he's asking him to go shopping or to cook. Little Zhang can't get any of his own things done at all.

2　你怎么了？一会儿哭，一会儿笑的。

你怎麼了？一會兒哭，一會兒笑的。

What's wrong with you? One minute you're crying, the next you're laughing.

3　这几天一会儿很冷，一会儿又很热，不少人都
感冒了。

這幾天一會兒很冷，一會兒又很熱，不少人都
感冒了。

In the last few days, one minute it's very cold, the next it's very hot. Many people have caught colds.

A WAY WITH WORDS

心事

小高一直没找到女朋友，（这）成了他父母的心病。

爸爸来邮件说妈妈又病了，所以小王今天心情不好。

Using the word/phrase in orange as a clue, try to figure out the meaning of the words/phrases in blue; consult a dictionary if necessary. Consider how the literal and extended senses are related in each case.

心事

小高一直沒找到女朋友，（這）成了他父母的心病。

爸爸來郵件說媽媽又病了，所以小王今天心情不好。

Language Practice

	Personality scale	PRESENTATIONAL

Rate the following characters' personalities on a scale of one to five, with one representing 一点也不开朗/一點也不開朗 (the least cheerful) and five 非常开朗/非常開朗 (the most cheerful).

Homer Simpson	1	2	3	4	5
Fred Flintstone	1	2	3	4	5
Ron Weasley	1	2	3	4	5
Hermione Granger	1	2	3	4	5
Batman	1	2	3	4	5
Superman	1	2	3	4	5
You	1	2	3	4	5

Then, based on your ratings, make comparisons among the characters and yourself, e.g.:

Homer没有Fred那么开朗。

Homer沒有Fred那麼開朗。

Fred比Homer开朗得多。

Fred比Homer開朗得多。

Finally, ask your class to vote on who has the most upbeat personality, using ⋯最开朗/ ⋯最開朗.

With the help of the pictures, discuss with a partner whether the characters share similar interests with each other and with you, e.g.:

Q: 张天明跟柯林的兴趣一样吗？

张天明跟柯林的興趣一樣嗎？

A: 在兴趣上，张天明跟柯林一样，都喜欢看球赛。

在興趣上，張天明跟柯林一樣，都喜歡看球賽。

[same]

Q: 柯林跟李哲的兴趣一样吗？

柯林跟李哲的興趣一樣嗎？

A: 在兴趣上，柯林跟李哲不一样，柯林喜欢看球赛，李哲喜欢看电影。

在興趣上，柯林跟李哲不一樣，柯林喜歡看球賽，李哲喜歡看電影。 [different]

1   **2**   **3**

4 you   **5**   you

Space cadet

With the help of the pictures, describe who forgot what and where, e.g.:

张天明把电脑拉在出租车上了。

張天明把電腦拉在出租車上了。

1

2

3

4

Then, ask three classmates to tell you who among their family and friends is forgetful and/or absentminded, e.g.:

Q: 你们家或者你的朋友谁常常忘这忘那？

你們家或者你的朋友誰常常忘這忘那？

A: 我妈妈常常忘这忘那、丢三拉四的。要么（or 一会儿）忘了买盐，要么（or 一会儿）把手机忘在车里。

我媽媽常常忘這忘那、丟三拉四的。要麼（or 一會兒）忘了買鹽，要麼（or 一會兒）把手機忘在車裡。

Ask three classmates about situations that would cause them to lose their cool, e.g.:

什么会让你着急（or 生气）？

什麼會讓你著急（or 生氣）？

First, list situations that would make them feel anxious, e.g.:

找不到钥匙/找不到鑰匙

_____

_____

Then, list situations that would cause your classmates to lose their tempers, e.g.:

开车/開車 发短信/發短信

_____

_____

Finally, report to your class what you have learned, e.g.:

找不到钥匙会让Marcia着急。

找不到鑰匙會讓Marcia著急。

看到有人一边开车一边发短信让Phil生气。

看到有人一邊開車一邊發短信讓Phil生氣。

A WAY WITH WORDS

开朗		開朗
小高今天考试考得不错，所以很开心。	Using the word/phrase in orange as a clue, try to figure out the meaning of the words/phrases in blue; consult a dictionary if necessary. Consider how the literal and extended senses are related in each case.	小高今天考試考得不錯，所以很開心。
小林的父母很开明，不太管小林选什么专业。		小林的父母很開明，不太管小林選什麼專業。

Something's up

INTERPERSONAL

When you sense that something is different or wrong, you can use 怎么了/怎麼了 to find out what's going on. Use the visuals to practice with a partner, e.g.:

Q: 他怎么了？　　A: 他发烧了。

他怎麼了？　　　他發燒了。

1

2

3

4

5

Make up your mind

INTERPERSONAL

Little Lin is indecisive about everything. His friends and acquaintances have gotten impatient and would like to get some answers. One of your classmates will be Little Lin. You and the rest of the class will pretend to be Little Lin's friends and family. Take turns with one another and use the cues to force Little Lin to make decisions, e.g.:

after graduation　　　find a job　　　go to graduate school

Q: 小林，你毕业以后做什么？

小林，你畢業以後做什麼？

A: 我还没决定（or 我还不知道）。可能找工作，也可能念研究生。

我還沒決定（or 我還不知道）。可能找工作，也可能念研究生。

Q: 你毕业以后到底找工作还是念研究生?

你畢業以後到底找工作還是念研究生?

A: _____

1	tomorrow	wear workout pants	wear jeans
2	next semester	take history	take philosophy
3	next year	live on campus	live off campus
4	after starting to date	tell your mother	not tell your mother
5	when shopping	care about the quality	care about the price

G | INTERPRETIVE | **We're through!** | PRESENTATIONAL |

Certain qualities in a friend can be deal-breakers. In your opinion, what characteristics could sour a friendship and make you call it quits?

不开朗/不開朗

容易生气/容易生氣

跟我兴趣爱好不同/跟我興趣愛好不同

跟我文化背景不同

跟我相处得不好/跟我相處得不好

忘这忘那、丢三拉四的/忘這忘那、丟三拉四的

做事非常马虎/做事非常馬虎

做错事不道歉/做錯事不道歉

Then you can say:

如果我的朋友_____, 我就不跟他/她交朋友了。

Finally, go around the class and listen to what your classmates have to say. Tally everyone's answers and see what the top deal-breaker is for you and your classmates.

Ideal mate

Here are some qualities that people look for in a prospective partner. Based on your own opinion, rank the qualities from one to eight, with the quality that is most important to you first. Add other qualities if they are not listed here.

很开朗/很開朗

很好看

钱很多/錢很多

兴趣爱好跟我一样/興趣愛好跟我一樣

文化背景跟我一样/文化背景跟我一樣

跟我相处得很好/跟我相處得很好

很在乎我

做事不马虎/做事不馬虎

After finishing your list, work with a partner and see if your lists are similar. Then, explain to one another what's important to you when dating. Try to include conjunctions or other devices to build a coherent and cohesive discourse.

七夕之约

七月初七

VALENTINE'S DAY AND THE
Qixi Festival

Valentine's Day (情人节/情人節) (Qíngrénjié) has been quite popular among young people in China in recent years. In addition, the Qixi Festival (七夕节/七夕節) (Qīxìjié), which falls on the seventh day of the seventh month of the lunar calendar, has been appropriated as a Chinese equivalent of Valentine's Day. The festival is based on an old legend in which a cowherd (牛郎) (niúláng) falls in love with the Weaver Girl (织女/織女) (Zhīnǚ), a celestial being. They become a couple and have two beautiful children. Fate intervenes, however: according to one version of the story, the Queen Mother of the West (王母娘娘) (Wángmǔ Niángniáng) recalls the Weaver Girl from the earth and cruelly separates the lovers by creating the "Silver River" (银河/銀河) (Yínhé)—which came to be the Chinese term for the Milky Way—with a flourish of her gold hairpin. A flock of magpies takes pity on the distraught couple; forming a bridge with their bodies, they allow the couple to be reunited. The Queen Mother of the West is moved to compassion, and agrees to let the lovers and their children come together as a family once a year on this bridge of magpies, 鹊桥/鵲橋 (quèqiáo). Interestingly enough, the seventh day of the seventh month used to be called 女儿节/女兒節 (Girls' Day); on this day, girls and young women would make offerings and pray to the Weaver Girl that they might have some of her dexterity and cleverness. For this reason the festival has also been called 乞巧节/乞巧節 (Qǐqiǎojié) (lit. Praying-for-Cleverness Day).

Idealized traits

Have any of the characters or language in IC ever struck you as overly coy? The traits that people look for in a potential mate vary from country to country. In China, some young women have sought to cultivate an image of girlish innocence, encapsulated in the recently popular Internet term 卖萌 / 賣萌 (*mài méng*), (lit. selling buds or sprouts). To many post-feminist Westerners the idea of a young woman acting juvenile or referring to herself as a "girl" (女孩子) may come across as retrograde. However, many people in China would not raise an eyebrow at the phenomenon.

COMPARE & CONTRAST

The thought of their pre-college children dating (早恋 / 早戀) (*zǎo liàn*) is something that worries many Chinese parents. In your culture, how young is considered too young to date? Do you see a disparity between your country and China in terms of parental attitudes toward dating?

A couple in Beijing

Courtship

Although customs and mores are changing, Western-style dating remains somewhat circumscribed in China. Instead, people speak of 谈朋友/談朋友 or 谈恋爱/談戀愛 (*tán liàn'ài*) when a man and a woman start going out. Teachers and parents usually discourage young people from forming romantic relationships at a young age. Parental opinion continues to play a large role in the choice of a marriage partner.

Lesson Wrap-Up

Project

More exercises

Role-play a mediation session with two partners. You and your Chinese roommate are not getting along and you have asked your RA to mediate. Your RA thinks that communication is part of the problem. As an exercise, your RA has asked you to put yourself in your roommate's shoes and to try to express yourself in a foreign language. Before the mediation session, you wrote down some of the situations that had led to conflict between you and your roommate. Being an intermediate-level Chinese speaker, you needed to look up some unfamiliar words, and wrote down the sources of conflict.

Possible sources of conflict:

- Your roommate is a soccer fan. During the soccer season, whenever there is a soccer match on TV, he/she will stay up and watch it. The sound of the TV makes it impossible for you to sleep.

- You are a 歌迷, particularly of country/rock and roll/heavy metal music; your roommate hates it ("dislikes it intensely"). He/she asks you to use headphones even though you don't think the sound is very loud ("big").

- You frequently forget to take your room card with you, so your roommate has to get up at night to open the door for you.

- He/she talks constantly on WeChat with his/her family and friends in China. You understand that your roommate misses home (想家), but you and your roommate should talk and become friends.

- Think of something else that a roommate might complain about.

Suggestions for the RA:

- Diffuse tension by thanking the roommates for coming.

- Explain the purpose of the meeting: 今天我们 (来) 谈谈你们俩为什么相处得不太好/今天我們 (來) 談談你們倆為什麼相處得不太好.

- Ask who would like to begin first or simply invite one of the roommates to start.

- Outline the rules: one roommate will speak first, to be followed by the other roommate.

- As one finishes, invite the other to speak, e.g., 现在请你说/現在請你說.

- If necessary, ask the other person to verify: 是不是这样/是不是這樣？

- Since feelings and perceptions play a big part in this type of situation, you may want to encourage them to express those by asking them, 你觉得/你覺得…, 你认为/你認為….

- Ask them if they can agree to do or not do certain things: 你们能不能同意…/你們能不能同意….

Study the following description; pay particular attention to how the highlighted parts help the sentences flow smoothly from one to the next. Notice how:

- pronouns (**他**) replace corresponding nouns when the subject remains unchanged (**张天明/張天明**)

- words, phrases, structures, or clauses that indicate time (**两个/兩個星期前,那天晚上,上个/上個星期六,八点的电影/八點的電影,丽莎等到八点一刻/麗莎等到八點一刻**) and adverbs (**一…就,才**) can serve as connective devices

张天明太马虎了

张天明人很好，很开朗，学习也不错。他是个球迷，电视里**一有**球赛，**就**非看不可。可是他非常马虎。**两个星期前**丽莎跟他约好去看一个演唱会，**那天晚上**他一直玩儿电脑，把演唱会的事儿忘得一干二净。**上个星期六**丽莎让他一起去看电影，他很高兴地答应了。**八点的电影**，**丽莎等到八点一刻**他还没到，给他打手机，**才**知道他跑到另一家电影院去了。这个天明，真马虎！

張天明太馬虎了

張天明人很好，很開朗，學習也不錯。他是個球迷，電視裡**一有**球賽，**就**非看不可。可是他非常馬虎。**兩個星期前**麗莎跟他約好去看一個演唱會，**那天晚上**他一直玩兒電腦，把演唱會的事兒忘得一乾二淨。**上個星期六**麗莎讓他一起去看電影，他很高興地答應了。**八點的電影**，**麗莎等到八點一刻**他還沒到，給他打手機，**才**知道他跑到另一家電影院去了。這個天明，真馬虎！

Describe a careless person (could be you, a classmate, or a friend). Use as many of the cohesive devices highlighted as possible to string together answers:

- 这个人怎么样？（很好,很开朗 or 不太开朗,喜欢帮别人的忙,学习很好 or 不太好……）

  這個人怎麼樣？（很好,很開朗 or 不太開朗,喜歡幫別人的忙,學習很好 or 不太好……）

- 因为这个人太喜欢……（玩电脑,玩手机,上网,听音乐）了，所以常常忘了……。

  因為這個人太喜歡……（玩電腦,玩手機,上網,聽音樂）了，所以常常忘了……。

- 能不能说出几件他（or 她）特别马虎的事儿？

  能不能說出幾件他（or 她）特別馬虎的事兒？

Can-Do Check List ✔ **I can**

Before proceeding to Lesson 7, make sure you can complete the following tasks in Chinese:

- ☐ Say if I have an upbeat personality
- ☐ State if I share similar interests with my friends
- ☐ Show my concern, ask if things are OK, and investigate further if necessary
- ☐ Describe a person who is absent-minded
- ☐ Give a simple description of the traits that I look for in a friend
- ☐ Tell what makes me anxious or angry

Lìshā zhè jǐ tiān hǎoxiàng yǒu *shénme*^a xīnshì. Zuótiān Lín Xuěméi wèn le tā *hǎo jǐ*^b cì, tā cái shuō tā gēn Zhāng Tiānmíng chǎo jià le.

Xuěméi gāng rènshi Lìshā de shíhou, tīng Lìshā shuō, tā hé Zhāng Tiānmíng zài gāozhōng jiù shì tóngxué. Tiānmíng rén hěn hǎo, hěn kāilǎng, xuéxí yě búcuò. Zài xìngqù *shang*¹ tā gēn Tiānmíng bú tài yíyàng, Tiānmíng shì ge qiúmí, diànshì li yì yǒu qiúsài, tā jiù fēi kàn bù kě, Lìshā shì ge gēmí, yì yǒu yǎnchànghuì jiù qù tīng. Lìshā shuō, tāmen de xìngqù àihào suīrán bù tóng^c, dànshì yìzhí xiāngchǔ de hěn hǎo.

Lín Xuěméi xiǎng lái xiǎng qù², xiǎng bù chū tāmen *dàodǐ* fāshēng le shénme shìr. Shì yīnwèi wénhuà bèijǐng bù tóng ma? Háishi Tiānmíng yǒu le xīn de nǚpéngyou? Zhènghǎo jīntiān wǎnshang yǒu kòng, Xuěméi jiù qù zhǎo Lìshā.

 Nǐ gēn Tiānmíng zěnme le?

 Bié tí le^d, tā xīn li *gēnběn* méiyǒu wǒ.

 Dàodǐ shì zěnme le?

 Liǎng ge xīngqī qián wǒ gēn tā yuē hǎo qù kàn yí ge yǎnchàng-huì, méi xiǎng dào tā nà tiān wǎnshang yìzhí wánr diànnǎo, bǎ yǎnchànghuì de shìr wàng de *yì gān èr jìng*. Nǐ shuō wǒ néng bù shēng qì ma?

 Bié shēng qì le, Kē Lín yě chángcháng zhèyàng, yí kàn qiúsài jiù shénme shìr dōu wàng le.

 Hái yǒu gèng *jiào*^e rén shēng qì de ne. Shàng ge xīngqīliù wǒ zhǎo tā péi wǒ qù kàn diànyǐng, tā hěn gāoxìng *de*³ dāying le, kěshì bā diǎn de diànyǐng, wǒ děng dào bā diǎn yí kè tā hái méi dào. Dǎ tā shǒujī, cái zhīdao tā *pǎo*^f dào lìng yì jiā diànyǐngyuàn qù le. Zhè xiē suīrán dōu shì xiǎo shìr, dànshì jiào wǒ fēicháng shēng qì, juéde tā gēnběn bú zàihu wǒ. Zhēn xiǎng gēn tā fēn shǒu.

 *Yuánlái*⁴ shì zhèyàng. Zhè ge Tiānmíng, zěnme *zhème*^g mǎhu! Hòulái ne?

 Hòulái tā jiàn dào wǒ, bùtíng de gěi wǒ dào qiàn, shuō duìbuqǐ, tàidu tèbié hǎo. Zhè ràng wǒ juéde tā xīn li hái shì yǒu wǒ.

Shì a, bié shēng qì le! Mǎhu gēn xīn li méiyǒu nǐ gēnběn bù tóng. Rúguǒ yǒu yì tiān bù chǎo le, shuōbudìng nǐmen jiù zhēn de huì fēn shǒu. *Shíjìshang, Kē Lín gēn Tiānmíng chàbuduō, chángcháng wàng zhè wàng nà*[h], diū sān là sì[5] de. *Tā yíhuìr wàng le wǒ de shēngrì, yíhuìr zhǎo bú dào yàoshi, yíhuìr yòu . . . Yǒude shíhou zhēn ràng rén zháojí.*

Shì ma? Yuánlái Kē Lín yě yǒu mǎhu de shíhou. Duì le, nǐ jiāo nán-péngyou de shìr, jiā li zhīdao ma?

Zhè ge ma . . . Wǒ hái méi bǎ wǒ gēn Kē Lín de shìr gàosu jiā li ne.

电脑和网络

電腦和網絡

COMPUTERS AND THE INTERNET

Learning Objectives

In this lesson, you will learn to:

- Find out if others are angry with you and apologize if so
- Avoid tension in a conversation by changing the subject
- Let people know about the trouble you had to go through because of their thoughtlessness or carelessness
- Name and discuss the activities you use the Internet for
- Discuss the pros and the cons of using the Internet

Relate & Get Ready

In your own culture/community:

- Is Internet access readily available?
- What consumer habits have changed because of the Internet?
- What impact has the Internet had on society as a whole?

课文

Text

Audio

Before You Study

Answer the following questions in Chinese to prepare for the reading.

1 你一般用手机还是用电脑上网？

2 你常常上网做什么？聊天、听音乐还是购物？

When You Study

Listen to the audio recording and skim the text; then answer the following questions in Chinese.

1 张天明整天在网上做什么？

2 大家约好了时间，张天明为什么迟到？

3 雪梅到底觉得网络时代怎么样？

张天明是个电脑迷，他的电脑从早到晚都开着。他在网上看新闻、查资料、玩儿游戏，有时候还在自己的网站上写博客，一会儿都离不开[1]电脑。他常常一上网，就忘了时间。昨天，丽莎、柯林、雪梅和他约好今天一起去唱卡拉OK，时间到了他也没来，打他的手机，也不接，就给他发了一个电子邮件。十分钟以后[2]，才看见天明急急忙忙地跑过来[3]。

对不起，对不起，我在网上下载了一个软件，又查了一点儿东西，结果忘了时间了。

查什么？

我要写一篇文章，查一些资料。

查资料？我们的教授不让我们用网上的东西，一定要用书或者杂志。他说网上的垃圾太多了。

你的教授太落伍了，网上有很多资料很可靠很有用啊。网络世界又大又方便，你可以叫外卖、购物，你可以租房子、买车，衣食住行，什么都查得到。

課文

Audio

張天明是個電腦迷，他的電腦從早到晚都開著。他在網上看新聞、查資料、玩兒遊戲，有時候還在自己的網站上寫博客，一會兒都離不開[1]電腦。他常常一上網，就忘了時間。昨天，麗莎、柯林、雪梅和他約好今天一起去唱卡拉OK，時間到了他也沒來，打他的手機，也不接，就給他發了一個電子郵件。十分鐘以後[2]，才看見天明急急忙忙地跑過來[3]。

對不起，對不起，我在網上下載了一個軟件[b]，又查了一點兒東西，結果忘了時間了。

查什麼？

我要寫一篇文章，查一些資料。

查資料？我們的教授不讓我們用網上的东西，一定要用書或者雜誌。他說網上的垃圾[c]太多了。

你的教授太落伍了，網上有很多資料很可靠很有用啊。網絡[d]世界又大又方便，你可以叫外賣、購物，你可以租房子、買車，衣食住行，什麼都查得到。

Before You Study

Answer the following questions in Chinese to prepare for the reading.

1 你一般用手機還是用電腦上網？

2 你常常上網做什麼？聊天、聽音樂還是購物？

When You Study

Listen to the audio recording and skim the text; then answer the following questions in Chinese.

1 張天明整天在網上做什麼？

2 大家約好了時間，張天明為什麼遲到？

3 雪梅到底覺得網絡時代怎麼樣？

对，特别方便。要是想交女朋友，也可以上网找。

哎，丽莎，你还在生我的气吗？

你说我该^e不该生气？你每次都迟到，老是害得大家等你。

对不起，对不起，是我不好。下次不敢了。

天明，你整天待在屋子^f里玩儿电脑，看起来真是玩儿上瘾了。

上瘾？没那么严重吧？现在是网络时代，当然离不开电脑。

我知道电脑和网络在我们的生活中越来越重要，我也用电脑帮助^g我做翻译练习，也上网比较价钱，可是不像你，常常忘了时间，忘了朋友。

天明，听丽莎说你不喜欢打电话，只喜欢发微信、发电邮。

微信、电邮不花钱。

没错！免费，又快又方便。

可是有的时候，看微信、看电邮没有打电话感觉好。

雪梅喜欢"电聊"^h。

"电聊"？什么是"电聊"？

對，特別方便。要是想交女朋友，也可以上網找。

哎，麗莎，你還在生我的氣嗎？

你說我該[e]不該生氣？你每次都遲到，老是害得大家等你。

對不起，對不起，是我不好。下次不敢了。

天明，你整天待在屋子[f]裡玩兒電腦，看起來真是玩兒上癮了。

上癮？沒那麼嚴重吧？現在是網絡時代，當然離不開電腦。

我知道電腦和網絡在我們的生活中越來越重要，我也用電腦幫助[g]我做翻譯練習，也上網比較價錢，可是不像你，常常忘了時間，忘了朋友。

天明，聽麗莎說你不喜歡打電話，只喜歡發微信、發電郵。

微信、電郵不花錢。

沒錯！免費，又快又方便。

可是有的時候，看微信、看電郵沒有打電話感覺好。

雪梅喜歡"電聊"[h]。

"電聊"？什麼是"電聊"？

就是打"电"话"聊"天儿。懂了吧? 一直聊、不停地聊、从早到晚地聊……

怎么? 听起来好像你不爱跟我聊天儿。

不,不,不,我不是那个意思[i],我是开玩笑。我当然爱跟你聊天儿。好了,好了,不说这些了,我们到底去哪家卡拉OK啊?

我上网查了,东边儿那家不错,那儿的歌都是丽莎喜欢的。你们看,我没忘了朋友吧?

Language Notes

a 一会儿都/一會兒都

一会儿都/一會兒都, 一点儿都/一點兒都, and 一个都/一個都 are all used in statements of emphatic negation. Respectively, they mean "not for a moment," "not in the least," and "not a single one" when followed by 不, 没/沒, or 没有/沒有.

b 软件/軟件

This is the term for "software." "Hardware" is 硬件 (yìngjiàn). In Taiwan, the terms for "software" and "hardware" are 软体/軟體 (ruǎntǐ) and 硬体/硬體 (yìngtǐ) respectively.

c 垃圾

垃圾 is pronounced lājī in Mainland China and lèsè in Taiwan.

d 网络/網絡

In Taiwan, the term 网路/網路 (wǎnglù) rather than 网络/網絡 (wǎngluò) is used.

e 该/該

该/該 is short for 应该/應該.

f 屋子

屋子 is more colloquial than 房间/房間.

g 帮助/幫助

Take care to distinguish 帮/幫, 帮助/幫助, and 帮忙/幫忙. Although they are synonymous with one another, they are used differently. 帮忙/幫忙 is a VO compound. To help me out or give me a hand is 帮我的忙/幫我的忙. 帮忙/幫忙 cannot take another object: [✗ 帮忙我/幫忙我]. 帮助/幫助 is a transitive verb, e.g., 帮助他学历史/幫助他學歷史. The main difference between 帮/幫 and 帮助/幫助 is that 帮助/幫助 is more formal than 帮/幫.

h 电聊/電聊

电聊/電聊 (to chat on the phone) is a facetious pun because it sounds the same as 电疗/電療 (diànliáo) (electrotherapy.)

i 我不是那个意思/ 我不是那個意思

The phrase 我不是那个意思/我不是那個意思 is used to dispel misunderstandings. It means, "That's not what I mean."

就是打"電"話"聊"天兒。懂了吧？一直聊、不停地聊、從早到晚地聊……

怎麼？聽起來好像你不愛跟我聊天兒。

不，不，不，我不是那個意思，我是開玩笑。我當然愛跟你聊天兒。好了，好了，不說這些了，我們到底去哪家卡拉OK啊？

我上網查了，東邊兒那家不錯，那兒的歌都是麗莎喜歡的。你們看，我沒忘了朋友吧？

View & Explore

For deeper language immersion and more cultural information, watch "Digital Generation," a short, supplemental video clip by Cheng & Tsui on this lesson's theme.

Video

Vocabulary

Audio

Flashcards

No.	Simplified	Traditional	Pinyin	Part of Speech	Definition
1	网络	網絡	*wǎngluò*	n	network, the Internet
2	新闻	新聞	*xīnwén*	n	news
3	资料	資料	*zīliào*	n	material (reference, academic)
4	游戏	遊戲	*yóuxì*	n	game
5	网站	網站	*wǎngzhàn*	n	website
6	博客	博客	*bókè*	n	blog
7	离开	離開	*lí kāi*	vc	to leave, to depart from
8	卡拉OK	卡拉OK	*kǎlā ōukēi*	n	karaoke
9	急忙	急忙	*jímáng*	adv	hastily, in a hurry
10	下载	下載	*xiàzài*	v	to download
11	软件	軟件	*ruǎnjiàn*	n	software
12	结果	結果	*jiéguǒ*	conj/n	as a result; result
13	杂志	雜誌	*zázhì*	n	magazine
14	垃圾	垃圾	*lājī*	n	garbage, trash
15	落伍	落伍	*luòwǔ*	v	to lag behind, to be outdated
16	可靠	可靠	*kěkào*	adj	dependable
17	有用	有用	*yǒuyòng*	adj	useful
18	外卖	外賣	*wàimài*	n	takeout
19	衣食住行	衣食住行	*yī shí zhù xíng*		basic necessities of life (lit. food, clothing, shelter, and transportation)
20	迟到	遲到	*chídào*	v	to arrive late

No.	Simplified	Traditional	Pinyin	Part of Speech	Definition
21	老是	老是	*lǎoshì*	adv	always
22	害	害	*hài*	v	to cause trouble, to harm
23	敢	敢	*gǎn*	mv	to dare
24	待	待	*dāi*	v	to stay
25	屋子	屋子	*wūzi*	n	room
26	上瘾	上癮	*shàng yǐn*	vo	to become addicted
27	严重	嚴重	*yánzhòng*	adj	serious, grave
28	时代	時代	*shídài*	n	era, age
29	重要	重要	*zhòngyào*	adj	important
30	帮助	幫助	*bāngzhù*	v/n	to help; help
31	翻译	翻譯	*fānyì*	v/n	to translate; interpreter, translation
32	免费	免費	*miǎnfèi*	vo	free of charge (lit. exempt from paying the fee)
33	感觉	感覺	*gǎnjué*	n/v	feeling, sense perception; to feel, to perceive

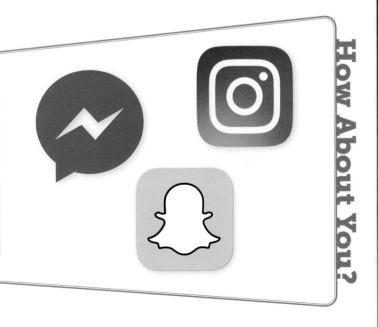

张天明喜欢发微信、发短信跟朋友聊天，因为又快又不花钱。你平常怎么跟朋友聊天儿？为什么？

張天明喜歡發微信、發短信跟朋友聊天，因為又快又不花錢。你平常怎麼跟朋友聊天兒？為什麼？

Grammar

---

1 | **Potential complements (III)**

There are several kinds of potential complements.

The first kind takes the form of "verb + 得 or 不 + resultative complement/directional complement." We studied this kind in Lessons 16 and 17, IC2. It indicates whether a result is achievable because of subjective conditions, as in (A) and (B), or external circumstances, as in (C) and (D).

A
我一会儿都离不开手机。

我一會兒都離不開手機。

I can't tear myself away from my cell phone, not even for a moment.

B
我的日文水平不高，看不懂日文杂志。

我的日文水平不高，看不懂日文雜誌。

My Japanese is not good enough for reading Japanese magazines.

C
房间的门太小，这张床搬不进去。

房間的門太小，這張床搬不進去。

This room's entryway is too small for the bed to fit through.

D
我的公寓很小，住不下两个人。

我的公寓很小，住不下兩個人。

My apartment is too small for two people.

Changing the potential complement to 不能 can affect the meaning. Compare (E) and (F):

E
我一会儿都离不开电脑。

我一會兒都離不開電腦。

I can't tear myself away from my computer, not even for a moment.

In (E), the inability has to do with the speaker.

F　我一会儿都不能离开电脑，离开了，电脑会出问题。

我一會兒都不能離開電腦，離開了，電腦會出問題。

I can't leave the computer even for a moment. If I do, something will go wrong
with the computer.
(Because of problems with the computer, I shouldn't be away from it.)

As we learned in IC2, this kind of potential complement usually occurs in negative form. In
affirmative statements we tend to use 能 + resultative complement/directional complement.
[See Grammar 2, Lesson 16 and Grammar 3, Lesson 17, IC2.]

In this lesson we encounter a second kind of potential complement, which takes the form
"verb + 得了 / 不了 (dé liǎo/bù liǎo)." This potential complement indicates whether
subjective or objective conditions permit the realization of a certain action. It also often appears
in negative form, as in (E) and (F), and is interchangeable with "（不）能 + verb."

G　我明天晚上有课，那个演唱会我去不了了。

我明天晚上有課，那個演唱會我去不了了。

or

我明天晚上有课，那个演唱会我不能去了。

我明天晚上有課，那個演唱會我不能去了。

I have class tomorrow evening. I won't be able to go to the concert.

H　那栋楼没有水电，住不了人。

那棟樓沒有水電，住不了人。

or

那栋楼没有水电，不能住人。

那棟樓沒有水電，不能住人。

That building doesn't have water or electricity. It's uninhabitable.

In questions, either the affirmative or the negative form can be used as seen in (I), (J), and (K). However, when using the negative form in a question, as in (J), the person asking the question already assumes a negative answer.

I

那个演唱会你去得了吗？

那個演唱會你去得了嗎？

Can you go to that concert?

J

那个演唱会你去不了吗？

那個演唱會你去不了嗎？

You can't go to that concert?

K

那个演唱会你去得了去不了？

那個演唱會你去得了去不了？

Can you go to that concert or not?

The potential complement "verb + 得了/不了" is more conversational than its counterpart "（不）能 + verb."

2　Connecting sentences (II)

In narrative sentences, time words can be used not only to express the time of an action but also as linking devices.

A

昨天丽莎、柯林、雪梅和他约好今天一起去唱卡拉OK，时间到了他也没来，打他的手机，也不接，就给他发了一个电子邮件。十分钟以后，（他们）才看见天明急急忙忙地跑过来。

昨天麗莎、柯林、雪梅和他約好今天一起去唱卡拉OK，時間到了他也沒來，打他的手機，也不接，就給他發了一個電子郵件。十分鐘以後，（他們）才看見天明急急忙忙地跑過來。

Yesterday, he, Lisa, Ke Lin, and Xuemei made plans to sing karaoke today. At the appointed time, he didn't show up. They called his cell, and no one answered. So they sent him an email. Ten minutes later, (they) saw Tianming running towards them in a hurry.

B （张天明）后天要去见教授，讨论选课的事，他想先找别的同学聊聊，听听他们的意见。**这一天下午**，他在篮球场上正好碰见大四的李哲，就一边和李哲打球，一边聊了起来。

（張天明）後天要去見教授，討論選課的事，他想先找別的同學聊聊，聽聽他們的意見。**這一天下午**，他在籃球場上正好碰見大四的李哲，就一邊和李哲打球，一邊聊了起來。

(Zhang Tianming) has to see his professor the day after tomorrow to discuss his course selections. He wants to talk with his schoolmates and hear their thoughts. One afternoon he happens to run into Li Zhe, a senior, on the basketball court, so he starts to play basketball and chat with him.

In the above two sentences, both 十分钟以后/十分鐘以後 and 这一天下午/這一天下午 serve a linking function. Without these two time expressions, the sentences would not be cohesive. Putting the time expressions after the subjects would make the sentences sound choppy, as seen in (C) and (D):

C 昨天丽莎、柯林、雪梅和他约好，今天一起去唱卡拉OK。时间到了他也没来，打他的手机，也不接，就给他发了一个电子邮件。他们**十分钟以后**，才看见天明急急忙忙地跑过来。

昨天麗莎、柯林、雪梅和他約好，今天一起去唱卡拉OK。時間到了他也沒來，打他的手機，也不接，就給他發了一個電子郵件。他們**十分鐘以後**，才看見天明急急忙忙地跑過來。

D （张天明）后天要去见他的教授，讨论选课的事，他想先找别的同学聊聊，听听他们的意见。他**这一天下午**，在篮球场上正好碰见大四的李哲，就一边和李哲打球，一边聊了起来。

（張天明）後天要去見他的教授，討論選課的事，他想先找別的同學聊聊，聽聽他們的意見。他**這一天下午**，在籃球場上正好碰見大四的李哲，就一邊和李哲打球，一邊聊了起來。

Place expressions can also be cohesive devices:

E 我昨天去购物中心买东西，在那儿看见了我好久不见的两个老同学。

我昨天去購物中心買東西，在那兒看見了我好久不見的兩個老同學。

I went to the shopping center yesterday to do some shopping. There I saw two old classmates whom I hadn't seen for a long time.

F 开学前我坐飞机来学校，在飞机上我看了一个很有意思的电影。

開學前我坐飛機來學校，在飛機上我看了一個很有意思的電影。

Before classes started, I took a flight to school. On the plane I saw a very interesting film.

Without the two place expressions, the above two sentences would not be cohesive. Furthermore, to serve as linking devices, the expressions must be placed at the beginning of the sentence or clause. Otherwise they wouldn't serve their cohesive purpose, as seen in (G) and (H):

G 我昨天去购物中心买东西。我在那儿看见了我好久不见的两个老同学。

我昨天去購物中心買東西。我在那兒看見了我好久不見的兩個老同學。

H 开学前我坐飞机来学校。我在飞机上看了一个很有意思的电影。

開學前我坐飛機來學校。我在飛機上看了一個很有意思的電影。

If a noun or pronoun serves such a purpose, it must also be placed at the beginning of a sentence or a clause:

I

我一叫他，他马上就来了。

我一叫他，他馬上就來了。

The minute I asked him, he came.

J

他去年去了中国三个月，我今年要去中国半年。

他去年去了中國三個月，我今年要去中國半年。

He went to China last year for three months. I'm going to China this year for half a year.

3 过来/過來 and 过去/過去 (to come over/to go over)

过来/過來 denotes a movement of a person or an object toward the speaker's standpoint (the point he/she is located at or he/she focuses on in his/her speech). The movement may pass a location as with the 桥/橋 (qiáo) (bridge) in 汽车开过桥来/汽車開過橋來 (The car came over crossing the bridge). It also may not pass a location, as seen in (A) and (B):

A

小张往我这边走过来，好像有什么事要跟我说。

小張往我這邊走過來，好像有什麼事要跟我說。

Little Zhang walked over to me, as if she had something to tell me.

[The standpoint is "me."]

B

同学们都往教室这里跑过来，想看看新来的音乐老师。

同學們都往教室這裡跑過來，想看看新來的音樂老師。

The students all came running over to the classroom, as they wanted to have a look at the new music teacher.

[The standpoint is "the classroom."]

Contrary to 过来/過來, 过去/過去 indicates the movement of a person or an object away from the speaker's standpoint. It may or may not pass a location.

C

小王从我身边走过去，没有看见我。

小王從我身邊走過去，沒有看見我。

Little Wang walked by me without seeing me.

[The standpoint is the location for "me," and Little Wang passed by "me."]

D

张老师很高兴地往她老朋友那边走过去。

張老師很高興地往她老朋友那邊走過去。

Teacher Zhang happily walked over to her old friend.

[The standpoint is where her old friend was.]

Chinese Chat

Zhang Tianming and Lin Xuemei are chatting on QZone. What would you say to Zhang Tianming?

11:01 PM   33%

< 动态   好友动态   +

张天明
今天10:15 PM

我玩儿电脑玩儿上瘾了，一上网就忘了时间。

👍 1人觉得很赞

林雪梅：我们明天还得考翻译，早点儿睡吧。
张天明：我还得下载一个软件。

张天明:
我玩兒電腦玩兒上瘾了，一上網就忘了時間。

林雪梅:
我們明天還得考翻譯，早點兒睡吧。

張天明:
我還得下載一個軟件。

Words & Phrases

A 从···到···/從···到··· (from...to...)

Examples of this common pattern include 从早到晚/從早到晚 (from morning till night), 从易到难/從易到難 (from easy to difficult), 从小到大/從小到大 (from childhood to adulthood), and 从我家到你家/從我家到你家 (from my house to yours).

1 他明年暑假要到中国去实习，所以从早到晚都在学习中文。

他明年暑假要到中國去實習，所以從早到晚都在學習中文。

He's going to intern in China next summer. That's why he's been studying Chinese from morning till night.

2 学跳舞要从易到难，慢慢儿来。

學跳舞要從易到難，慢慢兒來。

When it comes to learning how to dance, you have to go from easy to difficult, and take it slowly.

3 他妹妹从小到大都不喜欢穿牛仔裤。

他妹妹從小到大都不喜歡穿牛仔褲。

Since she was little, his younger sister has never liked wearing jeans.

4 从你家到我家坐地铁得四十分钟。

從你家到我家坐地鐵得四十分鐘。

It takes forty minutes by subway to get from your house to mine.

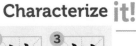

Characterize it!

Identify the common radical.

How does the radical relate to the overall meaning of the characters?

More characters

结果/結果 (as a result)

结果/結果 is a conjunction. Used in the second clause of a compound sentence, 结果/結果 expresses a result of the condition indicated in the first clause:

1
上高中的时候，他一天到晚踢球，不学习，结果高中念了五年才毕业。

上高中的時候，他一天到晚踢球，不學習，結果高中念了五年才畢業。

When he was in high school, he spent all his time playing soccer and didn't study. As a result, it took him five years to graduate from high school.

2
他常常麻烦别人，可是一点也不愿意帮助别人，结果一个朋友也没有。

他常常麻煩別人，可是一點也不願意幫助別人，結果一個朋友也沒有。

He often asks people for favors, but won't help others at all. Consequently, he doesn't have a single friend.

3
他原来听力不好，后来每天听录音，结果听力比我们都好。

他原來聽力不好，後來每天聽錄音，結果聽力比我們都好。

Originally, his listening comprehension wasn't very good, so he started listening to audio recordings every day. As a result, his listening comprehension is better than any of ours.

A WAY WITH WORDS

资料

他刚进我们公司工作，没有什么资历。

老周想开一家中国餐馆儿，可是资金不够。

Using the word/phrase in orange as a clue, try to figure out the meaning of the words/phrases in blue; consult a dictionary if necessary. Consider how the literal and extended senses are related in each case.

資料

他剛進我們公司工作，沒有什麼資歷。

老周想開一家中國餐館兒，可是資金不夠。

害得 / 害得 (to cause trouble so that, to do harm so that)

The verb 害 / 害 means "to harm" or "to impair." It's often used with the particle 得 to introduce a second clause describing the extent of the negative consequence caused by something or some action.

1

你昨天晚上没回来，害得我等了你一夜。

你昨天晚上沒回來，害得我等了你一夜。

You didn't come back last night. You made me wait for you all night.

2

女朋友一个星期没给他打电话，害得他吃不下饭，睡不好觉。

女朋友一個星期沒給他打電話，害得他吃不下飯，睡不好覺。

His girlfriend hasn't called him in a week. He hasn't been able to eat or sleep as a result.

3

弟弟把我的手机拿走了，没告诉我，害得我找了半天。

弟弟把我的手機拿走了，沒告訴我，害得我找了半天。

My younger brother took my cell phone and didn't tell me. As a result, I looked for it (in vain) for a long time.

D

看起来 / 看起來 (it seems)

This expression can be used before or after the subject.

1

李阿姨这几天看起来好像心里有什么事儿，到底怎么了？

李阿姨這幾天看起來好像心裡有什麼事兒，到底怎麼了？

It seems something has been bothering Auntie Li the past few days. What's going on with her?

2

天气不太好，很快就会下雨，我们看起来不能去公园打球了。

天氣不太好，很快就會下雨，我們看起來不能去公園打球了。

The weather isn't very good. It'll rain soon. It doesn't look like we'll be able to play ball in the park anymore.

Alternatively, the example in (2) could be reworded as:

3

天气不太好，很快就会下雨，看起来我们不能去公园打球了。

天氣不太好，很快就會下雨，看起來我們不能去公園打球了。

4 Person A

你念课文念得不太好，看起来昨天没有准备。

你念課文念得不太好，看起來昨天沒有準備。

You didn't read the text aloud very well. It seems like you didn't prepare yesterday.

Person B

对不起，老师，我下次一定好好儿准备。

對不起，老師，我下次一定好好兒準備。

I'm sorry, Teacher. I'll definitely be well prepared next time.

GET **Real** WITH **CHINESE**

You've just checked into your hotel room in Shanghai. While going up to your room in the elevator, you notice that the concierge has given you some promotional information along with your room key. What's being promoted on the back cover?

听起来/聽起來 (it sounds)

听起来/聽起來 means "it sounds like." What follows is the speaker's interpretation or conclusion based on what he/she has heard.

1   **Person A**   你怎么还不走？演唱会快开始了。

你怎麼還不走？演唱會快開始了。

How come you still haven't gone? The concert is about to start.

Person B   我文章还没写完，网上的资料特别多，我还……

我文章還沒寫完，網上的資料特別多，我還……

I still haven't finished my paper. There is so much information on the Internet. I still . . .

Person A   听起来你不想去了？算了吧！我自己去。

聽起來你不想去了？算了吧！我自己去。

Sounds like you don't want to go anymore. Forget it. I'll go by myself.

2   **Person A**   我找了一个公寓，离学校很近，房间很大，房租也不贵。

我找了一個公寓，離學校很近，房間很大，房租也不貴。

I found an apartment close to campus. The rooms are large and the rent is not expensive.

Person B   听起来挺不错的，你就租吧。

聽起來挺不錯的，你就租吧。

Sounds great. Why don't you rent it?

3   今天电视里有一个卖电脑的广告，听起来这个电脑又便宜又好，我真想订购一台。

今天電視裡有一個賣電腦的廣告，聽起來這個電腦又便宜又好，我真想訂購一台。

There was a commercial for a computer on TV today. The computer sounded very inexpensive and very good. I really wanted to order one.

Language Practice

INTERPERSONAL	**Plugged in**	PRESENTATIONAL

Make a list of the activities you engage in online, e.g., blogging, playing games, researching, downloading software, and chatting with friends. Then, list activities you never engage in online.

我常常上网……   我不上网……

我常常上網……   我不上網……

Then, in pairs, take turns asking about the activities your partner frequently and does not frequently engage in online.

你常常上网做什么？   你不上网做什么？

你常常上網做什麼？   你不上網做什麼？

Finally, report back to the class on the similarities and differences between your own and your partner's lists, e.g.:

Noah 跟我一样，都常常上网_____。

Noah 跟我一樣，都常常上網_____。

or

Aisha 跟我一样，都不上网_____。

Aisha 跟我一樣，都不上網_____。

A WAY WITH WORDS

Using the word/phrase in orange as a clue, try to figure out the meaning of the words/phrases in blue; consult a dictionary if necessary. Consider how the literal and extended senses are related in each case.

杂志		雜誌
我今天杂事儿太多，一点儿空都没有。		我今天雜事兒太多，一點兒空都沒有。
我们家门口有一个杂货店，我常常去那儿买东西。		我們家門口有一個雜貨店，我常常去那兒買東西。

Must-haves

INTERPERSONAL INTERPRETIVE

In pairs, take turns asking about gadgets that you cannot live without, such as a computer, a cell phone, a video game system, etc., e.g.:

张天明每天都得上网，他的生活离不开网络。

張天明每天都得上網，他的生活離不開網絡。

我每天都得_____，我的生活离不开_____。你呢？

我每天都得_____，我的生活離不開_____。你呢？

……

After listening to everyone's confessions, see if there is a most prized possession shared by a majority of the people in your class.

C

Pros and cons of the Internet

INTERPERSONAL PRESENTATIONAL

Ask three classmates about what positive and/or negative impact the Internet has had on their daily lives. Jot down their answers and report to the class.

D

Taking the hint

PRESENTATIONAL

Work with a partner and see if you can raise your EQ by expressing the following in Chinese:

1 It sounds like you're mad. What's the matter?

2 It seems that you're not pleased. What's going on?

3 Sorry! I've made you mad.

4 I am sorry. Are you angry with me?

5 Don't be angry. I was joking.

6 I didn't mean it. Please don't be mad at me.

7 Don't be mad. I apologize (to you).

8 How could I be so careless? I apologize (to you).

9 I am so sorry. It's all my fault.

10 It's my fault. I will not (dare to) do it again.

Moving on

INTERPERSONAL

We've all had moments when we've had to change the subject quickly or wrap up an awkward conversation. Some useful lines in such situations are:

- 好了，好了，别说了……

  好了，好了，別說了……

- 行，行，行，你别再说下去了……

  行，行，行，你別再說下去了……

- 行了，行了，我们别吵了……

  行了，行了，我們別吵了……

In pairs, compose a conversation between two people who fall into an extended argument. Have one of the characters end the argument by using one of these three pivot phrases. Then, act out the conversation you have composed, and ask your instructor and classmates to judge whether the pivot phrase was used appropriately.

F

Good grief

PRESENTATIONAL

Sometimes you just have to vent. Based on the images, practice complaining about everyday irritations, e.g.:

空调开得太冷，害得我感冒了。
空調開得太冷，害得我感冒了。

1

2

3

4

5

Story time

Based on the following sentences, narrate what happened to Little Lin yesterday. Don't forget to include the who, where, and when. Connect your sentences using time phrases, place expressions, and pronouns.

○ 小林昨天早上八点起床。

小林昨天早上八點起床。

○ 小林八点半去教室上课。

小林八點半去教室上課。

○ 小林在教室里看见同学们都在看电影，没上课，不知道为什么。

小林在教室裡看見同學們都在看電影，沒上課，不知道為什麼。

○ 小林过了一会儿才想起来，老师叫大家今天八点来看电影。

小林過了一會兒才想起來，老師叫大家今天八點來看電影。

○ 小林马上给老师道歉说："对不起，老师，我来晚了。"

小林馬上給老師道歉說："對不起，老師，我來晚了。"

小林昨天早上八点起床，_____去教室上课，_____看见同学们都在看电影，没上课，不知道为什么。_____才想起来，老师叫大家今天八点来看电影。_____给老师道歉说："对不起，老师，我来晚了。"

小林昨天早上八點起床，_____去教室上課，_____看見同學們都在看電影，沒上課，不知道為什麼。_____才想起來，老師叫大家今天八點來看電影。_____給老師道歉說："對不起，老師，我來晚了。"

BAIDU, ALIBABA, AND TENCENT

Three companies dominate the Chinese Internet: Baidu (百度) (*Bǎidù*), Alibaba (阿里巴巴) (*Ālǐbābā*), and Tencent (腾讯/騰訊) (*Téngxùn*). Baidu is China's largest search engine, Alibaba is an e-commerce platform, and Tencent operates the messaging services QQ and WeChat. However, all three companies have developed assets beyond their core businesses: Baidu, for example, operates an online editable encyclopedia similar to Wikipedia; Alibaba has expanded into mobile payments and cloud computing; and Tencent has through its investments become the world's largest gaming company.

The name Alibaba comes from "Ali Baba and the Forty Thieves," while Tencent's Chinese name, 腾讯/騰訊, literally means "jumping messages," a nod to the company's roots in messaging.

The origin of Baidu's name deserves particular mention. It means "hundreds of times" or "time and again," and comes from a Song dynasty poem by Xin Qiji, 辛弃疾/辛棄疾 (*Xīn Qíjí*; 1140–1207): 众里寻他千百度，蓦然回首，那人却在灯火阑珊处/眾裡尋他千百度，驀然回首，那人卻在燈火闌珊處 (*Zhòng lǐ xún tā qiān bǎi dù, mòrán huíshǒu, nà rén què zài dēnghuǒ lánshān chù*) ("A thousand times I search for her in the crowd, and suddenly turning my head, discover her where the lantern lights are dim"). 百度 also sounds identical to the word for "ferry" or "to ferry" (摆渡/擺渡), an apt connotation for a search engine, whose business is getting the user to the information that he/she is looking for.

Internet Lingo

Like people in many other countries, Chinese netizens frequently resort to abbreviations. *Pinyin* and English letters have thus become handy tools for this purpose. For instance, MM stands for 妹妹. Some abbreviations, such as 3Q, use a mix of Chinese and English. Try reading 3Q out loud and see if you can figure out what it means. Some numbers serve as onomatopoeia. What do you think 555 is supposed to sound like? Homonyms are also often used for facetious or satirical effect, such as 杯具 (*bēi jù*) (cups and utensils), which means 悲剧/悲劇 (*bēijù*) (tragedy). The originator of a comment chain is known as "master of the tower," 楼主/樓主 (*lóuzhǔ*), because a series of comments is thought to resemble a multistory building. Depending on their position on the chain individual comments are called "third floor," 三楼/三樓; "seventh floor," 七楼/七樓; "upstairs," 楼上/樓上; or "downstairs," 楼下/樓下. These slang terms are popular mainly among young people. A majority of older people would find them nonsensical or frown upon them. It's also doubtful that most of these terms will ever find their way into canonical dictionaries.

CHINESE CHARACTER THROWBACKS

Another fad among young Internet users is to appropriate and deliberately misuse very obscure characters. An example is 囧 (*jiǒng*), as in 今天考得很糟糕，真囧 (I messed up today's exam—I'm really down/embarrased). The appeal of the character is not difficult to see. The combination of 八 on top of 口 resembles a graphic depiction of a sad face with downcast eyebrows over the mouth, although the character is actually a variant of 炯, meaning "bright" or "brilliant." It sounds like 窘, meaning "embarrassing" or "awkward"; hence the usage. Reinvention of this character sparked an interest in breathing life back into obsolete characters. Another example is the creative adaptation of 槑 (*méi*), a rare variant of 梅 (flowering apricot). Because the character duplicates the character 呆 (*dāi*), which means "dull" or "dumb" and resembles someone standing around aimlessly, 槑 is now used to describe someone who is especially slow and always spacing out.

COMPARE & CONTRAST

Make a brief list of some of the abbreviations and Internet slang commonly used in your language. What similarities and differences can you spot between the Internet slang used in your country and Chinese Internet slang? How is wordplay in an alphabetic language different from that in a logographic one?

Lesson Wrap-Up

Project

More exercises

Prepare an oral presentation on Chinese Internet usage. Research the Chinese sites 百度, 淘宝网/淘寶網, 当当网/當當網, 微博/微博, and 搜狐. Choose one as the topic of your presentation. Navigate the site in order to describe it. Use slides to help your classmates follow your points. Include a screenshot of the site. In your presentation, be sure to elaborate on the following:

- explain how Chinese people use the site, e.g., 中国人常常上X购物/中國人常常上X購物
- suggest an overseas equivalent, e.g., X 有点像/有點像 Y, or X 和 Y 差不多/差不多
- give a sense of its popularity, scale, or importance, e.g., how many people use it, how it compares with its equivalent abroad
- end your presentation with a remark on the biggest surprise to you about this site if any, e.g., 没想到用 X 的人那么多/沒想到用X的人那麼多!

Keep It Flowing

Study the following description; pay particular attention to how the highlighted parts help the sentences flow smoothly from one to the next. Notice how:

- pronouns (他) replace corresponding nouns when the subject remains unchanged (张天明/張天明)
- words and phrases that indicate time (每天, 有时候/有時候, 的时候/的時候, 常常) can serve as connective devices

张天明是个电脑迷

　　张天明是个电脑迷。**每天**在网上看新闻、查资料、玩儿游戏，**有时候**还在自己的网站上写博客，一会儿都离不开电脑，**常常**一上网，就忘了时间。**他**写文章**的时候**，喜欢上网查资料，觉得网上很多资料很可靠很有用。别人说**他**玩儿电脑上瘾了。**他**说现在是网络时代，当然离不开电脑。

張天明是個電腦迷

　　張天明是個電腦迷，每天在網上看新聞，查資料，玩兒遊戲，有時候還在自己的網站上寫博客，一會兒都離不開電腦，常常一上網，就忘了時間。他寫文章的時候，喜歡上網查資料，覺得網上很多資料很可靠很有用。別人說他玩電腦玩上癮了，他說現在是網絡時代，當然離不開電腦。

Describe someone who is infatuated with or fixated on computers or cell phones. Use as many of the cohesive devices highlighted in the example as possible to string together your answers to the questions:

○ 这个人是个电脑迷还是个手机迷？
　　這個人是個電腦迷還是個手機迷？

○ 这个人整天用电脑（or 手机）做什么？
　　這個人整天用電腦（or 手機）做什麼？

○ 这个人离得开离不开电脑（or 手机）？
　　這個人離得開離不開電腦（or 手機）？

○ 他（or 她）为什么那么爱玩电脑（or 手机）？
　　他（or 她）為什麼那麼愛玩電腦（or 手機）？

○ 他（or 她）觉得自己玩电脑（or 手机）上瘾了吗？为什么？
　　他（or 她）覺得自己玩電腦（or 手機）上癮了嗎？為什麼？

Can-Do Check List

I can

Before proceeding to Lesson 8, make sure you can complete the following tasks in Chinese:

☐ Apologize after finding out I've made life difficult for others
☐ Change the subject during a conversation
☐ Complain about trouble caused by other people
☐ Talk about my online activities
☐ Discuss the positive and negative impacts of the Internet on my life

Zhāng Tiānmíng shì ge diànnǎomí, tā de diànnǎo *cóng zǎo dào wǎn* dōu kāi zhe. Tā zài wǎng shang kàn xīnwén, chá zīliào, wánr yóuxì, yǒu shíhou hái zài zìjǐ de wǎngzhàn shang xiě bókè, yíhuìr dōu[a] lí bù kāi[1] diànnǎo. Tā chángcháng yí shàng wǎng, jiù wàng le shíjiān. Zuótiān, Lìshā, Kē Lín, Xuěméi hé tā yuē hǎo jīntiān yìqǐ qù chàng kǎlāōukēi, shíjiān dào le tā yě méi lái, dǎ tā de shǒujī, yě bù jiē, jiù gěi tā fā le yí ge diànzǐ yóujiàn. Shí fēnzhōng yǐhòu[2], cái kàn jiàn Tiānmíng jí jí máng máng de pǎo guo lai[3].

 Duìbuqǐ, duìbuqǐ, wǒ zài wǎng shang xiàzài le yí ge ruǎnjiàn[b], yòu chá le yì diǎnr dōngxi, *jiéguǒ* wàng le shíjiān le.

 Chá shénme?

 Wǒ yào xiě yì piān wénzhāng, chá yì xiē zīliào.

 Chá zīliào? Wǒmen de jiàoshòu bú ràng wǒmen yòng wǎng shang de dōngxi, yídìng yào yòng shū huòzhě zázhì. Tā shuō wǎng shang de lājī[c] tài duō le.

 Nǐ de jiàoshòu tài luòwǔ le, wǎng shang yǒu hěn duō zīliào hěn kěkào hěn yǒuyòng a. Wǎngluò[d] shìjiè yòu dà yòu fāngbiàn, nǐ kěyǐ jiào wàimài, gòuwù, nǐ kěyǐ zū fángzi, mǎi chē, yī shí zhù xíng, shénme dōu chá de dào.

 Duì, tèbié fāngbiàn. Yàoshi xiǎng jiāo nǚpéngyou, yě kěyǐ shàng wǎng zhǎo.

 Āi, Lìshā, nǐ hái zài shēng wǒ de qì ma?

 Nǐ shuō wǒ gāi[e] bù gāi shēng qì? Nǐ měi cì dōu chídào, lǎoshì hài de dàjiā děng nǐ.

 Duìbuqǐ, duìbuqǐ, shì wǒ bù hǎo. Xià cì bù gǎn le.

 Tiānmíng, nǐ zhěngtiān dāi zài wūzi[f] li wánr diànnǎo, kàn qǐ lai zhēn shì wánr shàng yǐn le.

 Shàng yǐn? Méi nàme yánzhòng ba? Xiànzài shì wǎngluò shídài, dāngrán lí bù kāi diànnǎo.

 Wǒ zhīdao diànnǎo hé wǎngluò zài wǒmen de shēnghuó zhōng yuè lái yuè zhòngyào, wǒ yě yòng diànnǎo bāngzhù[g] wǒ zuò fānyì liànxí, yě shàng wǎng bǐjiào jiàqian, kěshì bú xiàng nǐ, chángcháng wàng le shíjiān, wàng le péngyou.

 Tiānmíng, tīng Lìshā shuō nǐ bù xǐhuan dǎ diànhuà, zhǐ xǐhuan fā Wēixìn, fā diànyóu.

 Wēixìn, diànyóu bù huā qián.

 Méi cuò! Miǎnfèi, yòu kuài yòu fāngbiàn.

 Kěshì yǒude shíhou, kàn Wēixìn, kàn diànyóu méiyǒu dǎ diànhuà gǎnjué hǎo.

 Xuěméi xǐhuan "diàn liáo"[h].

 "Diàn liáo"? Shénme shi "diàn liáo"?

 Jiùshi dǎ "diàn"huà "liáo"tiānr. Dǒng le ba? Yìzhí liáo, bùtíng de liáo, cóng zǎo dào wǎn de liáo . . .

 Zěnme? *Tīng qǐ lai* hǎoxiàng nǐ bú ài gēn wǒ liáo tiānr.

 Bù, bù, bù, wǒ bú shì nà ge yìsi[i], wǒ shì kāi wánxiào. Wǒ dāngrán ài gēn nǐ liáo tiānr. Hǎo le, hǎo le, bù shuō zhè xiē le, wǒmen dàodǐ qù nǎ jiā kǎlāōukēi a?

 Wǒ shàng wǎng chá le, dōngbianr nà jiā búcuò, nàr de gē dōu shì Lìshā xǐhuan de. Nǐmen kàn, wǒ méi wàng le péngyou ba?

打工

WORKING PART-TIME

Learning Objectives

In this lesson, you will learn to:

- Explain how people fund their education
- Discuss if you work part-time and why
- Name common jobs for students in China and in your country
- Talk about how students spend their pocket money

Relate & Get Ready

In your own culture/community:

- Are parents expected to financially support children in college?
- Do teenagers and college students often take part-time jobs?
- Do people generally have savings in the bank?
- Is it easy to apply for student loans?

课文

Text

Audio

Before You Study

Answer the following questions in Chinese to prepare for the reading.

1 你打过工吗？在哪儿打过工？

2 你觉得打工对学习有什么影响？

When You Study

Listen to the audio recording and skim the text; then answer the following questions in Chinese.

1 谁供张天明上学？张天明为什么想打工挣钱？

2 为什么中国的大学生一般不在餐馆儿打工？

3 丽莎的同屋为什么零用钱不够花，还想跟丽莎借钱？

张天明的父母希望孩子们能受到良好的教育，所以孩子一生下来[1]就开始给他们存[a]教育费。虽然张天明父母的收入不少，但是供[b]天明和姐姐上大学，经济上还是有些压力。张天明觉得自己已经是大人[c]了，应该找工作挣钱来[2]减轻父母的负担，所以就上网看看有没有适合自己的工作。这时候丽莎和雪梅走了[3]进来。

天明，你在网上看什么呢？

我想打点儿工，少花一点儿家里的钱。

打工会不会影响学习？

我想打工是想取得一些工作经验。如果打工时间不太多，不会影响学习。

我也想打工挣点儿零用钱。

你不是有奖学金吗？

奖学金不够交学费，我还申请了政府的学生贷款。雪梅，中国大学生也打工吗？

課文

Audio

張天明的父母希望孩子們能受到良好的教育，所以孩子一生下來[1]就開始給他們存[a]教育費。雖然張天明父母的收入不少，但是供[b]天明和姐姐上大學，經濟上還是有些壓力。張天明覺得自己已經是大人[c]了，應該找工作掙錢來[2]減輕父母的負擔，所以就上網看看有沒有適合自己的工作。這時候麗莎和雪梅走了[3]進來。

天明，你在網上看什麼呢？

我想打點兒工，少花一點兒家裡的錢。

打工會不會影響學習？

我想打工是想取得一些工作經驗。如果打工時間不太多，不會影響學習。

我也想打工掙點兒零用錢。

你不是有獎學金嗎？

獎學金不夠交學費，我還申請了政府的學生貸款。雪梅，中國大學生也打工嗎？

Before You Study

Answer the following questions in Chinese to prepare for the reading.

1 你打過工嗎？在哪兒打過工？

2 你覺得打工對學習有什麼影響？

When You Study

Listen to the audio recording and skim the text; then answer the following questions in Chinese.

1 誰供張天明上學？張天明為什麼想打工掙錢？

2 為什麼中國的大學生一般不在餐館兒打工？

3 麗莎的同屋為什麼零用錢不夠花，還想跟麗莎借錢？

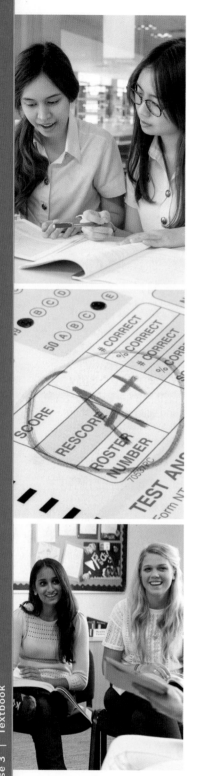

以前不用，因为那时候上大学不用交学费。现在大学收费了，所以不少大学生也想办法打工挣钱。

中国大学生一般在哪儿打工？在餐馆儿当服务员吗？

在餐馆儿打工的大学生也有，但是很少。中国城市里有很多从农村出来找工作的人，饭馆儿喜欢找他们，因为工资[d]比较低。

你打过工吗？

打过，我做过家教[e]，教英文。我的同学有的做翻译，有的管理电脑，也有的帮人遛狗或者喂猫。

看起来不少学生都是一边读书一边打工挣钱。

说到钱，我的同屋今天跟我借钱[f]。她说她妈妈生气了，不给她钱了。

为什么？

她父母把她这个学期的饭钱都交了，可是她不是叫外卖，就是跟同学去饭馆儿，还常常乱买东西，乱花钱，欠了银行和信用卡公司很多钱。上个月父母给的零用钱，以前不用，因為那時候上大學不用交學費。現在大學收費了，所以不少大學生也想辦法打工掙錢。

中國大學生一般在哪兒打工？在餐館兒當服務員嗎？

在餐館兒打工的大學生也有，但是很少。中國城市裡有很多從農村出來找工作的人，飯館兒喜歡找他們，因為工資[d]比較低。

你打過工嗎？

打過，我做過家教[e]，教英文。我的同學有的做翻譯，有的管理電腦，也有的幫人遛狗或者餵貓。

看起來不少學生都是一邊讀書一邊打工掙錢。

說到錢，我的同屋今天跟我借錢[f]。她說她媽媽生氣了，不給她錢了。

為什麼？

她父母把她這個學期的飯錢都交了，可是她不是叫外賣，就是跟同學去飯館兒，還常常亂買東西，亂花錢，欠了銀行和信用卡公司很多錢。上個月父母給的零用錢，

她不到^g十天就花完了，又跟妈妈要了一些，还是不够。

难怪她妈妈生气。她怎么不想想⁴，父母挣钱多不容易啊！

是啊，我们不应该乱花钱。

谁不知道⁴你是父母的乖孩子！好吧，你慢慢儿找工作，我们走了。

View & Explore

For deeper language immersion and more cultural information, watch "Part-Time Jobs," a short, supplemental video clip by Cheng & Tsui on this lesson's theme.

Video

她不到[g]十天就花完了，又跟媽媽要了一些，還是不夠。

難怪她媽媽生氣。她怎麼不想想[4]，父母掙錢多不容易啊！

是啊，我們不應該亂花錢。

誰不知道[4]你是父母的乖孩子！好吧，你慢慢兒找工作，我們走了。

Answer the following questions in Chinese.

1 麗莎怎麼交學費？你呢？

2 你覺得打工會不會影響學習？為什麼？

Language Notes

a 存

存 means to leave something somewhere for safekeeping, as in 在银行存钱/在銀行存錢 (to deposit money at a bank), 在超市 (chāoshì) 存包 (to check one's bag at a supermarket), and 把东西存在朋友家/把東西存在朋友家 (to leave things at a friend's place).

b 供

供 means to supply, as in 供水 (to supply water). It can also mean to provide financial support, as in 供孩子上学/供孩子上學 (to support one's children's education) and 供房子 (to pay one's mortgage).

c 大人

In standard Chinese, the antonym of 大人 is 小孩（子）or 小孩儿/小孩兒. It's not 小人, which refers to a despicable person. 小人 is the antonym of 君子 (jūnzǐ), a virtuous person.

d 工资/工資

Wages and salaries are 工资/工資 and 薪水/薪水 (xīnshuǐ), respectively. In Mainland China, 工资/工資 is used much more often than 薪水/薪水.

e 家教

家教 is short for 家庭教师/家庭教師.

f 借钱/借錢

借钱/借錢 can mean either to borrow or to lend money, depending on how the word is used: "X borrows money from Y" is X跟Y借钱/X跟Y借錢. However, "X lends money to Y" is X借钱给Y/X借錢給Y or X把钱借给Y/X把錢借給Y.

g 不到

不到 means "has not reached a certain number" or "less than," as in 认识不到一个月/認識不到一個月 (have known each other for less than a month), 现在不到六点/現在不到六點 (it's not yet six o'clock), and 机票不到一千元/機票不到一千元 (the airline ticket costs less than a thousand dollars).

Vocabulary

Audio

Flashcards

No.	Simplified	Traditional	Pinyin	Part of Speech	Definition
1	受到	受到	*shòu dào*	vc	to receive
2	良好	良好	*liánghǎo*	adj	good, fine (literary)
3	教育	教育	*jiàoyù*	n/v	education; to educate
4	生	生	*shēng*	v	to give birth to, to be born
5	存	存	*cún*	v	to deposit, to accumulate
6	收入	收入	*shōurù*	n	income
7	供	供	*gōng*	v	to provide, to support financially
8	压力	壓力	*yālì*	n	pressure
9	大人	大人	*dàren*	n	adult
10	减轻	減輕	*jiǎnqīng*	v	to lessen
11	负担	負擔	*fùdān*	n	burden
12	适合	適合	*shìhé*	v	to suit
13	影响	影響	*yǐngxiǎng*	v/n	to influence, to have an impact; influence
14	家庭	家庭	*jiātíng*	n	family, household
15	取得	取得	*qǔdé*	v	to obtain, to gain, to acquire
16	经验	經驗	*jīngyàn*	n/v	experience; to experience
17	零用钱	零用錢	*língyòngqián*	n	pocket money, spending money
18	奖学金	獎學金	*jiǎngxuéjīn*	n	scholarship money
19	交	交	*jiāo*	v	to hand over, to turn in

No.	Simplified	Traditional	Pinyin	Part of Speech	Definition
20	政府	政府	*zhèngfǔ*	n	government
21	贷款	貸款	*dàikuǎn*	n/vo	loan; to provide a loan
22	农村	農村	*nóngcūn*	n	countryside, village, rural area
23	工资	工資	*gōngzī*	n	wages, pay
24	低	低	*dī*	adj	low
25	家教	家教	*jiājiào*	n	tutor
26	遛	遛	*liù*	v	to walk (an animal), to stroll
27	喂	餵	*wèi*	v	to feed
28	猫	貓	*māo*	n	cat
29	读书	讀書	*dú shū*	vo	to attend school, to study, to read aloud
30	借	借	*jiè*	v	to borrow, to lend

林雪梅做过家教，教过英文。你打过什么工？如果你没打过工，你想打什么工？

林雪梅做過家教，教過英文。你打過什麼工？如果你沒打過工，你想打什麼工？

No.	Simplified	Traditional	Pinyin	Part of Speech	Definition
31	欠	欠	*qiàn*	v	to owe
32	银行	銀行	*yínháng*	n	bank
33	难怪	難怪	*nánguài*	adv	no wonder
34	乖	乖	*guāi*	adj	obedient, well-behaved (of children)

GET Real WITH CHINESE

After paying for a hotel room with a credit card, you are given this receipt. Determine which bank the credit card belongs to, then log onto their website to identify their current promotions.

Grammar

<u>1</u> **Directional complements (III)**

By definition, this type of complement has to do with direction: for instance, 来/來 signifies a movement toward the speaker and 上 indicates an upward movement. However, many directional complements do not actually deal with direction in a literal sense, but rather suggest a result or state of being. This lesson includes directional complements that express results.

A 他们希望孩子们能受到良好的教育，所以孩子一生下来就开始给他们存教育费。

他們希望孩子們能受到良好的教育，所以孩子一生下來就開始給他們存教育費。

They hoped that their children would get a good education. Therefore, they started to save for their educational expenses as soon as the children were born.

Here, 下来/下來 implies the detachment or separation of one thing from another. Similar examples are 从本子上撕 (sī) 下一张纸来/從本子上撕 (sī) 下一張紙來 (to tear a piece of paper from a notebook) and 把西瓜切 (qiē) 下来一块/把西瓜切 (qiē) 下來一塊 (to cut a slice off a watermelon).

B 每年开学的时候，家里还是得拿出很多钱来。

每年開學的時候，家裡還是得拿出很多錢來。

Every year at the beginning of the school year, (my) family still has to come up with a lot of money.

出来/出來 signifies the emergence of something from a hidden place into the open, or a change from having nothing to having something:

C 把你的问题说出来，我们大家帮你解决。

把你的問題說出來，我們大家幫你解決。

Get your problem out in the open. We will help you solve it.

D

我看出来他生气了。

我看出來他生氣了。

I could tell that he got angry.

E

给孩子想出来一个好名字。

給孩子想出來一個好名字。

Come up with a good name for the child.

上, 上来/上來, 上去, 下, 下来/下來, 下去, 出, 出来/出來, 过/過, 过来/過來, 过去/過去, 起/起, 起来/起來, 开/開, etc. can all convey a result. Directional complements of this kind are quite common. Try to memorize them together with their preceding verbs.

2 | Connecting two verb phrases using 来/來

来/來 can be used to connect two verbs. The second verb indicates the purpose of the first action. 来/來 has a similar meaning to "in order to."

A

张天明觉得自己已经是大人了，应该找工作挣钱来减轻父母的负担。

張天明覺得自己已經是大人了，應該找工作掙錢來減輕父母的負擔。

Zhang Tianming feels that he's a grown-up, and that he should get a job to ease the burden on his parents.

B

大家计划开一个舞会来给他过生日。

大家計劃開一個舞會來給他過生日。

Everybody planned to throw a dance party to celebrate his birthday.

C

我妹妹告诉我应该用听录音的办法来提高汉语水平。

我妹妹告訴我應該用聽錄音的辦法來提高漢語水平。

My younger sister tells me that I should listen to audio recordings to improve my Chinese.

The particle 了 (V)

You've learned that 了 can indicate the realization of an action or the emergence of a state. However, 了 is not always required with completed actions. Take this excerpt from the lesson text as an example:

A

张天明的父母收入虽然不少，但是供天明和姐姐上大学，经济上还是有些压力。他们希望孩子们能受到良好的教育，所以孩子一生下来就开始给他们存教育费。

張天明的父母收入雖然不少，但是供天明和姐姐上大學，經濟上還是有些壓力。他們希望孩子們能受到良好的教育，所以孩子一生下來就開始給他們存教育費。

Although Zhang Tianming's parents' income is not inconsiderable, sending Tianming and his sister to college does exert some financial pressure. They hope that their children will receive a good education. Therefore, they started saving for their children's education when their children were born.

In the above passage, 他们希望孩子们能受到良好的教育，所以孩子一生下来就开始给他们存教育费/他們希望孩子們能受到良好的教育，所以孩子一生下來就開始給他們存教育費 is a completed event. However, it is presented as part of the background information to the main narrative: 这时候丽莎和雪梅走了进来/這時候麗莎和雪梅走了進來. This is why the verb 存 does not take 了.

Characterize it!

What do the characters mean?	
What is the common radical?	
What does the radical mean?	
How does the radical relate to the overall meaning of the characters?	

More characters

4

Rhetorical questions

Rhetorical questions are interrogative in form, but are really used to emphasize a point. They are not real questions, and therefore do not require an answer.

A

他昨天根本没复习，能考一百分吗？

他昨天根本沒復習，能考一百分嗎？

He didn't review at all yesterday. Could he get a hundred on the test?

The speaker is saying that there is no way at all that the person in question could get full marks. The sentence is affirmative in form but negative in meaning.

B

他已经学了三年化学了，这么简单的问题他不会吗？

他已經學了三年化學了，這麼簡單的問題他不會嗎？

He's been studying chemistry for three years. Are you telling me he can't solve this simple problem?

The sentence is negative in form, but emphatically positive in meaning: "Surely, he should know how to solve the problem!"

Generally speaking, rhetorical questions that are affirmative in form carry an emphatically negative meaning; rhetorical questions that are negative in form carry an emphatically positive meaning. For more examples, see the following two sentences from this lesson:

C

她怎么不想想，父母挣钱多不容易啊？

她怎麼不想想，父母掙錢多不容易啊？

How come she doesn't give any thought to how hard it is for her parents to earn money?

[The speaker means that she should think about this issue.]

D

谁不知道你是父母的乖孩子！

誰不知道你是父母的乖孩子！

Who doesn't know you are an exemplary child?

[Everyone knows that you're an exemplary child.]

Words & Phrases

A

> ## 受到 (to receive)

受到 is often followed by an abstract noun, which is usually qualified as indicated parenthetically in Chinese: 受到（大家的）欢迎/歡迎 (receive [everyone's] welcome), 受到（良好的）教育 (receive [a very good] education), and 受到（老师的）影响/（老师的）影響 (receive [the teacher's] influence). It is easy to confuse 受到 with the similar-sounding word 收到, which is used in connection with concrete objects, e.g., 收到一封信 (receive a letter) and 收到一个礼物/收到一個禮物 (receive a gift). Notice the difference in tone: 受 (shòu) vs. 收 (shōu).

B

> ## 压力 / 壓力 (pressure)

压力/壓力 is a noun, often appearing in patterns such as 有压力/有壓力, 给⋯压力/給⋯壓力, or 对⋯的压力/對⋯的壓力.

1 考试考得不好，怕妈妈生气，我觉得有压力。

考試考得不好，怕媽媽生氣，我覺得有壓力。

I didn't do well on the exam and I'm worried that my mom will be mad. I feel a lot of pressure.

2 这次考研究生，我的教授给我很大的压力。

這次考研究生，我的教授給我很大的壓力。

As I take the entrance exam for graduate school this time around, my adviser is putting a lot of pressure on me.

3 今年经济很糟糕，我一直找不到工作，这对我的压力很大。

今年經濟很糟糕，我一直找不到工作，這對我的壓力很大。

The economy is doing really badly this year. I can't find a job, and this is putting a lot of pressure on me.

减轻/減輕 (to lessen)

减轻/減輕 is generally followed by an abstract noun, as in 减轻负担/減輕負擔 (to lessen a burden), 减轻压力/減輕壓力 (to alleviate pressure), and 减轻痛苦 (tòngkǔ) /減輕痛苦 (tòngkǔ) (to lessen pain).

1 学生希望老师少给一些功课，减轻他们的负担。

學生希望老師少給一些功課，減輕他們的負擔。

> The students wish that the teacher would assign less homework so as to lighten their burden.

2 找到工作了，他的压力减轻了不少。

找到工作了，他的壓力減輕了不少。

> Now that he's found a job, he feels a load has been taken off his shoulders.

3 医生想了很多办法来减轻他的痛苦 (tòngkǔ)。

醫生想了很多辦法來減輕他的痛苦 (tòngkǔ)。

> The doctor tried many different ways to ease his pain.

适合/適合 (to suit) and 合适/合適 (suitable)

In IC1, we learned 合适/合適 as an adjective meaning "suitable." This lesson teaches 适合/適合, meaning "to suit." 适合/適合 is a transitive verb, so it must be followed by a noun or occur in a "pivotal sentence" in which the object also serves as the subject of the following clause.

Compare how these two words are used differently in (1), (2), and (3):

1 这条牛仔裤不适合你穿，你妈妈穿可能合适。

這條牛仔褲不適合你穿，你媽媽穿可能合適。

> These jeans don't suit you. They might be suitable for your mom.

2

这种家具适合家里用，放在办公室不合适。

這種傢俱適合家裡用，放在辦公室不合適。

This kind of furniture suits home use (more). It's not suitable to put in an office.

3

这个专业不适合你，你还是选别的专业合适。

這個專業不適合你，你還是選別的專業合適。

This major doesn't suit you. You'd better pick another major.

E | 影响/影響 (to influence, to affect; influence)

影响/影響 can be a verb, as seen in (1) and (2):

1

睡觉的时间不够会影响健康。

睡覺的時間不夠會影響健康。

Not having enough time to sleep will affect one's health. *[verb]*

2

你看书吧，我坐在这儿不说话，不会影响你。

你看書吧，我坐在這兒不說話，不會影響你。

Why don't you study? I'll sit here quietly and won't distract you. *[verb]*

影响/影響 can also be a noun, often appearing in the pattern X对Y有影响/X對Y有影響 (X has an influence on Y).

3

你不去开这个会，对你找工作会有影响。

你不去開這個會，對你找工作會有影響。

If you don't go to the meeting, it'll affect your chances of getting a job. *[noun]*

F | 取得 (to obtain)

取得 is followed by abstract nouns such as 经验/經驗, 同意, 好成绩/好成績 (hǎo chéngjì) (success, a good grade), and 进步/進步 (jìnbù) (progress).

说到/說到 (speaking of)

To expand on a topic previously mentioned, use 说到/說到:

1   说到钱，我的同屋今天跟我说，她妈妈生气了，不给她钱了。

说到錢，我的同屋今天跟我說，她媽媽生氣了，不給她錢了。

Speaking of money, my roommate told me that her mom got angry and wouldn't give her any more money.

2

Person A   你想什么呢？

你想什麼呢？

What are you thinking about?

Person B   我在想下个学期选什么课呢。

我在想下個學期選什麼課呢。

I'm thinking about what classes I should take next semester.

Person A   说到下个学期的课，我们可以不选我们学校的课吗？

說到下個學期的課，我們可以不選我們學校的課嗎？

Speaking of next semester's classes, can we choose not to take our school's classes?

Person B   那你选哪儿的课？

那你選哪兒的課？

Then where will you take classes?

Person A   我想选旁边那个大学的课，可以吗？

我想選旁邊那個大學的課，可以嗎？

I want to go to take classes at the university nearby. Would that be okay?

Person B　我觉得不行。

我覺得不行。

I don't think so.

3　**Person A**　听说张天明的表哥打球打得很棒。

聽說張天明的表哥打球打得很棒。

I hear Zhang Tianming's cousin is a great ballplayer.

Person B　我也这么听说。说到打球，我们这个周末去打篮球好吗？

我也這麼聽說。說到打球，我們這個週末去打籃球好嗎？

Indeed, he is a great ballplayer. Speaking of playing ball, should we go play basketball this weekend?

H　**不是 X, 就是 Y (if it's not X, it's Y; either X or Y)**

This pattern is often used to describe two predictable scenarios:

1　她不是叫外卖，就是跟同学去饭馆儿吃饭。

她不是叫外賣，就是跟同學去飯館兒吃飯。

She either orders takeout or goes out to restaurants with her classmates.

2　现在租房子很不容易，不是价钱太贵，就是房子不好，麻烦得很。

現在租房子很不容易，不是價錢太貴，就是房子不好，麻煩得很。

It's really difficult to rent an apartment now. Either the rent is too expensive, or the rooms are bad. It's a real hassle.

3　昨天的晚会来的不是同学，就是朋友，他都认识。

昨天的晚會來的不是同學，就是朋友，他都認識。

Those who came to last night's party were either classmates or friends. He knew them all.

Q: 你们常常吃牛肉吗？

你們常常吃牛肉嗎？

Do you often eat beef?

A: 不，我们平常不是吃鸡，就是吃鱼，不吃牛肉。

不，我們平常不是吃雞，就是吃魚，不吃牛肉。

No, we usually have either chicken or fish. We don't eat beef.

难怪/難怪 (no wonder)

难怪/難怪 is an adverb used as an interjection, often at the beginning of a sentence.

1

难怪他不知道这件事，他根本不看新闻！

難怪他不知道這件事，他根本不看新聞！

No wonder he doesn't know this—he doesn't watch the news at all!

2

难怪他不申请念研究生，原来他已经找到工作了。

難怪他不申請念研究生，原來他已經找到工作了。

No wonder he is not applying to graduate school. Turns out, he's already found a job.

3

难怪这两天他不太高兴，原来他女朋友跟他分手了。

難怪這兩天他不太高興，原來他女朋友跟他分手了。

No wonder he's been in a bad mood the last couple of days. Turns out, his girlfriend broke up with him.

A WAY WITH WORDS

良好

学生宿舍太吵，可是学校还没有找到解决这个问题的良药。

Using the word/phrase in orange as a clue, try to figure out the meaning of the words/phrases in blue; consult a dictionary if necessary. Consider how the literal and extended senses are related in each case.

良好

學生宿舍太吵，可是學校還沒有找到解決這個問題的良藥。

小张觉得乱花父母的钱对不起自己的良心。

小張覺得亂花父母的錢對不起自己的良心。

多 (How . . . it is!)

多 can be used as an intensifier in exclamatory sentences:

1
父母挣钱多不容易啊！

父母掙錢多不容易啊！

How difficult it is for parents to make (enough) money!

2
小明，外边多冷呀，乖乖待在屋子里，别出去乱跑！

小明，外邊多冷呀，乖乖待在屋子裡，別出去亂跑！

Little Ming, it's really cold out. Be a good boy and stay indoors. Don't go out!

3
这套运动服多难看啊，谁买呀？送给我我都不要。

這套運動服多難看啊，誰買呀？送給我我都不要。

This tracksuit is so ugly! Who would buy it? I wouldn't take it even as a gift.

Chinese Chat

A friend is messaging you on LINE about getting together. How would you reply?

Marla:
明天下午一起唱卡拉OK吧！

You:
...

Marla:
你在哪儿打工？给我介绍一下吧，我也想挣点儿零用钱。

You:
...

Marla Eisenberg

明天下午一起唱卡拉OK吧！
11:36 AM

Read
11:37 AM

你在哪兒打工？给我介绍一下吧，我也想掙點兒零用錢。
11:39 AM

Read
11:40 AM

Language Practice

A | INTERPRETIVE | **On the money** | INTERPERSONAL |

1   It's good practice to write out your income and expenses on a monthly basis to see if you can balance your budget. Put together a hypothetical budget using the following chart.

收入

工资/工資: $_____

父母给的零用钱/父母給的零用錢: $_____

奖学金/奖學金: $_____

其他: $_____

支出 (zhīchū)

生活费/生活費

房租: $_____

水电费/水電費: $_____

饭钱、菜钱/飯錢、菜錢: $_____

车钱/車錢: $_____

手机费/手機費: $_____ 、

网络费/網絡費: $_____

其他: $_____

教育费/教育費

书钱/書錢: $_____

文具: $_____

其他: $_____

2 Then, in pairs, take turns asking about how your partner's income squares with his/her monthly expenses.

> **Q:** 你每个月的钱够不够付你的生活费和教育费？
>
> 你每個月的錢夠不夠付你的生活費和教育費？
>
> **A:** _____ 。

3 If your partner's expenses exceed his/her income, try to figure out possible solutions. Some suggestions are listed below. Pick the ones that suit your situation, then tell your partner what you plan to do. You can also add your own two cents on the last two lines.

> **Q:** 那你打算怎么办？
>
> 那你打算怎麼辦？
>
> **A:** _____ 。

- 跟银行借钱/跟銀行借錢

- 跟父母借钱/跟父母借錢

- 申请新的信用卡/申請新的信用卡

- 多打工

- 不乱花钱/不亂花錢

- 搬回家住，把房租、饭钱省下来/搬回家住，把房租、饭錢省下來

- _____

- _____

Part-time jobs

In pairs, use the images as prompts to identify places where you may be able to find a part-time job. Add your own pick to (6).

1   2   3

4    5   6 其他地方：_____

Then ask each other if you have worked in these places and answer based on your own situation, e.g.:

Q: 你在咖啡馆打过工吗？

你在咖啡館打過工嗎？

A: 我在咖啡馆打过工。

我在咖啡館打過工。

or

A: 我没在咖啡馆打过工。

我沒在咖啡館打過工。

Next, work with your partner to identify the following part-time jobs. After you are finished identifying the jobs, tell each other if you have done such work before, e.g.:

咖啡馆服务员 / 咖啡館服務員

我在咖啡馆当过服务员。

我在咖啡館當過服務員。

or

我没在咖啡馆当过服务员。

我沒在咖啡館當過服務員。

1 餐馆师傅/餐館師傅

2 商店售货员/商店售貨員

3 书店店员/書店店員

4 公共图书馆翻译/公共圖書館翻譯

5 旅行社导游/旅行社導遊

6 网络公司网站管理员/網絡公司網站管理員

Finally, poll your class and see what part-time jobs your classmates have had.

C INTERPERSONAL **Driven to distraction** PRESENTATIONAL

First, ask three to five of your classmates what would have a negative impact on their studies, e.g.:

Q: 什么会影响你学习？
   什麼會影響你學習？

A: 睡不好觉会影响我学习。
   睡不好覺會影響我學習。

Then record their answers, e.g.:

Jerry   睡不好觉/睡不好覺

_____   _____

_____   _____

_____   _____

Finally, share your list with a partner and see if any of the answers collected are the same. Then rank the answers and report back to the class.

D | **So predictable** | INTERPERSONAL

Some people always do the same things, eat the same food, buy the same clothes, etc. Working with a partner, describe how predictable Tianming, Lisha, Ke Lin, and Xuemei are, e.g.:

 free time   blogging/playing on the computer

Q: 张天明有空儿的时候做什么?

张天明有空兒的時候做什麼？

A: 张天明有空儿的时候，不是写博客，就是玩儿电脑游戏。

張天明有空兒的時候，不是寫博客，就是玩兒電腦遊戲。

1 free time   dog sitting/cat sitting

2 ordering in restaurants   steamed fish/beef with Chinese broccoli

3 out on the town   concert/karaoke

4 watching TV   basketball game/soccer game

Then, in pairs, take turns describing the routine activities you engage in in daily life.

E | **Getting down to work** | PRESENTATIONAL

Ask yourself what possible reasons would make you look for a part-time job: to earn some spending money, to get work experience, to help out your family, etc. Write these down in Chinese, and mark the most important reason with an asterisk. Then, in pairs, share the reasons that would make you take a part-time job:

我想打工，除了想＿＿＿＿＿＿＿＿，＿＿＿＿＿＿＿＿，
＿＿＿＿＿＿＿……以外，最重要的是想＿＿＿＿＿＿。

F INTERPERSONAL | **Full plate** | PRESENTATIONAL

In pairs, discuss and list the advantages and disadvantages of working while studying in school.

你觉得一边读书一边打工挣钱有什么好处？有什么坏处？

你覺得一邊讀書一邊打工掙錢有什麼好處？有什麼壞處？

好处/好處   坏处/壞處

1 _____   1 _____

2 _____   2 _____

3 _____   3 _____

....

Based on your list, compose a short report. Try to make sure that your points are smoothly connected.

我们觉得一边读书一边打工挣钱对_____很有帮助。
但我们也觉得一边读书一边打工挣钱可能对_____
有不好的影响。

我們覺得一邊讀書一邊打工掙錢對_____很有幫助。
但我們也覺得一邊讀書一邊打工掙錢可能對_____
有不好的影響。

A WAY WITH WORDS

经验		經驗
他在台湾生活了二十年，有很多有意思的经历。	Using the word/phrase in orange as a clue, try to figure out the meaning of the words/phrases in blue; consult a dictionary if necessary. Consider how the literal and extended senses are related in each case.	他在台灣生活了二十年，有很多有意思的經歷。
李老师五年前写的那本书，现在很多人都在看，已经成了经典了。		李老師五年前寫的那本書，現在很多人都在看，已經成了經典了。

TUITION & SCHOLARSHIPS

Although higher education in China was once free, the state began charging tuition at public institutions in the late 1980s. Surveys in recent years have repeatedly shown that education is the largest expense in the average household's annual budget—more than savings for retirement or housing expenditures. Both need- and merit-based scholarships are available. Parents, however, remain the main source of financial support for Chinese college students.

COMPARE & CONTRAST

While spending time at home and traveling with friends and family are popular activities for Chinese university students during the summer months, others choose to keep busy through part-time work. Typical summertime gigs range from tutoring and translating online materials to even running an online shop on Taobao or WeChat. How do these summer jobs compare to those popular in your community? What line of work would you be most likely to pursue in between semesters and why?

Working Students

An increasing number of Chinese college students work, either on or off campus, to offset living expenses. The most popular form of part-time employment is tutoring elementary and middle school students. Tutoring—especially with regard to musical instrument instruction—can be quite lucrative. College students also work part-time in sales, do creative work such as graphic design, or engage in translation services.

To find work, students can hire a part-time work agent, 兼职中介/兼職仲介 (*jiānzhí zhōngjiè*). Upon payment of a fee, usually around two hundred yuan, such agents will forward information about part-time job opportunities.

Mencius and manual labor

Mencius (孟子) (*Mèngzǐ*; 327–289 BCE), known as the "Second Sage of Confucianism," wrote: "Those who exert themselves intellectually rule others; those who exert themselves physically are ruled by others" (劳心者治人, 劳力者治于人/勞心者治人, 勞力者治於人) (*láo xīn zhě zhì rén, láo lì zhě zhì yú rén*). Traditionally, the Chinese elite dismissed manual labor as beneath them. Even today some of that prejudice lingers on. Parents are not always happy when their children express an interest in working part-time, especially in some menial capacity. Some parents feel that part-time jobs are distractions at best. However, that attitude is changing.

Lesson Wrap-Up

Project

More exercises

You work part-time at your university's international student office. Role-play a meeting with a Chinese student seeking information on employment opportunities while studying in your country. Study government guidelines such as those issued by the US Department of Homeland Security. Prepare answers to the questions on the following list. Choose four questions from the list for the first part of the meeting. For the second part, find out from your university's website what types of part-time jobs are available on campus and discuss which ones might be particularly appropriate for the student. You may want to:

- find out what the student's major is
- understand why the student wants to work part-time
- ask the student what he or she plans to do after graduation
- suggest one or two jobs to the student
- explain the advantages of these jobs

QUESTIONS:

○ 拿学生签证的国际学生能不能在校内打工?
   拿學生簽証的國際學生能不能在校內打工?

○ 国际学生什么时候可以开始打工?
   國際學生什麼時候可以開始打工?

○ 国际学生能打几份工?
   國際學生能打幾份工?

○ 国际学生每个星期能打多少个小时的工?
   國際學生每個星期能打多少個小時的工?

○ 国际学生如果想在校内打工需要什么文件 (wénjiàn) (document)?
   國際學生如果想在校內打工需要什麼文件 (wénjiàn) (document)?

○ 拿学生签证的国际学生能不能在校外打工?
   拿學生簽証的國際學生能不能在校外打工?

○ 国际学生在什么情况 (qíngkuàng) (circumstances) 下可以在校外打工?
   國際學生在什麼情況 (qíngkuàng) (circumstances) 下可以在校外打工?

Study the following description; pay particular attention to how the highlighted parts help the sentences flow smoothly from one to the next. Notice how:

- pronouns (他, 她们/她們) replace corresponding nouns when the subject remains unchanged (张天明/張天明, 丽莎/麗莎和雪梅)
- time words/phrases (有一天) can serve as connective devices
- conjunctions (所以, 如果, 除了…以外…) and adverbs (还/還) also join sentences together

张天明想打工

张天明觉得自己已经是大人了，应该少花一点儿家里的钱，所以想找个工作挣钱来减轻父母的负担。有一天，丽莎和雪梅来找他。她们问他在忙什么，他说想打工，在网上看有没有适合自己的工作。雪梅问天明打工影响不影响学习。天明说如果打工的时间不太多，不会影响学习。他还说，他打工，除了想挣一点钱以外，还想取得一些工作经验。

張天明想打工

張天明覺得自己已經是大人了，應該少花一點兒家裡的錢，所以想找個工作掙錢來減輕父母的負擔。有一天，麗莎和雪梅來找他。她們問他在忙什麼，他說想打工，在網上看有沒有適合自己的工作。雪梅問天明打工影響不影響學習。天明說如果打工的時間不太多，不會影響學習。他還說，他打工，除了想掙一點錢以外，還想取得一些工作經驗。

You, a classmate, or a friend must have worked part-time or been a volunteer. Describe your or someone else's experience. Use as many of the cohesive devices highlighted in the example as possible to string together your answers to the questions:

- 这个人在哪里打（过）工或者做（过）义工 (yìgōng)？
  這個人在哪裡打（過）工或者做（過）義工 (yìgōng)？

- 这个人打什么工或者做什么义工?
  這個人打什麼工或者做什麼義工？

- 这个人为什么打工或者做义工?
  這個人為什麼打工或者做義工？

- 这个人说打工或者做义工影响学习了吗?
  這個人說打工或者做義工影響學習了嗎？

- 这个人对学生一边学习一边打工或者做义工有什么看法?
  這個人對學生一邊學習一邊打工或者做義工有什麼看法？

Can-Do Check List ✓ **I can**

Before proceeding to Lesson 9, make sure you can complete the following tasks in Chinese:

- ☐ Describe how someone funds their education
- ☐ Talk about part-time common jobs for students
- ☐ Discuss the pros and cons of working part-time while in school
- ☐ Say if you work part-time and why
- ☐ Explain how students spend their pocket money

Zhāng Tiānmíng de fùmǔ xīwàng háizi men néng shòu dào liánghǎo de jiàoyù, suǒyǐ háizi yì shēng xia lai[1] jiù kāishǐ gěi tāmen cún[a] jiàoyù fèi. Suīrán Zhāng Tiānmíng fùmǔ de shōurù bù shǎo, dànshì gōng[b] Tiānmíng hé jiějie shàng dàxué, jīngjì shang háishi yǒu xiē yālì. Zhāng Tiānmíng juéde zìjǐ yǐjīng shì dàren[c] le, yīnggāi zhǎo gōngzuò zhèng qián lái[2] jiǎnqīng fùmǔ de fùdān, suǒyǐ jiù shàng wǎng kàn kan yǒu méiyǒu shìhé zìjǐ de gōngzuò. Zhè shíhou Lìshā hé Xuěméi zǒu le[3] jìn lai.

🙂 Tiānmíng, nǐ zài wǎng shang kàn shénme ne?

🙂 Wǒ xiǎng dǎ diǎnr gōng, shǎo huā yì diǎnr jiā li de qián.

🙂 Dǎ gōng huì bú huì yǐngxiǎng xuéxí?

🙂 Wǒ xiǎng dǎ gōng shì xiǎng qǔdé yì xiē gōngzuò jīngyàn. Rúguǒ dǎ gōng shíjiān bú tài duō, bú huì yǐngxiǎng xuéxí.

🙂 Wǒ yě xiǎng dǎ gōng zhèng diǎnr língyòng qián.

🙂 Nǐ bú shì yǒu jiǎngxuéjīn ma?

🙂 Jiǎngxuéjīn bú gòu jiāo xuéfèi, wǒ hái shēnqǐng le zhèngfǔ de xuéshēng dàikuǎn. Xuěméi, Zhōngguó dàxuéshēng yě dǎ gōng ma?

🙂 Yǐqián búyòng, yīnwèi nà shíhou shàng dàxué búyòng jiāo xuéfèi. Xiànzài dàxué shōu fèi le, suǒyǐ bù shǎo dàxuéshēng yě xiǎng bànfǎ dǎ gōng zhèng qián.

🙂 Zhōngguó dàxuéshēng yìbān zài nǎr dǎ gōng? Zài cānguǎnr dāng fúwùyuán ma?

🙂 Zài cānguǎnr dǎ gōng de dàxuéshēng yě yǒu, dànshì hěn shǎo. Zhōngguó chéngshì lǐ yǒu hěn duō cóng nóngcūn chū lai zhǎo gōngzuò de rén, fànguǎnr xǐhuan zhǎo tāmen, yīnwèi gōngzī[d] bǐjiào dī.

🙂 Nǐ dǎ guo gōng ma?

🙂 Dǎ guo, wǒ zuò guo jiājiào[e], jiāo Yīngwén. Wǒ de tóngxué yǒude zuò fānyì, yǒude guǎnlǐ diànnǎo, yě yǒude bāng rén liù gǒu huòzhě wèi māo.

Kàn qi lai bù shǎo xuésheng dōu shì yìbiān dú shū yìbiān dǎ gōng zhèng qián.

 Shuō dào qián, wǒ de tóngwū jīntiān gēn wǒ jiè qián[f]. Tā shuō tā māma shēng qì le, bù gěi tā qián le.

 Wèishénme?

 Tā fùmǔ bǎ tā zhè ge xuéqī de fàn qián dōu jiāo le, kěshì tā bú shì jiāo wàimài, jiù shì gēn tóngxué qù fànguǎnr, hái chángcháng luàn mǎi dōngxi, luàn huā qián, qiàn le yínháng hé xìnyòngkǎ gōngsī hěn duō qián. Shàng ge yuè fùmǔ gěi de língyòng qián, tā bú dào[g] shí tiān jiù huā wán le, yòu gēn māma yào le yì xiē, hái shì bú gòu.

 Nánguài tā māma shēngqì. Tā zěnme bù xiǎng xiǎng[4], fùmǔ zhèng qián duō bù róngyì a?

 Shì a, wǒmen bù yīnggāi luàn huā qián.

 Shéi bù zhīdào[4] nǐ shì fùmǔ de guāi háizi! Hǎo ba, nǐ màn mānr zhǎo gōngzuò, wǒmen zǒu le.

教育

EDUCATION

Learning Objectives

In this lesson, you will learn to:

- Comment on whether your parents packed your schedule with activities as a child
- Describe some typical classes offered in afterschool programs
- Indicate agreement or disagreement
- Present your opinions on children's education
- Talk about parents' aspirations for their children

Relate & Get Ready

In your own culture/community:

- Is it common for parents to enroll their children in afterschool programs?
- Do many people pursue graduate degrees?
- Do children have a say in family decisions?
- Is it common for both parents to be equally involved in their children's upbringing?

课文

Text

 Audio

Before You Study

Answer the following questions in Chinese to prepare for the reading.

1 你小时候学习的时间多还是玩儿的时间多?

2 你觉得孩子小时候学习外语好还是长大以后学习外语好? 为什么?

When You Study

Listen to the audio recording and skim the text; then answer the following questions in Chinese.

1 李哲的哥哥和嫂子最近为什么常常吵架?

2 李哲的嫂子怎么安排女儿的时间?

3 "望子成龙,望女成凤"是什么意思?

李哲的父母是墨西哥移民,他和他哥哥都是在加州出生、长大的。哥哥是电脑博士,设计软件、管理网站。李哲的嫂子十五年前从香港来美国留学,拿到硕士学位[a]以后找到工作,就在美国住了下来。哥哥和嫂子结婚十年了,生活一直很幸福。可是最近两年在女儿的教育问题上,意见常常不同,有时吵得很厉害。一天,李哲正在电话上跟侄女聊天儿,看见丽莎走了进来。

(李哲放下电话……)

丽莎,有事儿吗?

没什么事儿,我找天明,以为他在你这儿呢。对不起,害得你把电话挂了。

坐,坐,坐。刚才是我侄女给我打电话,我们正好说完了。

你有侄女? 今年多大了?

今年刚八岁。

她给你打电话有什么事啊?

課文

李哲的父母是墨西哥移民，他和他哥哥都是在加州出生、長大的。哥哥是電腦博士，設計軟件，管理網站。李哲的嫂子十五年前從香港來美國留學，拿到碩士學位[a]以後找到工作，就在美國住了下來。哥哥和嫂子結婚十年了，生活一直很幸福。可是最近兩年在女兒的教育問題上，意見常常不同，有時吵得很厲害。一天，李哲正在電話上跟侄女聊天兒，看見麗莎走了進來。

（李哲放下電話……）

🧑 麗莎，有事兒嗎？

👩 沒什麼事兒，我找天明，以為他在你這兒呢。對不起，害得你把電話掛了。

🧑 坐，坐，坐。剛才是我侄女給我打電話，我們正好說完了。

👩 你有侄女？今年多大了？

🧑 今年剛八歲。

👩 她給你打電話有什麼事啊？

Before You Study

Answer the following questions in Chinese to prepare for the reading.

1 你小時候學習的時間多還是玩兒的時間多？

2 你覺得孩子小時候學習外語好還是長大以後學習外語好？為什麼？

When You Study

Listen to the audio recording and skim the text; then answer the following questions in Chinese.

1 李哲的哥哥和嫂子最近為什麼常常吵架？

2 李哲的嫂子怎麼安排女兒的時間？

3 "望子成龍，望女成鳳"是什麼意思？

学习的事儿。我侄女才[1]小学三年级，我嫂子就安排她：星期一学钢琴[b]，星期二学画画儿，星期三学游泳，星期四学滑冰，只有星期五休息一天，星期六又叫她去上中文学校。她不喜欢学中文，所以就打电话到我这儿来，一边哭一边抱怨。

没那么严重吧？她怎么说？

她说小孩子也是人，有自己的爱好和兴趣，父母应该尊重孩子自己的选择。

她怎么这么会说话[c]？

这些话一定是跟我哥哥学的。我嫂子整天让她学这学那，我哥哥反对给孩子太大的压力，他认为[d]对孩子来说，最重要的是有一个快乐的童年。

我的童年很快乐。可是现在，每次上中文课我就想，要是我小时候父母就让我学中文，我现在就轻松多了。

没想到你跟我嫂子的看法一样！你同意我嫂子的做法？

我不完全同意，但我能理解。

學習的事兒。我侄女才[1]小學三年級，我嫂子就安排她：星期一學鋼琴[b]，星期二學畫畫兒，星期三學游泳，星期四學滑冰，只有星期五休息一天，星期六又叫她去上中文學校。她不喜歡學中文，所以就打電話到我這兒來，一邊哭一邊抱怨。

沒那麼嚴重吧？她怎麼說？

她說小孩子也是人，有自己的愛好和興趣，父母應該尊重孩子自己的選擇。

她怎麼這麼會說話[c]？

這些話一定是跟我哥哥學的。我嫂子整天讓她學這學那，我哥哥反對給孩子太大的壓力，他認為[d]對孩子來說，最重要的是有一個快樂的童年。

我的童年很快樂。可是現在，每次上中文課我就想，要是我小時候父母就讓我學中文，我現在就輕鬆多了。

沒想到你跟我嫂子的看法一樣！你同意我嫂子的做法？

我不完全同意，但我能理解。

很多父母望子成龙，望女成凤，希望自己的孩子小时候好好儿学习，将来能做出一番大事业。可是到现在我也想不清楚，孩子到底是将来"成龙""成凤"好[2]，还是有一个快乐的童年好？

我的看法是两个都重要。一个人当然应该有快乐的童年，但是长大以后也应该对社会有用，所以孩子最好还是在学校多学一些知识。

可是你别忘了，有些知识不是从书上学的，而是[3]从社会、从生活中学的。

李哲，你真成了哲学家[e]了。

Language Notes

a 学位/學位

The term for a bachelor's degree is 学士学位/學士學位. 博士学位/博士學位 and 硕士学位/碩士学位 are the terms for doctoral and master's degrees, respectively.

b 钢琴/鋼琴

Pianos are 钢琴/鋼琴 (lit. steel musical instrument). Violins are 小提琴 (xiǎotíqín) (lit. small, hand-carried musical instrument). Can you guess what 中提琴 and 大提琴 are?

c 会说话/會說話

Here, 会说话/會說話 means "very articulate."

d 认为/認為

认为/認為 differs from 对…来说/對…來說. While 对…来说/對…來說 can only convey the speaker's opinion, 认为/認為 may express either the opinion of the speaker or the opinion of the person being spoken about.

e 家

家 can be used as a suffix to mean an expert or established scholar in a particular field—画家/畫家, 哲学家/哲學家, 文学家/文學家, 历史学家/歷史學家, 化学家/化學家, etc. Out of modesty, many people refrain from using the suffix to refer to themselves. To call oneself a 画家/畫家 can sound a little grand. That's why people often just say what they do instead: 我画画儿/我畫畫兒 or 我是画画儿的/我是畫畫兒的 ("I'm someone who paints").

很多父母望子成龍，望女成鳳，希望自己的孩子小時候好好兒學習，將來能做出一番大事業。可是到現在我也想不清楚，孩子到底是將來"成龍""成鳳"好[2]，還是有一個快樂的童年好？

我的看法是兩個都重要。一個人當然應該有快樂的童年，但是長大以後也應該對社會有用，所以孩子最好還是在學校多學一些知識。

可是你別忘了，有些知識不是從書上學的，而是[3]從社會、從生活中學的。

李哲，你真成了哲學家[e]了。

After You Study

Answer the following questions in Chinese.

1 請介紹一下李哲的哥哥和嫂子的學習、家庭和工作。

2 你認為孩子小時候的教育什麼最重要？

View & Explore

For deeper language immersion and more cultural information, watch "Education," a short, supplemental video clip by Cheng & Tsui on this lesson's theme.

Video

Vocabulary

Audio

Flashcards

No.	Simplified	Traditional	Pinyin	Part of Speech	Definition
1	移民	移民	*yímín*	n/v	immigrant; to immigrate
2	博士	博士	*bóshì*	n	doctorate (academic title), Dr. (academic title)
3	设计	設計	*shèjì*	v/n	to design; design
4	嫂子	嫂子	*sǎozi*	n	older brother's wife
5	留学	留學	*liú xué*	vo	to study abroad
6	硕士	碩士	*shuòshì*	n	master's (academic title)
7	结婚	結婚	*jié hūn*	vo	to get married, to marry
8	幸福	幸福	*xìngfú*	n/adj	happiness; happy
9	厉害	厲害	*lìhai*	adj	terrible, formidable
10	侄女	侄女	*zhínǚ*	n	brother's daughter
11	小学	小學	*xiǎoxué*	n	elementary school
12	安排	安排	*ānpái*	v	to arrange
13	钢琴	鋼琴	*gāngqín*	n	piano
14	画画儿	畫畫兒	*huà huàr*	vo	to draw, to paint
15	抱怨	抱怨	*bàoyuàn*	v	to complain
16	尊重	尊重	*zūnzhòng*	v	to respect
17	选择	選擇	*xuǎnzé*	n/v	choice; to choose
18	反对	反對	*fǎnduì*	v	to oppose

This is a classroom in China where you are applying for a volunteer teaching position. As you prepare for your interview with the principal, you familiarize yourself with the meaning of the slogan above the blackboard. How would you explain your interpretation during the interview?

GET Real WITH CHINESE

No.	Simplified	Traditional	Pinyin	Part of Speech	Definition
19	认为	認為	rènwéi	v	to think, to consider
20	童年	童年	tóngnián	n	childhood
21	看法	看法	kànfǎ	n	point of view
22	做法	做法	zuòfǎ	n	way of doing things, course of action
23	完全	完全	wánquán	adv/adj	completely, fully; complete, whole
24	理解	理解	lǐjiě	v	to understand
25	望子成龙	望子成龍	wàng zǐ chéng lóng		to hope that one's son will become successful (lit. to hope that one's son will become a dragon)

No.	Simplified	Traditional	Pinyin	Part of Speech	Definition
26	望女成凤	望女成鳳	*wàng nǚ chéng fèng*		to hope that one's daughter will become successful (lit. to hope that one's daughter will become a phoenix)
27	番	番	*fān*	m	(measure word for type or kind)
28	事业	事業	*shìyè*	n	career, undertaking
29	社会	社會	*shèhuì*	n	society
30	知识	知識	*zhīshi*	n	knowledge
31	不是…， 而是…	不是…， 而是…	*búshì…, érshì…*		it's not … but … [See Grammar 3.]
32	墨西哥	墨西哥	*Mòxīgē*	pn	Mexico

李哲的嫂子让女儿学游泳和滑冰。你小的时候，你父母让你学什么？

李哲的嫂子讓女兒學游泳和滑冰。你小的時候，你父母讓你學什麼？

How About You?

Grammar

1 | The adverb 才 before numbers

才 is used before numbers to express a small quantity:

A

我每天上网才三个小时，时间不长。

我每天上網才三個小時，時間不長。

I go online for only three hours a day. That's not a lot of time.

B

现在才六点，球赛八点开始，不用这么早去。

現在才六點，球賽八點開始，不用這麼早去。

It's only six o'clock. The ball game starts at eight. There's no need to go so early.

C

你今年才二十岁，就想结婚？

你今年才二十歲，就想結婚？

You're just twenty years old, and you already want to get married?

When 才 is used after numbers and measure words or before verbs, it expresses slowness or lateness, as we have already learned.

D

我大哥二十岁就念完博士了，我二十岁才上大学。

我大哥二十歲就念完博士了，我二十歲才上大學。

My older brother finished his doctorate at the tender age of twenty. I didn't even start college until twenty.

Characterize it!

Identify the common radical.

How does the radical relate to the overall meaning of the characters?

More characters

2 | Adjectives as predicates

When an adjective is used as a predicate, the subject of the sentence can be a "noun + predicate" phrase:

A
你说，我们寒假去哪儿旅行好？

你說，我們寒假去哪兒旅行好？

Say, where should we travel during winter break?

B
今天晚上有一个生日舞会，我不知道穿什么衣服合适。

今天晚上有一個生日舞會，我不知道穿什麼衣服合適。

There's a birthday party tonight. I don't know what to wear.

C
你现在读书最重要，找工作的事儿不用着急。

你現在讀書最重要，找工作的事兒不用著急。

For you, the most important thing now is to study. There's no rush to find a job.

3 | 不是X，而是Y

The pattern "不是 X, 而是 Y" is used when, in response to a statement or situation, the speaker wishes to negate X and strongly affirm Y.

A
丽莎，你知道有些知识不是从书上学的，而是从社会、从生活中学的。

麗莎，你知道有些知識不是從書上學的，而是從社會、從生活中學的。

Lisha, you know that some knowledge can't be learned in school or from books. Rather, one learns it from society, from life.

B

我不是不希望孩子将来有一番大事业，而是不想给他太大的压力。

我不是不希望孩子將來有一番大事業，而是不想給他太大的壓力。

It's not that I don't want my child to have a great career in the future. It's just that I don't want to put too much pressure on him.

C

你这样做不是为他好，而是给他找麻烦。

你這樣做不是為他好，而是給他找麻煩。

What you're doing won't do him any good; on the contrary, it will bring him trouble.

D

Q: 你不叫我买这件衬衫，是怕我的钱不够，跟你借钱吗？

你不叫我買這件襯衫，是怕我的錢不夠，跟你借錢嗎？

You don't want me to buy this shirt. Is it because you're afraid that I don't have enough money and will borrow money from you?

A: 你想错了，我不是怕你跟我借钱，而是觉得这件衬衫质量不好，你不应该买。

你想錯了，我不是怕你跟我借錢，而是覺得這件襯衫質量不好，你不應該買。

You're wrong. I'm not afraid of you borrowing money from me. Rather, I feel that the quality of the shirt isn't great. You shouldn't get it.

E

Q: 刚才找你的人是你的女朋友吧?

剛才找你的人是你的女朋友吧？

Was that person who came looking for you just now your girlfriend?

A: 别乱说，她不是我的女朋友，而是我的嫂子。

別亂說，她不是我的女朋友，而是我的嫂子。

Don't talk nonsense. She's not my girlfriend, she's my sister-in-law.

Words & Phrases

| A | 一直 (all along, continuously) |

1 大学四年，小张一直住在学校宿舍里。

大學四年，小張一直住在學校宿舍裡。

Little Zhang has been living in the dorms for all four years of college.

2 她搬进新房子后，一直没交房租。

她搬進新房子後，一直沒交房租。

Since she moved into her new apartment, she hasn't been paying rent.

3 小林的专业是金融，毕业以后，一直在银行工作。

小林的專業是金融，畢業以後，一直在銀行工作。

Little Lin's major was finance. Ever since he graduated, he's been working in banking.

4 小张有两条毯子，只用了一条，另外的一条一直放在柜子里。

小張有兩條毯子，只用了一條，另外的一條一直放在櫃子裡。

Little Zhang has two blankets. She is only using one of them. The other one has been stored in the cabinet the whole time.

5 你从这儿一直往前走，很快就到地铁站了。

你從這兒一直往前走，很快就到地鐵站了。

Go straight forward from here, and you'll soon arrive at the subway station.

Comparing 幸福, 快乐/快樂, and 高兴/高興

幸福 means "to feel contented with life." It denotes a state of mind that has lasted for an extended period of time.

1　小王和小李结婚以后，生活一直很幸福。

　　小王和小李結婚以後，生活一直很幸福。

Since Little Wang and Little Li got married, their life has always been very happy.

快乐/快樂 refers to the happiness one feels when one's needs and concerns have been addressed and taken care of. It is not necessarily externalized, and can be a more sustained happiness than that suggested by 高兴/高興.

2　暑假回到父母家，有好吃的，有老同学一起玩儿，她很快乐。

　　暑假回到父母家，有好吃的，有老同學一起玩兒，她很快樂。

She was back at her parents' place for summer break. As there was good food and she could hang out with her former classmates, she was very happy.

3　上大学以后，他一直不快乐，因为他想家、想朋友。

　　上大學以後，他一直不快樂，因為他想家、想朋友。

Since he started college, he's been unhappy because he misses home and friends.

In celebratory greetings like 新年快乐/新年快樂 (Happy New Year) and 生日快乐/生日快樂 (Happy Birthday), 快乐/快樂 cannot be replaced with either 幸福 or 高兴/高興.

高兴/高興 suggests one's state of mind upon seeing someone they like or experiencing something they find gratifying. It can be externalized and possibly temporary.

4　听说好朋友周末来看他，他非常高兴。

　　聽說好朋友週末來看他，他非常高興。

On hearing that his good friend was coming to visit him over the weekend, he was very glad.

5　这次考试考得特别好，小王高兴得一直笑。

这次考試考得特別好，小王高興得一直笑。

As he did so well on the exam this time, Little Wang was so happy that he kept smiling.

6　你刚才还在笑，现在怎么不高兴了？

你剛才還在笑，現在怎麼不高興了？

You were smiling only a moment ago. Why are you unhappy now?

C　　厉害/厲害 (terrible, formidable)

As an adjective, 厉害/厲害 has the original meaning of "fierce":

1　他姐姐很厉害，你不要拿她的东西。

他姐姐很厲害，你不要拿她的東西。

His older sister is very fierce. Don't take her stuff.

2　那个老师很厉害，大家都怕他。

那個老師很厲害，大家都怕他。

That teacher is very scary, and everybody is afraid of him.

厉害/厲害 can also refer to strong ability:

3　一班的同学很厉害，篮球比赛每次都是第一。

一班的同學很厲害，籃球比賽每次都是第一。

The students in Class One are awesome. They have won every basketball game.

厉害/厲害 can follow a verb—as in the Text of this lesson—or another adjective to denote a very high degree. It is usually used to describe negative situations.

4

哥哥和嫂子结婚十年了，生活一直很幸福，可是最近两年在女儿的教育问题上，意见常常不同，有时吵得很厉害。

哥哥和嫂子結婚十年了，生活一直很幸福，可是最近兩年在女兒的教育問題上，意見常常不同，有時吵得很厲害。

My older brother and sister-in-law got married ten years ago. They've been happy since, but they have often differed with each other on the issue of their daughter's education in the last couple of years, sometimes arguing intensely.

5

小高昨天夜里肚子疼得很厉害，我跟他一起去医院看的病。

小高昨天夜裡肚子疼得很厲害，我跟他一起去醫院看的病。

Little Gao had a terrible stomachache last night, and I was the one to take him to the hospital.

6

孩子哭得很厉害，是不是饿了？

孩子哭得很厲害，是不是餓了？

The child is crying so hard. Is she hungry?

A WAY WITH WORDS

留学

我给小高打电话，他不在，我只好在电话上给他留言了。

我要回中国了，这本书就送给你留念吧。

Using the word/phrase in orange as a clue, try to figure out the meaning of the words/phrases in blue; consult a dictionary if necessary. Consider how the literal and extended senses are related in each case.

留學

我給小高打電話，他不在，我只好在電話上給他留言了。

我要回中國了，這本書就送給你留念吧。

最好 (had better, it's best)

1

吃完饭后，最好不要马上运动。

吃完飯後，最好不要馬上運動。

It's best not to exercise right after you eat.

2   Person A

我想学化学专业，将来好找工作。

我想學化學專業，將來好找工作。

I'd like to major in chemistry so that I can easily find a job.

Person B

你对化学有兴趣吗？如果没有，最好别学。

你對化學有興趣嗎？如果沒有，最好別學。

Are you interested in chemistry? If not, you'd better not study it.

3

这个电影很受欢迎，看的人多。你如果想看，最好
早点儿买票。

這個電影很受歡迎，看的人多。你如果想看，最好
早點兒買票。

This film is very popular. Many people want to see it. If you want to see it, you'd better get a ticket as soon as you can.

Language Practice

A [INTERPERSONAL] **Early years** [PRESENTATIONAL]

Put yourself in the shoes of your favorite actor, athlete, politician, or any other role model, and pretend you are being interviewed for a new biography. On a scale of one to five, rate "your" childhood in terms of happiness and stressfulness, with one being not at all happy or stressful and five being extremely happy or stressful.

On a name tag, write the name of the person you've chosen to be. Then go around the class and ask your classmates, who should also be in character:

1 你的童年快乐吗？

你的童年快樂嗎？

2 你的童年压力大吗？

你的童年壓力大嗎？

Finally, record and summarize their answers, e.g.:

Sasha, Jennifer, Matt 觉得他们的童年一点都不快乐，压力大得不得了。

Sasha, Jennifer, Matt 覺得他們的童年一點都不快樂，壓力大得不得了。

or

Kaitlin, Steve, Rosa 觉得他们的童年非常快乐，一点压力都没有。

Kaitlin, Steve, Rosa 覺得他們的童年非常快樂，一點壓力都沒有。

B **Extracurricular experiences** [INTERPERSONAL]

First, list Li Zhe's niece's extracurricular activities in Chinese. In addition, list any other common ones that you can think of. Once you're finished, work with a partner and take turns asking:

1 if you participated in any when you were growing up

2 if those you participated in were by your own choice

3 if any of those you participated in were by your parents' choice

4 if you enjoyed the activities, regardless of who arranged them

Helicopter parent

If you were a parent, what kind of afterschool schedule would you establish for your children to prepare them for the future? Use the chart to indicate the activities you would engage your child in.

	星期一	星期二	星期三	星期四	星期五	星期六	星期日
下午							
晚上							

Then, in pairs, examine your and your partner's schedules. Would they be too much for a child? Do they need some breathing room? Would the children complain? How much say would your child have in choosing his/her own activities?

D INTERPERSONAL **Expectations and accomplishments** PRESENTATIONAL

List the things that your parents hope you will have accomplished after completing your education. Then list the things that you expect to accomplish after graduation and the things that you hope your future children/nephews/nieces will accomplish when they grow up.

Look at the three lists and discuss with a partner if you're able to live up to your parents' expectations, how your own expectations for yourself are similar to or different from your parents' expectations for you, and whether you will be like your parents in your expectations of the next generation. Jot down what you have discussed and pay attention to the use of time phrases and pronouns/nouns as connectors, as well as other conjunctions, to build a more coherent and cohesive narrative. Finally, present your narrative to your class.

A WAY WITH WORDS

抱怨

我把你的电脑用坏了，真的很抱歉。

老张这两天不太舒服，但是还是抱病工作。

Using the word/phrase in orange as a clue, try to figure out the meaning of the words/phrases in blue; consult a dictionary if necessary. Consider how the literal and extended senses are related in each case.

抱怨

我把你的電腦用壞了，真的很抱歉。

老張這兩天不太舒服，但是還是抱病工作。

Fact checker

Pair up with a partner and get your facts straight based on the text of this lesson, e.g.:

李哲的父母是加拿大移民。

李哲的父母是加拿大移民。

Person A 我听说李哲的父母是加拿大移民。

我聽說李哲的父母是加拿大移民。

Person B 李哲的父母不是加拿大移民，而是墨西哥移民。

李哲的父母不是加拿大移民，而是墨西哥移民。

1 李哲的哥哥是电脑硕士。

 李哲的哥哥是電腦碩士。

2 李哲的哥哥同意给孩子很大的压力。

 李哲的哥哥同意給孩子很大的壓力。

3 丽莎同意李哲嫂子的做法。

 麗莎同意李哲嫂子的做法。

4 李哲的哥哥和嫂子在家庭经济问题上意见不同。

 李哲的哥哥和嫂子在家庭經濟問題上意見不同。

Taking sides

How do you indicate agreement or disagreement with others? Here are some options:

。 我同意（or 反对）……

 我同意（or 反對）……

- 我（不）同意＿＿＿＿＿的看法（or 做法 or 意见）。我认为（or 觉得）……

  我（不）同意＿＿＿＿＿的看法（or 做法 or 意見）。我認為（or 覺得）……

- 我觉得＿＿＿＿＿说的话很有道理（or 没有道理）。

  我覺得＿＿＿＿＿說的話很有道理（or 沒有道理）。

- 我不完全同意（or 反对）……

  我不完全同意（or 反對）……

Then use at least three of these four options to state your opinions in the following exercises.

1 李哲的侄女认为小孩子也是人，有自己的爱好和兴趣，父母应该尊重孩子自己的选择。你同意吗？

李哲的侄女認為小孩子也是人，有自己的愛好和興趣，父母應該尊重孩子自己的選擇。你同意嗎？

2 李哲的哥哥反对给孩子太大的压力。你觉得呢？

李哲的哥哥反對給孩子太大的壓力。你覺得呢？

3 丽莎觉得孩子应该有个快乐的童年，也应该好好儿学习。你的看法呢？

麗莎覺得孩子應該有個快樂的童年，也應該好好兒學習。你的看法呢？

G | **In my view** | INTERPERSONAL

Working with a partner, ask and answer the following questions according to your own perspective.

1 柯林对大一新生住在校内的看法是什么？你同意吗？为什么？

柯林對大一新生住在校內的看法是什麼？你同意嗎？為什麼？

2   张天明买衣服的标准是什么？你的看法呢？

张天明買衣服的標準是什麼？你的看法呢？

3   李哲大学毕业以后，打算念研究生。你有什么建议？

李哲大學畢業以後，打算念研究生。你有什麼建議？

4   虽然张天明常常忘这忘那，让丽莎生气，但丽莎没跟天明分手。你的看法是什么？

雖然張天明常常忘這忘那，讓麗莎生氣，但麗莎沒跟天明分手。你的看法是什麼？

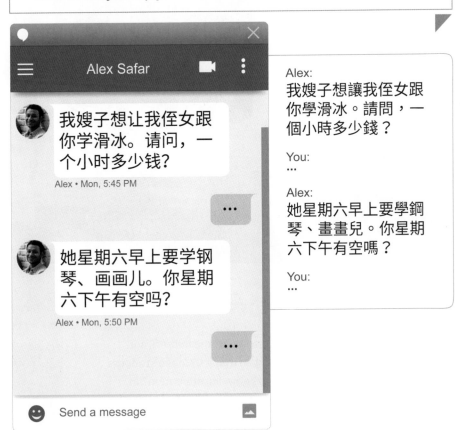

Chinese Chat

A potential client is chatting with you on Google Hangouts. How would you reply?

Alex Safar

我嫂子想让我侄女跟你学滑冰。请问，一个小时多少钱？

Alex • Mon, 5:45 PM

她星期六早上要学钢琴、画画儿。你星期六下午有空吗？

Alex • Mon, 5:50 PM

Send a message

Alex:
我嫂子想讓我侄女跟你學滑冰。請問，一個小時多少錢？

You:
...

Alex:
她星期六早上要學鋼琴、畫畫兒。你星期六下午有空嗎？

You:
...

Respect for Teachers

In keeping with the strong emphasis on education in Chinese culture is a special kind of respect for teachers. In Confucianism, relationships between teachers and students and between masters and disciples were comparable to those between fathers and sons. Indeed, as a cultural icon, the teacher, 师/師, was regularly worshiped in sacrificial ceremonies, ranking only after heaven, 天; earth, 地; the sovereign, 君 (jūn); and one's parents, 亲/親. In modern China, the traditional respect for teachers has been retained to a certain extent. Typically, elementary and some middle school students stand up and greet their teacher in chorus at the beginning of a class, and repeat the ritual to bid farewell to the teacher at the end of class. In Mainland China, September 10th is set aside as Teachers' Day, while in Taiwan teachers are celebrated on Confucius' birthday, September 28th.

COMPARE & CONTRAST

In your opinion, what are some of the cultural and social reasons compelling so many Chinese students to seek extracurricular or remedial education? In your country, do these reasons apply? How big is the comparable industry in your country? Have you ever gone to a cram school to prepare for an exam?

Parental Aspirations

龙/龍 is an animal with magical powers in ancient Chinese mythology and a symbol of imperial authority. 凤/鳳, short for 凤凰/鳳凰 (fènghuáng), is the sovereign of all birds in Chinese legend. The use of these symbols was tightly regulated. The elaborate imperial robe and ornate imperial throne were known as 龙袍/龍袍 (lóngpáo) and 龙座/龍座 respectively, and the empress' lavish headdress was called the "phoenix crown," 凤冠/鳳冠 (fèngguàn). That the dragon and phoenix in 望子成龙/望子成龍 and 望女成凤/望女成鳳 have become metaphors for outstanding talent speaks volumes about high parental expectations in China.

Metamorphosis into a dragon is also a metaphor for overcoming tremendous odds to achieve academic and career success. It comes from a legend in which a carp (鲤鱼/鯉魚) (lǐyú) turned into a dragon after leaping over the forbidding Dragon Gate (龙门/龍門) Gorge on the Yellow River. This legend (鲤鱼跳龙门/鯉魚跳龍門) is well known in China's neighbors Korea and Japan as well. In Chinese folk art, boys are often depicted riding carps. In Korea and Japan, colorful carp-shaped kites and streamers are flown to celebrate Children's Day on May 5th every year.

Cram School

A majority of the one hundred million pre-collegiate students in China attend cram schools, 补习班/補習班 (bǔxí bān)—extracurricular schools intended to enhance scholastic ability. Even young students attend cram schools, and it is estimated that ninety percent of urban elementary school students are enrolled. Especially in Mainland China, the competition on the college entrance exam is fierce, with the number of high school students outnumbering the number of positions available at universities. In addition, students aim for a high level of academic achievement in high school to increase the chance that they will be assigned to their first choice of major.

Lesson Wrap-Up

Project

More exercises

You've been invited to participate in a panel discussion on child education in America with a group of experts from China. You have decided to talk about the "Tiger Mom" controversy in the United States. To prepare for your presentation, read two reviews of Amy Chua's book *The Battle Hymn of the Tiger Mother*, and look up any new words you need for your presentation. Practice your talk with a partner and take questions from each other. As part of your conversation with your partner, be sure to:

- describe Amy Chua's background—who she is, what she does for a living, etc.

- explain what her book is about—how many daughters she has, what she made her daughters do, etc.

- summarize the main theme of her book

- elucidate her justification for what she did

- describe your childhood—were your parents like Amy Chua?

- give your thoughts on the pros and cons of Amy Chua's approach

Keep It Flowing

Study the following compare-and-contrast passage; pay particular attention to how the highlighted parts help the sentences flow smoothly from one to the next. Notice how:

- pronouns (他, 她) replace corresponding nouns when the subject remains unchanged (李哲的哥哥, 李哲的嫂子)

- certain prepositional phrases (在…上) can delimit issues or areas (教育的问题/教育的問題)

- certain verbs (认为/認為, 希望, 反对/反對) introduce opinions (three clauses following 认为/認為 in the first instance), desires (two clauses following 希望), and objections (one clause following 反对/反對).

- certain conjunctions (可是, 但是) and structures (不是…而是…) indicate contrast

- other conjunctions introduce causal relationships (所以)

- certain structures negate one thing and emphatically assert another (不是…而是…)

孩子的教育问题

　　李哲的哥哥和嫂子在女儿的教育问题上看法很不同。李哲的哥哥认为小孩也是人，有自己的爱好和兴趣，父母应该尊重孩子自己的选择。可是李哲的嫂子不这么看，她认为孩子太小，不知道学习很重要，所以整天安排女儿学这学那。李哲的哥哥反对给孩子太大的压力，他认为对孩子来说，最重要的是有一个快乐的童年。但是李哲的嫂子望子成龙，望女成凤，希望自己的孩子小时候好好儿学习，将来能做出一番大事业。李哲的哥哥不同意他嫂子的看法，他说，有些知识不是从书上学的，而是从社会、从生活中学的。

孩子的教育問題

　　李哲的哥哥和嫂子在女兒的教育問題上看法很不同。李哲的哥哥認為小孩也是人，有自己的愛好和興趣，父母應該尊重孩子自己的選擇。可是李哲的嫂子不這麼看，她認為孩子太小，不知道學習很重要，所以整天安排女兒學這學那。李哲的哥哥反對給孩子太大的壓力，他認為對孩子來說，最重要的是有一個快樂的童年。但是李哲的嫂子望子成龍，望女成鳳，希望自己的孩子小時候好好兒學習，將來能做出一番大事業。李哲不同意他嫂子的看法，他說，有些知識不是從書上學的，而是從社會、從生活中學的。

Compare and contrast your parents' view with that of Li Zhe's sister-in-law. Be sure to include different opinions. Use as many of the cohesive devices underlined in the example as possible to string together your answers to the questions:

- 你父母和李哲的嫂子在教育问题上看法一样吗？
  你父母和李哲的嫂子在教育問題上看法一樣嗎？

- 你父母认为孩子应该有一个什么样的童年？你同意吗？为什么？
  你父母認為孩子應該有一個什麼樣的童年？你同意嗎？為什麼？

- 你父母认为应该不应该给孩子压力？你的看法是什么？
  你父母認為應該不應該給孩子壓力？你的看法是什麼？

- 你父母希望孩子长大以后怎么样？
  你父母希望孩子長大以後怎麼樣？

- 你父母觉得知识是从哪儿学来的？
  你父母覺得知識是從哪兒學來的？

Can-Do Check List ✓

I can

Before proceeding to Lesson 10, make sure you can complete the following tasks in Chinese:

- ☐ Describe common afterschool classes and programs
- ☐ Express degrees of agreement or disagreement
- ☐ Phrase your opinion appropriately
- ☐ State your view on children's education
- ☐ Discuss parental hopes and expectations

Lǐ Zhé de fùmǔ shì Mòxīgē yímín, tā hé tā gēge dōu shì zài Jiāzhōu chūshēng, zhǎng dà de. Gēge shì diànnǎo bóshì, shèjì ruǎnjiàn, guǎnlǐ wǎngzhàn. Lǐ Zhé de sǎozi shíwǔ nián qián cóng Xiānggǎng lái Měiguó liú xué, ná dào shuòshì xuéwèi[a] yǐhòu zhǎo dào gōngzuò, jiù zài Měiguó zhù le xia lai. Gēge hé sǎozi jié hūn shí nián le, shēnghuó yìzhí hěn xìngfú. Kěshì zuìjìn liǎng nián zài nǚ'ér de jiàoyù wèntí shang, yìjiàn chángcháng bù tóng, yǒu shí chǎo de hěn lìhai. Yì tiān, Lǐ Zhé zhèngzài diànhuà shang gēn zhínǚ liáo tiānr, kàn jiàn Lìshā zǒu le jin lai.

(Lǐ Zhé fàng xià diànhuà . . .)

 Lìshā, yǒu shìr ma?

 Méi shénme shìr, wǒ zhǎo Tiānmíng, yǐwéi tā zài nǐ zhèr ne. Duìbuqǐ, hài de nǐ bǎ diànhuà guà le.

 Zuò, zuò, zuò. Gāngcái shì wǒ zhínǚ gěi wǒ dǎ diànhuà, wǒmen zhènghǎo shuō wán le.

 Nǐ yǒu zhínǚ? Jīnnián duō dà le?

 Jīnnián gāng bā suì.

 Tā gěi nǐ dǎ diànhuà yǒu shénme shì a?

 Xuéxí de shìr. Wǒ zhínǚ cái[1] xiǎoxué sān niánjí, wǒ sǎozi jiù ānpái tā: xīngqīyī xué gāngqín[b], xīngqī'èr xué huà huàr, xīngqīsān xué yóu yǒng, xīngqīsì xué huá bīng, zhǐyǒu xīngqīwǔ xiūxi yì tiān, xīngqīliù yòu jiào tā qù shàng Zhōngwén xuéxiào. Tā bù xǐhuan xué Zhōngwén, suǒyǐ jiù dǎ diànhuà dào wǒ zhèr lái, yìbiān kū yìbiān bàoyuàn.

 Méi nàme yánzhòng ba? Tā zěnme shuō?

 Tā shuō xiǎo háizi yě shì rén, yǒu zìjǐ de àihào hé xìngqù, fùmǔ yīnggāi zūnzhòng háizi zìjǐ de xuǎnzé.

 Tā zěnme zhème huì shuō huà[c]?

 Zhè xiē huà yídìng shì gēn wǒ gēge xué de. Wǒ sǎozi zhěngtiān ràng tā xué zhè xué nà, wǒ gēge fǎnduì gěi háizi tài dà de yālì, tā rènwéi[d] duì háizi lái shuō, zuì zhòngyào de shì yǒu yí ge kuàilè de tóngnián.

 Wǒ de tóngnián hěn kuàilè. Kěshì xiànzài, měi cì shàng Zhōngwén kè wǒ jiù xiǎng, yàoshi wǒ xiǎoshíhou fùmǔ jiù ràng wǒ xué Zhōngwén, wǒ xiànzài jiù qīngsōng duō le.

Méi xiǎng dào nǐ gēn wǒ sǎozi de kànfǎ yíyàng! Nǐ tóngyì wǒ sǎozi de zuòfǎ?

 Wǒ bù wánquán tóngyì, dàn wǒ néng lǐjiě.

 Hěn duō fùmǔ wàng zǐ chéng lóng, wàng nǚ chéng fèng, xīwàng zìjǐ de háizi xiǎoshíhou hǎo hāor xuéxí, jiānglái néng zuò chū yì fān dà shìyè. Kěshì dào xiànzài wǒ yě xiǎng bu qīngchu, háizi dàodǐ shì jiānglái "chéng lóng" "chéng fèng" hǎo[2], háishi yǒu yí ge kuàilè de tóngnián hǎo?

 Wǒ de kànfǎ shì liǎng ge dōu zhòngyào. Yí ge rén dāngrán yīnggāi yǒu kuàilè de tóngnián, dànshì zhǎng dà yǐhòu yě yīnggāi duì shèhuì yǒuyòng, suǒyǐ háizi zuìhǎo háishì zài xuéxiào duō xué yì xiē zhīshi.

 Kěshì nǐ bié wàng le, yǒu xiē zhīshi bú shì cóng shū shang xué de, ér shì[3] cóng shèhuì, cóng shēnghuó zhōng xué de.

 Lǐ Zhé, nǐ zhēn chéng le zhéxuéjiā[e] le.

中国地理

中國地理

GEOGRAPHY OF CHINA

Learning Objectives

In this lesson, you will learn to:

- Locate major Chinese cities, provinces, and geographic features on a map
- Compare basic geographic aspects of China and your own country
- Describe features of a tourist sight that would attract or deter you
- Discuss an itinerary for travel to China

Relate & Get Ready

In your own culture/community:

- How has local geography exerted an influence on development?
- What are considered the most desirable destinations for domestic tourism?
- What local features are popular among tourists, and what would you recommend to tourists planning a trip?

课文

Text

Audio

Before You Study

Answer the following questions in Chinese to prepare for the reading.

1 中国的人口是多少？

2 中国大还是你的国家(country)大？

When You Study

Listen to the audio recording and skim the text; then answer the following questions in Chinese.

1 张天明为什么想去南京看看？

2 丽莎想去哪些地方旅游？为什么？

3 他们最后决定去哪儿？为什么？

　　寒假快到了，张天明这几天一直在考虑旅行[a]的事儿。他的父母希望他去他们的家乡南京看看，张天明也很想当丽莎的导游，带她到中国的一些地方走走。除了南京以外，还应该去什么地方呢？为了决定旅行的路线，张天明拿出一张中国地图，看了起来[1]。

丽莎，你来看看中国地图，看到哪儿去旅行好。

看地图？你这个主意不错，我也正想学学中国地理呢。我对中国地理了解得太少了。

我们先到南京，我父母的家乡……在这里，在中国的东南。然后你想去哪儿？

这是哈尔滨，对吗？去哈尔滨吧。

你一下子要从东南边跑到最北边去？

昨天电视里介绍哈尔滨的冰灯了，好看极了。

冰灯好看是好看，可是哈尔滨现在冷得不得了，夏天再去吧。

好吧。不去北边，那坐火车去西边吧，听说新疆是个很特别的地方。

課文

Audio

寒假快到了，張天明這幾天一直在考慮旅行[a]的事兒。他的父母希望他去他們的家鄉南京看看，張天明也很想當麗莎的導遊，帶她到中國的一些地方走走。除了南京以外，還應該去什麼地方呢？為了決定旅行的路線，張天明拿出一張中國地圖，看了起來[1]。

麗莎，你來看看中國地圖，看到哪兒去旅行好。

看地圖？你這個主意不錯，我也正想學學中國地理呢。我對中國地理了解得太少了。

我們先到南京，我父母的家鄉⋯⋯在這裡，在中國的東南。然後你想去哪兒？

這是哈爾濱，對嗎？去哈爾濱吧。

你一下子要從東南邊跑到最北邊去？

昨天電視裡介紹哈爾濱的冰燈了，好看極了。

冰燈好看是好看，可是哈爾濱現在冷得不得了，夏天再去吧。

好吧。不去北邊，那坐火車去西邊吧，聽說新疆是個很特別的地方。

Before You Study

Answer the following questions in Chinese to prepare for the reading.

1 中國的人口是多少？

2 中國大還是你的國家(country)大？

When You Study

Listen to the audio recording and skim the text; then answer the following questions in Chinese.

1 張天明為什麼想去南京看看？

2 麗莎想去哪些地方旅遊？為什麼？

3 他們最後決定去哪兒？為什麼？

The Ice and Snow
Sculpture Festival in Harbin,
Heilongjiang Province

新疆在西北，十月就开始冷起来[1]了，现在去不合适。另外，坐火车太花时间，下次再去吧！

这是长江，这是黄河。我们坐船去看看长江或者黄河的风景吧。

坐船要花很长的时间。中国的河流[b]，大多从西往东流，如果从东往西走，时间更长。

为什么中国的河流大多从西往东流呢？

因为中国西部是高原，那儿有世界上最高的山。而[2]东边是平原和大海。

好像大城市都靠海或者离海不远。你看，在北边，这是北京、天津；东南边，这儿有上海、南京；南边这里，是广州和深圳。

你说的没错。中国的人口主要在东部[c]和南部。西南呢，高山、高原多，西北呢，沙漠多，自然条件不太好，所以人口比较少。

我觉得中国的地形和美国有点儿像。

你说的有道理。还有，中国和美国的面积也差不多，可是人口是美国的四倍多。听说，过节或者放假的时候，中国的旅游景点到处都是人山人海，挤得很。

是吗？

新疆在西北，十月就開始冷起來[1]了，現在去不合適。另外，坐火車太花時間，下次再去吧！

這是長江，這是黃河。我們坐船去看看長江或者黃河的風景吧。

坐船要花很長的時間。中國的河流[b]，大多從西往東流，如果從東往西走，時間更長。

為什麼中國的河流大多從西往東流呢？

因為中國西部是高原，那兒有世界上最高的山。而[2]東邊是平原和大海。

好像大城市都靠海或者離海不遠。你看，在北邊，這是北京、天津；東南邊，這兒有上海、南京；南邊這裡，是廣州和深圳。

你說的沒錯。中國的人口主要在東部[c]和南部。西南呢，高山、高原多，西北呢，沙漠多，自然條件不太好，所以人口比較少。

我覺得中國的地形和美國有點兒像。

你說的有道理。還有，中國和美國的面積也差不多，可是人口是美國的四倍多。聽說，過節或者放假的時候，中國的旅遊景點到處都是人山人海，擠得很。

是嗎？

Top to bottom:
The Moon-Embracing Pavilion, Tiger Leaping Gorge, and Jade Dragon Snow Mountain in Yunnan Province

还好，我们到中国的时候，学生还没放假，也不是过年过节。

中国这么大，我们的寒假那么短，到底去哪儿旅游好呢？

我觉得去云南最好不过了[3]。

云南在哪里？……我找到了，在这儿，是一个省，在西南部。那儿冬天不冷吗？

听说云南有些地方四季如春，一年四季都不冷不热。

我记得电视里说过[4]，云南风景好，少数民族[d]多，是个旅游的好地方。

好，云南，决定了，就去云南。

View & Explore

Video

For deeper language immersion and more cultural information, watch "China's Provinces," a short, supplemental video clip by Cheng & Tsui on this lesson's theme.

還好，我們到中國的時候，學生還沒放假，也不是過年過節。

中國這麼大，我們的寒假那麼短，到底去哪兒旅遊好呢？

我覺得去雲南最好不過了[3]。

雲南在哪裡？……我找到了，在這兒，是一個省，在西南部。那兒冬天不冷嗎？

聽說雲南有些地方四季如春，一年四季都不冷不熱。

我記得電視裡說過[4]，雲南風景好，少數民族[d]多，是個旅遊的好地方。

好，雲南，決定了，就去雲南。

Answer the following questions in Chinese.

1 請說說張天明和麗莎計劃的旅行路線。

2 請簡單地介紹一下中國的人口、面積、地形和河流。

Language Notes

a 旅行

旅行 and 旅游/旅遊 are roughly synonymous. The term 旅行 does not by itself imply a purpose for travel, and travel agencies are always 旅行社. However, 游/遊 means to wander, so 旅游/旅遊 specifically implies traveling for pleasure. To travel for business is 出差/出差 (chū chāi). Tourists are 游客/遊客. In Taiwan, the term 观光客/觀光客 (guānguāngkè) is also used; 观光/觀光 means "sightseeing."

b 河流

河流 is a collective noun. It can refer to rivers in general or all the rivers within a geographic area. 河 can refer to a specific river or several rivers.

c 东部/東部

部 is used with other characters to form multisyllabic words such as 东部/東部, 南部, 西南部. It is not used on its own. The term 中国的东部/中国的東部 (the eastern part of China) refers to the eastern region within China. By contrast, 中国的东边/中國的東邊 can refer either to "the East of China" (i.e., within China) or "east of China" (i.e., outside of China).

d 少数民族/少數民族

少数民族/少數民族 means "ethnic minority" (lit. minority nationality).

Vocabulary

No.	Simplified	Traditional	Pinyin	Part of Speech	Definition
1	地理	地理	dìlǐ	n	geography
2	家乡	家鄉	jiāxiāng	n	hometown, place of family origin
3	路线	路線	lùxiàn	n	route, itinerary
4	了解	了解	liǎojiě	v	to understand, to know about, to be informed
5	一下子	一下子	yíxiàzi	adv	in an instant, all of a sudden
6	冰灯	冰燈	bīngdēng	n	ice lantern
7	火车	火車	huǒchē	n	train
8	船	船	chuán	n	boat, ship
9	风景	風景	fēngjǐng	n	scenic landscape, scenery
10	河流	河流	héliú	n	river
11	大多	大多	dàduō	adv	mostly, for the most part
12	流	流	liú	v	to flow
13	部	部	bù	n	part, section
14	高原	高原	gāoyuán	n	plateau (lit. high field)
15	山	山	shān	n	mountain, hill
16	而	而	ér	conj	(conjunction to connect two clauses) [See Grammar 2.]
17	平原	平原	píngyuán	n	plain (lit. flat field)
18	海	海	hǎi	n	sea, ocean
19	人口	人口	rénkǒu	n	population
20	主要	主要	zhǔyào	adj	main, principal
21	沙漠	沙漠	shāmò	n	desert
22	自然	自然	zìrán	n/adj	nature; natural

No.	Simplified	Traditional	Pinyin	Part of Speech	Definition
23	条件	條件	*tiáojiàn*	n	condition
24	地形	地形	*dìxíng*	n	terrain, topography
25	面积	面積	*miànjī*	n	area (of land)
26	倍	倍	*bèi*	m	(measure word for times by which something is multiplied)
27	过节	過節	*guò jié*	vo	to celebrate a holiday
28	旅游	旅遊	*lǚyóu*	v/n	to travel (for pleasure); (pleasure) travel
29	景点	景點	*jǐngdiǎn*	n	scenic spot, tourist spot
30	到处	到處	*dàochù*	adv	all around, all over
31	人山人海	人山人海	*rén shān rén hǎi*		huge crowds of people (lit. mountains and seas of people)
32	挤	擠	*jǐ*	adj/v	crowded; to push against, to squeeze
33	短	短	*duǎn*	adj	short

丽莎想去哈尔滨旅游，因为哈尔滨的冰灯好看极了。你想去中国的什么地方旅游？为什么？

麗莎想去哈爾濱旅遊，因為哈爾濱的冰燈好看極了。你想去中國的什麼地方旅遊？為什麼？

You've received this flyer from a travel agency. Identify key details, including the price and destination of the package. Using resources online, find out what is popular to see and do there to help you plan your travel itinerary.

GET
Real
WITH CHINESE

免费上门来接，轻松带您游

周
价格：

😊 上海一日游

价格：230元/人（含门票、船票）

游览景点：
乘浦江游船饱览两岸美景、东
方明珠（上塔263、259m悬空
观光廊）历史发展陈列馆、车
游浦东新区南浦大桥、城隍庙
自由活动、外滩南京路步行街。

游览景点：
乘坐环镇水
第一水乡、
富安桥、古
福寺（寺庙
选择）等精

旅游标准：另有登88层金茂大厦线路请来电咨询
空调旅游车、导游服务。（注：餐费自理）

旅游标
空调旅

😊 乌镇

No.	Simplified	Traditional	Pinyin	Part of Speech	Definition
34	省	省	*shěng*	n	province (administrative division)
35	四季如春	四季如春	*sìjì rú chūn*		spring-like all year round
36	少数	少數	*shǎoshù*	n	few, minority (lit. small number)
37	民族	民族	*mínzú*	n	ethnic group, nationality
38	南京	南京	*Nánjīng*	pn	Nanjing
39	哈尔滨	哈爾濱	*Hā'ěrbīn*	pn	Harbin
40	新疆	新疆	*Xīnjiāng*	pn	Xinjiang
41	长江	長江	*Chángjiāng*	pn	Yangtze River
42	黄河	黃河	*Huánghé*	pn	Yellow River
43	天津	天津	*Tiānjīn*	pn	Tianjin
44	广州	廣州	*Guǎngzhōu*	pn	Guangzhou
45	深圳	深圳	*Shēnzhèn*	pn	Shenzhen
46	云南	雲南	*Yúnnán*	pn	Yunnan

Grammar

---

1 | **Indicating the beginning of a state using 起来/起來**

As we learned in IC2, 起来/起來 can indicate that an action is starting to take place. [See Grammar 2, Lesson 15, IC2.]

A　张天明拿出一张中国地图，看了起来。

張天明拿出一張中國地圖，看了起來。

Zhang Tianming took out a map of China and started studying it.

B　听她说完那些话，大家都笑了起来。

聽她說完那些話，大家都笑了起來。

After listening to what she said, everybody began to laugh.

C　你怎么哭起来了？

你怎麼哭起來了？

How come you started crying?

D　吃完晚饭，没有什么事儿，他就看起杂志来。

吃完晚飯，沒有什麼事兒，他就看起雜誌來。

After dinner he had a free moment, so he began to flip through some magazines.

When there is an object, it must be placed between 起/起 and 来/來, as in (D).

起来/起來 can also be used after adjectives to indicate the start and continuation of a state.

E　今天是周末，购物中心里的人多起来了。

今天是週末，購物中心裡的人多起來了。

It's the weekend today. The malls are starting to fill up with people.

F　他走进房间打开灯，房间里一下子亮 (liàng) 起来了。

他走進房間打開燈，房間裡一下子亮 (liàng) 起來了。

He walked into the room and turned on the light. The room brightened up instantly.

起来/起來 is often used with adjectives such as 亮/亮 (liàng) (bright; to brighten up), 大, 高, 多, 快, and 热闹/熱鬧 (rènao) (lively). Like 起来/起來, 下来/下來 can follow a verb or adjective to indicate the start of an action or condition, but the verb or adjective usually suggests a diminution or decrease in size, volume, quantity, speed, intensity, etc. For instance, 下来/下來 is often used with 暗 (àn) (dark; to darken), 小, 低, 少, 慢, 安静/安靜, and 停 (tíng) (to stop).

G　刚才他开车开得很快，进城以后，他开得慢下来了。

　　刚才他開車開得很快，進城以後，他開得慢下來了。

刚才他開車開得很快，進城以後，他開得慢下來了。

Just now, he was driving very fast. After he entered the city, he began to slow down.

H　屋子里的灯慢慢暗下来了。

　　屋子裡的燈慢慢暗下來了。

The light in the room slowly began to dim.

I　上课了，教室里安静了下来。

　　上課了，教室裡安靜了下來。

Class started, and the room began quieting down.

Seasonal weather changes can also be expressed with 起来/起來, as in 夏天热起来了/夏天熱起來了 and 冬天冷起来了/冬天冷起來了.

2　　　　　　　　　　**The conjunction 而**

而 is used to connect two clauses that present different or contrasting characteristics or situations. It has a literary flavor.

A　中国西部是高原，那儿有世界上最高的山。而东边是平原和大海。

　　中國西部是高原，那兒有世界上最高的山。而東邊是平原和大海。

The western part of China is plateaus; there, you'll find the world's tallest mountain. By contrast, in the east are plains and the ocean.

B

小林毕业以后计划回中国工作，而不准备留在美国。

小林畢業以後計劃回中國工作，而不準備留在美國。

Little Lin plans to go back to China to work rather than stay in the United States.

C

我想去学校图书馆打工，而我的同屋想去校外打工。

我想去學校圖書館打工，而我的同屋想去校外打工。

I want to work at the school library, but my roommate wants to work off campus.

D

我哥哥已经拿到硕士学位了，而我才高中毕业。

我哥哥已經拿到碩士學位了，而我才高中畢業。

My older brother has already gotten his master's degree. I, on the other hand, have just graduated from high school.

3 　　　最 adjective 不过了/最 adjective 不過了

"X 最 adjective 不过了/X 最 adjective 不過了" has the same meaning as "没有比 X 更 adjective 的/沒有比 X 更 adjective 的" (nothing can surpass X). It is a rather strong expression, e.g.:

A

她过生日，买花送她最好不过了。

她過生日，買花送她最好不過了。

Nothing would be a better gift for her birthday than flowers.

B

这本书对世界经济的介绍最清楚不过了。

這本書對世界经济的介紹最清楚不過了。

This book's introduction to the global economy surpasses all others in clarity.

C

这个实习工作对化学系的学生来说，最合适不过了。

這個實習工作對化學系的學生來說，最合適不過了。

For a chemistry major, there's no internship more appropriate than this one.

As we learned in IC2, to express that someone has experience doing something, the dynamic particle 过/過 is used. It differs from 了 in two ways. [See Grammar 5, Lesson 13, IC2.]

First, 了 is descriptive in nature and is used to relate the occurrence of an action.

A 我去年去了一次中国，在北京实习了三个月，别的地方都没去，就回来了。

我去年去了一次中國，在北京實習了三個月，別的地方都沒去，就回來了。

Last year, I went to China to intern in Beijing for three months. I really didn't go anywhere else, and then just came back.

B 第二天早上，我很早就起来了，起床后就去运动场跑步。

第二天早上，我很早就起來了，起床後就去運動場跑步。

The next morning I got up really early. After I got up, I went jogging at the athletic field.

C 客人们进来以后，找到了自己的位子，坐了下来。

客人們進來以後，找到了自己的位子，坐了下來。

The guests walked in, found their seats, and sat down.

过/過, on the other hand, is explanatory in nature. It is used to explain the reasoning for a following statement. In other words, the emphasis is on the impact a past action has had on the present situation:

D （以前）我们在一起学过英文，我知道他英文很好。

（以前）我們在一起學過英文，我知道他英文很好。

We used to study English together. I know his English is very good.
(Because we studied English together, I know his English is very good.)

E Person A 你去过中国，请告诉我们去哪儿旅游最好。

你去過中國，請告訴我們去哪兒旅遊最好。

You've been to China. Give us some tips on the best places to go.
(Because you've been to China, you can give us some tips on where some of the best places to go are.)

Person B 云南的旅游景点多，少数民族的文化也很有意思，是旅游的好地方。

雲南的旅遊景點多，少數民族的文化也很有意思，是旅遊的好地方。

Yunnan has plenty of tourist sights, and the cultures of the minority ethnic groups are also intriguing. It's a good place to visit.

F 他学过好几年中文，都能看中文报纸、杂志了。

他學過好幾年中文，都能看中文報紙、雜誌了。

He's been studying Chinese for several years. He can even read Chinese newspapers and magazines.
(Because he's been studying Chinese for several years, he can understand Chinese newspapers and magazines.)

In (D), (E), and (F), the clauses containing 过/過 all serve as explanatory background to the clauses that follow. 过/過 indicates the impact or influence of a past action on the present.

Second, 了 generally requires a specific time phrase, unless the sentence forms part of an extended narrative in which the temporal background has already been stated or is implicitly understood as in (C); 过/過 does not. When we use 过/過, the time implied is often rather vague: "before" or "in the past." Only when we want to be more precise—usually, to refute or prove a point—do we use a time phrase, as in the second part of (G).

G Person A 我听说你没去过别的国家，是真的吗？

我聽說你沒去過別的國家，是真的嗎？

I heard that you've never been abroad. Is that true?

Person B 谁说的？我去年去过日本。

誰說的？我去年去過日本。

Who said that? I went to Japan last year.

Note that when 过/過 is used in the experiential sense, it usually cannot be followed by 了.

Words & Phrases

为了/為了 and 因为/因為

为了/為了 denotes purpose, whereas 因为/因為 denotes cause.

1
为了把中文学得更好，我明年要去中国留学。

為了把中文學得更好，我明年要去中國留學。

In order to improve my Chinese, I'm going to study abroad in China next year.

2
因为在中国学中文条件更好，所以我明年去中国留学。

因為在中國學中文條件更好，所以我明年去中國留學。

Because the conditions in China are better for learning Chinese, I'm going to China to study next year.

3
为了解决学费的问题，他一边上学一边打工。

為了解決學費的問題，他一邊上學一邊打工。

In order to solve the problem of school tuition, he works part time while going to school.

4
因为得交学费，所以他一边上学一边打工。

因為得交學費，所以他一邊上學一邊打工。

Because he has to pay for school tuition, he works part time while going to school.

5
因为这个学校很有名，所以我申请。

因為這個學校很有名，所以我申請。

Because this school is very famous, I'm applying to it.

6
我申请这个学校，是为了能跟我的女朋友在一起。

我申請這個學校，是為了能跟我的女朋友在一起。

I'm applying to this school so that I can be with my girlfriend.

Comparing 理解/理解 and 了解/了解

理解/理解 means "to understand."

1 她现在学习压力大，不能帮助我，我理解。

她現在學習壓力大，不能幫助我，我理解。

She's under a lot of pressure with her studies and can't help me. I understand.

2 老师刚才说的意思，你没有完全理解。

老師剛才說的意思，你沒有完全理解。

You didn't completely understand what the teacher just said.

3 做这件事很容易，我不理解你为什么怕这怕那。

做這件事很容易，我不理解你為什麼怕這怕那。

It's very easy to do this. I don't understand why you're being so timid.

了解/了解, on the other hand, means to have a clear knowledge of something.

4 我在那个国家住过几年，对那里比较了解。

我在那個國家住過幾年，對那裡比較了解。

I lived in that country for a few years, and know things there pretty well.

5 你了解她的过去吗？

你了解她的過去嗎？

Do you know her past?

6 我们老师对每个学生在学习上的问题都很了解。

我們老師對每個學生在學習上的問題都很了解。

Our teacher has a clear knowledge of each student's problems with regard to studying.

一下子 (all of a sudden, in an instant)

一下子 is equivalent to 一下. It means "not much time has gone by," and it's often used to depict how fast or how soon actions or things happen.

1

你一下子就要从南边跑到最北边去？

你一下子就要從南邊跑到最北邊去？

All of a sudden, you want to go from the south to the northernmost part?

2

你说的那个商店我一下子就找到了，不难找。

你說的那個商店我一下子就找到了，不難找。

I found the store you mentioned right away. It wasn't difficult to find.

3

妈妈给他的零用钱他一下子就花完了。

媽媽給他的零用錢他一下子就花完了。

He went through the allowance that his mother had given him in no time.

A WAY WITH WORDS

Using the word/phrase in orange as a clue, try to figure out the meaning of the words/phrases in blue; consult a dictionary if necessary. Consider how the literal and extended senses are related in each case.

风景

这几年很多中国城市都有出国旅游的风气。

听说有些中国人买房子前会先看看房子的风水怎么样。

風景

這幾年很多中國城市都有出國旅遊的風氣。

聽說有些中國人買房子前會先看看房子的風水怎麼樣。

大多 (mostly)

大多 is an adverb meaning "for the most part" or "mostly." It cannot be used before nouns.

1

我们班的同学**大多**住在学校宿舍。

我們班的同學**大多**住在學校宿舍。

Our classmates mostly live in the school dorms.

2

美国的大山和河流的名字，我弟弟**大多**说不对。

美國的大山和河流的名字，我弟弟**大多**說不對。

My younger brother couldn't get the names of most of the big mountains and rivers of the U.S. right.

3

我们学校教授的研究，我**大多**都了解，你不用上网看了。

我們學校教授的研究，我**大多**都了解，你不用上網看了。

I'm familiar with most of our school's professors' research. You don't need to go online to find out.

Indicating a pause in speech using 呢

This particle occurs after a subject or topic and is followed by a pause in speech. It usually appears in enumerative sentences suggesting contrast:

1

你说的没错，中国的人口主要在东部和南部。西南呢，高山、高原多，西北呢，沙漠多，自然条件不太好，所以人口比较少。

你說的沒錯，中國的人口主要在東部和南部。西南呢，高山、高原多，西北呢，沙漠多，自然條件不太好，所以人口比較少。

You put it correctly. China's population is primarily in the east and south. As for the southwest, there are numerous big mountains and plateaus. The northwest, on the other hand, has many deserts with unfavorable natural conditions. That's why the population there is relatively sparse.

2 Q: 你们寒假准备做什么？

你們寒假準備做什麼？

What do you plan to do over winter break?

A: 我呢，要回家，小张呢，要留在学校打工，小李要做
什么，我不知道。

我呢，要回家，小張呢，要留在學校打工，小李要做
什麼，我不知道。

I'm going home. Little Zhang, on the other hand, has to stay at school and work.
I don't know what Little Li will do.

3 选什么专业好，我还没想清楚。学医呢，没有意思，
学文学呢，怕以后不好找工作。

選什麼專業好，我還沒想清楚。學醫呢，沒有意思，
學文學呢，怕以後不好找工作。

What's a good major to choose? I haven't figured it out. Studying medicine, on the
one hand, is boring. On the other hand, I'm worried that if I study literature, I won't
be able to find a job.

Chinese Chat

A friend is texting you about your plans for winter break. How would
you reply?

Friend:
寒假你想去哪儿旅行？

You:
...

Friend:
最好不要去太冷的地方。

You:
...

寒假你想去哪兒旅行？

...

最好不要去太冷的地方。

...

Messages   Contact

Send

Language Practice

A | INTERPRETIVE | **Goes with the territory** | PRESENTATIONAL |

Refer to the map of China at the top of page 318 to locate these provinces.

1 四川省

2 广东省/廣東省

3 湖南省

4 云南省/雲南省

5 山东省/山東省

6 A province of your choice

Then work with a partner and describe to each other where these provinces are located in China.

_____在中国的_____部。_____呢，
在中国的_____部。……

_____在中國的_____部。_____呢，
在中國的_____部。……

B | INTERPRETIVE | **Talk of the town** | INTERPERSONAL |

Refer to the map of China at the top of page 318 to locate these cities. Then order them according to latitude with the northernmost city first.

1 上海

2 北京

3 南京

4 天津

5 深圳

6 广州/廣州

7 杭州

8 哈尔滨/哈爾濱

9 A city of your choice

Finally, answer this question with a partner:

哪些城市靠海或者离海不远？

哪些城市靠海或者離海不遠？

Geography whiz

In pairs, locate 长江/長江 and 黄河/黃河 on the map of China at the bottom of page 318 and answer this question:

长江在黄河的北边还是南边？

長江在黃河的北邊還是南邊？

Then work with your partner to locate a mountain, a plateau, and a plain on another map of China. Write down the full names of the mountain, plateau, and plain, asking your instructor to help you pronounce them if necessary. Finally, tell your class where they are located.

1 _____山在_____省的____部。

2 _____高原在中国/中國的____部。

3 _____平原在中国/中國的____部。

D INTERPRETIVE **In the region** PRESENTATIONAL

Check the boxes to indicate the regions in which most of China's major mountain ranges, deserts, plateaus, and plains are located, referring to the map at the bottom of page 318.

	东南/東南	西南	东北/東北	西北
高山	☐	☐	☐	☐
高原	☐	☐	☐	☐
沙漠/沙漠	☐	☐	☐	☐
平原	☐	☐	☐	☐

First, recap your assertions in a short, organized paragraph.

Second, briefly describe the direction in which many major rivers run.

Third, describe how the population is distributed along the coast vs. in plateau areas.

In pairs, connect your three points with appropriate cohesive devices, and decide if there's anything else about Chinese geography that you can add.

Finally, present your basic introduction to the geography of China to your class. For a challenge, create a slideshow to enhance your presentation or film a presentation and upload it to YouTube.

Country to country

In pairs, collaborate to match the topics in the first column with the details pertaining to China or the U.S. in the second column, then work together to prepare an oral report comparing China and the U.S. Add other details to flesh out your report based on your own interests and knowledge. Avoid repetition and make sure your report flows well.

面积/面積	Beijing
人口	3.71 million mi^2
首都	more than 300 million
政治中心	New York
经济中心/經濟中心	more than 1.3 billion
文化中心	Shanghai
……	Washington, DC
	3.80 million mi^2
	…

F

INTERPERSONAL

Weighing the options

PRESENTATIONAL

Work with a partner to list the pros and cons of visiting the following places. Take into consideration location, climate, transportation, costs, tourist population, tourist sights, etc., e.g.:

北京◇名胜古迹多/名勝古蹟多◇人太多

Q: 去北京旅游有什么好？有什么不好？
去北京旅遊有什麼好？有什麼不好？

A: 北京的名胜古迹多，不过每個景點都是人山人海。
北京的名勝古蹟多，不過每個景點都是人山人海。

1 上海

2 南京

3 杭州

4 深圳

5 香港

6 台北

7 哈尔滨/哈爾濱

8 A city of your choice

Then recommend one destination that you think would be ideal to visit in summer or winter, e.g.:

夏天（or 冬天）去＿＿＿＿＿＿旅游最好不过了，因为
＿＿＿＿＿＿，＿＿＿＿＿＿；另外（or 再说），
＿＿＿＿＿＿……

夏天（or 冬天）去＿＿＿＿＿＿旅遊最好不過了，因為
＿＿＿＿＿＿，＿＿＿＿＿＿；另外（or 再說），
＿＿＿＿＿＿……

After listening to everyone's recommendations, group people with the same recommendations together. Open the floor to debate. Each group should defend its recommendations and point out why other places are not as good.

Words you can use to present your arguments in a coherent and cohesive manner include, but are not limited to:

认为/認為	不见得/不見得	考虑/考慮
同意	比较/比較	比方说/比方說
反对/反對	实际上/實際上	呢…呢…
看法	结果/結果	不是…，而是…
恐怕	建议/建議	

要么…，要么…/要麼…，要麼…

Finally, the class should vote on the best place in China to visit.

去＿＿＿＿＿＿旅游最好（or 最合适）。

去＿＿＿＿＿＿旅遊最好（or 最合適）。

Characterize it!

More characters

❶ 济　❷ 挤

Identify the common component.

What does the component represent?

❶ 濟　❷ 擠

Happy travels

Step 1 Divide the class into two groups: tour consultants and potential clients.

Step 2 As a group, the tour consultants should create a comprehensive list of possible questions in Chinese to help clients plan their trips. Make sure to include questions on travel dates, destinations, budgets, preferences for transportation, preferences for accommodations, etc.

Meanwhile, the clients should pair up and plan a travel itinerary. Make sure to include essential information on travel dates, destinations, means of transportation, accommodation, budget, etc. Then, brainstorm questions to ask a travel consultant to obtain the best service and advice possible.

Step 3 Finally, hold a travel fair as a class. In pairs, the consultants should set up travel booths to provide service.

Prospective clients should take turns visiting each stand. After visiting all the consultants, the clients should rate and comment on the consultants' services. Clients may offer feedback on whether the consultants were able to give suggestions based on their knowledge of the climate and geography of China; provide guidance on whether it's practical or realistic to travel to certain destinations with the given time frame, budget constraints, and personal preferences; and present alternatives by pointing out the advantages of different options.

The consultants should decide which of the clients' questions were most challenging yet reasonable, and whose itinerary was most intriguing yet feasible in terms of time and budget.

A WAY WITH WORDS

特别

你想到我们公司工作？
告诉我你有什么特长
(*cháng*)。

这个学校有很多特点，
所以给我留下很好的
印象。

Using the word/phrase in orange as a clue, try to figure out the meaning of the words/phrases in blue; consult a dictionary if necessary. Consider how the literal and extended senses are related in each case.

特別

你想到我們公司工作？
告訴我你有什麼特長
(*cháng*)。

這個學校有很多特點，
所以給我留下很好的
印象。

A woman of the Yao ethnic minority of Yunnan Province

REGIONAL DIFFERENCES

The contrast between Heilongjiang Province in the northeast and Yunnan Province in the southwest is illustrative of China's vast geographic variation.

Heilongjiang Province lies on the border with Russia and is well known for its long winters; the capital, Harbin, features historic Russian-style architecture. Since 1963, Harbin has hosted an annual ice and snow festival that draws many tourists from near and far. The festival includes an ice-sculpture contest and numerous colorful ice lanterns.

Yunnan Province could not be more different: much of Yunnan is mountainous, and its climate ranges from temperate to tropical. The rugged terrain and varied climate support a wide range of fauna and flora. Yunnan has been called a biodiversity hotspot, and an estimated fifteen thousand plant species and almost half of China's birds and mammals are found in Yunnan. There are fifty-six officially recognized nationalities in China. Yunnan Province is home to twenty-five distinct ethnic minorities, making it one of the country's most culturally diverse regions.

Yunnan Province is indicated on the map at the top of page 318. With the knowledge that Harbin is its capital, can you locate Heilongjiang Province?

One of the most famous early modern Chinese geographers was the late Ming traveler 徐霞客 (*Xú Xiákè*) (1587–1641). For thirty years, Xu explored many far-flung corners of the country and kept meticulous records of his travels. He was the first writer to describe the karst topography formed by the disintegration of limestone and gypsum that characterizes parts of southern China.

He also explored the source of the Yangtze River and corrected the widespread misconception that the Yangtze had its origin in the mountains of northwestern Sichuan. Unfortunately, no complete manuscript of his diaries has survived. Even so, his descriptions of the geography, climate, fauna, flora, and folk customs of China remain a rich mine of information for historians and scientists.

Xu Xiake

The karst landscape of Guilin

COMPARE & CONTRAST

1 Who is the most important or famous geographer or explorer in your country? What is his/her claim to fame?

2 The flooding of the North China Plain by the Yellow River has exerted a substantial influence on the course of Chinese history. One hypothesis states that the emphasis on stability in Chinese statecraft arose out of a need for greater organization in the face of the calamitous effects of the river's unpredictability. In your country, is there a geographic region that has historically been considered representative of a national story or struggle? What concepts and ideas about your country are embedded in notions of this region, and do they exert an effect on contemporary social and political culture?

MAJOR RIVERS

The Yangtze River in Nanjing

The Yellow River has historically been considered the cradle of Chinese civilization. Its middle reach is heavily silted with loess soil (黃土/黄土) from the Loess Plateau (黃土高原/黄土高原); silt deposition is responsible for the color of the river and the elevation of the riverbed many meters above surrounding areas. Loess soil is crumbly and porous; hence, areas abutting the river are fertile and easy to farm, but are also subject to monumental devastation when the river floods.

The longest river in China, the Yangtze River, is the third longest in the world. Some of China's most agriculturally productive land is found along the middle and lower parts of the river, and the river has historically been essential to transport in China's interior. Many of the country's most important cities are located along the Yangtze, including Chongqing, Wuhan, Nanjing, and Shanghai. The Three Gorges Dam, one of the world's largest hydropower stations, is near Chongqing.

SELECTED ADMINISTRATIVE DIVISIONS AND CITIES OF CHINA

北
西 东/東
南

哈尔滨/哈爾濱

新疆

北京

天津

山东/山東

南京

上海

四川

杭州

湖南

云南/雲南

These maps of China indicate the locations of every administrative division (labeled in black), city (labeled in red), and topographic feature you've learned so far. Research the names and locations of other administrative divisions, cities, and topographic features. Note that 北京, 天津, and 上海 are provincial-level cities.

广州/廣州

广东/廣東

深圳

TOPOGRAPHY OF CHINA

北
西 东/東
南

黄河/黃河

长江/長江

Legend
- ☐ 沙漠/沙漠
- ☐ 高原
- ☐ 平原
- ☐ 山
- ☐ 高山

Lesson Wrap-Up

Your home state or province has a trade office in China, and has asked a Chinese friend of yours
to prepare a presentation introducing the state or province. You've offered to help your friend.

- Using the list of topics below as a guide, conduct research on your state or province.

- Try to contextualize your facts, e.g., _____州在美国/美國
的____部，面积/面積是_____，是美国面积/美國面積（
最大 or 最小 or 第____大）的州. Use connective phrases to make sure that your
presentation flows, e.g., if the political and economic centers of your state or province do
not coincide, you can say: 虽然/雖然 X 是 Y （州 or 省）的政治中心，但
是 Y （州 or 省）的经济中心/經濟中心是 Z.

- Prepare a slideshow based on your research and share it with your friend/the class.

TOPICS:

o 地理方位

o 面积/面積

o 人口

o 州的首府 (shǒufǔ) 或者省的省会/省會 (shěnghuì)

o 自然条件/自然條件（靠海不靠海，是不是沙漠/
沙漠、平原、高原）

o 政治中心

o 经济中心/經濟中心

o 文化中心

o 最高的山

o 最长的河/最長的河

o 语言/語言 (yǔyán)

o 教育（有名的大学/大學）

o 运动/運動

o 旅游/旅遊（有哪些名胜古迹/名勝古蹟）

First, study the following description; pay particular attention to how the highlighted parts help the sentences flow smoothly from one to the next. Notice how:

- conjunctions (**而, 所以, 因为/因為**) and adverbs (**也**) can join sentences together
- place words (**那儿/那兒**) can serve as connective devices

中国地理

中国的面积很大。西边是高原，**那儿**有世界上最高的山，**而**东边是平原和大海，**所以**中国的河流，大多是从西往东流。**因为**东部和南部自然条件比较好，**所以**人口主要在这些地方，大城市**也**都靠海或者离海不远。**而**中国的西南，高山、高原多，西北呢，沙漠多，自然条件不太好，**所以**人口比较少。

中國地理

中國的面積很大。西邊是高原，**那兒**有世界上最高的山，**而**東邊是平原和大海，**所以**中國的河流，大多是從西往東流。**因為**東部和南部自然條件比較好，**所以**人口主要在這些地方，大城市**也**都靠海或者離海不遠。**而**中國的西南，高山、高原多，西北呢，沙漠多，自然條件不太好，**所以**人口比較少。

Second, briefly describe your country's geography. Study the cohesive devices highlighted in the example, and use as many as possible to string together your answers to the questions:

○ 你的国家的面积大不大？

你的國家的面積大不大？

○ 你的国家的大山主要在哪里？

你的國家的大山主要在哪裡？

○ 你的国家的河大多从哪儿往哪儿流？

你的國家的河大多從哪兒往哪兒流？

○ 大城市在哪些地方？

大城市在哪些地方？

○ 人口主要在哪些地方（东部，西部，中部……）？
为什么？

人口主要在哪些地方（東部，西部，中部……）？
為什麼？

○ 哪些地方人口比较少（东部，西部，中部……）？
为什么？

哪些地方人口比較少（東部，西部，中部……）？
為什麼？

Can-Do Check List ✓ **I can**

Before proceeding to Volume 4, make sure you can complete the following tasks in Chinese:

☐ Name cities located in China's north, southeast, and south
☐ Give a brief account of China's geographic features
☐ Describe similarities and differences between China and my own country in terms of territorial size, population, and terrain
☐ Talk about factors pertinent to selecting a travel destination
☐ Discuss an itinerary for travel to China, keeping in mind geography, climate, time, and budget

Hánjià kuài dào le, Zhāng Tiānmíng zhè jǐ tiān yìzhí zài kǎolǜ lǚxíng[a] de shìr. Tā de fùmǔ xīwàng tā qù tāmen de jiāxiāng Nánjīng kàn kan, Zhāng Tiānmíng yě hěn xiǎng dāng Lìshā de dǎoyóu, dài tā dào Zhōngguó de yì xiē dìfang zǒu zou. Chúle Nánjīng yǐwài, hái yīnggāi qù shénme dìfang ne? Wèile juédìng lǚxíng de lùxiàn, Zhāng Tiānmíng ná chu yì zhāng Zhōngguó dìtú, kàn le qǐ lai[1].

Lìshā, nǐ lái kàn kan Zhōngguó dìtú, kàn dào nǎr qù lǚxíng hǎo.

Kàn dìtú? Nǐ zhè ge zhúyi búcuò, wǒ yě zhèng xiǎng xué xue Zhōngguó dìlǐ ne. Wǒ duì Zhōngguó dìlǐ liǎojiě de tài shǎo le.

Wǒmen xiān dào Nánjīng, wǒ fùmǔ de jiāxiāng . . . Zài zhèli, zài Zhōngguó de dōngnán. Ránhòu nǐ xiǎng qù nǎr?

Zhè shì Hā'ěrbīn, duì ma? Qù Hā'ěrbīn ba.

Nǐ yíxiàzi yào cóng dōngnánbian pǎo dào zuì běibian qù?

Zuótiān diànshì li jièshào Hā'ěrbīn de bīngdēng le, hǎokàn jí le.

Bīngdēng hǎokàn shì hǎokàn, kěshì Hā'ěrbīn xiànzài lěng de bù déliǎo, xiàtiān zài qù ba.

Hǎo ba. Bú qù běibian, nà zuò huǒchē qù xībian ba, tīng-shuō Xīnjiāng shì ge hěn tèbié de dìfang.

Xīnjiāng zài xīběi, shíyuè jiù kāishǐ lěng qǐ lai[1] le, xiànzài qù bù héshì. Lìngwài, zuò huǒchē tài huā shí-jiān, xiàcì zài qù ba!

Zhè shì Chángjiāng, zhè shì Huánghé. Wǒmen zuò chuán qù kàn kan Chángjiāng huòzhě Huánghé de fēngjǐng ba.

Zuò chuán yào huā hěn cháng de shíjiān. Zhōngguó de héliú[b], dàduō cóng xī wǎng dōng liú, rúguǒ cóng dōng wǎng xī zǒu, shíjiān gèng cháng.

Wèishénme Zhōngguó de héliú dàduō cóng xī wǎng dōng liú ne?

Yīnwèi Zhōngguó xībù shì gāoyuán, nàr yǒu shìjiè shang zuì gāo de shān. Ér[2] dōngbian shì píngyuán hé dà hǎi.

Hǎoxiàng dà chéngshì dōu kào hǎi huòzhě lí hǎi bù yuǎn. Nǐ kàn, zài běibian, zhè shì Běijīng, Tiānjīn; dōng-nánbian, zhèr yǒu Shànghǎi, Nánjīng, nánbian zhèli, shì Guǎngzhōu hé Shēnzhèn.

Nǐ shuō de méi cuò. Zhōngguó de rénkǒu zhǔyào zài dōngbù[c] hé nánbù. Xīnán ne, gāoshān, gāoyuán duō, xīběi ne, shāmò duō, zìrán tiáojiàn bú tài hǎo, suǒyǐ rénkǒu bǐjiào shǎo.

Wǒ juéde Zhōngguó de dìxíng hé Měiguó yǒu diǎnr xiàng.

Nǐ shuō de yǒu dàoli. Hái yǒu, Zhōngguó hé Měiguó de miànjī yě chàbuduō, kěshì rénkǒu shì Měiguó de sì bèi duō. Tīngshuō, guò jié huòzhě fàng jià de shíhou, Zhōng-guó de lǚyóu jǐngdiǎn dàochù dōu shì rén shān rén hǎi, jǐ de hěn.

Shì ma?

Háihǎo, wǒmen dào Zhōngguó de shíhou, xuésheng hái méi fàng jià, yě bú shì guò nián guò jié.

Zhōngguó zhème dà, wǒmen de hánjià nàme duǎn, dàodǐ qù nǎr lǚyóu hǎo ne?

Wǒ juéde qù Yúnnán zuì hǎo búguò le[3].

Yúnnán zài nǎli? . . .Wǒ zhǎo dào le, zài zhèr, shì yí ge shěng, zài xīnánbù. Nàr dōngtiān bù lěng ma?

Tīngshuō Yúnnán yǒu xiē dìfang sìjì rú chūn, yì nián sìjì dōu bù lěng bú rè.

Wǒ jìde diànshì li shuō guo[4], Yúnnán fēngjǐng hǎo, shǎoshù mínzú[d] duō, shì ge lǚyóu de hǎo dìfang.

Hǎo, Yúnnán, juédìng le, jiù qù Yúnnán.

A | **Chinese character crossword puzzles**

Many of the new words and phrases from Lessons 6–10 share the same characters. In these puzzles, the common character is positioned in the center of the cluster of bubbles. The triangular points indicate which way you should read the words. Work with a partner and see how many association bubbles you can complete, adding more bubbles if you can think of additional words/phrases, e.g.:

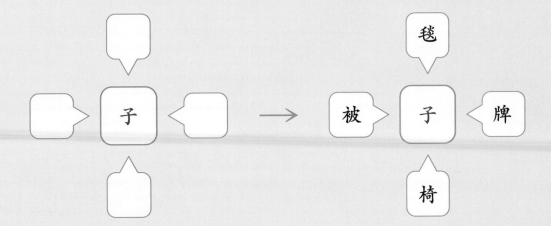

1

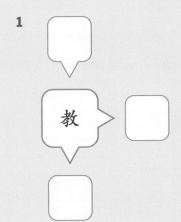

2

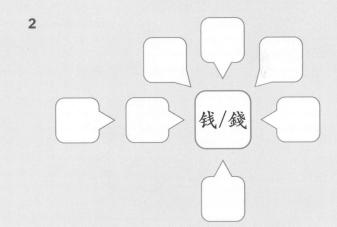

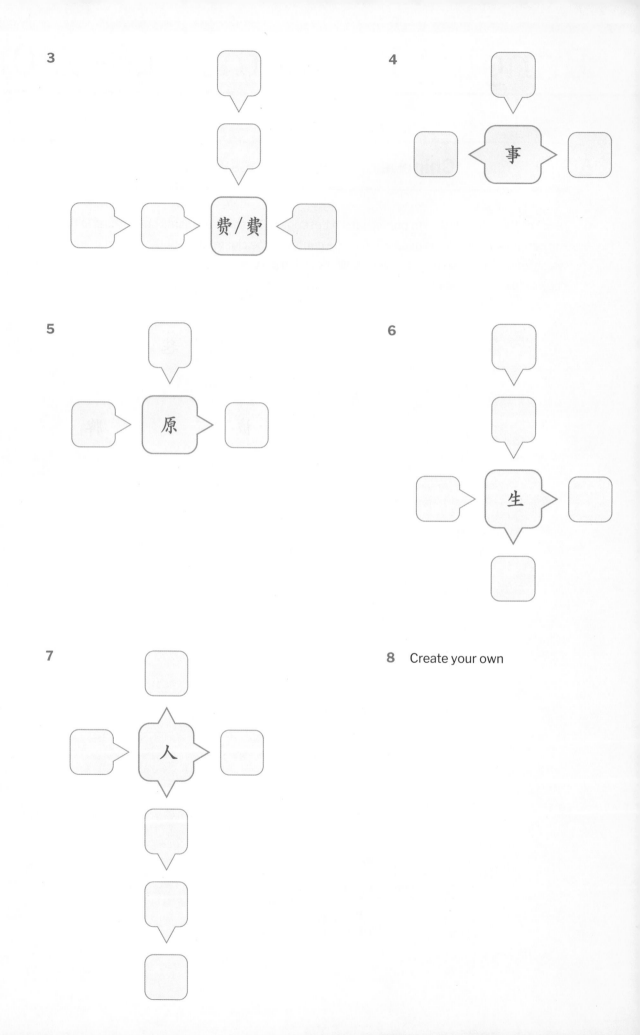

Matching words

Draw lines to connect each verb with its proper object.

交	玩笑
安排	资料/資料
解决/解決	看法
受（到）	经验/經驗
减轻/減輕	学费/學費
取得	软件/軟件
查	负担/負擔
下载/下載	教育
同意	问题/問題
开/開	时间/時間

Make a word list

First, brainstorm with a partner and ask each other what words come to mind when you want to:

- describe a compatible boyfriend/girlfriend
- talk about the role that the Internet plays in your daily life
- discuss how to shop intelligently
- debate how to strike a balance between study and play
- plan a trip to China

Then, brainstorm with your partner and ask each other what words or phrases will help if you wish to:

- agree or disagree
- inquire if everything is OK
- apologize for your language or behavior
- discuss the pros and cons of something
- make comparisons
- make suggestions

D | Organize your thoughts

Select a topic from the first list in (C). In pairs, discuss:

- what you want to say
- what words or phrases from the second list in (C) will help your express your opinion
- what should be said first, next, and last
- what transitions may be needed
- what cohesive devices should be used to connect your sentences

It's a good idea to jot down sentences that you wish to say, then number them in the order you think they should be presented. Consider how you can make your list into a coherent discourse. Once you've finished, present your work to the class.

E | Go with the flow

How would you make the following flow better in paragraph form? Don't forget to pay attention to time words, place expressions, and pronouns.

昨天是星期六，我去同学家给他过生日	昨天是星期六，我去同學家給他過生日
我开车去他家	我開車去他家
我看见了很多同学，有男同学，也有女同学	我看見了很多同學，有男同學，也有女同學
我们唱卡拉OK	我們唱卡拉OK
我们吃生日蛋糕了	我們吃生日蛋糕了
我玩得很高兴	我玩得很高興
我很晚才回家	我很晚才回家

_____

_____

_____

_____

The Chinese-English index is alphabetized according to *pinyin*. Words containing the same Chinese characters are first grouped together. Homonyms appear in the order of their tonal pronunciation (i.e., first tones first, second tones second, third tones third, fourth tones fourth, and neutral tones last).

Simplified	Traditional	Pinyin	Part of Speech	English	Lesson
A					
哎	哎	āi	excl	(exclamatory particle to express surprise or dissatisfaction or to remind)	1
哎呀	哎呀	āiyā	interj	gosh, ah (an exclamation to express surprise)	4
爱好	愛好	àihào	n/v	hobby, interest; to love (something)	6
安排	安排	ānpái	v	to arrange	9
安全	安全	ānquán	adj	safe	1
B					
摆	擺	bǎi	v	to put, to place	2
搬家	搬家	bān jiā	vo	to move (one's residence)	1
帮忙	幫忙	bāng máng	vo	to help	1
帮助	幫助	bāngzhù	v/n	to help; help	7
抱怨	抱怨	bàoyuàn	v	to complain	9
倍	倍	bèi	m	(measure word for times by which something is multiplied)	10
背景	背景	bèijǐng	n	background	6
被子	被子	bèizi	n	comforter, quilt	2
比方说	比方說	bǐfāng shuō		for example	3
比较	比較	bǐjiào	adv/v	relatively, comparatively, rather; to compare	1
毕业	畢業	bì yè	vo	to graduate	5
标准	標準	biāozhǔn	n/adj	criterion; standard	4
冰灯	冰燈	bīngdēng	n	ice lantern	10
菠菜	菠菜	bōcài	n	spinach	3

Simplified	Traditional	Pinyin	Part of Speech	English	Lesson
博客	博客	*bókè*	n	blog	7
博士	博士	*bóshì*	n	doctorate (academic degree), Dr. (academic title)	9
部	部	*bù*	n	part, section	10
不见得	不見得	*bújiànde* [*bùjiànde*]*		not necessarily	1
不是…而是…	不是…而是…	*búshì…érshì…* [*bùshì…érshì…*]		it's not…but…	9
不停	不停	*bùtíng*	adv	continuously, incessantly	6
不同	不同	*bù tóng*		different, not the same	6

C

Simplified	Traditional	Pinyin	Part of Speech	English	Lesson
菜单	菜單	*càidān*	n	menu	3
餐馆儿	餐館兒	*cānguǎnr*	n	restaurant	2
餐巾	餐巾	*cānjīn*	n	napkin	3
层	層	*céng*	m	(measure word for stories of a building)	2
长	長	*cháng*	adj	long	1
长江	長江	*Chángjiāng*	pn	Yangtze River	10
吵架	吵架	*chǎo jià*	vo	to quarrel	6
迟到	遲到	*chídào*	v	to arrive late	7
出生	出生	*chūshēng*	v	to be born	1
船	船	*chuán*	n	boat, ship	10
纯棉	純棉	*chúnmián*	adj	pure cotton, one-hundred-percent cotton	4
存	存	*cún*	v	to deposit, to accumulate	8

D

Simplified	Traditional	Pinyin	Part of Speech	English	Lesson
答应	答應	*dāying*	v	to agree (to do something), to promise, to answer	6
打交道	打交道	*dǎ jiāodào*	vo	to deal with	5

* For vocabulary items starting with 不 or 一, we have included the *pinyin* with the stand-alone tone of these two characters in square brackets. However, the *pinyin* listed first indicates how the characters are conventionally pronounced as a lexical unit.

Simplified	Traditional	Pinyin	Part of Speech	English	Lesson
大多	大多	dàduō	adv	mostly, for the most part	10
大人	大人	dàren	n	adult	8
待	待	dāi	v	to stay	7
贷款	貸款	dàikuǎn	n/vo	loan; to provide a loan	8
到处	到處	dàochù	adv	all around, all over	10
到底	到底	dàodǐ	adv	what on earth, what in the world, in the end	6
道理	道理	dàoli	n	reason, sense	4
道歉	道歉	dào qiàn	vo	to apologize	6
低	低	dī	adj	low	8
地道	地道	dìdao	adj	authentic, genuine	2
地理	地理	dìlǐ	n	geography	10
地形	地形	dìxíng	n	terrain, topography	10
电影院	電影院	diànyǐngyuàn	n	movie theater	6
丢三拉四	丟三拉四	diū sān là sì		scatterbrained, forgetful	6
栋	棟	dòng	m	(measure word for buildings)	2
读书	讀書	dú shū	vo	to attend school, to study, to read aloud	8
短	短	duǎn	adj	short	10

E

Simplified	Traditional	Pinyin	Part of Speech	English	Lesson
而	而	ér	conj	(conjunction to connect two clauses)	10

F

Simplified	Traditional	Pinyin	Part of Speech	English	Lesson
发生	發生	fāshēng	v	to happen, to occur, to take place	6
番	番	fān	m	(measure word for type or kind)	9
翻译	翻譯	fānyì	v/n	to translate; interpreter, translation	7
反对	反對	fǎnduì	v	to oppose	9

Simplified	Traditional	Pinyin	Part of Speech	English	Lesson
非…不可	非…不可	*fēi…bù kě*		have to, nothing but … would do	4
分手	分手	*fēn shǒu*	vo	to break up, to part company	6
风景	風景	*fēngjǐng*	n	scenic landscape, scenery	10
负担	負擔	*fùdān*	n	burden	8
G					
干衣机	乾衣機	*gānyījī*	n	(clothes) dryer	2
敢	敢	*gǎn*	mv	to dare	7
感觉	感覺	*gǎnjué*	n/v	feeling, sense perception; to feel, to perceive	7
钢琴	鋼琴	*gāngqín*	n	piano	9
高原	高原	*gāoyuán*	n	plateau (lit. high field)	10
高中	高中	*gāozhōng*	n	senior high school	6
各	各	*gè*	pr	each, every	3
根本	根本	*gēnběn*	adv	at all, simply	6
弓	弓	*gōng*	n	bow (for archery)	1
供	供	*gōng*	v	to provide, to support financially	8
工学院	工學院	*gōng xuéyuàn*	n	school of engineering	5
工资	工資	*gōngzī*	n	wages, pay	8
购物	購物	*gòuwù*	vo	to shop	4
挂	掛	*guà*	v	to hang, to hang up	2
乖	乖	*guāi*	adj	obedient, well-behaved (of children)	8
管	管	*guǎn*	v	to control, manage, to mind, to care about	5
管理学院	管理學院	*guǎnlǐ xuéyuàn*	n	school of management	5
广东	廣東	*Guǎngdōng*	pn	Guangdong	3
广州	廣州	*Guǎngzhōu*	pn	Guangzhou	10

Simplified	Traditional	Pinyin	Part of Speech	English	Lesson
柜子	櫃子	*guìzi*	n	cabinet, cupboard	2
过几天	過幾天	*guò jǐ tiān*		in a few days	2
过节	過節	*guò jié*	vo	to celebrate a holiday	10
H					
哈尔滨	哈爾濱	*Hā'ěrbīn*	pn	Harbin	10
海	海	*hǎi*	n	sea, ocean	10
害	害	*hài*	v	to cause trouble, to harm	7
杭州	杭州	*Hángzhōu*	pn	Hangzhou	3
好处	好處	*hǎochu*	n	advantage, benefit	1
好看	好看	*hǎokàn*	adj	nice-looking, attractive	4
河流	河流	*héliú*	n	river	10
湖南	湖南	*Húnán*	pn	Hunan	3
画画儿	畫畫兒	*huà huàr*	vo	to draw, to paint	9
化学	化學	*huàxué*	n	chemistry	5
黄河	黃河	*Huánghé*	pn	Yellow River	10
火车	火車	*huǒchē*	n	train	10
J					
鸡	雞	*jī*	n	chicken	3
急忙	急忙	*jímáng*	adv	hastily, in a hurry	7
挤	擠	*jǐ*	adj/v	crowded; to push against, to squeeze	10
加	加	*jiā*	v	to add	4
家教	家教	*jiājiào*	n	tutor	8
家庭	家庭	*jiātíng*	n	family, household	8
家乡	家鄉	*jiāxiāng*	n	hometown, place of family origin	10

Simplified	Traditional	Pinyin	Part of Speech	English	Lesson
价钱	價錢	*jiàqian*	n	price	4
减轻	減輕	*jiǎnqīng*	v	to lessen	8
建议	建議	*jiànyì*	n/v	suggestion; to suggest	5
将来	將來	*jiānglái*	n	future	5
奖学金	獎學金	*jiǎngxuéjīn*	n	scholarship money	8
交	交	*jiāo*	v	to hand over, to turn in	8
交朋友	交朋友	*jiāo péngyou*	vo	to make friends	6
叫	叫	*jiào*	v	to make (someone do something)	6
叫（菜）	叫（菜）	*jiào (cài)*	v (o)	to order (food)	3
教授	教授	*jiàoshòu*	n	professor	5
教育	教育	*jiàoyù*	n/v	education; to educate	8
结果	結果	*jiéguǒ*	conj/n	as a result; result	7
结婚	結婚	*jié hūn*	vo	to get married, to marry	9
解决	解決	*jiějué*	v	to solve, to resolve	5
借	借	*jiè*	v	to borrow, to lend	8
芥兰	芥蘭	*jièlán*	n	Chinese broccoli	3
金融	金融	*jīnróng*	n	finance, banking	5
经济	經濟	*jīngjì*	n	economics, economy	5
经验	經驗	*jīngyàn*	n/v	experience; to experience	5
景点	景點	*jǐngdiǎn*	n	scenic spot, tourist spot	10
旧	舊	*jiù*	adj	old (of things)	2
决定	決定	*juédìng*	v/n	to decide; decision	5
K					
卡拉OK	卡拉OK	*kǎlā ōukēi*	n	karaoke	7
开朗	開朗	*kāilǎng*	adj	extroverted, open and sunny in disposition	6

Simplified	Traditional	Pinyin	Part of Speech	English	Lesson
开玩笑	開玩笑	*kāi wánxiào*	vo	to crack a joke, to joke	3
开学	開學	*kāi xué*	vo	to begin a new semester	1
看法	看法	*kànfǎ*	n	point of view	9
考虑	考慮	*kǎolǜ*	v	to consider	3
柯林	柯林	*Kē Lín*	pn	(a personal name)	1
可靠	可靠	*kěkào*	adj	dependable	7
空	空	*kōng*	adj	empty	2
空调	空調	*kōngtiáo*	n	air conditioning	2
恐怕	恐怕	*kǒngpà*	adv	I'm afraid that, I think perhaps, probably	2
口味	口味	*kǒuwèi*	n	(personal) taste	3
筷子	筷子	*kuàizi*	n	chopsticks	3

L

Simplified	Traditional	Pinyin	Part of Speech	English	Lesson
垃圾	垃圾	*lājī*	n	garbage, trash	7
拉	拉	*là*	v	to leave (something) behind inadvertently (colloq.)	1
辣	辣	*là*	adj	spicy	3
老是	老是	*lǎoshì*	adv	always	7
离开	離開	*lí kāi*	vc	to leave, to depart from	7
理解	理解	*lǐjiě*	v	to understand	9
李哲	李哲	*Lǐ Zhé*	pn	(a personal name)	5
厉害	厲害	*lìhai*	adj	terrible, formidable	9
丽莎	麗莎	*Lìshā*	pn	(a personal name)	3
历史	歷史	*lìshǐ*	n	history	5
良好	良好	*liánghǎo*	adj	good, fine (literary)	8
辆	輛	*liàng*	m	(measure word for vehicles)	1

Simplified	Traditional	Pinyin	Part of Speech	English	Lesson
了解	了解	*liǎojiě*	v	to understand, to know about, to be informed	10
林雪梅	林雪梅	*Lín Xuěméi*	pn	(a personal name)	3
零用钱	零用錢	*língyòngqián*	n	allowance, spending money	8
流	流	*liú*	v	to flow	10
留学	留學	*liú xué*	vo	to study abroad	9
留学生	留學生	*liúxuéshēng*	n	study-abroad student	3
遛	遛	*liù*	v	to walk (an animal), to stroll	8
路线	路線	*lùxiàn*	n	route, itinerary	10
旅游	旅遊	*lǚyóu*	v/n	to travel (for pleasure); (pleasure) travel	10
落伍	落伍	*luòwǔ*	v	to lag behind, to be outdated	7

M

Simplified	Traditional	Pinyin	Part of Speech	English	Lesson
马虎	馬虎	*mǎhu*	adj	careless, perfunctory, mediocre	6
马路	馬路	*mǎlù*	n	road, street	2
猫	貓	*māo*	n	cat	8
毛巾	毛巾	*máojīn*	n	towel	4
毛衣	毛衣	*máoyī*	n	woolen sweater	4
门	門	*mén*	n	door	2
门	門	*mén*	m	(measure word for academic courses)	5
门口	門口	*ménkǒu*	n	doorway, entrance	3
迷	迷	*mí*	n/v	fan; to be infatuated with	6
免费	免費	*miǎnfèi*	v/vo	free of charge [lit. exempt from paying the fee]	7
面积	面積	*miànjī*	n	area (of land)	10
民族	民族	*mínzú*	n	ethnic group, nationality	10

Simplified	Traditional	Pinyin	Part of Speech	English	Lesson
名牌	名牌	*míngpái*	n	famous brand, name brand	4
墨西哥	墨西哥	*Mòxīgē*	pn	Mexico	9
N					
难怪	難怪	*nánguài*	adv	no wonder	8
南京	南京	*Nánjīng*	pn	Nanjing	10
嫩	嫩	*nèn*	adj	tender	3
牛仔裤	牛仔褲	*niúzǎikù*	n	jeans	4
农村	農村	*nóngcūn*	n	countryside, village, rural area	8
P					
牌子	牌子	*páizi*	n	brand	4
陪	陪	*péi*	v	to accompany	6
碰见	碰見	*pèng jiàn*	vc	to run into (a person by chance)	5
平原	平原	*píngyuán*	n	plain (lit. flat field)	10
Q					
其他	其他	*qítā*	pr	other, else	5
欠	欠	*qiàn*	v	to owe	8
清淡	清淡	*qīngdàn*	adj	light in flavor	3
轻松	輕鬆	*qīngsōng*	adj	light, relaxed	5
清蒸	清蒸	*qīngzhēng*	v	to steam (food without heavy sauce)	3
取得	取得	*qǔdé*	v	to obtain, to gain, to acquire	8
R					
人口	人口	*rénkǒu*	n	population	10
人山人海	人山人海	*rén shān rén hǎi*		huge crowds of people (lit. mountains and seas of people)	10

Simplified	Traditional	Pinyin	Part of Speech	English	Lesson
认为	認為	*rènwéi*	v	to think, to consider	9
日用品	日用品	*rìyòngpǐn*	n	daily necessities	2
软件	軟件	*ruǎnjiàn*	n	software	7
S					
嫂子	嫂子	*sǎozi*	n	older brother's wife	9
沙漠	沙漠	*shāmò*	n	desert	10
山	山	*shān*	n	mountain, hill	10
上瘾	上癮	*shàng yǐn*	vo	to become addicted	7
少数	少數	*shǎoshù*	n	few, minority (lit. small number)	10
社会	社會	*shèhuì*	n	society	9
设计	設計	*shèjì*	v/n	to design; design	9
申请	申請	*shēnqǐng*	v	to apply (to a school or job)	5
深圳	深圳	*Shēnzhèn*	pn	Shenzhen	10
生	生	*shēng*	v	to give birth to, to be born	8
生活	生活	*shēnghuó*	n/v	(day-to-day) life; to live	1
生气	生氣	*shēng qì*	vo	to get angry	6
省	省	*shěng*	n	province (administrative division)	10
省钱	省錢	*shěng qián*	vo	to save money, to economize	1
省下来	省下來	*shěng xia lai*	vc	to save (money, time)	5
时代	時代	*shídài*	n	era, age	7
实际上	實際上	*shíjìshang*	adv	in fact, in reality, actually	6
时髦	時髦	*shímáo*	adj	fashionable, stylish	4
适合	適合	*shìhé*	v	to suit	8
世界	世界	*shìjiè*	n	world	5

Simplified	Traditional	Pinyin	Part of Speech	English	Lesson
事业	事業	*shìyè*	n	career, undertaking	9
适应	適應	*shìyìng*	v	to adapt, to become accustomed to	1
收入	收入	*shōurù*	n	income	8
受不了	受不了	*shòu bu liǎo*	vc	cannot take it, unable to bear	5
受到	受到	*shòu dào*	vc	to receive	8
数字	數字	*shùzì*	n	numeral, figure, digit	5
税	稅	*shuì*	n	tax	4
说不定	說不定	*shuōbudìng*	adv	perhaps, maybe	6
硕士	碩士	*shuòshì*	n	master's (academic degree)	9
四川	四川	*Sìchuān*	pn	Sichuan	3
四季如春	四季如春	*sìjì rú chūn*		spring-like all year round	10

			T		
台	台	*tái*	m	(measure word for machines)	2
态度	態度	*tàidu*	n	attitude	6
谈	談	*tán*	v	to talk, to discuss	5
毯子	毯子	*tǎnzi*	n	blanket	2
讨论	討論	*tǎolùn*	v	to discuss	5
T恤衫	T恤衫	*tīxùshān*	n	T-shirt	4
提	提	*tí*	v	to mention, to bring up	6
天津	天津	*Tiānjīn*	pn	Tianjin	10
条件	條件	*tiáojiàn*	n	condition	10
童年	童年	*tóngnián*	n	childhood	9
同屋	同屋	*tóngwū*	n	roommate	2
同意	同意	*tóngyì*	v	to agree	4

Simplified	Traditional	Pinyin	Part of Speech	English	Lesson
				W	
外卖	外賣	*wàimài*	n	takeout	7
完全	完全	*wánquán*	adv/adj	completely, fully; complete, whole	9
网络	網絡	*wǎngluò*	n	network, the Internet	7
网站	網站	*wǎngzhàn*	n	website	7
望女成凤	望女成鳳	*wàng nǚ chéng fèng*		to hope that one's daughter will become successful (lit. to hope that one's daughter will become a phoenix)	9
望子成龙	望子成龍	*wàng zǐ chéng lóng*		to hope that one's son will become successful (lit. to hope that one's son will become a dragon)	9
微信	微信	*Wēixìn*	pn	WeChat	3
喂	餵	*wèi*	v	to feed	8
味道	味道	*wèidao*	n	taste, flavor (of food)	3
卫生纸	衛生紙	*wèishēngzhǐ*	n	toilet paper	4
文具	文具	*wénjù*	n	stationery, writing supplies	2
文学	文學	*wénxué*	n	literature	5
文章	文章	*wénzhāng*	n	essay, article	5
屋子	屋子	*wūzi*	n	room	7
无论	無論	*wúlùn*	conj	regardless of . . . , whether it be . . .	4
				X	
洗	洗	*xǐ*	v	to wash	2
洗衣粉	洗衣粉	*xǐyīfěn*	n	laundry powder	4
洗衣机	洗衣機	*xǐyījī*	n	washing machine	2
系	系	*xì*	n	academic department (of a college or university)	5
下载	下載	*xiàzài*	v	to download	7

Simplified	Traditional	Pinyin	Part of Speech	English	Lesson
咸	鹹	*xián*	adj	salty	3
现金	現金	*xiànjīn*	n	cash	4
香	香	*xiāng*	adj	fragrant, pleasant-smelling	3
相处	相處	*xiāngchǔ*	v	to get along	6
像	像	*xiàng*	v	to resemble, to be like	4
小学	小學	*xiǎoxué*	n	elementary school	9
校内	校內	*xiào nèi*		on campus	1
校外	校外	*xiào wài*		off campus	1
心	心	*xīn*	n	heart, mind	6
心事	心事	*xīnshì*	n	something that weighs on one's mind	6
新疆	新疆	*Xīnjiāng*	pn	Xinjiang	10
新生	新生	*xīnshēng*	n	new student	1
新闻	新聞	*xīnwén*	n	news	7
新鲜	新鮮	*xīnxian*	adj	fresh	3
幸福	幸福	*xìngfú*	n/adj	happiness; happy	9
需要	需要	*xūyào*	v/n	to need; needs	4
选	選	*xuǎn*	v	to choose	5
选择	選擇	*xuǎnzé*	n/v	choice; to choose	9
学分	學分	*xuéfēn*	n	academic credit	5
学位	學位	*xuéwèi*	n	academic degree	5

Y

Simplified	Traditional	Pinyin	Part of Speech	English	Lesson
压力	壓力	*yālì*	n	pressure	8
牙膏	牙膏	*yágāo*	n	toothpaste	4
研究生	研究生	*yánjiūshēng*	n	graduate student	1

Simplified	Traditional	Pinyin	Part of Speech	English	Lesson
严重	嚴重	*yánzhòng*	adj	serious, grave	7
演唱会	演唱會	*yǎnchànghuì*	n	vocal concert	6
要么···, 要么···	要麼···, 要麼···	*yàome ..., yàome ...*	conj	if it's not ... it's ..., either ... or ...	5
钥匙	鑰匙	*yàoshi*	n	key	6
衣柜	衣櫃	*yīguì*	n	wardrobe	2
衣食住行	衣食住行	*yī shí zhù xíng*		basic necessities of life (lit. food, clothing, shelter, and transportation)	7
一会儿	一會兒	*yíhuìr [yīhuìr]*	n+m	in a moment, a little while	4
一下子	一下子	*yíxiàzi [yīxiàzi]*	adv	in an instant, all of a sudden	10
一般	一般	*yìbān [yībān]*	adv	generally	2
一干二净	一乾二淨	*yì gān èr jìng [yī gān èr jìng]*		completely, thoroughly	6
移民	移民	*yímín*	n/v	immigrant; to immigrate	9
意见	意見	*yìjiàn*	n	opinion	5
银行	銀行	*yínháng*	n	bank	8
影响	影響	*yǐngxiǎng*	v/n	to influence, to have an impact; influence	8
油	油	*yóu*	n/adj	oil; oily	3
游戏	遊戲	*yóuxì*	n	game	7
有机	有機	*yǒujī*	adj	organic	3
有用	有用	*yǒuyòng*	adj	useful	7
原来	原來	*yuánlái*	adv/adj	as a matter of fact; original, former	6
云南	雲南	*Yúnnán*	pn	Yunnan	10
Z					
杂志	雜誌	*zázhì*	n	magazine	7
在乎	在乎	*zàihu*	v	to mind, to care	4

Simplified	Traditional	Pinyin	Part of Speech	English	Lesson
张天明	張天明	*Zhāng Tiānmíng*	pn	(a personal name)	1
着急	著急	*zháojí*	v	to worry	2
哲学	哲學	*zhéxué*	n	philosophy	5
真的	真的	*zhēn de*	adv	really, truly	2
整天	整天	*zhěng tiān*		all day long	5
政府	政府	*zhèngfǔ*	n	government	8
正好	正好	*zhènghǎo*	adv	coincidentally	3
挣钱	掙錢	*zhèng qián*	vo	to earn money	5
知识	知識	*zhīshi*	n	knowledge	9
侄女	侄女	*zhínǚ*	n	brother's daughter	9
只好	只好	*zhǐhǎo*	adv	to be forced to, to have no choice but	4
质量	質量	*zhìliàng*	n	quality	4
重要	重要	*zhòngyào*	adj	important	7
主意	主意	*zhúyi*	n	idea	3
主要	主要	*zhǔyào*	adj	main, principal	10
资料	資料	*zīliào*	n	material (reference, academic)	7
自然	自然	*zìrán*	n/adj	nature; natural	10
自由	自由	*zìyóu*	adj	free, unconstrained	1
尊重	尊重	*zūnzhòng*	v	to respect	9
做法	做法	*zuòfǎ*	n	way of doing things, course of action	9

Vocabulary Index (English-Chinese), Volume 3

The English-Chinese index is organized based on the alphabetical order of the English definitions. For ease of reference, indefinite articles and definite articles are omitted when they are the beginning of a phrase.

English	Simplified	Traditional	Pinyin	Part of Speech	Lesson
A					
academic credit	学分	學分	xuéfēn	n	5
academic degree	学位	學位	xuéwèi	n	5
academic department (of a college or university)	系	系	xì	n	5
accompany	陪	陪	péi	v	6
adapt, become accustomed to	适应	適應	shìyìng	v	1
add	加	加	jiā	v	4
adult	大人	大人	dàren	n	8
advantage, benefit	好处	好處	hǎochu	n	1
agree	同意	同意	tóngyì	v	4
agree (to do something), promise, answer	答应	答應	dāying	v	6
air conditioning	空调	空調	kōngtiáo	n	2
all around, all over	到处	到處	dàochù	adv	10
all day long	整天	整天	zhěng tiān		5
allowance, spending money	零用钱	零用錢	língyòngqián	n	8
always	老是	老是	lǎoshì	adv	7
apologize	道歉	道歉	dào qiàn	vo	6
apply (to a school or job)	申请	申請	shēnqǐng	v	5
area (of land)	面积	面積	miànjī	n	10
arrange	安排	安排	ānpái	v	9
arrive late	迟到	遲到	chídào	v	7

English	Simplified	Traditional	Pinyin	Part of Speech	Lesson
as a matter of fact; original, former	原来	原來	yuánlái	adv/adj	6
as a result; result	结果	結果	jiéguǒ	conj/n	7
at all, simply	根本	根本	gēnběn	adv	6
attend school, study, read aloud	读书	讀書	dú shū	vo	8
attitude	态度	態度	tàidu	n	6
authentic, genuine	地道	地道	dìdao	adj	2
B					
background	背景	背景	bèijǐng	n	6
bank	银行	銀行	yínháng	n	8
basic necessities of life (lit. food, clothing, shelter, and transportation)	衣食住行	衣食住行	yī shí zhù xíng		7
be born	出生	出生	chūshēng	v	1
be forced to, have no choice but	只好	只好	zhǐhǎo	adv	4
become addicted	上瘾	上癮	shàng yǐn	vo	7
begin a new semester	开学	開學	kāi xué	vo	1
blanket	毯子	毯子	tǎnzi	n	2
blog	博客	博客	bókè	n	7
boat, ship	船	船	chuán	n	10
borrow, lend	借	借	jiè	v	8
bow (for archery)	弓	弓	gōng	n	1
brand	牌子	牌子	páizi	n	4
break up, part company	分手	分手	fēn shǒu	vo	6
brother's daughter	侄女	侄女	zhínǚ	n	9
burden	负担	負擔	fùdān	n	8

English	Simplified	Traditional	Pinyin	Part of Speech	Lesson
		C			
cabinet, cupboard	柜子	櫃子	*guìzi*	n	2
cannot take it, unable to bear	受不了	受不了	*shòu bu liǎo*	vc	5
career, undertaking	事业	事業	*shìyè*	n	9
careless, perfunctory, mediocre	马虎	馬虎	*mǎhu*	adj	6
cash	现金	現金	*xiànjīn*	n	4
cat	猫	貓	*māo*	n	8
cause trouble, harm	害	害	*hài*	v	7
celebrate a holiday	过节	過節	*guò jié*	vo	10
chemistry	化学	化學	*huàxué*	n	5
chicken	鸡	雞	*jī*	n	3
childhood	童年	童年	*tóngnián*	n	9
Chinese broccoli	芥兰	芥蘭	*jièlán*	n	3
choice; choose	选择	選擇	*xuǎnzé*	n/v	9
choose	选	選	*xuǎn*	v	5
chopsticks	筷子	筷子	*kuàizi*	n	3
(clothes) dryer	干衣机	乾衣機	*gānyījī*	n	2
coincidentally	正好	正好	*zhènghǎo*	adv	3
comforter, quilt	被子	被子	*bèizi*	n	2
complain	抱怨	抱怨	*bàoyuàn*	v	9
completely, fully; complete, whole	完全	完全	*wánquán*	adv/adj	9
completely, thoroughly	一干二净	一乾二淨	*yì gān èr jìng*		6
condition	条件	條件	*tiáojiàn*	n	10

English	Simplified	Traditional	Pinyin	Part of Speech	Lesson
(conjunction to connect two clauses)	而	而	*ér*	conj	10
consider	考虑	考慮	*kǎolù*	v	3
continuously, incessantly	不停	不停	*bùtíng*	adv	6
control, manage, mind, care about	管	管	*guǎn*	v	5
countryside, village, rural area	农村	農村	*nóngcūn*	n	8
crack a joke, joke	开玩笑	開玩笑	*kāi wánxiào*	vo	3
criterion; standard	标准	標準	*biāozhǔn*	n/adj	4
crowded; push against, squeeze	挤	擠	*jǐ*	adj/v	10

D

English	Simplified	Traditional	Pinyin	Part of Speech	Lesson
daily necessities	日用品	日用品	*rìyòngpǐn*	n	2
dare	敢	敢	*gǎn*	mv	7
deal with	打交道	打交道	*dǎ jiāodào*	vo	5
decide; decision	决定	決定	*juédìng*	v/n	5
dependable	可靠	可靠	*kěkào*	adj	7
deposit, accumulate	存	存	*cún*	v	8
desert	沙漠	沙漠	*shāmò*	n	10
design; design	设计	設計	*shèjì*	v/n	9
different, not the same	不同	不同	*bù tóng*		6
discuss	讨论	討論	*tǎolùn*	v	5
doctorate (academic degree), Dr. (academic title)	博士	博士	*bóshì*	n	9
door	门	門	*mén*	n	2
doorway, entrance	门口	門口	*ménkǒu*	n	3
download	下载	下載	*xiàzài*	v	7
draw, paint	画画儿	畫畫兒	*huà huàr*	vo	9

|---------|-----------|-------------|--------|----------------|--------|
		E			
each, every	各	各	*gè*	pr	3
earn money	挣钱	掙錢	*zhèng qián*	vo	5
economics, economy	经济	經濟	*jīngjì*	n	5
education; educate	教育	教育	*jiàoyù*	n/v	8
elementary school	小学	小學	*xiǎoxué*	n	9
empty	空	空	*kōng*	adj	2
era, age	时代	時代	*shídài*	n	7
essay, article	文章	文章	*wénzhāng*	n	5
ethnic group, nationality	民族	民族	*mínzú*	n	10
(exclamatory particle to express surprise or dissatisfaction or to remind)	哎	哎	*āi*	excl	1
experience; experience	经验	經驗	*jīngyàn*	n/v	8
extroverted, open and sunny in disposition	开朗	開朗	*kāilǎng*	adj	6
		F			
family, household	家庭	家庭	*jiātíng*	n	8
famous brand, name brand	名牌	名牌	*míngpái*	n	4
fan; be infatuated with	迷	迷	*mí*	n/v	6
fashionable, stylish	时髦	時髦	*shímáo*	adj	4
feed	喂	餵	*wèi*	v	8
feeling, sense perception; to feel, to perceive	感觉	感覺	*gǎnjué*	n/v	7
few, minority (lit. small number)	少数	少數	*shǎoshù*	n	10
finance, banking	金融	金融	*jīnróng*	n	5
flow	流	流	*liú*	v	10

English	Simplified	Traditional	Pinyin	Part of Speech	Lesson
for example	比方说	比方說	bǐfāng shuō		3
fragrant, pleasant-smelling	香	香	xiāng	adj	3
free, unconstrained	自由	自由	zìyóu	adj	1
free of charge [lit. exempt from paying the fee]	免费	免費	miǎnfèi	v	7
fresh	新鲜	新鮮	xīnxian	adj	3
future	将来	將來	jiānglái	n	5

<table>
<tr><td colspan="6" align="center">G</td></tr>
</table>

English	Simplified	Traditional	Pinyin	Part of Speech	Lesson
game	游戏	遊戲	yóuxì	n	7
garbage, trash	垃圾	垃圾	lājī	n	7
generally	一般	一般	yìbān [yībān]	adv	2
geography	地理	地理	dìlǐ	n	10
get along	相处	相處	xiāngchǔ	v	6
get angry	生气	生氣	shēng qì	vo	6
get married, marry	结婚	結婚	jié hūn	vo	9
give birth to, be born	生	生	shēng	v	8
gosh, ah (an exclamation to express surprise)	哎呀	哎呀	āiyā	interj	4
government	政府	政府	zhèngfǔ	n	8
graduate	毕业	畢業	bì yè	vo	5
graduate student	研究生	研究生	yánjiūshēng	n	1
Guangdong	广东	廣東	Guǎngdōng	pn	3
Guangzhou	广州	廣州	Guǎngzhōu	pn	10

<table>
<tr><td colspan="6" align="center">H</td></tr>
</table>

English	Simplified	Traditional	Pinyin	Part of Speech	Lesson
hand over, turn in	交	交	jiāo	v	8
hang, hang up	挂	掛	guà	v	2

English	Simplified	Traditional	Pinyin	Part of Speech	Lesson
Hangzhou	杭州	杭州	*Hángzhōu*	pn	3
happen, occur, take place	发生	發生	*fāshēng*	v	6
happiness; happy	幸福	幸福	*xìngfú*	n/adj	9
Harbin	哈尔滨	哈爾濱	*Hā'ěrbīn*	pn	10
hastily, in a hurry	急忙	急忙	*jímáng*	adv	7
have to, nothing but … would do	非…不可	非…不可	*fēi … bù kě*		4
heart, mind	心	心	*xīn*	n	6
help	帮忙	幫忙	*bāng máng*	vo	1
help; help	帮助	幫助	*bāngzhù*	v/n	7
history	历史	歷史	*lìshǐ*	n	5
hobby, interest; love (something)	爱好	愛好	*àihào*	n/v	6
hometown, place of family origin	家乡	家鄉	*jiāxiāng*	n	10
hope that one's daughter will become successful (lit. to hope that one's daughter will become a phoenix)	望女成凤	望女成鳳	*wàng nǚ chéng fèng*		9
hope that one's son will become successful (lit. to hope that one's son will become a dragon)	望子成龙	望子成龍	*wàng zǐ chéng lóng*		9
huge crowds of people (lit. mountains and seas of people)	人山人海	人山人海	*rén shān rén hǎi*		10
Hunan	湖南	湖南	*Húnán*	pn	3

I

English	Simplified	Traditional	Pinyin	Part of Speech	Lesson
I'm afraid that, I think perhaps, probably	恐怕	恐怕	*kǒngpà*	adv	2
ice lantern	冰灯	冰燈	*bīngdēng*	n	10
idea	主意	主意	*zhúyi*	n	3
if it's not … it's …, either … or …	要么…，要么…	要麼…，要麼…	*yàome …, yàome …*	conj	5

English	Simplified	Traditional	Pinyin	Part of Speech	Lesson
immigrant; immigrate	移民	移民	yímín	n/v	9
important	重要	重要	zhòngyào	adj	7
in a few days	过几天	過幾天	guò jǐ tiān		2
in a moment, a little while	一会儿	一會兒	yíhuìr	n+m	4
in an instance, all of a sudden	一下子	一下子	yíxiàzi [yīxiàzi]	adv	10
in fact, in reality, actually	实际上	實際上	shíjìshang	adv	6
income	收入	收入	shōurù	n	8
influence, have an impact; influence	影响	影響	yǐngxiǎng	v/n	8
it's not … but …	不是…而是…	不是…而是…	búshì … érshì …		9

J

English	Simplified	Traditional	Pinyin	Part of Speech	Lesson
jeans	牛仔裤	牛仔褲	niúzǎikù	n	4

K

English	Simplified	Traditional	Pinyin	Part of Speech	Lesson
karaoke	卡拉OK	卡拉OK	kǎlā ōukēi	n	7
Ke Lin (a personal name)	柯林	柯林	Kē Lín	pn	1
key	钥匙	鑰匙	yàoshi	n	6
knowledge	知识	知識	zhīshi	n	9

L

English	Simplified	Traditional	Pinyin	Part of Speech	Lesson
lag behind, be outdated	落伍	落伍	luòwǔ	v	7
laundry powder	洗衣粉	洗衣粉	xǐyīfěn	n	4
leave, depart from	离开	離開	lí kāi	vc	7
leave (something) behind inadvertently (colloq.)	拉	拉	là	v	1
lessen	减轻	減輕	jiǎnqīng	v	8
Li Zhe (a personal name)	李哲	李哲	Lǐ Zhé	pn	5
(day-to-day) life; to live	生活	生活	shēnghuó	n/v	1

English	Simplified	Traditional	Pinyin	Part of Speech	Lesson
light in flavor	清淡	清淡	qīngdàn	adj	3
light, relaxed	轻松	輕鬆	qīngsōng	adj	5
Lin Xuemei (a personal name)	林雪梅	林雪梅	Lín Xuěméi	pn	3
Lisha (a personal name)	丽莎	麗莎	Lìshā	pn	3
[literary] good, fine	良好	良好	liánghǎo	adj	8
literature	文学	文學	wénxué	n	5
loan; provide a loan	贷款	貸款	dàikuǎn	n/vo	8
long	长	長	cháng	adj	1
low	低	低	dī	adj	8
M					
magazine	杂志	雜誌	zázhì	n	7
main, principal	主要	主要	zhǔyào	adj	10
make (someone do something)	叫	叫	jiào	v	6
make friends	交朋友	交朋友	jiāo péngyou	vo	6
master's (academic degree)	硕士	碩士	shuòshì	n	9
material (reference, academic)	资料	資料	zīliào	n	7
(measure word for academic courses)	门	門	mén	m	5
(measure word for buildings)	栋	棟	dòng	m	2
(measure word for machines)	台	台	tái	m	2
(measure word for stories of a building)	层	層	céng	m	2
(measure word for times by which something is multiplied)	倍	倍	bèi	m	10
(measure word for type or kind)	番	番	fān	m	9
(measure word for vehicles)	辆	輛	liàng	m	1

English	Simplified	Traditional	Pinyin	Part of Speech	Lesson
mention, bring up	提	提	*tí*	v	6
menu	菜单	菜單	*càidān*	n	3
Mexico	墨西哥	墨西哥	*Mòxīgē*	pn	9
mind, care	在乎	在乎	*zàihu*	v	4
mostly, for the most part	大多	大多	*dàduō*	adv	10
mountain, hill	山	山	*shān*	n	10
move (one's residence)	搬家	搬家	*bān jiā*	vo	1
movie theater	电影院	電影院	*diànyǐngyuàn*	n	6

N

English	Simplified	Traditional	Pinyin	Part of Speech	Lesson
Nanjing	南京	南京	*Nánjīng*	pn	10
napkin	餐巾	餐巾	*cānjīn*	n	3
nature; natural	自然	自然	*zìrán*	n/adj	10
need; needs	需要	需要	*xūyào*	v/n	4
network, the Internet	网络	網絡	*wǎngluò*	n	7
new student	新生	新生	*xīnshēng*	n	1
news	新闻	新聞	*xīnwén*	n	7
nice-looking, attractive	好看	好看	*hǎokàn*	adj	4
no wonder	难怪	難怪	*nánguài*	adv	8
not necessarily	不见得	不見得	*bújiànde*	adv	1
numeral, figure, digit	数字	數字	*shùzì*	n	5

O

English	Simplified	Traditional	Pinyin	Part of Speech	Lesson
obedient, well-behaved (of children)	乖	乖	*guāi*	adj	8
obtain, gain, acquire	取得	取得	*qǔdé*	v	8
off campus	校外	校外	*xiào wài*		1

English	Simplified	Traditional	Pinyin	Part of Speech	Lesson
oil; oily	油	油	*yóu*	n/adj	3
old (of things)	旧	舊	*jiù*	adj	2
older brother's wife	嫂子	嫂子	*sǎozi*	n	9
on campus	校内	校內	*xiào nèi*		1
opinion	意见	意見	*yìjiàn*	n	5
oppose	反对	反對	*fǎnduì*	v	9
order (food)	叫（菜）	叫（菜）	*jiào (cài)*	v (o)	3
organic	有机	有機	*yǒujī*	adj	3
other, else	其他	其他	*qítā*	pr	5
owe	欠	欠	*qiàn*	v	8
P					
part, section	部	部	*bù*	n	10
perhaps, maybe	说不定	說不定	*shuōbudìng*	adv	6
philosophy	哲学	哲學	*zhéxué*	n	5
piano	钢琴	鋼琴	*gāngqín*	n	9
plain (lit. flat field)	平原	平原	*píngyuán*	n	10
plateau (lit. high field)	高原	高原	*gāoyuán*	n	10
point of view	看法	看法	*kànfǎ*	n	9
population	人口	人口	*rénkǒu*	n	10
pressure	压力	壓力	*yālì*	n	8
price	价钱	價錢	*jiàqian*	n	4
professor	教授	教授	*jiàoshòu*	n	5
provide, support financially	供	供	*gōng*	v	8
province (administrative division)	省	省	*shěng*	n	10

English	Simplified	Traditional	Pinyin	Part of Speech	Lesson
pure cotton, one-hundred-percent cotton	纯棉	純棉	chúnmián	adj	4
put, place	摆	擺	bǎi	v	2
Q					
quality	质量	質量	zhìliàng	n	4
quarrel	吵架	吵架	chǎo jià	vo	6
R					
really, truly	真的	真的	zhēn de	adv	2
reason, sense	道理	道理	dàoli	n	4
receive	受到	受到	shòu dào	vc	8
regardless of . . . , whether it be . . .	无论	無論	wúlùn	conj	4
relatively, comparatively, rather; compare	比较	比較	bǐjiào	adv/v	1
resemble, be like	像	像	xiàng	v	4
respect	尊重	尊重	zūnzhòng	v	9
restaurant	餐馆儿	餐館兒	cānguǎnr	n	2
river	河流	河流	héliú	n	10
road, street	马路	馬路	mǎlù	n	2
room	屋子	屋子	wūzi	n	7
roommate	同屋	同屋	tóngwū	n	2
route, itinerary	路线	路線	lùxiàn	n	10
run into (a person by chance)	碰见	碰見	pèng jiàn	vc	5
S					
safe	安全	安全	ānquán	adj	1
salty	咸	鹹	xián	adj	3

English	Simplified	Traditional	Pinyin	Part of Speech	Lesson
save (money, time)	省下来	省下來	*shěng xia lai*	vc	5
save money, economize	省钱	省錢	*shěng qián*	vo	1
scatterbrained, forgetful	丢三拉四	丢三拉四	*diū sān là sì*		6
scenic landscape, scenery	风景	風景	*fēngjǐng*	n	10
scenic spot, tourist spot	景点	景點	*jǐngdiǎn*	n	10
scholarship money	奖学金	獎學金	*jiǎngxuéjīn*	n	8
school of engineering	工学院	工學院	*gōng xuéyuàn*	n	5
school of management	管理学院	管理學院	*guǎnlǐ xuéyuàn*	n	5
sea, ocean	海	海	*hǎi*	n	10
senior high school	高中	高中	*gāozhōng*	n	6
serious, grave	严重	嚴重	*yánzhòng*	adj	7
Shenzhen	深圳	深圳	*Shēnzhèn*	pn	10
shop	购物	購物	*gòuwù*	vo	4
short	短	短	*duǎn*	adj	10
Sichuan	四川	四川	*Sìchuān*	pn	3
society	社会	社會	*shèhuì*	n	9
software	软件	軟件	*ruǎnjiàn*	n	7
solve, resolve	解决	解決	*jiějué*	v	5
something that weighs on one's mind	心事	心事	*xīnshì*	n	6
spicy	辣	辣	*là*	adj	3
spinach	菠菜	菠菜	*bōcài*	n	3
spring-like all year round	四季如春	四季如春	*sìjì rú chūn*		10
stationery, writing supplies	文具	文具	*wénjù*	n	2
stay	待	待	*dāi*	v	7

English	Simplified	Traditional	Pinyin	Part of Speech	Lesson
steam (food without heavy sauce)	清蒸	清蒸	qīngzhēng	v	3
study-abroad student	留学生	留學生	liúxuéshēng	n	3
study abroad	留学	留學	liú xué	vo	9
suggestion; suggest	建议	建議	jiànyì	n/v	5
suit	适合	適合	shìhé	v	8
T					
T-shirt	T恤衫	T恤衫	tìxùshān	n	4
takeout	外卖	外賣	wàimài	n	7
talk, discuss	谈	談	tán	v	5
(personal) taste	口味	口味	kǒuwèi	n	3
taste, flavor (of food)	味道	味道	wèidao	n	3
tax	税	稅	shuì	n	4
tender	嫩	嫩	nèn	adj	3
terrain, topography	地形	地形	dìxíng	n	10
terrible, formidable	厉害	厲害	lìhai	adj	9
think, consider	认为	認為	rènwéi	v	9
Tianjin	天津	天津	Tiānjīn	pn	10
toilet paper	卫生纸	衛生紙	wèishēngzhǐ	n	4
toothpaste	牙膏	牙膏	yágāo	n	4
towel	毛巾	毛巾	máojīn	n	4
train	火车	火車	huǒchē	n	10
translate; interpreter, translation	翻译	翻譯	fānyì	v/n	7
travel (for pleasure); (pleasure) travel	旅游	旅遊	lǚyóu	v/n	10
tutor	家教	家教	jiājiào	n	8

English	Simplified	Traditional	Pinyin	Part of Speech	Lesson
U					
understand	理解	理解	lǐjiě	v	9
understand, know about, be informed	了解	了解	liǎojiě	v	10
useful	有用	有用	yǒuyòng	adj	7
V					
vocal concert	演唱会	演唱會	yǎnchànghuì	n	6
W					
wages, pay	工资	工資	gōngzī	n	8
walk (an animal), stroll	遛	遛	liù	v	8
wardrobe	衣柜	衣櫃	yīguì	n	2
wash	洗	洗	xǐ	v	2
washing machine	洗衣机	洗衣機	xǐyījī	n	2
way of doing things, course of action	做法	做法	zuòfǎ	n	9
website	网站	網站	wǎngzhàn	n	7
WeChat	微信	微信	Wēixìn	pn	3
what on earth, what in the world, in the end	到底	到底	dàodǐ	adv	6
woolen sweater	毛衣	毛衣	máoyī	n	4
world	世界	世界	shìjiè	n	5
worry	着急	着急	zháojí	v	2
X					
Xinjiang	新疆	新疆	Xīnjiāng	pn	10

English	Simplified	Traditional	Pinyin	Part of Speech	Lesson
Y					
Yangtze River	长江	長江	*Chángjiāng*	pn	10
Yellow River	黄河	黃河	*Huánghé*	pn	10
Yunnan	云南	雲南	*Yúnnán*	pn	10
Z					
Zhang Tiaming (a personal name)	张天明	張天明	*Zhāng Tiānmíng*	pn	1

Vocabulary Index (Chinese-English), Volumes 1–2

The Chinese-English index is alphabetized according to *pinyin*. Words containing the same Chinese characters are first grouped together. Homonyms appear in the order of their tonal pronunciation (i.e., first tones first, second tones second, third tones third, fourth tones fourth, and neutral tones last).

Simplified	Traditional	Pinyin	Part of Speech	English	Lesson
A					
啊	啊	*a*	p	(a sentence-final particle of exclamation, interrogation, etc.)	6
阿姨	阿姨	*āyí*	n	aunt	20
哎	哎	*āi*	excl	(exclamatory particle to express surprise or dissatisfaction)	13
爱	愛	*ài*	v	to love, to like, to be fond of	14
安静	安靜	*ānjìng*	adj	quiet	17
B					
把	把	*bǎ*	m	(measure word for things with handles, for handfuls of things)	14
把	把	*bǎ*	prep	(indicating disposition, arrangement, or settlement of something)	15
爸爸	爸爸	*bàba*	n	father, dad	2
吧	吧	*ba*	p	(a sentence-final particle)	5
白英爱	白英愛	*Bái Yīng'ài*	pn	(a personal name)	2
百	百	*bǎi*	nu	hundred	9
班	班	*bān*	n	class	14
搬	搬	*bān*	v	to move	16
半	半	*bàn*	nu	half, half an hour	3
半天	半天	*bàntiān*		half a day, a long time	18
办	辦	*bàn*	v	to handle, to do	11

Simplified	Traditional	Pinyin	Part of Speech	English	Lesson
办法	辦法	bànfǎ	n	method, way (of doing something)	15
办公室	辦公室	bàngōngshì	n	office	6
帮	幫	bāng	v	to help	6
棒	棒	bàng	adj	fantastic, super [colloq.]	18
包	包	bāo	n	bag, sack, bundle, package	20
保险	保險	bǎoxiǎn	n/adj	insurance; secure	15
抱	抱	bào	v	to hold or carry in the arms	18
报纸	報紙	bàozhǐ	n	newspaper	17
杯	杯	bēi	m	(measure word for things contained in a cup or glass)	5
北	北	běi	n	north	13
北京	北京	Běijīng	pn	Beijing	1
被	被	bèi	prep	by	18
本	本	běn	m	(measure word for books)	14
鼻子	鼻子	bízi	n	nose	14
笔	筆	bǐ	n	pen	7
比	比	bǐ	prep/v	compared with (comparison marker); to compare	11
比赛	比賽	bǐsài	n/v	game, match, competition; to compete	18
遍	遍	biàn	m	(measure word for complete courses of an action or instances of an action)	15
表姐	表姐	biǎojiě	n	older female cousin	14
别	別	bié	adv	don't	6
别人	別人	biérén	n	other people, another person	4
冰茶	冰茶	bīngchá	n	iced tea	12
冰箱	冰箱	bīngxiāng	n	refrigerator	15
病人	病人	bìngrén	n	patient	15

Simplified	Traditional	Pinyin	Part of Speech	English	Lesson
不	不	bù	adv	not, no	1
不错	不錯	búcuò [bùcuò]	adj	pretty good	4
不但…，而且…	不但…，而且…	búdàn…, érqiě… [bùdàn…, érqiě…]	conj	not only…, but also…	11
不过	不過	búguò [bùguò]	conj	however, but	9
不好意思	不好意思	bù hǎoyìsi		to feel embarrassed	10
不用	不用	bú yòng [bù yòng]		need not	9
C					
才	才	cái	adv	not until, only then	5
菜	菜	cài	n	dish, cuisine	3
餐厅	餐廳	cāntīng	n	dining room, cafeteria	8
厕所	廁所	cèsuǒ	n	restroom, toilet	15
茶	茶	chá	n	tea	5
查	查	chá	v	to check, to look into	19
差不多	差不多	chàbuduō	adv/adj	almost, nearly; similar	17
常常	常常	chángcháng	adv	often	4
常老师	常老師	Cháng lǎoshī	pn	Teacher Chang	6
长城	長城	Chángchéng	pn	the Great Wall	19
长短	長短	chángduǎn	n	length	9
场	場	chǎng	n	field	13
唱歌（儿）	唱歌（兒）	chàng gē(r)	vo	to sing (a song)	4
超重	超重	chāozhòng	v	to be overweight (of luggage, freight, etc.)	20
吵	吵	chǎo	v/adj	to quarrel; noisy	17
衬衫	襯衫	chènshān	n	shirt	9

Simplified	Traditional	Pinyin	Part of Speech	English	Lesson
成	成	*chéng*	v	to become	16
城市	城市	*chéngshì*	n	city	10
吃	吃	*chī*	v	to eat	3
吃坏	吃壞	*chī huài*	vc	to get sick because of bad food	15
宠物	寵物	*chǒngwù*	n	pet	17
初	初	*chū*	n	beginning	19
出去	出去	*chūqu*	vc	to go out	10
出租	出租	*chūzū*	v	to rent out	17
出租汽车	出租汽車	*chūzū qìchē*	n	taxi	10
厨房	廚房	*chúfáng*	n	kitchen	17
除了…以外	除了…以外	*chúle … yǐwài*	conj	in addition to, besides	8
穿	穿	*chuān*	v	to wear, to put on	9
窗户	窗戶	*chuānghu*	n	window	19
春天	春天	*chūntiān*	n	spring	11
次	次	*cì*	m	(measure word for frequency)	13
聪明	聰明	*cōngming*	adj	smart, bright, clever	14
从	從	*cóng*	prep	from	13
错	錯	*cuò*	adj	wrong	12

D

打车	打車	*dǎ chē*	vo	to take a taxi	10
打电话	打電話	*dǎ diànhuà*	vo	to make a phone call	6
打工	打工	*dǎ gōng*	vo	to work at a temporary job (often part time)	19
打球	打球	*dǎ qiú*	vo	to play ball	4
打扫	打掃	*dǎsǎo*	v	to clean up (a room, apartment or house)	16

Simplified	Traditional	Pinyin	Part of Speech	English	Lesson
打算	打算	*dǎsuàn*	v/n	to plan; plan	19
打折	打折	*dǎ zhé*	vo	to sell at a discount, to give a discount	19
打针	打針	*dǎ zhēn*	vo	to get an injection	15
大	大	*dà*	adj	big, old	3
大哥	大哥	*dàgē*	n	eldest/oldest brother	2
大家	大家	*dàjiā*	pr	everybody	7
大姐	大姐	*dàjiě*	n	eldest/oldest sister	2
大小	大小	*dàxiǎo*	n	size	9
大学生	大學生	*dàxuéshēng*	n	college student	2
带	帶	*dài*	v	to bring, to take, to carry, to come with	12
单程	單程	*dānchéng*	n	one-way trip	19
担心	擔心	*dān xīn*	vo	to worry	18
蛋糕	蛋糕	*dàngāo*	n	cake	14
但是	但是	*dànshì*	conj	but	6
当	當	*dāng*	v	to serve as, to be	17
当然	當然	*dāngrán*	adv	of course	18
导游	導遊	*dǎoyóu*	n	tour guide	19
到	到	*dào*	v	to go to, to arrive	6
的	的	*de*	p	(a possessive or descriptive particle)	2
地	地	*de*	p	(particle to link adverbial and verb)	20
得	得	*de*	p	(a structural particle)	7
得	得	*děi*	av	must, to have to	6
登机口	登機口	*dēngjīkǒu*	n	boarding gate	20
登机牌	登機牌	*dēngjīpái*	n	boarding pass	20

Simplified	Traditional	Pinyin	Part of Speech	English	Lesson
等	等	*děng*	v	to wait, to wait for	6
第	第	*dì*	prefix	(prefix for ordinal numbers)	7
弟弟	弟弟	*dìdi*	n	younger brother	2
地方	地方	*dìfang*	n	place	13
地铁	地鐵	*dìtiě*	n	subway	10
地图	地圖	*dìtú*	n	map	13
点	點	*diǎn*	m	o'clock (lit. dot, point, thus "points on the clock")	3
点菜	點菜	*diǎn cài*	vo	to order food	12
点（儿）	點（兒）	*diǎn(r)*	m	a little, a bit, some	5
电	電	*diàn*	n	electricity	16
电脑	電腦	*diànnǎo*	n	computer	8
电视	電視	*diànshì*	n	television	4
电影	電影	*diànyǐng*	n	movie	4
电子邮件	電子郵件	*diànzǐ yóujiàn*	n	email/electronic mail	10
订	訂	*dìng*	v	to reserve, to book (a ticket, a hotel room, etc.)	19
东	東	*dōng*	n	east	13
东京	東京	*Dōngjīng*	pn	Tokyo	13
东西	東西	*dōngxi*	n	things, objects	9
冬天	冬天	*dōngtiān*	n	winter	11
懂	懂	*dǒng*	v	to understand	7
都	都	*dōu*	adv	both, all	2
豆腐	豆腐	*dòufu*	n	tofu, bean curd	12
肚子	肚子	*dùzi*	n	belly, abdomen, stomach	15
对	對	*duì*	adj	right, correct	4

Simplified	Traditional	Pinyin	Part of Speech	English	Lesson
对不起	對不起	duìbuqǐ	v	sorry	5
多	多	duō	adv	how many/much, to what extent	3
多	多	duō	adj	many, much	7
多少	多少	duōshao	qpr	how much/how many	9
		E			
饿	餓	è	adj	hungry	12
儿子	兒子	érzi	n	son	2
二姐	二姐	èrjiě	n	second oldest sister	2
		F			
发短信	發短信	fā duǎnxìn	vo	to send a text message (lit. to send a short message)	10
发烧	發燒	fā shāo	vo	to have a fever	15
发音	發音	fāyīn	n	pronunciation	8
饭	飯	fàn	n	meal, (cooked) rice	3
饭馆（儿）	飯館（兒）	fànguǎn(r)	n	restaurant	12
饭卡	飯卡	fànkǎ	n	meal card	12
饭桌	飯桌	fànzhuō	n	dining table	17
方便	方便	fāngbiàn	adj	convenient	6
房间	房間	fángjiān	n	room	16
房租	房租	fángzū	n	rent	17
放	放	fàng	v	to put, to place	12
放假	放假	fàng jià	vo	go on vacation, have time off	19
非常	非常	fēicháng	adv	very, extremely, exceedingly	11
飞机	飛機	fēijī	n	airplane	10
（飞）机场	（飛）機場	(fēi)jīchǎng	n	airport	10

Simplified	Traditional	Pinyin	Part of Speech	English	Lesson
费	費	fèi	v	to spend, to take (effort)	16
费	費	fèi	n	fee, expenses	17
分	分	fēn	m	(measure word for 1/100 of a kuai [equivalent of a cent])	9
分钟	分鐘	fēnzhōng	n	minute	17
份	份	fèn	m	(measure word for meal orders, jobs)	19
封	封	fēng	m	(measure word for letters)	8
服务员	服務員	fúwùyuán	n	waiter, attendant	12
附近	附近	fùjìn	n	vicinity, neighborhood, nearby area	17
父母	父母	fùmǔ	n	parents, father and mother	19
付钱	付錢	fù qián	vo	to pay money	9
复习	復習	fùxí	v	to review	7
G					
干净	乾淨	gānjìng	adj	clean	17
赶快	趕快	gǎnkuài	adv	right away, quickly, in a hurry	15
感冒	感冒	gǎnmào	v	to have a cold	15
刚	剛	gāng	adv	just	12
刚才	剛才	gāngcái	t	just now, a moment ago	11
高速公路	高速公路	gāosù gōnglù	n	highway	10
高文中	高文中	Gāo Wénzhōng	pn	(a personal name)	2
高小音	高小音	Gāo Xiǎoyīn	pn	(a personal name)	5
高兴	高興	gāoxìng	adj	happy, pleased	5
告诉	告訴	gàosu	v	to tell	8
哥哥	哥哥	gēge	n	older brother	2
个	個	gè/ge	m	(measure word for many common everyday objects)	2

Simplified	Traditional	Pinyin	Part of Speech	English	Lesson
给	給	gěi	v	to give	5
给	給	gěi	prep	to, for	6
跟	跟	gēn	prep	with	6
更	更	gèng	adv	even more	11
公共汽车	公共汽車	gōnggòng qìchē	n	bus	10
公司	公司	gōngsī	n	company	19
公寓	公寓	gōngyù	n	apartment	17
公园	公園	gōngyuán	n	park	11
功课	功課	gōngkè	n	homework, schoolwork	7
工作	工作	gōngzuò	n/v	job; to work	2
狗	狗	gǒu	n	dog	14
够	夠	gòu	adj	enough	12
谷歌	谷歌	Gǔgē	pn	Google	13
拐	拐	guǎi	v	to turn	13
广告	廣告	guǎnggào	n	advertisement	17
贵	貴	guì	adj	honorable, expensive	1
国际	國際	guójì	adj	international	18
过	過	guò	v	to live (a life), to observe (a holiday), to celebrate (a festival), to pass	14
过敏	過敏	guòmǐn	v	to be allergic to	15
过	過	guo	p	(particle used after a verb to indicate a past experience)	13
H					
还	還	hái	adv	also, too, as well	3
还是	還是	háishi	conj	or	3
孩子	孩子	háizi	n	child	2

Simplified	Traditional	Pinyin	Part of Speech	English	Lesson
海伦	海倫	*Hǎilún*	pn	Helen	14
寒假	寒假	*hánjià*	n	winter vacation	10
汉字	漢字	*Hànzì*	n	Chinese characters	7
航班	航班	*hángbān*	n	scheduled flight	19
航空	航空	*hángkōng*	n	aviation	19
好	好	*hǎo*	adj	fine, good, nice, OK, it's settled	1
好吃	好吃	*hǎochī*	adj	delicious	12
好几	好幾	*hǎo jǐ*		quite a few	15
好久	好久	*hǎo jiǔ*		a long time	4
好玩儿	好玩兒	*hǎowánr*	adj	fun, amusing, interesting	11
好像	好像	*hǎoxiàng*	v	to seem, to be like	12
号	號	*hào*	m	(measure word for a position in a numerical series, day of the month)	3
号	號	*hào*	n	size	9
号码	號碼	*hàomǎ*	n	number	16
喝	喝	*hē*	v	to drink	5
和	和	*hé*	conj	and	2
合适	合適	*héshì*	adj	suitable	9
黑	黑	*hēi*	adj	black	9
很	很	*hěn*	adv	very	3
红	紅	*hóng*	adj	red	9
红绿灯	紅綠燈	*hónglǜdēng*	n	traffic light	13
红烧	紅燒	*hóngshāo*	v	to braise in soy sauce (to red-cook)	12
后来	後來	*hòulái*	t	later	8

Simplified	Traditional	Pinyin	Part of Speech	English	Lesson
后天	後天	*hòutiān*	t	the day after tomorrow	16
护照	護照	*hùzhào*	n	passport	19
花	花	*huā*	v	to spend	10
花	花	*huā*	n	flower	14
滑冰	滑冰	*huá bīng*	vo	to ice skate	11
欢迎	歡迎	*huānyíng*	v	to welcome	20
还	還	*huán*	v	to return (something)	17
换	換	*huàn*	v	to exchange, to change	9
黄	黃	*huáng*	adj	yellow	9
黄瓜	黃瓜	*huánggua*	n	cucumber	12
回家	回家	*huí jiā*	vo	to go home	5
回来	回來	*huí lai*	vc	to come back	6
回去	回去	*huí qu*	vc	to go back, to return	11
会	會	*huì*	mv	can, know how to	8
会	會	*huì*	mv	will	11
活动	活動	*huódòng*	n	activity	13
或者	或者	*huòzhě*	conj	or	10

		J			
极	極	*jí*	adv	extremely	12
几	幾	*jǐ*	nu	how many, some, a few	2
记得	記得	*jìde*	v	to remember	16
计划	計劃	*jìhuà*	v/n	to plan; plan	19
家	家	*jiā*	n	family, home	2
家常	家常	*jiācháng*	n	home-style	12

Simplified	Traditional	Pinyin	Part of Speech	English	Lesson
家具	傢俱	*jiājù*	n	furniture	17
加州	加州	*Jiāzhōu*	pn	California	11
检查	檢查	*jiǎnchá*	v	to examine	15
简单	簡單	*jiǎndān*	adj	simple	18
件	件	*jiàn*	m	(measure word for shirts, dresses, jackets, coats, etc.)	9
见	見	*jiàn*	v	to see	3
见面	見面	*jiàn miàn*	vo	to meet up, to meet with	6
健康	健康	*jiànkāng*	adj/n	healthy; health	15
教	教	*jiāo*	v	to teach	7
脚	腳	*jiǎo*	n	foot	18
饺子	餃子	*jiǎozi*	n	dumplings (with vegetable and/or meat filling)	12
叫	叫	*jiào*	v	to be called, to call	1
教室	教室	*jiàoshì*	n	classroom	8
接	接	*jiē*	v	to catch, to meet, to welcome	14
节	節	*jié*	m	(measure word for class periods)	6
姐姐	姐姐	*jiějie*	n	older sister	2
介绍	介紹	*jièshào*	v	to introduce	5
今年	今年	*jīnnián*	t	this year	3
今天	今天	*jīntiān*	t	today	3
紧张	緊張	*jǐnzhāng*	adj	nervous, anxious	10
近	近	*jìn*	adj	near	13
进	進	*jìn*	v	to enter	5
进来	進來	*jìn lai*	vc	to come in	5
九月	九月	*jiǔyuè*	n	September	3

Simplified	Traditional	Pinyin	Part of Speech	English	Lesson
就	就	*jiù*	adv	precisely, exactly	6
就	就	*jiù*	adv	just, only (indicating a small number)	16
觉得	覺得	*juéde*	v	to feel, to think	4
K					
咖啡	咖啡	*kāfēi*	n	coffee	5
咖啡色	咖啡色	*kāfēisè*	n	brown, coffee color	9
开车	開車	*kāi chē*	vo	to drive a car	10
开会	開會	*kāi huì*	vo	to have a meeting	6
开始	開始	*kāishǐ*	v/n	to begin, to start; beginning	7
看	看	*kàn*	v	to watch, to look, to read	4
看病	看病	*kàn bìng*	vo	to see a doctor	15
考试	考試	*kǎo shì*	vo/n	to give or take a test; test	6
烤鸭	烤鴨	*kǎoyā*	n	roast duck	20
靠	靠	*kào*	v	to lean on, to lean against, to be next to	19
渴	渴	*kě*	adj	thirsty	12
可爱	可愛	*kě'ài*	adj	cute, lovable	14
可乐	可樂	*kělè*	n	cola	5
可能	可能	*kěnéng*	mv/adj	may; possible	17
可是	可是	*kěshì*	conj	but	3
可以	可以	*kěyǐ*	mv	can, may	5
刻	刻	*kè*	m	quarter (of an hour)	3
课	課	*kè*	n	class, course, lesson	6
课文	課文	*kèwén*	n	text of a lesson	7
客气	客氣	*kèqi*	adj	polite	6

Simplified	Traditional	Pinyin	Part of Speech	English	Lesson
客厅	客廳	*kètīng*	n	living room	17
空（儿）	空（兒）	*kòng(r)*	n	free time	6
口	口	*kǒu*	m	(measure word for number of family members)	2
哭	哭	*kū*	v	to cry, to weep	20
酷	酷	*kù*	adj	cool (appearance, behavior)	7
裤子	褲子	*kùzi*	n	pants	9
块	塊	*kuài*	m	(measure word for the basic Chinese monetary unit [equivalent of a dollar])	9
快	快	*kuài*	adj/adv	fast, quick; quickly	5
快乐	快樂	*kuàilè*	adj	happy	10

L

Simplified	Traditional	Pinyin	Part of Speech	English	Lesson
来	來	*lái*	v	to come	5
蓝	藍	*lán*	adj	blue	10
篮球	籃球	*lánqiú*	n	basketball	18
懒	懶	*lǎn*	adj	lazy	15
老师	老師	*lǎoshī*	n	teacher	1
了	了	*le*	p	(a dynamic particle)	5
累	累	*lèi*	adj	tired	8
冷	冷	*lěng*	adj	cold	11
离	離	*lí*	prep	away from	13
梨	梨	*lí*	n	pear	14
里边	裡邊	*lǐbian*	n	inside	13
礼物	禮物	*lǐwù*	n	gift, present	14
李友	李友	*Lǐ Yǒu*	pn	(a personal name)	1
力气	力氣	*lìqi*	n	strength, effort	16

Simplified	Traditional	Pinyin	Part of Speech	English	Lesson
俩	倆	liǎ	nu+m	two [colloq.]	16
连	連	lián	prep	even	17
脸	臉	liǎn	n	face	14
练习	練習	liànxí	v	to practice	6
凉拌	涼拌	liángbàn	v	(of food) cold "blended", cold tossed	12
两	兩	liǎng	nu	two, a couple of	2
聊天（儿）	聊天（兒）	liáo tiān(r)	vo	to chat	5
另外	另外	lìngwài	conj	furthermore, in addition	17
楼	樓	lóu	n	multi-storied building, floor (of a multi-level building)	14
路	路	lù	n	route, road	10
路口	路口	lùkǒu	n	intersection	13
录音	錄音	lùyīn	n/vo	sound recording; to record	7
旅馆	旅館	lǚguǎn	n	hotel	19
旅行	旅行	lǚxíng	v	to travel	16
旅行社	旅行社	lǚxíngshè	n	travel agency	19
绿	綠	lǜ	adj	green	10
律师	律師	lǜshī	n	lawyer	2
乱	亂	luàn	adv	randomly, arbitrarily, messily	15
M					
妈妈	媽媽	māma	n	mother, mom	2
麻烦	麻煩	máfan	adj	troublesome	10
马上	馬上	mǎshàng	adv	immediately, right away	19
吗	嗎	ma	qp	(question particle)	1
买	買	mǎi	v	to buy	9

Simplified	Traditional	Pinyin	Part of Speech	English	Lesson
卖完	賣完	*mài wán*	vc	to be sold out	12
慢	慢	*màn*	adj	slow	7
忙	忙	*máng*	adj	busy	3
毛	毛	*máo*	m	(measure word for 1/10 of a kuai [equivalent of a dime])	9
没	沒	*méi*	adv	not	2
没关系	沒關係	*méi guānxi*		it doesn't matter	12
每	每	*měi*	pr	every, each	10
美国	美國	*Měiguó*	pn	America	1
美式	美式	*Měishì*	adj	American-style	18
美元	美元	*Měiyuán*	n	American dollar (USD)	17
妹妹	妹妹	*mèimei*	n	younger sister	2
米饭	米飯	*mǐfàn*	n	cooked rice	12
面试	面試	*miànshì*	v/n	to interview; interview (for a job or school admission)	11
名胜古迹	名勝古蹟	*míngshèng gǔjì*		famous scenic spots and historic sites	19
明天	明天	*míngtiān*	t	tomorrow	3
名字	名字	*míngzi*	n	name	1
N					
拿	拿	*ná*	v	to take, to get	13
哪	哪	*nǎ/něi*	qpr	which	6
哪里	哪裡	*nǎli*	pr	where	7
哪儿	哪兒	*nǎr*	qpr	where	5
那	那	*nà*	pr	that	2
那	那	*nà*	conj	in that case, then	4
那里	那裡	*nàli*	pr	there	17

Simplified	Traditional	Pinyin	Part of Speech	English	Lesson
那么	那麼	*nàme*	pr	(indicating degree) so, such	11
那儿	那兒	*nàr*	pr	there	8
奶奶	奶奶	*nǎinai*	n	paternal grandmother	20
男	男	*nán*	adj	male	2
南	南	*nán*	n	south	13
难	難	*nán*	adj	difficult	7
难受	難受	*nánshòu*	adj	hard to bear, uncomfortable	18
呢	呢	*ne*	qp	(question particle)	1
能	能	*néng*	mv	can, to be able to	8
你	你	*nǐ*	pr	you	1
年级	年級	*niánjí*	n	grade in school	6
念	念	*niàn*	v	to read aloud	7
您	您	*nín*	pr	you (honorific for 你)	6
牛肉	牛肉	*niúròu*	n	beef	12
纽约	紐約	*Niǔyuē*	pn	New York	1
暖和	暖和	*nuǎnhuo*	adj	warm	11
女	女	*nǚ*	adj	female	2
女儿	女兒	*nǚ'ér*	n	daughter	2
P					
怕	怕	*pà*	v	to fear, to be afraid of	18
拍	拍	*pāi*	n	racket	18
盘	盤	*pán*	n	plate, dish	12
旁边	旁邊	*pángbiān*	n	side	13
胖	胖	*pàng*	adj	fat	18

Simplified	Traditional	Pinyin	Part of Speech	English	Lesson
跑步	跑步	*pǎo bù*	vo	to jog	18
朋友	朋友	*péngyou*	n	friend	3
篇	篇	*piān*	m	(measure word for essays, articles, etc.)	8
便宜	便宜	*piányi*	adj	cheap, inexpensive	9
片	片	*piàn*	m	(measure word for tablets, slices, etc.)	15
票	票	*piào*	n	ticket	10
漂亮	漂亮	*piàoliang*	adj	pretty	5
瓶	瓶	*píng*	m/n	(measure word for bottled liquid, etc.)	5
平常	平常	*píngcháng*	adv	usually	7
苹果	蘋果	*píngguǒ*	n	apple	14

Q

Simplified	Traditional	Pinyin	Part of Speech	English	Lesson
起床	起床	*qǐ chuáng*	vo	to get up	8
起飞	起飛	*qǐfēi*	v	(of airplanes) to take off	20
千	千	*qiān*	nu	thousand	19
签证	簽證	*qiānzhèng*	n	visa	19
钱	錢	*qián*	n	money	9
前	前	*qián*	n	forward, ahead	13
前面	前面	*qiánmiàn*	n	ahead, in front of	13
青菜	青菜	*qīngcài*	n	green, leafy vegetable	12
清楚	清楚	*qīngchu*	adj	clear	12
请	請	*qǐng*	v	please (polite form of request), to treat or to invite (somebody)	1
请客	請客	*qǐng kè*	vo	to invite someone (to dinner, coffee, etc.), to play the host	4

Simplified	Traditional	Pinyin	Part of Speech	English	Lesson
秋天	秋天	*qiūtiān*	n	autumn, fall	11
去	去	*qù*	v	to go	4
去年	去年	*qùnián*	t	last year	14
R					
然后	然後	*ránhòu*	adv	then	10
让	讓	*ràng*	v	to allow or cause (somebody to do something)	10
热	熱	*rè*	adj	hot	11
人	人	*rén*	n	people, person	1
人民币	人民幣	*rénmínbì*	n	renminbi (RMB, Chinese currency)	17
认识	認識	*rènshi*	v	to be acquainted with, to recognize	3
日本	日本	*Rìběn*	pn	Japan	13
日记	日記	*rìjì*	n	diary	8
日文	日文	*Rìwén*	pn	Japanese (language)	13
容易	容易	*róngyì*	adj	easy	7
肉	肉	*ròu*	n	meat	12
如果…的话	如果…的話	*rúguǒ … de huà*	conj	if	9
S					
沙发	沙發	*shāfā*	n	sofa	17
商店	商店	*shāngdiàn*	n	store, shop	9
上	上	*shàng*	v	to go [colloq.]	13
上菜	上菜	*shàng cài*	vo	to serve food	12
上次	上次	*shàng cì*		last time	15
上大学	上大學	*shàng dàxué*	vo	to attend college/university	18

Simplified	Traditional	Pinyin	Part of Speech	English	Lesson
上个	上個	*shàng ge*		previous, last	7
上海	上海	*Shànghǎi*	pn	Shanghai	12
上课	上課	*shàng kè*	vo	to go to a class, to start a class, to be in class	7
上网	上網	*shàng wǎng*	vo	to go online, to surf the internet	8
上午	上午	*shàngwǔ*	t	morning	6
谁	誰	*shéi*	qpr	who, whom	2
身体	身體	*shēntǐ*	n	body, health	15
什么	什麼	*shénme*	qpr	what	1
生病	生病	*shēng bìng*	vo	to get sick	15
生词	生詞	*shēngcí*	n	new words, vocabulary	7
生日	生日	*shēngrì*	n	birthday	3
师傅	師傅	*shīfu*	n	master worker	12
十八	十八	*shíbā*	nu	eighteen	3
十二	十二	*shí'èr*	nu	twelve	3
时候	時候	*shíhou*	n	(a point in) time, moment, (a duration of) time	4
时间	時間	*shíjiān*	n	time	6
实习	實習	*shíxí*	v	to intern	19
是	是	*shì*	v	to be	1
试	試	*shì*	v	to try	9
事（儿）	事（兒）	*shì(r)*	n	matter, affair, event	3
收	收	*shōu*	v	to receive, to accept	9
手	手	*shǒu*	n	hand	18
手机	手機	*shǒujī*	n	cell phone	10
首都	首都	*shǒudū*	n	capital city	19

Simplified	Traditional	Pinyin	Part of Speech	English	Lesson
首都机场	首都機場	Shǒudū Jīchǎng	pn	the Capital Airport (in Beijing)	20
瘦	瘦	shòu	adj	thin, skinny, lean	20
售货员	售貨員	shòuhuòyuán	n	shop assistant, salesclerk	9
书	書	shū	n	book	4
书店	書店	shūdiàn	n	bookstore	13
书架	書架	shūjià	n	bookcase, bookshelf	17
书桌	書桌	shūzhuō	n	desk	17
舒服	舒服	shūfu	adj	comfortable	11
叔叔	叔叔	shūshu	n	uncle	20
属	屬	shǔ	v	to belong to	14
暑假	暑假	shǔjià	n	summer vacation	19
暑期	暑期	shǔqī	n	summer term	14
刷卡	刷卡	shuā kǎ	vo	to pay with a credit card	9
帅	帥	shuài	adj	handsome	7
双	雙	shuāng	m	(measure word for a pair)	9
水	水	shuǐ	n	water	5
水果	水果	shuǐguǒ	n	fruit	14
水平	水平	shuǐpíng	n	level, standard	18
睡觉	睡覺	shuì jiào	vo	to sleep	4
说	說	shuō	v	to say, to speak	6
说话	說話	shuō huà	vo	to talk	7
送	送	sòng	v	to see off or out, to take (someone somewhere)	10
送	送	sòng	v	to give as a gift	14
素	素	sù	adj	vegetarian (lit. plain)	12

Simplified	Traditional	Pinyin	Part of Speech	English	Lesson
素餐	素餐	*sùcān*	n	vegetarian meal	19
宿舍	宿舍	*sùshè*	n	dormitory	8
酸	酸	*suān*	adj	sour	12
酸辣汤	酸辣湯	*suānlàtāng*	n	hot-and-sour soup	12
算了	算了	*suàn le*		forget it, never mind	4
虽然	雖然	*suīrán*	conj	although	9
岁	歲	*suì*	n	year (of age)	3
所以	所以	*suǒyǐ*	conj	so	4
T					
他	他	*tā*	pr	he, him	2
她	她	*tā*	pr	she, her	2
它	它	*tā*	pr	it	9
台北	台北	*Táiběi*	pn	Taipei	19
太…了	太…了	*tài…le*		too, extremely	3
汤姆	湯姆	*Tāngmǔ*	pn	Tom	14
糖醋鱼	糖醋魚	*tángcùyú*	n	sweet-and-sour fish	12
躺下	躺下	*tǎng xià*	vc	to lie down	15
套	套	*tào*	m	(measure word for things that come in a set/sets)	17
特别	特別	*tèbié*	adv	especially	10
疼死	疼死	*téng sǐ*	adj + c	really painful	15
踢	踢	*tī*	v	to kick	18
提高	提高	*tígāo*	v	to improve, to raise, to heighten	18
天	天	*tiān*	n	day	3
天气	天氣	*tiānqì*	n	weather	11

Simplified	Traditional	Pinyin	Part of Speech	English	Lesson
甜	甜	*tián*	adj	sweet	12
条	條	*tiáo*	m	(measure word for pants and long, thin objects)	9
跳舞	跳舞	*tiào wǔ*	vo	to dance	4
听	聽	*tīng*	v	to listen	4
听说	聽說	*tīngshuō*	v	to be told, to hear of	13
挺	挺	*tǐng*	adv	very, rather	9
同	同	*tóng*	adj	same	16
同学	同學	*tóngxué*	n	classmate	3
图书馆	圖書館	*túshūguǎn*	n	library	5
托运	托運	*tuōyùn*	v	to check (luggage)	20
W					
外国	外國	*wàiguó*	n	foreign country	4
玩（儿）	玩（兒）	*wán(r)*	v	to have fun, to play	5
碗	碗	*wǎn*	n	bowl	12
晚	晚	*wǎn*	adj	late	7
晚饭	晚飯	*wǎnfàn*	n	dinner, supper	3
晚上	晚上	*wǎnshang*	t	evening, night	3
王红	王紅	*Wáng Hóng*	pn	a personal name	14
王朋	王朋	*Wáng Péng*	pn	(a personal name)	1
往	往	*wǎng*	prep	towards	13
往返	往返	*wǎngfǎn*	v	make a round trip, go there and back	19
网球	網球	*wǎngqiú*	n	tennis	18
网上	網上	*wǎng shang*		on the Internet	11
忘	忘	*wàng*	v	to forget	12

Simplified	Traditional	Pinyin	Part of Speech	English	Lesson
危险	危險	*wēixiǎn*	adj	dangerous	18
喂	喂	*wéi/wèi*	interj	(on the phone) Hello!, Hey!	6
位	位	*wèi*	m	(polite measure word for people)	6
位子	位子	*wèizi*	n	seat	12
味精	味精	*wèijīng*	n	monosodium glutamate (MSG)	12
为了	為了	*wèile*	prep	for the sake of	18
为什么	為什麼	*wèishénme*	qpr	why	3
卫生间	衛生間	*wèishēngjiān*	n	bathroom	17
文化	文化	*wénhuà*	n	culture	19
问	問	*wèn*	v	to ask (a question)	1
问题	問題	*wèntí*	n	question, problem	6
我	我	*wǒ*	pr	I, me	1
我们	我們	*wǒmen*	pr	we, us	3
卧室	臥室	*wòshì*	n	bedroom	17
午饭	午飯	*wǔfàn*	n	lunch, midday meal	8
舞会	舞會	*wǔhuì*	n	dance party, ball	14

		X			
西	西	*xī*	n	west	13
西北航空公司	西北航空公司	*Xīběi Hángkōng Gōngsī*	pn	Northwest Airlines	19
西瓜	西瓜	*xīgua*	n	watermelon	14
希望	希望	*xīwàng*	v/n	to hope; hope	8
喜欢	喜歡	*xǐhuan*	v	to like	3
洗澡	洗澡	*xǐ zǎo*	vo	to take a bath/shower	8
下车	下車	*xià chē*	vo	to get off (a bus, train, etc.)	10

Simplified	Traditional	Pinyin	Part of Speech	English	Lesson
下个	下個	*xià ge*		next	6
下午	下午	*xiàwǔ*	t	afternoon	6
下雪	下雪	*xià xuě*	vo	to snow	11
下雨	下雨	*xià yǔ*	vo	to rain	11
夏天	夏天	*xiàtiān*	n	summer	11
先	先	*xiān*	adv	first	10
先生	先生	*xiānsheng*	n	Mr., husband, teacher	1
线	線	*xiàn*	n	line	10
现在	現在	*xiànzài*	t	now	3
香港	香港	*Xiānggǎng*	pn	Hong Kong	19
箱子	箱子	*xiāngzi*	n	suitcase, box	20
想	想	*xiǎng*	av	to want to, would like to	4
想	想	*xiǎng*	v	to think	16
想起来	想起來	*xiǎng qi lai*	vc	to remember, to recall	16
像	像	*xiàng*	v	to be like, to look like, to take after	14
小	小	*xiǎo*	adj	small, little	4
小白菜	小白菜	*xiǎo báicài*	n	baby bok choy	12
小姐	小姐	*xiǎojiě*	n	Miss, young lady	1
小时	小時	*xiǎoshí*	n	hour	15
小心	小心	*xiǎoxīn*	v	to be careful	20
笑	笑	*xiào*	v	to laugh at, to laugh, to smile	8
些	些	*xiē*	m	(measure word for an indefinite amount), some	12
鞋	鞋	*xié*	n	shoes	9
写	寫	*xiě*	v	to write	7

Simplified	Traditional	Pinyin	Part of Speech	English	Lesson
谢谢	謝謝	*xièxie*	v	to thank	3
新	新	*xīn*	adj	new	8
新年	新年	*xīnnián*	n	new year	10
信	信	*xìn*	n	letter (correspondence)	8
信用卡	信用卡	*xìnyòngkǎ*	n	credit card	9
星期	星期	*xīngqī*	n	week	3
星期四	星期四	*xīngqīsì*	n	Thursday	3
行	行	*xíng*	v	all right, OK	6
行李	行李	*xíngli*	n	luggage	20
姓	姓	*xìng*	v/n	(one's) family name is . . . ; family name	1
兴趣	興趣	*xìngqù*	n	interest	17
休息	休息	*xiūxi*	v	to take a break, to rest	15
学	學	*xué*	v	to study, to learn	7
学期	學期	*xuéqī*	n	school term, semester, quarter	8
学生	學生	*xuésheng*	n	student	1
学习	學習	*xuéxí*	v	to study, to learn	7
学校	學校	*xuéxiào*	n	school	5

Y

Simplified	Traditional	Pinyin	Part of Speech	English	Lesson
压	壓	*yā*	v	to press, to hold down, to weigh down	18
押金	押金	*yājīn*	n	security deposit	17
呀	呀	*ya*	p	(interjectory particle used to soften a question)	5
淹死	淹死	*yān sǐ*	vc	to drown	18
盐	鹽	*yán*	n	salt	12

Simplified	Traditional	Pinyin	Part of Speech	English	Lesson
颜色	顏色	*yánsè*	n	color	9
演	演	*yǎn*	v	to show (a film), to perform	16
眼睛	眼睛	*yǎnjing*	n	eye	14
痒	癢	*yǎng*	adj	itchy	15
养	養	*yǎng*	v	to raise	17
样子	樣子	*yàngzi*	n	style	9
药	藥	*yào*	n	medicine	15
药店	藥店	*yàodiàn*	n	pharmacy	15
要	要	*yào*	v	to want	5
要	要	*yào*	mv	will, to be going to; to want to, to have a desire to	6
要不然	要不然	*yàobùrán*	conj	otherwise	15
要是	要是	*yàoshi*	conj	if	6
爷爷	爺爺	*yéye*	n	paternal grandfather	20
也	也	*yě*	adv	too, also	1
夜里	夜裡	*yè lǐ*	n	at night	15
衣服	衣服	*yīfu*	n	clothes	9
医生	醫生	*yīshēng*	n	doctor, physician	2
医院	醫院	*yīyuàn*	n	hospital	15
一定	一定	*yídìng [yīdìng]*	adj/adv	certain, definite; certainly, definitely	14
一共	一共	*yígòng [yīgòng]*	adv	altogether	9
一路平安	一路平安	*yí lù píng'ān [yī lù píng'ān]*		have a good trip, bon voyage	20
一下	一下	*yí xià [yī xià]*	n+m	once, a bit	5
一样	一樣	*yíyàng [yīyàng]*	adj	same, alike	9

Simplified	Traditional	Pinyin	Part of Speech	English	Lesson
一边	一邊	yìbiān [yībiān]	adv	simultaneously, at the same time	8
一房一厅	一房一廳	yì fáng yì tīng [yī fáng yī tīng]		one bedroom and one living room	17
一起	一起	yìqǐ [yīqǐ]	adv	together	5
一言为定	一言為定	yì yán wéi dìng [yī yán wéi dìng]		that settles it, that's settled, it's decided	16
一直	一直	yìzhí [yīzhí]	adv	straight, continuously	13
以后	以後	yǐhòu	t	after, from now on, later on	6
以前	以前	yǐqián	t	before	8
以为	以為	yǐwéi	v	to assume erroneously	14
已经	已經	yǐjīng	adv	already	8
椅子	椅子	yǐzi	n	chair	17
因为	因為	yīnwèi	conj	because	3
音乐	音樂	yīnyuè	n	music	4
音乐会	音樂會	yīnyuèhuì	n	concert	8
饮料	飲料	yǐnliào	n	beverage	14
印象	印象	yìnxiàng	n	impression	16
应该	應該	yīnggāi	mv	should, ought to	18
英国	英國	Yīngguó	pn	Britain	3
英文	英文	Yīngwén	n	the English language	2
用	用	yòng	v	to use	8
用功	用功	yònggōng	adj	hard-working, diligent, studious	14
游泳	游泳	yóu yǒng	vo	to swim	18
有	有	yǒu	v	to have, to exist	2
有的	有的	yǒude	pr	some	4
有名	有名	yǒumíng	adj	famous, well-known	19

Simplified	Traditional	Pinyin	Part of Speech	English	Lesson
有意思	有意思	*yǒu yìsi*	adj	interesting	4
又	又	*yòu*	adv	again	11
右	右	*yòu*	n	right	13
鱼	魚	*yú*	n	fish	12
语法	語法	*yǔfǎ*	n	grammar	7
预报	預報	*yùbào*	v/n	to forecast; forecast	11
预习	預習	*yùxí*	v	to preview	7
圆	圓	*yuán*	adj	round	14
元	元	*yuán*	m	(measure word for the basic Chinese monetary unit), *yuan*	17
远	遠	*yuǎn*	adj	far	13
愿意	願意	*yuànyì*	mv	to be willing	18
约	約	*yuē*	v	to make an appointment	11
月	月	*yuè*	n	month	3
越来越	越來越	*yuè lái yuè*	adv	more and more	15
运动	運動	*yùndòng*	n	sports	13
运动服	運動服	*yùndòngfú*	n	sportswear, athletic clothing	18
Z					
在	在	*zài*	prep	at, in, on	5
在	在	*zài*	v	to be present, to be at (a place)	6
再	再	*zài*	adv	again	9
再见	再見	*zàijiàn*	v	goodbye, see you again	3
再说	再說	*zàishuō*	conj	moreover	15
糟糕	糟糕	*zāogāo*	adj	in a terrible mess, how terrible	11

Simplified	Traditional	Pinyin	Part of Speech	English	Lesson
早	早	*zǎo*	adj	early	7
早饭	早飯	*zǎofàn*	n	breakfast	8
早上	早上	*zǎoshang*	t	morning	7
怎么	怎麼	*zěnme*	qpr	how, how come	7
怎么样	怎麼樣	*zěnmeyàng*	qpr	Is it OK? How is that? How does that sound?	3
站	站	*zhàn*	m	(measure word for bus stops, train stops, etc.)	10
张	張	*zhāng*	m	(measure word for flat objects such as paper, pictures, etc.)	7
长	長	*zhǎng*	v	to grow, to appear	14
长大	長大	*zhǎng dà*	vc	to grow up	14
找	找	*zhǎo*	v	to look for	4
找（钱）	找（錢）	*zhǎo (qián)*	v(o)	to give change	9
照顾	照顧	*zhàogu*	v	to look after, to care for, to attend to	20
照片	照片	*zhàopiàn*	n	picture, photo	2
这	這	*zhè*	pr	this	2
这么	這麼	*zhème*	pr	so, this (late, etc.)	7
这儿	這兒	*zhèr*	pr	here	9
真	真	*zhēn*	adv	really	7
整理	整理	*zhěnglǐ*	v	to put in order	16
正在	正在	*zhèngzài*	adv	in the middle of (doing something)	8
政治	政治	*zhèngzhì*	n	politics	19
枝	枝	*zhī*	m	(measure word for long, thin, inflexible objects such as pens, pencils, etc.)	7
知道	知道	*zhīdao*	v	to know	8

Simplified	Traditional	Pinyin	Part of Speech	English	Lesson
直飞	直飛	*zhí fēi*		fly directly	19
只	只	*zhǐ*	adv	only	4
纸	紙	*zhǐ*	n	paper	7
中	中	*zhōng*	adj	medium, middle	9
中国	中國	*Zhōngguó*	pn	China	1
中国城	中國城	*Zhōngguóchéng*	n	Chinatown	13
中国国际航空公司	中國國際航空公司	*Zhōngguó Guójì Hángkōng Gōngsī*	pn	Air China	19
中间	中間	*zhōngjiān*	n	middle	13
中文	中文	*Zhōngwén*	n	the Chinese language	6
中午	中午	*zhōngwǔ*	t	noon	8
中心	中心	*zhōngxīn*	n	center	13
中学	中學	*zhōngxué*	n	middle school, secondary school	14
钟头	鐘頭	*zhōngtóu*	n	hour	14
种	種	*zhǒng*	m	(measure word for kinds, sorts, types)	9
重	重	*zhòng*	adj	heavy, serious	14
周末	週末	*zhōumò*	n	weekend	4
祝	祝	*zhù*	v	to wish (well)	8
住	住	*zhù*	v	to live (in a certain place)	14
专业	專業	*zhuānyè*	n	major (in college), specialty	8
转机	轉機	*zhuǎn jī*	vo	change planes	19
准	准	*zhǔn*	v	to allow, to be allowed	17
准备	準備	*zhǔnbèi*	v	to prepare	6
桌子	桌子	*zhuōzi*	n	table	12

Simplified	Traditional	Pinyin	Part of Speech	English	Lesson
字	字	zì	n	character	7
自己	自己	zìjǐ	pr	oneself	10
走	走	zǒu	v	to go by way of, to walk	10
走道	走道	zǒudào	n	aisle	19
走路	走路	zǒu lù	vo	to walk	17
租	租	zū	v	to rent	19
足球	足球	zúqiú	n	soccer, football	18
嘴	嘴	zuǐ	n	mouth	14
最	最	zuì	adv	most, (of superlative degree) -est	14
最好	最好	zuìhǎo	adv	had better	15
最后	最後	zuìhòu		final, last	10
最近	最近	zuìjìn	t	recently	8
昨天	昨天	zuótiān	t	yesterday	4
左	左	zuǒ	n	left	13
做	做	zuò	v	to do	2
做饭	做飯	zuò fàn	vo	to cook, to prepare a meal	17
坐	坐	zuò	v	to sit	5
坐	坐	zuò	v	to travel by	10

The English-Chinese index is organized based on the alphabetical order of the English definitions. For ease of reference, indefinite articles and definite articles are omitted when they are the beginning of a phrase.

English	Simplified	Traditional	Pinyin	Part of Speech	Lesson
A					
activity	活动	活動	huódòng	n	13
advertisement	广告	廣告	guǎnggào	n	17
after, from now on, later on	以后	以後	yǐhòu	t	6
afternoon	下午	下午	xiàwǔ	t	6
again	再	再	zài	adv	9
again	又	又	yòu	adv	11
ahead, in front of	前面	前面	qiánmiàn	n	13
Air China	中国国际航空公司	中國國際航空公司	Zhōngguó Guójì Hángkōng Gōngsī	pn	19
airplane	飞机	飛機	fēijī	n	10
airport	（飞）机场	（飛）機場	(fēi)jīchǎng	n	10
aisle	走道	走道	zǒudào	n	19
all right, OK	行	行	xíng	v	6
allow, be allowed	准	准	zhǔn	v	17
allow or cause (somebody to do something)	让	讓	ràng	v	10
almost, nearly; similar	差不多	差不多	chàbuduō	adv/adj	17
already	已经	已經	yǐjīng	adv	8
also, too, as well	还	還	hái	adv	3
although	虽然	雖然	suīrán	conj	9

English	Simplified	Traditional	Pinyin	Part of Speech	Lesson
altogether	一共	一共	*yígòng*	adv	9
America	美国	美國	*Měiguó*	pn	1
American-style	美式	美式	*Měishì*	adj	18
American dollar (USD)	美元	美元	*Měiyuán*	n	17
and	和	和	*hé*	conj	2
apartment	公寓	公寓	*gōngyù*	n	17
apple	苹果	蘋果	*píngguǒ*	n	14
ask (a question)	问	問	*wèn*	v	1
assume erroneously	以为	以為	*yǐwéi*	v	14
at, in, on	在	在	*zài*	prep	5
at night	夜里	夜裡	*yè lǐ*	n	15
aunt	阿姨	阿姨	*āyí*	n	20
autumn, fall	秋天	秋天	*qiūtiān*	n	11
aviation	航空	航空	*hángkōng*	n	19
away from	离	離	*lí*	prep	13

B

English	Simplified	Traditional	Pinyin	Part of Speech	Lesson
baby bok choy	小白菜	小白菜	*xiǎo báicài*	n	12
bag, sack, bundle, package	包	包	*bāo*	n	20
Bai Ying'ai	白英爱	白英愛	*Bái Yīng'ài*	pn	2
basketball	篮球	籃球	*lánqiú*	n	18
bathroom	卫生间	衛生間	*wèishēngjiān*	n	17
be	是	是	*shì*	v	1
be acquainted with, recognize	认识	認識	*rènshi*	v	3
be allergic to	过敏	過敏	*guòmǐn*	v	15

English	Simplified	Traditional	Pinyin	Part of Speech	Lesson
be called, call	叫	叫	*jiào*	v	1
be careful	小心	小心	*xiǎoxīn*	v	20
be like, look like, take after	像	像	*xiàng*	v	14
be overweight (of luggage, freight, etc.)	超重	超重	*chāozhòng*	v	20
be present, be at (a place)	在	在	*zài*	v	6
be sold out	卖完	賣完	*mài wán*	vc	12
be told, hear of	听说	聽說	*tīngshuō*	v	13
be willing	愿意	願意	*yuànyì*	mv	18
because	因为	因為	*yīnwèi*	conj	3
become	成	成	*chéng*	v	16
bedroom	卧室	臥室	*wòshì*	n	17
beef	牛肉	牛肉	*niúròu*	n	12
before	以前	以前	*yǐqián*	t	8
begin, start; beginning	开始	開始	*kāishǐ*	v/n	7
beginning	初	初	*chū*	n	19
Beijing	北京	北京	*Běijīng*	pn	1
belly, abdomen, stomach	肚子	肚子	*dùzi*	n	15
belong to	属	屬	*shǔ*	v	14
beverage	饮料	飲料	*yǐnliào*	n	14
big, old	大	大	*dà*	adj	3
birthday	生日	生日	*shēngrì*	n	3
black	黑	黑	*hēi*	adj	9
blue	蓝	藍	*lán*	adj	10
boarding gate	登机口	登機口	*dēngjīkǒu*	n	20

English	Simplified	Traditional	Pinyin	Part of Speech	Lesson
boarding pass	登机牌	登機牌	*dēngjīpái*	n	20
body, health	身体	身體	*shēntǐ*	n	15
book	书	書	*shū*	n	4
bookcase, bookshelf	书架	書架	*shūjià*	n	17
bookstore	书店	書店	*shūdiàn*	n	13
both, all	都	都	*dōu*	adv	2
bowl	碗	碗	*wǎn*	n	12
braise in soy sauce (to red-cook)	红烧	紅燒	*hóngshāo*	v	12
breakfast	早饭	早飯	*zǎofàn*	n	8
bring, take, carry, come with	带	帶	*dài*	v	12
Britain	英国	英國	*Yīngguó*	pn	3
brown, coffee color	咖啡色	咖啡色	*kāfēisè*	n	9
bus	公共汽车	公共汽車	*gōnggòng qìchē* n		10
busy	忙	忙	*máng*	adj	3
but	可是	可是	*kěshì*	conj	3
but	但是	但是	*dànshì*	conj	6
buy	买	買	*mǎi*	v	9
by	被	被	*bèi*	prep	18
C					
cake	蛋糕	蛋糕	*dàngāo*	n	14
California	加州	加州	*Jiāzhōu*	pn	11
can, able to	能	能	*néng*	mv	8
can, know how to	会	會	*huì*	mv	8
can, may	可以	可以	*kěyǐ*	mv	5

English	Simplified	Traditional	Pinyin	Part of Speech	Lesson
Capital Airport (in Beijing)	首都机场	首都機場	Shǒudū Jīchǎng	pn	20
capital city	首都	首都	shǒudū	n	19
catch, meet, welcome	接	接	jiē	v	14
cell phone	手机	手機	shǒujī	n	10
center	中心	中心	zhōngxīn	n	13
certain, definite; certainly, definitely	一定	一定	yídìng	adj/adv	14
chair	椅子	椅子	yǐzi	n	17
change planes	转机	轉機	zhuǎn jī	vo	19
character	字	字	zì	n	7
chat	聊天（儿）	聊天（兒）	liáo tiān(r)	vo	5
cheap, inexpensive	便宜	便宜	piányi	adj	9
check, look into	查	查	chá	v	19
check (luggage)	托运	托運	tuōyùn	v	20
child	孩子	孩子	háizi	n	2
China	中国	中國	Zhōngguó	pn	1
Chinatown	中国城	中國城	Zhōngguóchéng	n	13
Chinese characters	汉字	漢字	Hànzì	n	7
Chinese language	中文	中文	Zhōngwén	n	6
city	城市	城市	chéngshì	n	10
class	班	班	bān	n	14
class, course, lesson	课	課	kè	n	6
classmate	同学	同學	tóngxué	n	3
classroom	教室	教室	jiàoshì	n	8
clean	干净	乾淨	gānjìng	adj	17

English	Simplified	Traditional	Pinyin	Part of Speech	Lesson
clean up (a room, apartment or house)	打扫	打掃	dǎsǎo	v	16
clear	清楚	清楚	qīngchu	adj	12
clothes	衣服	衣服	yīfu	n	9
coffee	咖啡	咖啡	kāfēi	n	5
cola	可乐	可樂	kělè	n	5
cold	冷	冷	lěng	adj	11
college student	大学生	大學生	dàxuéshēng	n	2
color	颜色	顏色	yánsè	n	9
come	来	來	lái	v	5
come back	回来	回來	huí lai	vc	6
come in	进来	進來	jìn lai	vc	5
comfortable	舒服	舒服	shūfu	adj	11
company	公司	公司	gōngsī	n	19
compared with (comparison marker), to compare	比	比	bǐ	prep/v	11
computer	电脑	電腦	diànnǎo	n	8
concert	音乐会	音樂會	yīnyuèhuì	n	8
convenient	方便	方便	fāngbiàn	adj	6
cook, prepare a meal	做饭	做飯	zuò fàn	vo	17
cooked rice	米饭	米飯	mǐfàn	n	12
cool (appearance, behavior)	酷	酷	kù	adj	7
credit card	信用卡	信用卡	xìnyòngkǎ	n	9
cry, weep	哭	哭	kū	v	20
cucumber	黄瓜	黃瓜	huánggua	n	12

English	Simplified	Traditional	Pinyin	Part of Speech	Lesson
culture	文化	文化	*wénhuà*	n	19
cute, lovable	可爱	可愛	*kě'ài*	adj	14
D					
dance	跳舞	跳舞	*tiào wǔ*	vo	4
dance party, ball	舞会	舞會	*wǔhuì*	n	14
dangerous	危险	危險	*wēixiǎn*	adj	18
daughter	女儿	女兒	*nǚ'ér*	n	2
day	天	天	*tiān*	n	3
day after tomorrow	后天	後天	*hòutiān*	t	16
delicious	好吃	好吃	*hǎochī*	adj	12
desk	书桌	書桌	*shūzhuō*	n	17
diary	日记	日記	*rìjì*	n	8
difficult	难	難	*nán*	adj	7
dining room, cafeteria	餐厅	餐廳	*cāntīng*	n	8
dining table	饭桌	飯桌	*fànzhuō*	n	17
dinner, supper	晚饭	晚飯	*wǎnfàn*	n	3
dish, cuisine	菜	菜	*cài*	n	3
do	做	做	*zuò*	v	2
doctor, physician	医生	醫生	*yīshēng*	n	2
dog	狗	狗	*gǒu*	n	14
don't	别	別	*bié*	adv	6
dormitory	宿舍	宿舍	*sùshè*	n	8
drink	喝	喝	*hē*	v	5
drive a car	开车	開車	*kāi chē*	vo	10

English	Simplified	Traditional	Pinyin	Part of Speech	Lesson
drown	淹死	淹死	*yān sǐ*	vc	18
dumplings (with vegetable and/or meat filling)	饺子	餃子	*jiǎozi*	n	12
(dynamic particle)	了	了	*le*	p	5
		E			
early	早	早	*zǎo*	adj	7
east	东	東	*dōng*	n	13
easy	容易	容易	*róngyì*	adj	7
eat	吃	吃	*chī*	v	3
eighteen	十八	十八	*shíbā*	nu	3
eldest/oldest brother	大哥	大哥	*dàgē*	n	2
eldest/oldest sister	大姐	大姐	*dàjiě*	n	2
electricity	电	電	*diàn*	n	16
email/electronic mail	电子邮件	電子郵件	*diànzǐ yóujiàn*	n	10
English language	英文	英文	*Yīngwén*	n	2
enough	够	夠	*gòu*	adj	12
enter	进	進	*jìn*	v	5
especially	特别	特別	*tèbié*	adv	10
even	连	連	*lián*	prep	17
even more	更	更	*gèng*	adv	11
evening, night	晚上	晚上	*wǎnshang*	t	3
every, each	每	每	*měi*	pr	10
everybody	大家	大家	*dàjiā*	pr	7
examine	检查	檢查	*jiǎnchá*	v	15
exchange, change	换	換	*huàn*	v	9

English	Simplified	Traditional	Pinyin	Part of Speech	Lesson
(exclamatory particle to express surprise or dissatisfaction)	哎	哎	āi	excl	13
extremely	极	極	jí	adv	12
eye	眼睛	眼睛	yǎnjing	n	14
F					
face	脸	臉	liǎn	n	14
family, home	家	家	jiā	n	2
famous, well-known	有名	有名	yǒumíng	adj	19
famous scenic spots and historic sites	名胜古迹	名勝古蹟	míngshèng gǔjì	n	19
fantastic, super [colloq.]	棒	棒	bàng	adj	18
far	远	遠	yuǎn	adj	13
fast, quick; quickly	快	快	kuài	adj/adv	5
fat	胖	胖	pàng	adj	18
father, dad	爸爸	爸爸	bàba	n	2
fear, be afraid of	怕	怕	pà	v	18
fee, expenses	费	費	fèi	n	17
feel, think	觉得	覺得	juéde	v	4
feel embarrassed	不好意思	不好意思	bù hǎoyìsi		10
female	女	女	nǚ	adj	2
field	场	場	chǎng	n	13
final, last	最后	最後	zuìhòu		10
fine, good, nice, OK, it's settled	好	好	hǎo	adj	1
first	先	先	xiān	adv	10
fish	鱼	魚	yú	n	12
flower	花	花	huā	n	14

English	Simplified	Traditional	Pinyin	Part of Speech	Lesson
fly directly	直飞	直飛	zhí fēi		19
foot	脚	腳	jiǎo	n	18
for the sake of	为了	為了	wèile	prep	18
forecast; forcast	预报	預報	yùbào	v/n	11
foreign country	外国	外國	wàiguó	n	4
forget	忘	忘	wàng	v	12
forget it, never mind	算了	算了	suàn le		4
forward, ahead	前	前	qián	n	13
free time	空（儿）	空（兒）	kòng(r)	n	6
friend	朋友	朋友	péngyou	n	3
from	从	從	cóng	prep	13
fruit	水果	水果	shuǐguǒ	n	14
fun, amusing, interesting	好玩儿	好玩兒	hǎowánr	adj	11
furniture	家具	傢俱	jiājù	n	17
furthermore, in addition	另外	另外	lìngwài	conj	17
G					
game, match, competition; to compete	比赛	比賽	bǐsài	n/v	18
Gao Wenzhong	高文中	高文中	Gāo Wénzhōng	pn	2
Gao Xiaoyin	高小音	高小音	Gāo Xiǎoyīn	pn	5
get an injection	打针	打針	dǎ zhēn	vo	15
get off (a bus, train, etc.)	下车	下車	xià chē	vo	10
get sick	生病	生病	shēng bìng	vo	15
get sick because of bad food	吃坏	吃壞	chī huài	vc	15
get up	起床	起床	qǐ chuáng	vo	8

English	Simplified	Traditional	Pinyin	Part of Speech	Lesson
gift, present	礼物	禮物	lǐwù	n	14
give	给	給	gěi	v	5
give as a gift	送	送	sòng	v	14
give change	找（钱）	找（錢）	zhǎo (qián)	v(o)	9
give or take a test; test	考试	考試	kǎo shì	vo/n	6
go	去	去	qù	v	4
go [colloq.]	上	上	shàng	v	13
go back, return	回去	回去	huí qu	vc	11
go by way of, walk	走	走	zǒu	v	10
go home	回家	回家	huí jiā	vo	5
go on vacation, have time off	放假	放假	fàng jià	vo	19
go online, surf the internet	上网	上網	shàng wǎng	vo	8
go out	出去	出去	chūqu	vc	10
go to, arrive	到	到	dào	v	6
go to a class, start a class, be in class	上课	上課	shàng kè	vo	7
goodbye, see you again	再见	再見	zàijiàn	v	3
Google	谷歌	谷歌	Gǔgē	pn	13
grade in school	年级	年級	niánjí	n	6
grammar	语法	語法	yǔfǎ	n	7
Great Wall	长城	長城	Chángchéng	pn	19
green	绿	綠	lǜ	adj	10
green, leafy vegetable	青菜	青菜	qīngcài	n	12
grow, appear	长	長	zhǎng	v	14
grow up	长大	長大	zhǎng dà	vc	14

English	Simplified	Traditional	Pinyin	Part of Speech	Lesson
H					
had better	最好	最好	*zuìhǎo*	adv	15
half, half an hour	半	半	*bàn*	nu	3
half a day, a long time	半天	半天	*bàntiān*		18
hand	手	手	*shǒu*	n	18
handle, do	办	辦	*bàn*	v	11
handsome	帅	帥	*shuài*	adj	7
happy	快乐	快樂	*kuàilè*	adj	10
happy, pleased	高兴	高興	*gāoxìng*	adj	5
hard to bear, uncomfortable	难受	難受	*nánshòu*	adj	18
hard-working, diligent, studious	用功	用功	*yònggōng*	adj	14
have, exist	有	有	*yǒu*	v	2
have a cold	感冒	感冒	*gǎnmào*	v	15
have a fever	发烧	發燒	*fā shāo*	vo	15
have a good trip, bon voyage	一路平安	一路平安	*yí lù píng'ān*		20
have a meeting	开会	開會	*kāi huì*	vo	6
have fun, play	玩（儿）	玩（兒）	*wán(r)*	v	5
he, him	他	他	*tā*	pr	2
healthy; health	健康	健康	*jiànkāng*	adj/n	15
heavy, serious	重	重	*zhòng*	adj	14
Helen	海伦	海倫	*Hǎilún*	pn	14
Hello!, Hey! (on the phone)	喂	喂	*wéi/wèi*	interj	6
help	帮	幫	*bāng*	v	6
here	这儿	這兒	*zhèr*	pr	9

English	Simplified	Traditional	Pinyin	Part of Speech	Lesson
highway	高速公路	高速公路	gāosù gōnglù	n	10
hold or carry in the arms	抱	抱	bào	v	18
home-style	家常	家常	jiācháng	n	12
homework, schoolwork	功课	功課	gōngkè	n	7
Hong Kong	香港	香港	Xiānggǎng	pn	19
honorable, expensive	贵	貴	guì	adj	1
hope; hope	希望	希望	xīwàng	v/n	8
hospital	医院	醫院	yīyuàn	n	15
hot	热	熱	rè	adj	11
hot-and-sour soup	酸辣汤	酸辣湯	suānlàtāng	n	12
hotel	旅馆	旅館	lǚguǎn	n	19
hour	钟头	鐘頭	zhōngtóu	n	14
hour	小时	小時	xiǎoshí	n	15
how, how come	怎么	怎麼	zěnme	qpr	7
how many, some, a few	几	幾	jǐ	nu	2
how many/much, to what extent	多	多	duō	adv	3
how much/many	多少	多少	duōshao	qpr	9
however, but	不过	不過	búguò	conj	9
hundred	百	百	bǎi	nu	9
hungry	饿	餓	è	adj	12

I

English	Simplified	Traditional	Pinyin	Part of Speech	Lesson
I, me	我	我	wǒ	pr	1
ice skate	滑冰	滑冰	huá bīng	vo	11
iced tea	冰茶	冰茶	bīngchá	n	12

English	Simplified	Traditional	Pinyin	Part of Speech	Lesson
if	要是	要是	*yàoshi*	conj	6
if	如果…的话	如果…的話	*rúguǒ…de huà*	conj	9
immediately, right away	马上	馬上	*mǎshàng*	adv	19
impression	印象	印象	*yìnxiàng*	n	16
improve, raise, heighten,	提高	提高	*tígāo*	v	18
in a terrible mess, how terrible	糟糕	糟糕	*zāogāo*	adj	11
in addition to, besides	除了…以外	除了…以外	*chúle…yǐwài*	conj	8
in that case, then	那	那	*nà*	conj	4
in the middle of (doing something)	正在	正在	*zhèngzài*	adv	8
(indicating degree) so, such	那么	那麼	*nàme*	pr	11
(indicating disposition, arrangement, or settlement of something)	把	把	*bǎ*	prep	15
inside	里边	裡邊	*lǐbian*	n	13
insurance; secure	保险	保險	*bǎoxiǎn*	n/adj	15
interest	兴趣	興趣	*xìngqù*	n	17
interesting	有意思	有意思	*yǒu yìsi*	adj	4
(interjectory particle used to soften a question)	呀	呀	*ya*	p	5
intern	实习	實習	*shíxí*	v	19
international	国际	國際	*guójì*	adj	18
intersection	路口	路口	*lùkǒu*	n	13
interview, interview (for a job or school admission)	面试	面試	*miànshì*	v/n	11
introduce	介绍	介紹	*jièshào*	v	5

English	Simplified	Traditional	Pinyin	Part of Speech	Lesson
invite someone (to dinner, coffee, etc.), play the host	请客	請客	qǐng kè	vo	4
Is it OK? How is that? How does that sound?	怎么样	怎麼樣	zěnmeyàng	qpr	3
it	它	它	tā	pr	9
it doesn't matter	没关系	沒關係	méi guānxi		12
itchy	痒	癢	yǎng	adj	15
J					
Japan	日本	日本	Rìběn	pn	13
Japanese (language)	日文	日文	Rìwén	pn	13
job; to work	工作	工作	gōngzuò	n/v	2
jog	跑步	跑步	pǎo bù	vo	18
just	刚	剛	gāng	adv	12
just, only (indicating a small number)	就	就	jiù	adv	16
just now, a moment ago	刚才	剛才	gāngcái	t	11
K					
kick	踢	踢	tī	v	18
kitchen	厨房	廚房	chúfáng	n	17
know	知道	知道	zhīdao	v	8
L					
last time	上次	上次	shàng cì		15
last year	去年	去年	qùnián	t	14
late	晚	晚	wǎn	adj	7
later	后来	後來	hòulái	t	8
laugh at, laugh, smile	笑	笑	xiào	v	8

English	Simplified	Traditional	Pinyin	Part of Speech	Lesson
lawyer	律师	律師	lǜshī	n	2
lazy	懒	懶	lǎn	adj	15
lean on, lean against, be next to	靠	靠	kào	v	19
left	左	左	zuǒ	n	13
length	长短	長短	chángduǎn	n	9
letter (correspondence)	信	信	xìn	n	8
level, standard	水平	水平	shuǐpíng	n	18
Li You	李友	李友	Lǐ Yǒu	pn	1
library	图书馆	圖書館	túshūguǎn	n	5
lie down	躺下	躺下	tǎng xià	vc	15
like	喜欢	喜歡	xǐhuan	v	3
line	线	線	xiàn	n	10
listen	听	聽	tīng	v	4
little, a bit, some	点（儿）	點（兒）	diǎn(r)	m	5
live (a life), observe (a holiday), celebrate (a festival), pass	过	過	guò	v	14
live (in a certain place)	住	住	zhù	v	14
living room	客厅	客廳	kètīng	n	17
long time	好久	好久	hǎo jiǔ		4
look after, care for, attend to	照顾	照顧	zhàogu	v	20
look for	找	找	zhǎo	v	4
love, like, be fond of	爱	愛	ài	v	14
luggage	行李	行李	xíngli	n	20
lunch, midday meal	午饭	午飯	wǔfàn	n	8

English	Simplified	Traditional	Pinyin	Part of Speech	Lesson
		M			
major (in college), specialty	专业	專業	*zhuānyè*	n	8
make a phone call	打电话	打電話	*dǎ diànhuà*	vo	6
make a round trip, go there and back	往返	往返	*wǎngfǎn*	v	19
make an appointment	约	約	*yuē*	v	11
male	男	男	*nán*	adj	2
many, much	多	多	*duō*	adj	7
map	地图	地圖	*dìtú*	n	13
master worker	师傅	師傅	*shīfu*	n	12
matter, affair, event	事（儿）	事（兒）	*shì(r)*	n	3
may; possible	可能	可能	*kěnéng*	mv/adj	17
meal, (cooked) rice	饭	飯	*fàn*	n	3
meal card	饭卡	飯卡	*fànkǎ*	n	12
(measure word for a pair)	双	雙	*shuāng*	m	9
(measure word for a position in a numerical series, day of the month)	号	號	*hào*	m	3
(measure word for an indefinite amount), some	些	些	*xiē*	m	12
(measure word for books)	本	本	*běn*	m	14
(measure word for bottled liquid, etc.)	瓶	瓶	*píng*	m/n	5
(measure word for bus stops, train stops, etc.)	站	站	*zhàn*	m	10
(measure word for class periods)	节	節	*jié*	m	6
(measure word for complete courses of an action or instances of an action)	遍	遍	*biàn*	m	15
(measure word for essays, articles, etc.)	篇	篇	*piān*	m	8

English	Simplified	Traditional	Pinyin	Part of Speech	Lesson
(measure word for flat objects such as paper, pictures, etc.)	张	張	zhāng	m	7
(measure word for frequency)	次	次	cì	m	13
(measure word for kinds, sorts, types)	种	種	zhǒng	m	9
(measure word for letters)	封	封	fēng	m	8
(measure word for long, thin, inflexible objects such as pens, pencils, etc.)	枝	枝	zhī	m	7
(measure word for many common everyday objects)	个	個	gè/ge	m	2
(measure word for meal orders, jobs)	份	份	fèn	m	19
(measure word for number of family members)	口	口	kǒu	m	2
(measure word for pants and long, thin objects)	条	條	tiáo	m	9
(measure word for people [polite])	位	位	wèi	m	6
(measure word for shirts, dresses, jackets, coats, etc.)	件	件	jiàn	m	9
(measure word for tablets, slices, etc.)	片	片	piàn	m	15
(measure word for the basic Chinese monetary unit [equivalent of a dollar])	块	塊	kuài	m	9
(measure word for the basic Chinese monetary unit), *yuan*	元	元	yuán	m	17
(measure word for things contained in a cup or glass)	杯	杯	bēi	m	5
(measure word for things that come in a set/sets)	套	套	tào	m	17

English	Simplified	Traditional	Pinyin	Part of Speech	Lesson
(measure word for things with handles, for handfuls of things)	把	把	bǎ	m	14
(measure word for 1/100 of a kuai [equivalent of a cent])	分	分	fēn	m	9
(measure word for 1/10 of a kuai [equivalent of a dime])	毛	毛	máo	m	9
meat	肉	肉	ròu	n	12
medicine	药	藥	yào	n	15
medium, middle	中	中	zhōng	adj	9
meet up/with	见面	見面	jiàn miàn	vo	6
method, way (of doing something)	办法	辦法	bànfǎ	n	15
middle	中间	中間	zhōngjiān	n	13
middle school, secondary school	中学	中學	zhōngxué	n	14
minute	分钟	分鐘	fēnzhōng	n	17
Miss, young lady	小姐	小姐	xiǎojiě	n	1
money	钱	錢	qián	n	9
monosodium glutamate (MSG)	味精	味精	wèijīng	n	12
month	月	月	yuè	n	3
more and more	越来越	越來越	yuè lái yuè	adv	15
moreover	再说	再說	zàishuō	conj	15
morning	上午	上午	shàngwǔ	t	6
morning	早上	早上	zǎoshang	t	7
most, (of superlative degree) -est	最	最	zuì	adv	14
mother, mom	妈妈	媽媽	māma	n	2
mouth	嘴	嘴	zuǐ	n	14

English	Simplified	Traditional	Pinyin	Part of Speech	Lesson
move	搬	搬	*bān*	v	16
movie	电影	電影	*diànyǐng*	n	4
Mr., husband, teacher	先生	先生	*xiānsheng*	n	1
multi-story building, floor (of a multi-level building)	楼	樓	*lóu*	n	14
music	音乐	音樂	*yīnyuè*	n	4
must, have to	得	得	*děi*	av	6
N					
name	名字	名字	*míngzi*	n	1
near	近	近	*jìn*	adj	13
need not	不用	不用	*bú yòng*		9
nervous, anxious	紧张	緊張	*jǐnzhāng*	adj	10
new	新	新	*xīn*	adj	8
new words, vocabulary	生词	生詞	*shēngcí*	n	7
new year	新年	新年	*xīnnián*	n	10
New York	纽约	紐約	*Niǔyuē*	pn	1
newspaper	报纸	報紙	*bàozhǐ*	n	17
next one	下个	下個	*xià ge*		6
noon	中午	中午	*zhōngwǔ*	t	8
north	北	北	*běi*	n	13
Northwest Airlines	西北航空公司	西北航空公司	*Xīběi Hángkōng Gōngsī*	pn	19
nose	鼻子	鼻子	*bízi*	n	14
not	没	沒	*méi*	adv	2
not, no	不	不	*bù*	adv	1

English	Simplified	Traditional	Pinyin	Part of Speech	Lesson
not only . . . , but also . . .	不但···, 而且···	不但···， 而且···	búdàn . . . , érqiě . . .	conj	11
not until, only then	才	才	cái	adv	5
now	现在	現在	xiànzài	t	3
number	号码	號碼	hàomǎ	n	16

O

English	Simplified	Traditional	Pinyin	Part of Speech	Lesson
o'clock (lit. dot, point, thus "points on the clock")	点	點	diǎn	m	3
(of airplanes) take off	起飞	起飛	qǐfēi	v	20
of course	当然	當然	dāngrán	adv	18
(of food) cold "blended", cold tossed	凉拌	涼拌	liángbàn	v	12
office	办公室	辦公室	bàngōngshì	n	6
often	常常	常常	chángcháng	adv	4
older brother	哥哥	哥哥	gēge	n	2
older female cousin	表姐	表姐	biǎojiě	n	14
older sister	姐姐	姐姐	jiějie	n	2
on the Internet	网上	網上	wǎng shang		11
once, a bit	一下	一下	yí xià	n+m	5
one bedroom and one living room	一房一厅	一房一廳	yì fáng yì tīng		17
(one's) family name is . . . ; family name	姓	姓	xìng	v/n	1
oneself	自己	自己	zìjǐ	pr	10
one-way trip	单程	單程	dānchéng	n	19
only	只	只	zhǐ	adv	4
or	还是	還是	háishi	conj	3
or	或者	或者	huòzhě	conj	10

English	Simplified	Traditional	Pinyin	Part of Speech	Lesson
order food	点菜	點菜	diǎn cài	vo	12
other people, another person	别人	別人	biérén	n	4
otherwise	要不然	要不然	yàobùrán	conj	15
P					
pants	裤子	褲子	kùzi	n	9
paper	纸	紙	zhǐ	n	7
parents, father and mother	父母	父母	fùmǔ	n	19
park	公园	公園	gōngyuán	n	11
(particle to link adverbial and verb)	地	地	de	p	20
(particle used after a verb to indicate a past experience)	过	過	guo	p	13
passport	护照	護照	hùzhào	n	19
paternal grandfather	爷爷	爺爺	yéye	n	20
paternal grandmother	奶奶	奶奶	nǎinai	n	20
patient	病人	病人	bìngrén	n	15
pay money	付钱	付錢	fù qián	vo	9
pay with a credit card	刷卡	刷卡	shuā kǎ	vo	9
pear	梨	梨	lí	n	14
pen	笔	筆	bǐ	n	7
people, person	人	人	rén	n	1
pet	宠物	寵物	chǒngwù	n	17
pharmacy	药店	藥店	yàodiàn	n	15
picture, photo	照片	照片	zhàopiàn	n	2
place	地方	地方	dìfang	n	13

English	Simplified	Traditional	Pinyin	Part of Speech	Lesson
plan; plan	打算	打算	dǎsuàn	v/n	19
plan; plan	计划	計劃	jìhuà	v/n	19
plate, dish	盘	盤	pán	n	12
play ball	打球	打球	dǎ qiú	vo	4
please (polite form of request), to treat or to invite (somebody)	请	請	qǐng	v	1
polite	客气	客氣	kèqi	adj	6
politics	政治	政治	zhèngzhì	n	19
(possessive or descriptive particle)	的	的	de	p	2
practice	练习	練習	liànxí	v	6
precisely, exactly	就	就	jiù	adv	6
(prefix for ordinal numbers)	第	第	dì	prefix	7
prepare	准备	準備	zhǔnbèi	v	6
press, hold down, weigh down	压	壓	yā	v	18
pretty	漂亮	漂亮	piàoliang	adj	5
pretty good	不错	不錯	búcuò	adj	4
preview	预习	預習	yùxí	v	7
previous one	上个	上個	shàng ge		7
pronunciation	发音	發音	fāyīn	n	8
put, place	放	放	fàng	v	12
put in order	整理	整理	zhěnglǐ	v	16
Q					
quarrel; noisy	吵	吵	chǎo	v/adj	17
quarter (of an hour)	刻	刻	kè	m	3

English	Simplified	Traditional	Pinyin	Part of Speech	Lesson
(question particle)	吗	嗎	*ma*	qp	1
(question particle)	呢	呢	*ne*	qp	1
question, problem	问题	問題	*wèntí*	n	6
quiet	安静	安靜	*ānjìng*	adj	17
quite a few	好几	好幾	*hǎo jǐ*		15

R

English	Simplified	Traditional	Pinyin	Part of Speech	Lesson
racket	拍	拍	*pāi*	n	18
rain	下雨	下雨	*xià yǔ*	vo	11
raise	养	養	*yǎng*	v	17
randomly, arbitrarily, messily	乱	亂	*luàn*	adv	15
read aloud	念	念	*niàn*	v	7
really	真	真	*zhēn*	adv	7
really painful	疼死	疼死	*téng sǐ*	adj+c	15
receive, accept	收	收	*shōu*	v	9
recently	最近	最近	*zuìjìn*	t	8
red	红	紅	*hóng*	adj	9
refrigerator	冰箱	冰箱	*bīngxiāng*	n	15
remember	记得	記得	*jìde*	v	16
remember, recall	想起来	想起來	*xiǎng qi lai*	vc	16
renminbi (RMB, Chinese currency)	人民币	人民幣	*rénmínbì*	n	17
rent	房租	房租	*fángzū*	n	17
rent	租	租	*zū*	v	19
rent out	出租	出租	*chūzū*	v	17
reserve, book (a ticket, a hotel room, etc.)	订	訂	*dìng*	v	19

English	Simplified	Traditional	Pinyin	Part of Speech	Lesson
restaurant	饭馆（儿）	飯館（兒）	fànguǎn(r)	n	12
restroom, toilet	厕所	廁所	cèsuǒ	n	15
return	还	還	huán	v	17
review	复习	復習	fùxí	v	7
right	右	右	yòu	n	13
right, correct	对	對	duì	adj	4
right away, quickly, in a hurry	赶快	趕快	gǎnkuài	adv	15
roast duck	烤鸭	烤鴨	kǎoyā	n	20
room	房间	房間	fángjiān	n	16
round	圆	圓	yuán	adj	14
route, road	路	路	lù	n	10

S

English	Simplified	Traditional	Pinyin	Part of Speech	Lesson
salt	盐	鹽	yán	n	12
same, alike	一样	一樣	yíyàng	adj	9
same, alike	同	同	tóng	adj	16
say, speak	说	說	shuō	v	6
scheduled flight	航班	航班	hángbān	n	19
school	学校	學校	xuéxiào	n	5
school term, semester, quarter	学期	學期	xuéqī	n	8
seat	位子	位子	wèizi	n	12
second oldest sister	二姐	二姐	èrjiě	n	2
security deposit	押金	押金	yājīn	n	17
see	见	見	jiàn	v	3
see a doctor	看病	看病	kàn bìng	vo	15

English	Simplified	Traditional	Pinyin		
see off or out, take (someone somewhere)	送	送	sòng		
seem, be like	好像	好像	hǎoxiàng	adv	
sell at a discount, give a discount	打折	打折	dǎ zhé	vo	19
send a text message (lit. send a short message)	发短信	發短信	fā duǎnxìn	vo	10
(sentence-final particle of exclamation, interrogation, etc.)	啊	啊	a	p	6
(sentence-final particle)	吧	吧	ba	p	5
September	九月	九月	jiǔyuè	p	3
serve as, to be	当	當	dāng	v	17
serve food	上菜	上菜	shàng cài	vo	12
Shanghai	上海	上海	Shànghǎi	pn	12
she, her	她	她	tā	pr	2
shirt	衬衫	襯衫	chènshān	n	9
shoes	鞋	鞋	xié	n	9
shop assistant, salesclerk	售货员	售貨員	shòuhuòyuán	n	9
should, ought to	应该	應該	yīnggāi	mv	18
show (a film), perform	演	演	yǎn	v	16
side	旁边	旁邊	pángbiān	n	13
simple	简单	簡單	jiǎndān	adj	18
simultaneously, at the same time	一边	一邊	yìbiān	adv	8
sing (a song)	唱歌（儿）	唱歌（兒）	chàng gē(r)	vo	4
sit	坐	坐	zuò	v	5
size	大小	大小	dàxiǎo	n	9
size	号	號	hào	n	9

	Simplified	Traditional	Pinyin	Part of Speech	Lesson
...ep	睡觉	睡覺	*shuì jiào*	vo	4
slow	慢	慢	*màn*	adj	7
small, little	小	小	*xiǎo*	adj	4
smart, bright, clever	聪明	聰明	*cōngming*	adj	14
snow	下雪	下雪	*xià xuě*	vo	11
so	所以	所以	*suǒyǐ*	conj	4
so, this (late, etc.)	这么	這麼	*zhème*	pr	7
soccer, football	足球	足球	*zúqiú*	n	18
sofa	沙发	沙發	*shāfā*	n	17
some	有的	有的	*yǒude*	pr	4
son	儿子	兒子	*érzi*	n	2
sorry	对不起	對不起	*duìbuqǐ*	v	5
sound recording; record	录音	錄音	*lùyīn*	n/vo	7
sour	酸	酸	*suān*	adj	12
south	南	南	*nán*	n	13
spend	花	花	*huā*	v	10
spend, take (effort)	费	費	*fèi*	v	16
sports	运动	運動	*yùndòng*	n	13
sportswear, athletic clothing	运动服	運動服	*yùndòngfú*	n	18
spring	春天	春天	*chūntiān*	n	11
store, shop	商店	商店	*shāngdiàn*	n	9
straight, continuously	一直	一直	*yìzhí*	adv	13
strength, effort	力气	力氣	*lìqi*	n	16
(structural particle)	得	得	*de*	p	7

English	Simplified	Traditional	Pinyin	Part of Speech	Lesson
student	学生	學生	*xuésheng*	n	1
study, learn	学	學	*xué*	v	7
study, learn	学习	學習	*xuéxí*	v	7
style	样子	樣子	*yàngzi*	n	9
subway	地铁	地鐵	*dìtiě*	n	10
suitable	合适	合適	*héshì*	adj	9
suitcase, box	箱子	箱子	*xiāngzi*	n	20
summer	夏天	夏天	*xiàtiān*	n	11
summer term	暑期	暑期	*shǔqī*	n	14
summer vacation	暑假	暑假	*shǔjià*	n	19
sweet	甜	甜	*tián*	adj	12
sweet-and-sour fish	糖醋鱼	糖醋魚	*tángcùyú*	n	12
swim	游泳	游泳	*yóu yǒng*	vo	18
T					
table	桌子	桌子	*zhuōzi*	n	12
Taipei	台北	台北	*Táiběi*	pn	19
take, get	拿	拿	*ná*	v	13
take a bath/shower	洗澡	洗澡	*xǐ zǎo*	vo	8
take a break, to rest	休息	休息	*xiūxi*	v	15
take a taxi	打车	打車	*dǎ chē*	vo	10
talk	说话	說話	*shuō huà*	vo	7
taxi	出租汽车	出租汽車	*chūzū qìchē*	n	10
tea	茶	茶	*chá*	n	5
teach	教	教	*jiāo*	v	7

English	Simplified	Traditional	Pinyin	Part of Speech	Lesson
teacher	老师	老師	lǎoshī	n	1
Teacher Chang	常老师	常老師	Cháng lǎoshī	pn	6
television	电视	電視	diànshì	n	4
tell	告诉	告訴	gàosu	v	8
tennis	网球	網球	wǎngqiú	n	18
text of a lesson	课文	課文	kèwén	n	7
thank	谢谢	謝謝	xièxie	v	3
that	那	那	nà	pr	2
that settles it, that's settled, it's decided	一言为定	一言為定	yì yán wéi dìng		16
then	然后	然後	ránhòu	adv	10
there	那儿	那兒	nàr	pr	8
there	那里	那裡	nàli	pr	17
thin, skinny, lean	瘦	瘦	shòu	adj	20
things, objects	东西	東西	dōngxi	n	9
think	想	想	xiǎng	v	16
thirsty	渴	渴	kě	adj	12
this	这	這	zhè	pr	2
this year	今年	今年	jīnnián	t	3
thousand	千	千	qiān	nu	19
Thursday	星期四	星期四	xīngqīsì	n	3
ticket	票	票	piào	n	10
time	时间	時間	shíjiān	n	6
time (a point in), moment, time (a duration of)	时候	時候	shíhou	n	4
tired	累	累	lèi	adj	8

English	Simplified	Traditional	Pinyin	Part of Speech	Lesson
to, for	给	給	*gěi*	prep	6
today	今天	今天	*jīntiān*	t	3
tofu, bean curd	豆腐	豆腐	*dòufu*	n	12
together	一起	一起	*yìqǐ*	adv	5
Tokyo	东京	東京	*Dōngjīng*	pn	13
Tom	汤姆	湯姆	*Tāngmǔ*	pn	14
tomorrow	明天	明天	*míngtiān*	t	3
too, also	也	也	*yě*	adv	1
too, extremely	太…了	太…了	*tài … le*		3
tour guide	导游	導遊	*dǎoyóu*	n	19
towards	往	往	*wǎng*	prep	13
traffic light	红绿灯	紅綠燈	*hónglǜdēng*	n	13
travel	旅行	旅行	*lǚxíng*	v	16
travel agency	旅行社	旅行社	*lǚxíngshè*	n	19
travel by	坐	坐	*zuò*	v	10
troublesome	麻烦	麻煩	*máfan*	adj	10
try	试	試	*shì*	v	9
turn	拐	拐	*guǎi*	v	13
twelve	十二	十二	*shí'èr*	nu	3
two [colloq.]	俩	倆	*liǎ*	nu+m	16
two, a couple of	两	兩	*liǎng*	nu	2
U					
uncle	叔叔	叔叔	*shūshu*	n	20
understand	懂	懂	*dǒng*	v	7

English	Simplified	Traditional	Pinyin	Part of Speech	Lesson
use	用	用	*yòng*	v	8
usually	平常	平常	*píngcháng*	adv	7
V					
vegetarian (lit. plain)	素	素	*sù*	adj	12
vegetarian meal	素餐	素餐	*sùcān*	n	19
very	很	很	*hěn*	adv	3
very, extremely, exceedingly	非常	非常	*fēicháng*	adv	11
very, rather	挺	挺	*tǐng*	adv	9
vicinity, neighborhood, nearby area	附近	附近	*fùjìn*	n	17
visa	签证	簽證	*qiānzhèng*	n	19
W					
wait, wait for	等	等	*děng*	v	6
waiter, attendant	服务员	服務員	*fúwùyuán*	n	12
walk	走路	走路	*zǒu lù*	vo	17
Wang Hong	王红	王紅	*Wáng Hóng*	pn	14
Wang Peng	王朋	王朋	*Wáng Péng*	pn	1
want	要	要	*yào*	v	5
want to, would like to	想	想	*xiǎng*	av	4
warm	暖和	暖和	*nuǎnhuo*	adj	11
watch, look, read	看	看	*kàn*	v	4
water	水	水	*shuǐ*	n	5
watermelon	西瓜	西瓜	*xīgua*	n	14
we, us	我们	我們	*wǒmen*	pr	3

English	Simplified	Traditional	Pinyin	Part of Speech	Lesson
wear, put on	穿	穿	chuān	v	9
weather	天气	天氣	tiānqì	n	11
week	星期	星期	xīngqī	n	3
weekend	周末	週末	zhōumò	n	4
welcome	欢迎	歡迎	huānyíng	v	20
west	西	西	xī	n	13
what	什么	什麼	shénme	qpr	1
where	哪儿	哪兒	nǎr	qpr	5
where	哪里	哪裡	nǎli	pr	7
which	哪	哪	nǎ/něi	qpr	6
who, whom	谁	誰	shéi	qpr	2
why	为什么	為什麼	wèishénme	qpr	3
will	会	會	huì	mv	11
will, be going to; want to, have a desire to	要	要	yào	mv	6
window	窗户	窗戶	chuānghu	n	19
winter	冬天	冬天	dōngtiān	n	11
winter vacation	寒假	寒假	hánjià	n	10
wish (well)	祝	祝	zhù	v	8
with	跟	跟	gēn	prep	6
work at a temporary job (often part time)	打工	打工	dǎ gōng	vo	19
worry	担心	擔心	dān xīn	vo	18
write	写	寫	xiě	v	7
wrong	错	錯	cuò	adj	12

English	Simplified	Traditional	Pinyin	Part of Speech	Lesson
		Y			
year (of age)	岁	歲	*suì*	n	3
yellow	黄	黃	*huáng*	adj	9
yesterday	昨天	昨天	*zuótiān*	t	4
you	你	你	*nǐ*	pr	1
you (honorific for 你)	您	您	*nín*	pr	6
younger brother	弟弟	弟弟	*dìdi*	n	2
younger sister	妹妹	妹妹	*mèimei*	n	2

Lesson 1

Text

Zhang Tianming is a college freshman. School's about to start. His home is very far from the university, so he has to take a plane to get to school. He's on the plane for more than two hours. After he gets off the plane, he immediately hails a cab. In no time, he arrives at his school dormitory.

Zhang Tianming: There's so many people here!

Ke Lin: You must be a freshman.

Zhang Tianming: Yes, I'm a freshman. How about you?

Ke Lin: I'm a grad student. I'm here to help the freshmen move. What's your name?

Zhang Tianming: My name is Zhang Tianming.

Ke Lin: Zhang Tianming? Is that a Chinese name?

Zhang Tianming: That's right. My mom and dad are from China, but I was born and grew up in America. Your name is…?

Ke Lin: I'm studying Chinese. My Chinese name is Ke Lin. What are the characters for your name?

Zhang Tianming: Zhang with *gong* (bow) [on the left] and *chang* (long) [on the right], same character as the one for "piece" as in "a piece of paper," *tian* as in "weather," *ming* as in "tomorrow."

Ke Lin: How did you get to school?

Zhang Tianming: I flew. From the airport I took a taxi. Ke Lin, do you also live here?

Ke Lin: No, this is the freshman dorm. I live off campus.

Zhang Tianming: Is that so? Why do you live off campus? Do you think it's better to live on or off campus?

Ke Lin: Some people like to live on campus. They think it's both convenient and safe. Some people like to live off campus because off-campus housing is cheaper. I live off campus. Besides wanting to save some money, I also want my freedom. On top of that, it's not necessarily that convenient to live on campus.

Zhang Tianming: Really? Then I'll move off campus, too, in the future.

Ke Lin: You've just arrived, so it's good for you to live on campus and get used to school life. If you want to live off campus later, I can help you find a place.

Zhang Tianming: OK. If I want to move later, I'll definitely ask you for help.

Ke Lin: There's no one in front of you now. I'll help you move your bags into your room.

Zhang Tianming: OK. Thanks. Hey, where's my computer? Shoot, I might have left it in the cab!

Text

Zhang Tianming's room is not very big: two people can live there. His roommate has already arrived. There isn't a lot of furniture in the room. Against the windows are two desks, and in front of each desk there is a chair. Next to the desks are the beds, upon which are quilts and blankets. There are two wardrobes next to the bed. There are some clothes hanging inside. To the right of the door are two bookshelves, still empty.

Zhang Tianming: It's so hot. How come there's no air conditioning in the room?

Ke Lin: This building is pretty old. I used to live here as a freshman.

Zhang Tianming: The bathroom is pretty small, too. It must be very inconvenient to live here, right?

Ke Lin: No, it's very convenient here. The dining hall is right downstairs, and next to it there's a small store selling daily necessities and stationery. The classroom buildings aren't far from here, only a five- or six-minute walk.

Zhang Tianming: Is it convenient to do laundry here?

Ke Lin: Extremely convenient. On this floor there are three washing machines and three dryers.

Zhang Tianming: Is it noisy here?

Ke Lin: No, it's not. The major roads are far from here. It's very quiet.

Zhang Tianming: I hear that dining hall food is, generally speaking, not very good. What about here?

Ke Lin: You're right. The food in the dining hall is really not that good.

Zhang Tianming: Then what should I do?

Ke Lin: Don't worry. There are many restaurants nearby. There's even a Chinese restaurant.

Zhang Tianming: I think there aren't that many good Chinese restaurants in America.

Ke Lin: That's not necessarily true. The food at that Chinese restaurant nearby is very authentic. My girlfriend and I go there all the time.

Zhang Tianming: Really? Then could you take me there in a few days to check it out?

Ke Lin: Sure. No problem.

Lesson 3 | Text

Today's the weekend, and having already finished his homework, Zhang Tianming sends Ke Lin a WeChat message, saying that he and his girlfriend Lisha would like to eat Chinese food. He asks Ke Lin if he would like to go. Ke Lin says it so happens that he also wants to have Chinese food, so he asks Zhang Tianming and Lisha to wait for him outside the dorm. He'll come pick them up.

Half an hour later, Ke Lin's car arrives. Zhang Tianming and Lisha get into the car and see a girl. Ke Lin introduces her, saying that she is an international student from China named Lin Xuemei. In a few minutes, they arrive at a Chinese restaurant.

Waiter:	Here's the menu.
Ke Lin:	Thanks. Lisha, Tianming, what would you like to eat?
Zhang Tianming:	What's good here?
Ke Lin:	Their chicken is done very well. So is their fish, especially the steamed fish. It tastes amazing.
Lin Xuemei:	Their beef with Chinese broccoli is also quite good—it's both tender and fragrant.
Lisha:	Can we order a soup?
Ke Lin:	Of course. Their spinach-and-tofu soup is very good. Let's order one.
Lin Xuemei:	Let's order another vegetable dish.
Waiter:	Are you ready to order?
Ke Lin:	Yes. One steamed fish, one beef with Chinese broccoli, and one spinach-and-tofu soup. What fresh vegetables do you have today?
Waiter:	How about baby bok choy?
Ke Lin:	Is it organic?
Waiter:	Yes.
Ke Lin:	Okay. We'd like our food a bit light. Please don't make it too salty. Not too much oil, no MSG.
Zhang Tianming:	Please bring us four glasses of ice water first, four pairs of chopsticks, and give us some more napkins.
Waiter:	Sure, no problem. Oh, that's right. Do you want rice?
Lin Xuemei:	We don't "want rice" [like beggars]. We'd like four bowls of rice.
Waiter:	You're right. You'd like four bowls of rice.
Lin Xuemei:	Sorry! I was kidding around with you.
	. . .

Zhang Tianming:	Lin Xuemei, Ke Lin says that the Chinese dishes here are very authentic. Is that true?
Lin Xuemei:	Their dishes are very good, but not as good as those in our restaurants in Hangzhou.
Zhang Tianming:	My parents say that the food is very different all over China. Which place has the best food?
Lin Xuemei:	That depends on your personal preferences. Take me for example. I like it sweet. That's why I like Shanghainese cuisine. Ke Lin loves spicy food, so he likes Sichuanese and Hunanese food. If you like your food light, you can have Cantonese dishes . . .
Ke Lin:	Xuemei, let's go to China over the winter break.
Lin Xuemei:	Go to China to have Chinese food? I'd consider it.
Lisha:	That's a good idea. I'd also consider it.
Zhang Tianming:	Food and fun? Of course I'll consider it, too.
Lin Xuemei:	Really? Awesome! Let's all go.
Lisha:	If I could go to China to study Chinese, that would be even better.
Ke Lin:	Hey, our food's here.

Lesson 4

	Text

When Zhang Tianming came [to school] from home, his mom bought him some clothes—like T-shirts, sweaters, jeans, and so on—but he doesn't think they're that good either in style or color. Today is Sunday, and it just so happens that Lin Xuemei and Lisha need to buy some daily necessities such as toilet paper, toothpaste, towels, and laundry detergent, so Ke Lin takes them to the biggest shopping center nearby.

Ke Lin: What clothes do you want to buy?

Zhang Tianming: I'd like to buy a tracksuit.

Ke Lin: They're here. Look at this one. The style, size, and length are all very suitable. Plus, it's twenty percent off.

Zhang Tianming: The color is good, too. How much money? What's the brand?

Lin Xuemei: The price is not expensive. I've never heard of the brand.

Lisha: But it's pure cotton.

Zhang Tianming: It's not okay if it's not a good brand. I want to buy name brand.

Ke Lin: Aren't you fashionable, wearing name brands! That one looks like it's name brand. Oh wow, way too expensive.

Zhang Tianming: When it comes to shopping, I only buy name brand or I won't buy, because name-brand clothes are better quality.

Lisha: That's right. Some clothes are inexpensive, but they aren't from a good brand. After you've worn them once or twice, you don't want to wear them anymore and you have to buy another set. That way, it's probably more money to buy two pieces of clothing than just one piece of clothing from a name brand.

Lin Xuemei: What you say makes sense.

Ke Lin: Of course it's not good if you only consider price when shopping for clothes, but you don't have to insist on name brands. My criteria for buying clothes is first, whether they're comfortable; second, whether they're good quality; and third, whether the price is reasonable. What brand they are and whether the style is fashionable, I totally don't care. That's because clothes are for yourself, not for others to look at.

Zhang Tianming:	I don't agree. Do you like to see Lin Xuemei wear unattractive clothes?
Ke Lin:	Xuemei looks good in whatever clothes she's wearing. Isn't that right?
Lin Xuemei:	OK, OK, enough said.
Zhang Tianming:	Ke Lin, how come the clothes you have on are name brand? I thought you didn't wear name brand.
Ke Lin:	I said that it isn't necessary to buy name brand, but I never said I don't wear name brands. I bought this when it was on sale.
Lin Xuemei:	Lisha, let's go over to the daily necessities to take a look.
Zhang Tianming:	You go ahead. I'll go pay first. We'll see each other in a little bit.

(Zhang Tianming is paying . . .)

Sales clerk:	Sir, cash or credit card?
Zhang Tianming:	I'll swipe my credit card.
Sales clerk:	Sir, with tax, altogether it's $186.40.
Zhang Tianming:	All right . . . Thank you! Bye.

Lesson 5

> Text

Zhang Tianming is taking four courses this semester: World History, Computer Science, Political Science, and Chinese. These classes are all very interesting, and he's learned a lot. Because Zhang Tianming often speaks Chinese with his parents at home, first-year Chinese for him is very easy in terms of listening and speaking; only writing Chinese characters is a little difficult. Apart from Chinese, preparing for his other classes takes up a lot of his time, and he also has to write many essays, so he finds his course load a bit too much. This semester is half over. Soon he'll have to choose next semester's classes. Zhang Tianming hopes that he can relax a bit more next semester. The day after tomorrow, he will see his professor to discuss course selection, and he wants to talk with other schoolmates first and hear their thoughts. This afternoon he happens to run into Li Zhe, who's a senior, on the basketball court. He and Li Zhe chat as they play basketball.

Zhang Tianming: So, have you finished picking your classes for next semester?

Li Zhe: Not yet. How about you?

Zhang Tianming: I definitely want to take Chinese. As for the other two classes, I'm still thinking. Oh yeah, how many classes do you still have to take before you can graduate?

Li Zhe: I want to double major, so I still need four more classes. I want to take another chemistry class, an econ class, plus two classes with the Department of Computer Science. Then I'll have enough credits.

Zhang Tianming: That's it. I've decided. I'll also take Economics and Computer Science. My problem is solved. This is great. I'll tell my professor the day after tomorrow when I see him, and get some suggestions from him. Li Zhe, what do you want to do after you graduate?

Li Zhe: I'd like to go to grad school, either engineering or management school. I haven't discussed it yet with my professor. Tianming, what do you want to major in?

Zhang Tianming: I'd like to study literature, but my mom says it won't be easy to find a job if I study literature. Besides, I won't make much money. She hopes that I'll study finance, but I'm not interested in finance. How boring—dealing with numbers all day long.

Li Zhe: My parents aren't too different from yours. If I could pick my own major, it would be philosophy because I like to think about [philosophical] problems. Many of our classmates have more freedom than we do. Their parents don't care what majors they pick.

Zhang Tianming: Which schools do you want to apply to?

Li Zhe: I'd like to apply to a school near my sister's place. That way I can move into her house and save money on room and board.

Zhang Tianming: But staying at your sister's place might be a bit constricting.

Li Zhe: What you say is true, but staying at my sister's place has many advantages. I need to think about it some more.

Text

Something's been weighing on Lisha's mind the past few days. Only after Lin Xuemei asked her about it several times yesterday did Lisha say that she had had a fight with Zhang Tianming.

When Xuemei first met Lisha, she heard Lisha say that she and Zhang Tianming were classmates in high school. Tianming is a good guy—very outgoing and a good student, too. In terms of interests, she and Tianming are not that similar. Tianming is a sports buff. Whenever there is a ball game on TV, he has to watch it. Lisha is a music fan. Whenever there is a concert, she goes and listens. Lisha says although they have different interests and hobbies, they have always gotten along well.

Lin Xuemei racked her brain, but she still couldn't figure out what had really happened to the two of them. Was it because their cultural backgrounds were different? Or was it because Tianming had a new girlfriend? This evening Lin Xuemei happens to have some free time, so she goes looking for Lisha.

Lin Xuemei:	What's up with you and Tianming?
Lisha:	I don't want to talk about it. I just don't matter to him.
Lin Xuemei:	What's really wrong?
Lisha:	Two weeks ago he and I were supposed to go to a concert. Who knew? He spent the night playing on his computer. He completely forgot about the concert. How could I have not gotten upset?
Lin Xuemei:	Don't be upset. Ke Lin is often like that, too. Whenever he starts watching a ball game, he forgets about everything else.
Lisha:	There was something even more maddening. Last Saturday I wanted him to go with me to the movies. He happily agreed. The film was at eight o'clock. I waited till eight fifteen. He still hadn't arrived. I called his cell, and only then did I find out that he had gone to another movie theater. These were all small matters, but they made me really upset. I think I really don't matter to him. I really just want to break up with him.
Lin Xuemei:	So that's what happened. How could Tianming be so scatterbrained? What happened after that?
Lisha:	When he saw me later, he kept apologizing to me. He seemed sincerely sorry and made me feel that he genuinely cared about me.
Lin Xuemei:	That's right. Don't be upset. Being scatterbrained and not caring about you are totally different. If you stop fighting, you may well go your separate ways. Actually, Ke Lin is not much different from Tianming. He often forgets this or that and always leaves things behind. One minute he forgets my birthday, the next he can't find his keys, or something else . . . He sometimes really has me worried.
Lisha:	Really? Turns out Ke Lin has his moments of carelessness. Oh yeah, does your family know you have a boyfriend?
Lin Xuemei:	No . . . I haven't told them yet.

Lesson 7 (Text)

Zhang Tianming is a computer fanatic. His computer is on from morning till night. He reads news, does research, and plays games online. Sometimes he writes his blog on his own website. He can't leave his computer for a moment. When he goes online, very often he loses track of time. Yesterday, he, Lisha, Ke Lin, and Xuemei made plans to sing karaoke today, but at the appointed time he didn't show up. They called his cell, but he didn't answer. So they sent him an email. Ten minutes later they see him running toward them.

Zhang Tianming: Sorry, sorry. I downloaded some software, searched for a few things, and lost track of time.

Ke Lin: What were you searching for?

Zhang Tianming: I have to write an article. I needed to look up some information.

Lin Xuemei: Looking for information? Our professor doesn't allow us to use anything from the Internet. We have to use books and journals. He says there is too much junk on the Internet.

Zhang Tianming: Your professor is too out of touch. Lots of information on the Internet is very reliable and useful. The online world is huge and convenient. You can order takeout, shop, you can rent housing, buy a car, from clothes to food, from housing to transportation, you can find all kinds of information.

Lisha: That's right, it's really convenient. If you want to find a girlfriend, you can also go online.

Zhang Tianming: Hey, Lisha, are you still mad at me?

Lisha: You tell me if I should be mad or not. You're late every time. You always keep everyone waiting.

Zhang Tianming: I'm sorry. I'm really sorry. It's my fault. There won't be a next time.

Ke Lin: Tianming, you stay all day in your room playing on your computer. Seems like you're addicted.

Zhang Tianming: Addicted? Surely it's not as serious as that? It's the age of the Internet. Of course we can't be away from our computers.

Lisha:	I know that computers and the Internet are becoming more and more important in our lives. I also use my computer to do my translation exercises and go online to compare prices, but I'm not like you, always forgetting the time and your friends.
Lin Xuemei:	I hear Lisha say that you don't like to make phone calls. You only like to send WeChat messages and emails.
Ke Lin:	You don't have to pay for WeChat or email.
Zhang Tianming:	That's right. They are free, quick, and convenient.
Lin Xuemei:	But sometimes, reading WeChat messages and emails doesn't feel as good as a phone call.
Ke Lin:	Xuemei likes "tele-chatting."
Lisha:	"Tele-chatting"? What's "tele-chatting"?
Ke Lin:	Chatting on the phone. Got it? Chatting continuously, chatting non-stop, from morning till night . . .
Lin Xuemei:	What? Sounds like you don't like chatting with me.
Ke Lin:	No, no. That's not what I meant. I was joking. Of course I love chatting with you. OK, that's enough. No more talk of this. Where are we going to sing karaoke?
Zhang Tianming:	I looked online. There's a place on the east side that's quite good. They have all the songs that Lisha likes. See, I didn't forget my friends.

Lesson 8

(Text)

Zhang Tianming's parents hope for their children to be able to receive a good education, so when their children were born, they started putting money away for their children's educational expenses. Although Zhang Tianming's parents' income is not inconsiderable, sending both Tianming and his sister to college puts some financial pressure on them. Tianming thinks that he's already an adult and that he should work to alleviate his parents' burden; so, he goes online to check out whether there are any suitable jobs. As he does so, Lisha and Xuemei walk in.

Lisha:	Tianming, what are you looking at online?
Zhang Tianming:	I want to work a little so that I can spend less of my family's money.
Lin Xuemei:	Wouldn't working impact your studies?
Zhang Tianming:	I'd like to work so that I can get a little work experience. If I don't spend too much time working, it shouldn't affect my studies.
Lisha:	I also want to work to make some spending money.
Lin Xuemei:	Don't you have a scholarship?
Lisha:	The scholarship isn't enough to cover tuition. I also applied for a government student loan. Xuemei, do Chinese college students also work?
Lin Xuemei:	They didn't have to before, because then they didn't have to pay for college tuition. Now universities charge tuition, so many students try to find ways to work and make money.
Lisha:	Where do Chinese students usually work? In restaurants as waiters?
Lin Xuemei:	There are students who work in restaurants, but not many. In Chinese cities there are many people from rural areas looking for jobs. Restaurants like to hire them because their wages are relatively low.
Lisha:	Have you worked before?
Lin Xuemei:	Yes, I have. I've been a tutor—I taught English. Among my classmates, some worked as translators, some worked in computer management, and some worked as dog- or cat-sitters.
Zhang Tianming:	Seems like many students go to school and work part-time to make money at the same time.
Lisha:	Speaking of money, today my roommate borrowed money from me. She said her mom was upset and stopped giving her any money.
Lin Xuemei:	Why?
Lisha:	Her parents paid for her food this semester, but she ordered takeout or she went to restaurants with classmates. She also spent money recklessly on other things, and owes the bank and credit-card companies a lot of money. Last month she spent the allowance that her parents had given her in less than ten days, and then asked for some more from her mother. That still wasn't enough.
Lin Xuemei:	No wonder her mom is angry. Why doesn't she give any thought to how hard it is for her parents to make money?
Zhang Tianming:	I'm with you. We shouldn't spend money recklessly.
Lisha:	We all know you're such a model child! All right, you take your time looking for jobs. We're leaving.

Lesson 9 — Text

Li Zhe's parents are Mexican immigrants. He and his older brother were both born and grew up in California. His older brother has a doctoral degree in Computer Science—he designs software and manages websites. Li Zhe's sister-in-law came from Hong Kong to the United States fifteen years ago to study. After she got a master's degree and found a job, she settled in America. Li Zhe's older brother and sister-in-law have been married for ten years. They've always been very happy, but in the last couple of years, their opinions have differed over their daughter's education, sometimes causing big arguments. One day, Li Zhe is chatting with his niece on the phone when he sees Lisha walk in.

(Li Zhe hangs up.)

Li Zhe: Lisha, is something up?

Lisha: Nothing's up. I came to look for Tianming. I thought he was here with you. I'm sorry, I made you hang up.

Li Zhe: Sit, please sit. My niece called me just now, but we just finished talking.

Lisha: You have a niece? How old is she?

Li Zhe: She just turned eight this year.

Lisha: What did she want to talk about?

Li Zhe: It was about her studies. She's just started third grade. And my sister-in-law is already scheduling her: Monday, piano lessons; Tuesday, painting lessons; Wednesday, swimming; Thursday, ice skating; her only break on Friday; and Saturday, Chinese lessons. She doesn't like studying Chinese. That's why she called me. She cried and complained.

Lisha: Is it that serious? What did she say?

Li Zhe: She says that kids are people too—they have their own interests and hobbies, and parents should respect their children's choices.

Lisha: She sure knows how to express herself!

Li Zhe: She must have learned it from my older brother. My sister-in-law always wants her to study this or that, but my older brother objects to putting too much pressure on kids. He thinks that the most important thing for a kid is to have a happy childhood.

Lisha: I had a very happy childhood, but now every time I'm in Chinese class I just think, if my parents had made me learn Chinese when I was a child, I would have a much easier time.

Li Zhe: Who knew you would have the same view as my sister-in-law! Does that mean you agree with my sister-in-law's methods?

Lisha:	I don't agree entirely, but I can understand.
Li Zhe:	Many parents hope that their children will rise above the others. They all hope that their children study well when they are young so that they can have successful careers, but even now I still haven't figured it out whether it's better for children to become high achievers in the future or have a happy childhood.
Lisha:	My view is that both are important. A person should have a happy childhood, but also make a contribution to society after they grow up. So it's best for children to learn as much as they can in school.
Li Zhe:	But don't forget: some knowledge isn't learned from books. It must be learned from society, from life.
Lisha:	Oh, Li Zhe, you've really turned into a bona fide philosopher.

Lesson 10 (Text)

It'll soon be winter break. Zhang Tianming has been thinking about his travel plans over the last couple of days. His parents hope that he'll go visit their hometown, Nanjing. Zhang Tianming also very much wants to be Lisha's tour guide and take her to a few places in China. Besides Nanjing, where else should they go? In order to decide on their itinerary, he takes out a map of China and begins to study it.

Zhang Tianming: Lisha, come take a look at this map of China and see where we want to go.

Lisha: Look at the map? Great idea. I want to learn about Chinese geography. I know so little about Chinese geography.

Zhang Tianming: We'll first go to Nanjing, my parents' hometown . . . It's here, in southeastern China. Where do you want to go next?

Lisha: This is Harbin, isn't it? Let's go to Harbin.

Zhang Tianming: How come you want to go from the southeast all the way to the extreme north?

Lisha: Yesterday on TV there was a program on Harbin's ice lanterns. They were really beautiful.

Zhang Tianming: Ice lanterns are nice, but it's really cold there now. Let's go in the summer.

Lisha: OK. We won't go to the north. Then let's take a train to the west. I hear that Xinjiang is a very special place.

Zhang Tianming: Xinjiang is in the northwest. It starts to get cold in October. Now is not a good time to go. Besides, trains take too long. Let's go next time.

Lisha: This is the Yangtze River, and this is the Yellow River. Let's take a boat to look at the landscape along the Yangtze or the Yellow River.

Zhang Tianming: Taking a boat takes a long time. Most of China's rivers flow from west to east. Going from east to west would take an even longer amount of time.

Lisha: Why do most of China's rivers flow from west to east?

Zhang Tianming: Because China's western part is a plateau. The world's tallest mountain is there. In the eastern part, there are plains and oceans.

Lisha: It seems that all the big cities are by the sea or not too far away from it. See, in the north are Beijing and Tianjin. In the southeast are Shanghai and Nanjing. In the south are Guangzhou and Shenzhen.

Zhang Tianming: What you say is correct. China's population is mainly in the east and south. In the southwest there are many tall mountains and plateaus. In the northwest there are many deserts. The natural conditions are not very good, so the population is sparse.

Lisha: I think China's topography is a little like America's.

Zhang Tianming:	What you say makes sense. Also, the land area is about the same. But China's population is more than four times that of the U.S. I hear that during holidays or school breaks there are huge crowds in all the scenic areas.
Lisha:	Really?
Zhang Tianming:	Luckily, when we go, students will still be in school and it won't be around any major holidays.
Lisha:	China is so big. Our break is so short. Where should we go?
Zhang Tianming:	I think Yunnan is the best place to go.
Lisha:	Where is Yunnan? . . . Oh, I found it. It's here. It's a province in the southwest. Is it cold there in winter?
Zhang Tianming:	I've heard that some places in Yunnan are spring-like year round. Throughout the year, in all four seasons, it's not too cold or too hot.
Lisha:	I heard on TV that Yunnan has beautiful scenery and many ethnic minorities. It's a great place to visit.
Zhang Tianming:	It's decided then. We'll go to Yunnan.